Chinese Foreign Policy

This updated and expanded third edition of *Chinese Foreign Policy* seeks to explain the processes, actors and current history behind China's international relations, as well as offering an in-depth look at the key areas of China's modern global relations.

Among the key issues are:

- The expansion of Chinese foreign policy from regional to international interests
- China's growing economic power in an era of global financial uncertainty
- Modern security challenges, including maritime security, counter-terrorism and protection of overseas economic interests
- The shifting power relationship with the United States, as well as with the European Union, Russia and Japan
- China's engagement with a growing number of international and regional institutions and legal affairs
- The developing great power diplomacy of China.

New chapters address not only China's evolving foreign policy interests but also recent changes in the international system and the effects of China's domestic reforms. In response to current events, sections addressing Chinese trade, bilateral relations, and China's developing strategic interest in Russia and the Polar Regions have been extensively revised and updated.

This book will be essential reading for students of Chinese foreign policy and Asian international relations, and highly recommended for students of diplomacy, international security and IR in general.

Marc Lanteigne is Senior Research Fellow at the Norwegian Institute of International Affairs (NUPI), Oslo. He is the author/editor of four books on China as well as several articles on Chinese and Asian international relations.

Chinese Foreign Policy

An introduction

Third edition

Marc Lanteigne

Routledge
Taylor & Francis Group

LONDON AND NEW YORK

First published 2016
by Routledge
2 Park Square, Milton Park, Abingdon, Oxon OX14 4RN

and by Routledge
711 Third Avenue, New York, NY 10017

Routledge is an imprint of the Taylor & Francis Group, an informa business

© 2016 Marc Lanteigne

The right of Marc Lanteigne to be identified as author of this work has been asserted by him/her in accordance with sections 77 and 78 of the Copyright, Designs and Patents Act 1988.

British Library Cataloguing-in-Publication Data
A catalogue record for this book is available from the British Library

Library of Congress Cataloging-in-Publication Data
Names: Lanteigne, Marc, author.
Title: Chinese foreign policy : an introduction / Marc Lanteigne.
Description: Third edition. | New York, NY : Routledge, 2016. | Includes
     bibliographical references and index.
Identifiers: LCCN 2015028349
Subjects: LCSH: China--Foreign relations--1976- | China--Foreign
     economic relations.
Classification: LCC JZ1734 .L367 2016 | DDC 327.51--dc23
LC record available at http://lccn.loc.gov/2015028349

ISBN: 978-1-138-93568-6 (hbk)
ISBN: 978-1-138-93569-3 (pbk)
ISBN: 978-1-315-67722-4 (ebk)

Typeset in Times New Roman
by HWA Text and Data Management, London

Contents

Boxes

Acronyms

A2 / AD	anti-access / area denial
ABM	anti-ballistic missile
ACFTA	ASEAN–China Free Trade Agreement
ADB	Asian Development Bank
ADIZ	Air Defence Identification Zone
AFC	Asian financial crisis (1997–8)
AFRICOM	United States Africa Command
AIIB	Asian Infrastructure Investment Bank
AMS	Chinese Academy of Military Sciences
ANU	Australia National University
ANZUS	Australia–New Zealand–United States Security Treaty
APEC	Asia-Pacific Economic Cooperation
APT	ASEAN-Plus-Three
ARF	ASEAN Regional Forum
ASAT	anti-satellite weapon
ASB	air-sea battle
ASCEL	active strategic counterattacks on exterior lines
ASEAN	Association of Southeast Asian Nations
ASEAN-ISIS	ASEAN Institutes for Strategic and International Studies
ASEM	Asia–Europe Meeting
AU	African Union
BAT	Beidu, Alibaba and Tencent (Chinese internet firms)
BCIM	Bangladesh–China–India–Myanmar trade corridor (proposed)
BRICS	Brazil, Russia, India, China and South Africa
C_4I	command, control, communication, computers and information
C_4ISTAR	command, control, communications, computers, intelligence, surveillance, target acquisition and reconnaissance
CACF	China–Arab Cooperation Forum
CASS	Chinese Academy of Social Sciences
CC	Central Committee of the Chinese Communist Party
CCG	China Coast Guard
CCP	Communist Party of China
CCTV	China Central Television
CFSP	Common Foreign and Security Policy (European Union)
CIA	(US) Central Intelligence Agency

CICA	Conference on Interaction and Confidence Building in Asia
CICIR	China Institutes of Contemporary International Relations
CIIS	China Institute of International Studies
CNNIC	Chinese Internet Network Information Centre
CNOOC	Chinese National Offshore Oil Corporation
CNPC	Chinese National Petroleum Corporation
COC	code of conduct
COMECON	Council for Mutual Economic Assistance
CPPCC	Chinese People's Political Consultative Committee
CSCAP	Council of Security Cooperation in the Asia-Pacific
CSI	Container Security Initiative
CYL	Communist Youth League
DMZ	demilitarised zone
DPP	Democratic Progressive Party (Taiwan)
DPRK	Democratic People's Republic of Korea (North Korea)
EAS	East Asian Summit
EC	European Commission
ECFA	China–Taiwan Economic Cooperation Framework Agreement
ECS	East China Sea
EEU	Eurasian Economic Union
EEZ	exclusive economic zone
EFTA	European Free Trade Association
ETIM	East Turkestan Independence Movement
EU	European Union
EurAsEC	Eurasian Economic Community
FOCAC	Forum on China–Africa Cooperation
FSU	former Soviet Union
FTA	free trade agreement
FTAAP	Free Trade Area of the Asia-Pacific
FVEY	"Five Eyes" intelligence coalition
G-2	Group of Two (China and United States)
G-7	Group of Seven
GATT	General Agreement on Tariffs and Trade
GCC	Gulf Cooperation Council
GDP	gross domestic product
GWoT	global war on terror
IAEA	International Atomic Energy Agency
IASC	International Arctic Scientific Committee
ICBM	inter-continental ballistic missile
ICC	International Criminal Court
ICCPR	International Covenant on Civil and Political Rights
ICESCR	International Covenant on Economic, Social and Cultural Rights
IMF	International Monetary Fund
ISI	import-substitution industrialisation
ISIL	Islamic State in Iraq and the Levant (also "Islamic State")
JAM-GC	Joint Concept for Access and Manoeuvre in the Global Commons
KEDO	Korean Peninsula Energy Development Organisation
KMT	Kuomintang (Nationalist Party, Taiwan)

KWP	(North) Korean Workers' Party
LAC	Line of Actual Control
LAS	League of Arab States (Arab League)
MERCOSUR	South American Common Market
MERS	Middle East respiratory syndrome
MES	market economy status
MFA	Multi-Fibre Agreement
MII	Ministry of Information Industry, China
MIIT	Ministry of Industry and Information Technology, China
MITI	Ministry of International Trade and Industry, Japan
MoFA	Ministry of Foreign Affairs, China
MOFCOM	Chinese Ministry of Commerce
MOOTW	military operations other than war
MPS	Ministry of Public Security, China
MSG	Melanesian Spearhead Group
MSR	Maritime Silk Road
MSS	Ministry of State Security, China
MTCR	Missile Technology Control Regime
NAFTA	North American Free Trade Agreement
NAM	Non-Aligned Movement
NATO	North American Treaty Organisation
NDB	New Development Bank
NEAT	Network of East Asian Think Tanks
NFU	"no first use" (of nuclear weapons)
NGO	non-governmental organisation
NIEO	New International Economic Order
NLD	National League of Democracy, Myanmar
NPC	National People's Congress, PRC
NPT	nuclear non-proliferation treaty
NSC	"new security concept"
NSR	Northern Sea Route
OAS	Organisation of American States
OBOR	"one belt and one road"
ODA	overseas development assistance
OECD	Organisation for Economic Cooperation and Development
OSCE	Organisation for Security and Cooperation in Europe
P5	Permanent Five members of the UN Security Council
PAP	People's Armed Police
PCA	Partnership and Cooperation Agreement (China and European Union)
PIF	Pacific Islands Forum
PLA	People's Liberation Army
PLAAF	PLA Air Force
PLAGF	PLA Ground Forces
PLAN	PLA Navy
PPP	purchasing power parity
PRC	People's Republic of China
PTA	preferential trade agreement
RATS	regional anti-terrorism structure

RCEP	Regional Comprehensive Economic Partnership
ReCAAP	Regional Cooperation Agreement on Combating Piracy and Armed Robbery against Ships in Asia
RMB	*renminbi*, currency of the PRC (currency unit = "yuan", also "¥" or "元")
RMSI	Regional Maritime Security Initiative
ROC	Republic of China (Taiwan)
ROK	Republic of Korea (South Korea)
SAARC	South Asian Association for Regional Cooperation
SACU	Southern African Customs Union
SAR	special autonomous region
SARS	severe acute respiratory syndrome
SCO	Shanghai Cooperation Organisation
SCS	South China Sea
SEATO	Southeast Asian Treaty Organisation
S&ED	(US–China) Strategic and Economic Dialogue
SETC	State Economic and Trade Commission, China
SEZ	special economic zone
SIGINIT	signals intelligence
SIIS	Shanghai Institute of International Studies
SLBM	submarine-launched ballistic missile
SLoCs	sea lanes of communication
SLORC	State Law and Order Restoration Council, Myanmar
SOE	state-owned enterprise
SPT	Six-Party Talks (on the Korean Peninsula)
TAC	Treaty of Amity and Cooperation
THAAD	terminal high altitude area defence
TIP	Turkistan Independence Party
TMD	theatre missile defence
TPP	Trans-Pacific Partnership
UAV	unmanned aerial vehicle
UN	United Nations
UNASUR	Union of South American Nations
UNCLOS	United Nations Convention on the Law of the Sea
UNGA	United Nations General Assembly
UNSC	United Nations Security Council
UNSMIS	UN Supervision Mission in Syria
US	United States
USSR	Union of Soviet Socialist Republics
VPN	virtual private networks
WTO	World Trade Organisation

Acknowledgements

In wisdom, desire roundness, and in conduct, desire squareness.
Liu Su, Tang Dynasty, quoted in *A Manual of Chinese Quotations: Being a Translation of the Ch'êng Yü K'ao* (1893)

This, the third edition of *Chinese Foreign Policy*, is the result of new research and fieldwork not only in China but also in Northeast Asia, Oceania, the United States and Northern Europe, and came about due in no small part to many persons who provided me with information, recommendations and encouragement as I sought to piece together China's expanding international interests under a new government and an ever-changing global milieu.

Many individuals and organisations were of invaluable assistance in the research and preparations for this book. A special thank-you must go first to Lynn Gardinier and Bjørnar Sverdrup-Thygeson for their diligent and indispensible editing work, and to Andrew Humphrys at Routledge for his oversight of this book project dating back to the first edition and the tentative scribble-notes before that.

I would also like to give warm thanks to all my colleagues at the Norwegian Institute of International Affairs (NUPI) in Oslo for their help and encouragement during the writing of the third edition of this book, especially to Ulf Sverdrup for all his support, and to Wrenn Yennie Lindgren, Cedric de Coning, Ane Teksum Isbrekken, Indra Øverland, Mikkel Pedersen, Elana Wilson Rowe and Åsmund Weltzien.

During my research in China, many local scholars, specialists and officials were extremely helpful during the data collection process for this work, especially in emerging areas of China's foreign policy interests such as the BRICS, new financial institutions, polar policies, economic security and cross-regional diplomacy. I am very grateful for all of their assistance!

Colleagues who also greatly aided this work with their comments, thoughts and support include Maria Ackrén, Stephen Aris, Robert Ayson, Alyson Bailes, Sebastian Bersick, Rasmus Gjedssø Bertelsen, Margrét Cela, Enrico Fels, Katie Foley, Gao Yang, Gunhild Hoogensen Gjørv, Nadine Godehardt, Maria-Fernanda Gonzalez Rojas, Joanne Hall, Pia Hansson, Bertel Heurlin, Miwa Hirono, Emmi Ikonen, Nargis Kassenova, Togzhan Kassenova, Nusta Carranza Ko, Vaclav Kopecky, Natasha Kuhrt, Stephen Levine, Li Dongkun, Teemu Naarajärvi, Silja Bára Ómarsdóttir, Merja Polvinen, David Santoro, Kristinn Schram, Katharina Serrano, Aglaya Snetkov, Lili Song, Ian Storey, Camilla T. N. Sørensen, May-Britt Stumbaum, Su Ping, Monique Taylor, Page Wilson, Nicki Wrighton and Jason Young.

Finally, very warm thanks to my family, who have supported me (and this book project) in too many ways to count and who continue to be an invaluable inspiration to me.

Marc Lanteigne

1 Introduction

The reconstruction of Chinese foreign policy

The rise of China (*Zhongguo* 中国) within the international system has been heralded as one of the most significant changes in turn-of-the-century global relations. Much has been written and discussed about China's growth in power, often referred to as a "rise" or an "ascent" from an isolated state to a regional power to a potential great power capable of exerting much influence not only within the Asia-Pacific region but also on an international level. This growth and influence can be examined in a variety of international relations areas, from security to economy to culture and the environment, all of which leads to the question of which directions the country will take as the "rise" continues. Will China become a global power (or superpower) alongside the United States, and if it does, what kind of global power will it be? Assuming China's power continues to increase, these questions become ever more important in understanding changes to Chinese foreign policy.

Foreign policy has often been described as interplay between various political *agents* (including individuals with specific needs and wants), and *structures* formed by social relationships (such as the state, as well as organisations and rules which are commonly constructed).[1] In the case of China, the biggest change in the development of that country's foreign policy has been the expansion both of the number of "agents" involved, directly or indirectly, in Beijing's foreign policymaking processes, and in the number of China's international interests as well as global-level "structures" with which it can interact. These structures have been both formal, such as international organisations, and also informal, such as global norms and behaviours. In the space of seventy years, China's foreign policy interests, originally far more limited to regional issues, have grown to encompass many more international concerns which can truly be called "global". As with other countries, especially great powers, in the age of globalisation and interdependence, identifying a clear separation between China's domestic political interests and its foreign policy can be very difficult. In the case of China, the dividing line has become increasingly blurry as the number of Chinese international interests and responsibilities grows and more actors, both individuals and groups, within China become involved with global affairs.

At first glance, the decision-making process in foreign policy matters appears more centralised in China in comparison to other states, including those in the West. Part of the reason for this perception has been the shape of China's government since 1949, when the country's Communist government assumed power and has since been dominated by a single political actor, namely the Chinese Communist Party (*Zhongguo Gongchandang* 中国共产党) or CCP. However, the Chinese government in Beijing still must undertake frequent balancing between its domestic interests, including improving standards of living, promoting stability, maintaining the dominant role of the CCP in Chinese governance, and continuing with the process of economic and governmental reform begun in the late 1970s, while also developing a modern foreign policy. This ongoing process of simultaneous government bargaining in domestic and foreign relations, often referred to as a "two-level game",[2] has become ever more complex in the Chinese case since Beijing must maintain the momentum of socio-economic reforms in the country, while simultaneously overseeing the country's rapid rise in power within the international system.

From the beginning of the twenty-first century, China's foreign policy interests expanded well beyond the Asia-Pacific region, and can now be observed worldwide. This process has been accelerated under the government of President Xi Jinping, who assumed the presidency of China in March 2013. The foreign policy expansion has taken place in tandem with the development of Chinese economic power which assumed even greater prominence in the wake of the post-2008 global financial crisis and the announcement in early 2011 that China had overtaken Japan as the second-largest economy in the world, after the United States. In 2014, it was widely reported that China had, according to some economic measurements such as purchasing power parity (PPP), actually overtaken the US as the largest economic power in terms of financial output.[3] However, income per person remained well below that of Western economies, and policymakers in Beijing continued to stress that the economic reform process in China was far from over.

This book examines the main issues and challenges facing China in the realm of foreign policy, through two major themes. First, China is a rising power in the international system and is now a "great power" on the regional (Asia-Pacific) level as well as increasingly on the international level. While the country has not yet achieved the status of "global power" or "superpower", a designation shared by both the United States and the then-Soviet Union, it is now in a strong position to become one. It has been frequently demonstrated throughout the history of international relations that great powers have very distinct, and often more numerous, foreign policy interests than other states, and as China grows in global strength and capabilities a similar pattern has emerged. Many of the cases examined here will reflect the effects of China's rapid growth and its growing international interests, including diplomatic, economic and strategic.

Second, China's foreign policy is not only undergoing a process of expansion (*kuozhang* 扩张) but also of *reconstruction* (*chongjian* 重建). This process is taking place in a variety of ways. The institutions within China which are responsible for foreign policy development

---

Box 1.1 The foreign policy roles of the Chinese Communist Party
"The political hybrid that the CCP is attempting to become today is born out of its study of the reasons that the Soviet and East European regimes collapsed but also very much informed of its study of other modernising and newly-industrialised states, particularly in East Asia, Western Europe and Latin America."
         – David Shambaugh, *China's Communist Party: Atrophy and Adaptation*
            (Washington DC: Woodrow Wilson Centre Press, 2008), 6.

"Currently four principal forces shape Chinese views toward, and actions in, the world: domestic politics and other internal constraints; global interdependence; realist foreign policy thinking; and technology-driven action–reaction dynamics."
         – David Lampton, *Following the Leader: Ruling China, From Deng Xiaoping*
            to Xi Jinping (Berkeley: University of California Press, 2014), 109.

are, by necessity, undergoing reform, permitting them to adjust to changing domestic and international circumstances. In addition, the number of actors, including sectors of the Chinese government but also non-state actors and individuals within China, interested in and participating in the creation of Chinese foreign policy, continues to grow. Studying China's international relations through only a small group of government actors is becoming less and less a viable approach for scholars of this subject. However, equally as important is the fact that *ideas* about international relations in China, both within its government and other actors, are also slowly being reconstructed. Outdated ideas are being discarded, previously ignored concepts from a variety of eras are being given a fresh airing, and there is a greater willingness in China to learn from other states and other international players, such as organisations. This reconstruction is affecting all aspects of China's interests abroad, and will affect much current and future thinking relating to the country's foreign policy goals.

Chinese power and "bigness" in the world today

Rarely in history has a single state, regardless of size, grown so quickly in such a number of ways, and the case of China's rapid development presents a distinct set of questions for modern foreign policy study. Those examining Chinese growth have a variety of measurements to choose from, and from myriad viewpoints China can justifiably be referred to as a "big state" (*daguo* 大国). From a geographic point of view, China has historically been viewed as a large entity, with the third-biggest landmass in the world (after that of the Russian Federation and Canada and ahead of the United States and Brazil). The country also has a long coastline which opens up to the Pacific Ocean and the greater Asia-Pacific, a region which has been viewed for the past two decades as a part of the world expanding in both power and influence. From the beginning of the current century, many political economists began to view the Asia-Pacific region as the inexorable new hub of the global economy, in relation to the traditional financial powers of Europe and the United States.

At the same time, China has many neighbours in East, South and Central Asia, as it borders on fourteen other states, including Russia, India, Pakistan, Vietnam, the Republic of Korea (South Korea), the Democratic People's Republic of Korea (DPRK / North Korea), Kazakhstan and Myanmar (Burma). Thus, China has more neighbours than any country except the Russian Federation, which also has fourteen states on its land borders. China also possesses maritime boundaries, some disputed, with six other states, including Japan and the Philippines; seven if one includes the island of Taiwan, which Beijing claims as part of its sovereign territory but which has maintained a separate government and economy since 1949. For much of the Cold War, many of these borders were sources of real or potential conflict for Beijing, and in one case a dispute over its border with the USSR almost resulted in a full-scale war between two nuclear powers in 1969.

Since the 1990s, China has sought to improve relations with as many of its neighbours as possible, including settling leftover border disputes with the former Soviet Union, and since 2008 relations with Taiwan have warmed considerably with the establishment of business links, tourism and a 2010 preferential trade agreement. China remains involved in ongoing land and maritime border disputes, including disputed territorial claims with India, and claims to the majority of the South China Sea (SCS) which since 2010 have resulted in a cooling of diplomatic relations between China on one side and parts of Southeast Asia on the other. Some Southeast Asian states, including the Philippines and Vietnam, have also claimed sections of the SCS, and since 2010 there has been a series of incidents involving vessels from China and these states. These included a mid-2012 standoff between Chinese and Philippine vessels near the disputed Scarborough Shoal, known in Chinese as Huangyan Island (*Huangyan dao* 黄岩岛), and the placement of a Chinese offshore oil rig in disputed waters near the Paracel Islands (*Xisha qundao* 西沙群岛), which angered the government of Vietnam, which also claims the islands.

The boundary of the East China Sea (ECS) is also disputed between China and Japan, an issue which has affected bilateral relations and was exacerbated by incidents including in September 2010 when a Chinese fishing vessel collided with a Japanese coastguard ship, and in November 2013 when Beijing announced the installation of an Air Defence Identification Zone (ADIZ) over a region of the ECS which included the Senkaku Islands (*Diaoyu dao* 钓鱼岛) which have been claimed by China, Japan and Taiwan. The ECS disputes have also become involved in the contentious foreign policies of Xi Jinping and Japanese Prime minister Shinzo Abe, who after an unsuccessful and short tenure as Japanese leader in 2006–7, returned to office in December 2012 promising a harder line against Chinese military pressures. Under Abe, Sino-Japanese relations cooled considerably, leading to anti-Japan protests in Chinese cities in mid-2012 and heightened global concerns that the disputed ECS islands may lead to a military incident. A meeting and awkward handshake between the two leaders in November 2014 lowered tensions somewhat, but the ultimate status of the Senkaku / Diaoyu islands region remains a sore point.

China also possesses the largest population in the world, with about 1.36 billion persons as of 2014 (India is second with 1.21 billion), forming slightly less than 20 per cent of the world's total population. The country also contains some of the world's largest cities and municipalities, including the capital Beijing (21 million), Shanghai (24 million), Chongqing (29.5 million), Guangzhou (15 million) and Shenzhen (10.6 million). The "bigness" of China's populace therefore has a major influence on many global matters relating to population, including migration, labour and increasingly the environment. Indeed, substantive international-level decisions on these issues can no longer be undertaken without China's input. Moreover, much of China's population is becoming more affluent and increasingly urbanised. In 2011, China's urban population numbers overtook its rural population for the first time, reaching 690.79 million or 51.27 per cent of China's total population.

From a security perspective, China is viewed as a rising military power, albeit one which still lags far behind the West in many key areas. On the one hand, China is a nuclear power, having tested its first warhead in 1964. By contrast, its conventional weaponry remains largely underdeveloped in comparison with that of the United States and other parts of Asia, although since the turn of the century China has been seeking to address those gaps. In examining China's army, navy and air force, one can recognise that its ability to project power beyond its borders, while improving, remains limited with much of its military still dedicated to the self-defence of the country itself, with less emphasis on projecting power abroad.

China has, however, been upgrading its military to be less dependent upon strength of numbers and with a greater focus on high technology. China's armed forces, the People's Liberation Army (*renmin jiefangjun* 人民解放军) or PLA, have developed new weaponry, including fighter jets and submarines, and have purchased weapons from other states, especially Russia. In the past, Beijing purchased destroyers and submarines from Moscow which were seen as more capable of potentially facing off against the West, but from the turn of the century China began to rely more on indigenous military development. As well, China began concentrating on upgrading its maritime power and improving its ability to send vessels further afield from Chinese waters, and the People's Liberation Army Navy, or PLAN, has been especially active in building new vessels both to better patrol Chinese waters and to extend Chinese naval power further into the Indian and Pacific Oceans. Chinese navy ships have participated in joint military operations, such as patrolling for pirate vessels in the Indian Ocean since 2009 and assisting in the evacuation of thousands of Chinese nationals from Libya when the state collapsed into civil war in 2011. The ability to better project maritime power away from Chinese waters was further augmented with the deployment of the PLA Navy's first aircraft carrier, the *Liaoning* (辽宁舰), which began sea trials in 2011. In March 2013, it was announced that China's civilian maritime security bodies would be unified under a Chinese Coast Guard (*Zhongguo haijing* 中国海警) or CCG.

The country also has an estimated 60–70 missiles capable of intercontinental flight and the delivery of nuclear weapons, including an estimated 240–400 warheads. The exact number remains a closely-guarded secret. At the same time, China has been developing space technology for both civilian and military use. After a failed attempt to develop a manned space programme in the 1970s to match those of the United States and Soviet Union, China restarted its efforts after 1992 under "Project 921". In October 2003, China sent its first "taikonaut" or astronaut from China, Yang Liwei, into space, becoming only the third country to do so, and in June 2012 sent its first female taikonaut (Liu Yang) into space. In January 2007, the country created much international alarm by conducting its first test of an anti-satellite (ASAT) weapon, knocking down one of its own satellites which had ceased to function. Since the turn of the century, China has also been developing greater capabilities in the area of "cyberwarfare" (*wangluo zhanzheng* 网络战争) and has developed the concept of "information confrontation" (*xinxi duikang* 信息对抗) within its military thinking.

Western policymakers and scholars are frequently divided over whether China's military modernisation poses a direct threat to the international status quo or whether such updating is merely one aspect of China's overall modernisation policies. Since the 1990s, China's military budget has grown from a comparatively low starting point with steady annual increases. In March 2015, the annual Chinese military budget was announced to be 886.9 billion *yuan* or approximately US$145 billion, a fraction of American annual military spending. The idea of direct military confrontation with the United States is seen by many China scholars as highly unlikely since both states are nuclear powers, but also a direct military confrontation with the United States is seen as too risky for Beijing. Nevertheless, debate about a "China Threat" (*Zhongguo weixie* 中国威胁), both from an economic and security viewpoint, continues in the West including in the United States, with scholars arguing whether it is better to "contain" China, along the same lines as the classic American containment policy against the USSR during the Cold War, or to "engage" it, encouraging it to cooperate with international norms and organisations in the hopes of discouraging China from using force to get what it wants.

In late 2011, the United States under President Barack Obama announced a new strategic initiative in the Asia-Pacific, an initiative which has alternately been termed a "pivot" or a "rebalancing" of US forces there. As part of the policy, American forces would be stationed in Darwin in northern Australia, military ties with regional allies including Japan and the Philippines would be upgraded, ties with other partners including Singapore and Vietnam would be augmented, and more American forces would be stationed on the islands of Guam and Hawaii in the Pacific. US naval forces would also be redistributed with a greater focus on the Pacific Ocean. Although the Obama government repeatedly stressed that the pivot policy was not a response to China's military modernisation, these moves have nonetheless been widely regarded in China and outside as a response to Beijing's growing military presence in the region. The future effectiveness of the pivot/rebalancing policy, however, is open for debate, given post-2008 strains on the American economy, the development of other security crises appearing in the Middle East and North Africa since the pivot was announced, and the border conflict between Russia and Ukraine since 2014. As China's security interests push further out into the Pacific, there is the question of whether the two great powers, China and the United States, can accommodate their respective strategic interests in the region. During a July 2013 summit meeting with Barack Obama, Chinese President Xi downplayed any talk of a Pacific rivalry, noting that "the vast Pacific Ocean has enough space for the two large countries of China and the United States".[4]

Finally, after harbouring much suspicion about multilateral security cooperation, Beijing has altered its views considerably since the turn of the century, favouring multilateral security cooperation in areas such as arms control agreements and United Nations peacekeeping missions. By the end of 2014, Chinese personnel were serving in UN peacekeeping missions including in Lebanon, Mali, Sudan/South Sudan and Western Sahara, and at that time China was the largest contributor of UN peacekeeping personnel among the "permanent five" (P5) members of the UN Security Council. Overall, China has become more open to participating in multilateral security operations and has closely examined the benefits of developing policies related to "military operations other than war" or MOOTW.

Further evidence of China's growth and influence in international relations can be observed in its economy. The transformation of China from an isolated command economy to one of the largest market forces in the world in a period of 30 years is unparalleled in history. Until the end of the 1970s, Beijing closely followed its own version of the closed Soviet communist model of economics, including state control over almost all assets and strong discouragement of international investment. These policies were exacerbated, to disastrous effect, during the Great Leap Forward (*dayuejin* 大跃进) campaign under the country's first communist leader, Mao Zedong, in 1958–61 which plunged millions into poverty, accelerated widespread famine, and very nearly destroyed the Chinese economy. As well, after the death of Soviet leader Joseph Stalin in 1954, relations between China and the USSR deteriorated. Stalin's successor, Nikita Khrushchev, often disagreed with Mao on many issues, ranging from ideology to security concerns to relations with the United States.

Box 1.2 China and world order

"At this early stage of development, Chinese ideas about alternative world orders remain inchoate and contested within China itself. Accordingly, these visions have not yet gained traction within or beyond China. We suspect, however, that they will develop into a more appealing and consequential alternative ideology as they become more coherent and as China increases its power and prestige."

– Randall L. Schweller and Xiaoyu Pu, "After Unipolarity: China's Visions of International Order in an Era of U.S. Decline", *International Security* 36(1) (Summer 2011): 52.

"In order to pursue foreign policies appropriate to a post-hegemonic order all states, China and the United States included, must adjust to a new reality of negotiated asymmetry. The old status quo is dead. The new status quo, the 'status ad quem', must emerge. Our attention should shift from the familiar 'situation from which' of the hegemonic status quo to a more forward-looking 'situation to which' – a status ad quem of what is sustainable in a diversified and globalized world system."

– Brantly Womack, "China and the Future Status Quo", *Chinese Journal of International Politics* 8(2) (Summer 2015): 115–37.

By the beginning of the 1960s the two large communist states had essentially severed all ties with each other, leaving Beijing with few trading partners and no access to the widely developing global markets, led at that time by the United States, Europe and Japan. Worse for China, the decision to launch a party purification campaign, to be known as the Cultural Revolution (*wenhua dageming* 文化大革命), which began in 1966 and did not fully dissipate until Mao's death in 1976, created massive upheaval and chaos in both Chinese society and the CCP itself, taking place within a period of the country's most acute international isolation.

Following the sweeping economic reforms of Deng Xiaoping in the late 1970s, China's economy rapidly opened up to the world and the country attempted to revive its economy, starting with the acceptance of financial assistance from international donors, and later with the acceptance of international investment in the 1980s. From the late 1990s, Beijing began to encourage Chinese firms to "go out" (*zouchuqu* 走出去) and join the international market, creating global brands and joining with foreign partners. China had joined the World Trade Organisation (WTO) in 2001, and had begun to engage in increased trade and investment in markets well beyond Asia. Although China is a latecomer to globalisation theory and the ruling Chinese Communist Party remains wary of too much economic liberalisation which might prompt unwanted political change, China's impact on modern globalisation has been significant. China is now viewed as the factory of the world, producing many products for global markets. As has been argued in international relations theory, the purpose of foreign economic relations is largely to make the domestic politics of state more compatible with the global economy.[5]

In the case of China, while this goal has been realised in many cases, there remains much progress to be achieved. It is important to note that much of the Chinese economy remains in state hands (directly or indirectly), including state-owned enterprises or SOEs (*guoyouqiye* 国有企业), and there is ongoing government supervision of the financial sector, key commodity markets, and currency trade. Beijing has also changed its policies concerning free trade in the past decade, supporting the efforts of the WTO to liberalise global trade and becoming more willing to strike out on its own and negotiate preferential trade agreements both bilaterally, with developing and increasingly with developed economies, as well as with regional organisations. China's enthusiasm for free trade even extended into its relations with Taiwan, with both sides taking advantage of the post-2008 diplomatic thaw to construct an Economic Cooperation Framework Agreement (ECFA) in 2010 which removed numerous trade tariffs and opened the door for increased bilateral trade, investment and economic ties.

Economic growth in the country has hovered around 9–10 per cent since the turn of the century, and despite numerous predictions since the 1990s that what goes up must come down, the Chinese economy has weathered many shocks with little evidence of a slowdown, the most recent being the 2008 "credit crunch" and subsequent global economic crisis in the West. Following its entry into the WTO in 2001, Beijing developed its ability to significantly influence trade talks, while before the recession both the US and Europe worried about an influx of cheap Chinese goods, including everything from textiles to computers, in global markets. By the end of 2015, China was able to accumulate a staggering US$3.5 trillion in foreign currency reserves, a significant amount of that in American dollars, giving the state much influence in international investment.[6] The large Chinese market has not only affected developed economies in the United States, Japan and the European Union but also the economies of developing states, all of which became dependent upon Chinese products. As a result of China's rapid economic growth, the country is hungry for a large variety of commodities and energy products, and this need has helped to shape much Chinese diplomacy in Africa, Central Asia and Latin America.

In the aftermath of the recession, China found itself one of the main linchpins of the global economy as it moved to prevent an economic downturn created by a drop in demand for Chinese goods, especially in the shaky American and Western European markets. In November 2008, the Chinese government implemented an ambitious economic stimulus package worth about US$586 billion to improve domestic infrastructure and move the country away from an over-reliance on exports. Nevertheless, as the global slowdown began, debate in China continued as to how much longer the country could maintain such high growth rates, should the global economy remain sluggish, and even Beijing policymakers began to speak of a cooling off of Chinese growth. Markets became wary of the possibility of an economic "hard landing" for China and its potential effect on the global economy. However, since taking office the Xi government has been concentrating on preparing the Chinese economy for a more mundane "new normal" (*xin changtai* 新常态) for the Chinese economy, with slower economic growth rates (closer to 7 per cent GDP growth), to reflect the condition of the overall global economy and China's deeper engagement with it.

China, despite its economic progress and the envy of other developing states, is still a developing economy by many international standards, with many parts of the country, especially the interior, still struggling with high poverty levels. As China began to take off economically since the turn of the century, there was talk of a "Beijing Consensus" (*Beijing Gongshi* 北京共识), a model of Chinese-influenced economic growth, as opposed to the traditional "Washington Consensus" which was promoted since the 1990s by the United States and international economic organisations such as the International Monetary Fund (IMF) as the best way to develop economies.[7] While the latter promoted liberalisation and reducing state power, the former emphasises innovation and sovereignty rights. A Chinese model of economics, despite ongoing debate as to its structure, has arguably given China something it could never hope to achieve under Mao, namely *soft power* (*ruan shili* 软实力), meaning power based on attraction rather than force or coercion.

A question now often being asked by international political economy (IPE) specialists is whether China's experience in economic growth constitutes a "model" which could be transplanted, in whole or in part, to other developing states. The global recession only intensified this debate about the role of government in economic development, partially as a result of China's relative lack of damage from the economic downturn, and the question of a Chinese economic model has been wrapped up in the greater debate both within government and among international relations specialists, as to the benefits of "state capitalism" whereby the state retains a strong oversight role in production and key markets. This model has been taken up by other states to varying degrees, most notably by the government of Vladimir Putin in Russia, but also in smaller developing states.

While President Hu Jintao was concerned about promising too much regarding the growth of the Chinese economy, Xi Jinping, shortly after assuming the presidency, began to speak of a "Chinese Dream" (*Zhongguo meng* 中国梦) which not only suggested a greater degree of confidence in the country's economic future despite domestic and international challenges, but was also tied to the idea of the "rejuvenation" (*fuxing* 复兴) of China as a great economic power. Later in Xi's administration, there was discussion about expanding these ideas to a regional level, as the Chinese leader began to speak of an "Asia-Pacific dream" (*YaTai meng* 亚太梦) which would unify China and other parts of Asia in mutual development and prosperity.

Despite the rapid growth of globalisation which has resulted in an increase of ideas and media as well as capital into China, Beijing remains concerned about maintaining its sovereignty and remains wary of international calls for greater democracy and human rights, arguing that such areas must be addressed only by Beijing and at a pace with which China itself is most comfortable. The "colour revolutions" in the former Soviet Union in 2003–5, affecting Georgia, Ukraine and Kyrgyzstan, which saw autocratic governments being toppled by popular uprisings, raised concern in Beijing about a "demonstration effect", or a similar situation arising in China, and greater safeguards were undertaken to ensure that such a revolution, which the Chinese government has suggested was largely influenced by the work of Western agencies such as non-governmental organisations (NGOs), would not take place in the PRC. The colour revolutions in the former USSR acted as proof to many in the Chinese government that a peaceful evolution strategy is still being undertaken by the West, and as a result the CCP called for a "smokeless war" (*meiyouxiaoyan de zhanzheng* 没有硝烟的战争) against such influences.[8] The subsequent "Euromaidan" protests in Ukraine starting in late 2013 which resulted in the fall of the government of Viktor Yanukovych and subsequent Russian intervention in Crimea and Eastern Ukraine were also widely viewed in Chinese policy circles as being sparked by Western political interests.

In late 2010, the "Arab Spring" protest movements flared across Southwest Asia and North Africa, unseating long-entrenched governments in Egypt, Libya, Tunisia and Yemen, and touching off a civil war in Syria starting in 2011. The backlash from these events also contributed to a subsequent civil war in Libya since 2014 and the rise of an extremist quasi-state known as the Islamic State of Iraq and the Levant (ISIL), also known as ISIS or the "Islamic State", carved out of lawless regions in Iraq and war-torn Syria.

These events again created concerns in China about US and Western interference in other states' domestic political affairs. Beijing again sought to prevent a demonstration effect in China itself, going so far in 2011 as banning the word "jasmine" (*molihua* 茉莉花), the name for the Tunisian revolution, from internet sites and social media. These case studies suggest that the Chinese state is still seeking to better manage the forces of globalisation for the betterment of the state, while ensuring that the Communist Party maintains its paramount role in Chinese governance. Since Maoist times, Beijing has been concerned about so-called "peaceful evolution" (*heping yanbian* 和平演变), namely the concentrated attempt by outside actors, especially the West, to undermine socialism in China through a variety of political, socio-economic and cultural pressures. In 1991, the fall of the Soviet Union, the largest communist state and long-time rival to the United States, further sharpened Chinese sensitivities to Western interference in China from within.

Much of China's foreign policy in the area of state-to-state relations has been based on the Maoist era doctrine of the Five Principles of Peaceful Co-existence (*heping gongchu wuxiang yuanze* 和平共处五项原则), which calls for "mutual respect for each other's territorial integrity and sovereignty, mutual non-aggression, mutual non-interference in each other's internal affairs, equality and mutual benefit, and peaceful co-existence". Today, much of modern Chinese foreign policy remains guided by a strong Westphalian view on the importance of maintaining the sovereignty of states. There has also traditionally been an emphasis on the "four 'no's" (*sibu* 四不), namely no hegemony, no power politics, no military alliances and no arms racing.[9] However, those who see China as a potential threat suggest that the state may be waiting until its strength is further solidified before gradually shedding these ideals and behaving more like traditional rising powers. Beijing has countered these views with the assertion that it is interested in a peaceful rising in the international system and wishes to promote greater international harmony. As President Xi stated during a policy speech in January 2013,

Pursuing peaceful development is what the fine traditional Chinese culture calls for, and is a natural choice made by the Chinese people who have suffered so much in modern times. With the agonising sufferings inflicted by war etched in our memory, we Chinese cherish peace and stability. What we abhor is turbulence, what we want is stability and what we hope to see is world peace.[10]

China's diplomatic power is also on the rise, including within international organisations and regimes. After the Communist Revolution in 1949, Mao Zedong frequently railed against many international organisations which he claimed were proxies of imperialist powers such as the United States. China was shut out of the United Nations for much of the Cold War, with Taiwan acting on Mainland China's behalf. However, from the point at which Beijing regained its UN seat in 1971, China became one of the permanent five members with veto powers on the United Nations Security Council (UNSC) along with the United States, the Soviet Union / Russian Federation, Great Britain and France, giving it much power to make or break many international security initiatives. At the same time, China's current support for international intervention stands in contrast to its opposition to the policy during the Maoist era. This stance was partially a product of the 1950–3 Korean War, which saw Chinese volunteer forces, heeding Mao's call to "Resist America. Assist Korea" (*kangMei yuanChao* 抗美援朝), by fighting alongside the communist North Koreans against South Korea, the United States and other UN forces. However, even after the Cold War China has insisted that international intervention must be guided by the UN and especially its Security Council.

As a result, Beijing has been supportive of many UN peace operations, but has also been openly critical of non-UN missions such as the intervention by the North Atlantic Treaty Organisation (NATO) in Kosovo in 1999, and was ambivalent, but not obstructionist, about the American-led "coalition of the willing" operations in Iraq in 2003–11, US operations in Afghanistan in 2001–14, and NATO's air support for Libyan rebels seeking the overthrow of the Muammar Gaddafi regime during that civil conflict in 2011. Beijing's views on humanitarian intervention missions have evolved with China's insistence that the UN is the best actor to engage in such activity. By 2010, China was providing the largest number of United Nations peacekeeping personnel out of the permanent five members of the UN Security Council. However, Beijing has shown no reluctance to veto UN resolutions which it views as being too interventionist in states' sovereign affairs, including resolutions which featured condemnations of governments in Myanmar and Sudan. Since the beginning of the civil war in Syria, China joined Russia in vetoing UNSC resolutions which would have pressured Syrian president Bashar Assad to step down in the wake of escalating antigovernment violence.

Beijing's engagement in other types of international institutions is also growing. From the time of its admission to the WTO, the country has been an active member and has often defended the rights of developing states to a new global trade deal which better reflects their interests. At the same time, China's enthusiasm for free trade on a regional scale has also grown, supporting liberalised trade with Southeast Asia and to a lesser degree with Japan and South Korea. China is also a driving force within the Asia-Pacific Economic Cooperation (APEC) forum, which seeks to liberalise trade across the Pacific Rim to better compete with the European Union and North America. As well, China has been at the forefront of new Asian political and economic communities, including the ASEAN-plus-three (APT) organisation uniting Northeast and Southeast Asian economies, and the newer East Asia Summit (EAS), created in 2005 as a dialogue group for Asian economies. The Shanghai Cooperation Organisation (SCO) was founded in 2001 and brought together China, Russia and most of Central Asia for security and trade cooperation, with China contributing much to the organisation's policymaking. In May 2014, Beijing hosted the Conference on Interaction and Confidence Building Measures in Asia (CICA), a security organisation which includes governments from across Asia and the Middle East. At the event, Xi spoke of the need to move further beyond Cold War thinking and develop solutions to regional security issues which better reflected Asia itself.

In short, China has been very much a "joiner" of international institutions and remains wary of any such organisations of which it is not a member. For example, China has been sensitive to perceived attempts by the United States to establish a security regime in the Asia-Pacific by tying together all of its regional bilateral partners into a group which might seek to balance Chinese power. More specifically, Beijing reacted with concerns when the Trans-Pacific Partnership (TPP), originally a small-scale, four-member free trade agreement in the Pacific in 2005, added the United States as a member after 2010 along with other regional economies including Australia, Canada, Japan, Malaysia and Vietnam, and began working in 2011 towards liberalising mutual trade well beyond APEC guidelines, with a tentative agreement struck in October 2015. Beijing was not included in TPP meetings despite its economic presence, and questions were raised in China as to whether the TPP might be used as means of checking Beijing's regional economic power, and was simply another arm of the US "pivot" policy.

However, since taking office, President Xi has been more active in developing newer international regimes which better reflect Beijing's foreign policy interests. China is a major shaper of the "BRICS" group (which also includes Brazil, Russia, India and South Africa), and supported the 2014 development of a BRICS financial institution, the New Development Bank (NDB) which would act as an alternative to the traditional, Western-backed lending institutions of the International Monetary Fund (IMF) and the World Bank. Also in 2014, President Xi proposed and began to develop another financing body, known as the Asian Infrastructure Investment Bank or AIIB which would support infrastructure development in the Asia-Pacific region. Finally, in response to Beijing's exclusion from the TPP, during the annual APEC leadership summit in Beijing in November 2014, President Xi proposed a revival of a "Free Trade of the Asia-Pacific" framework which, long-discussed within APEC since the 1990s, would result in liberalised trade across the region, including with China.

The more ambitious foreign policy designs of the Xi government have been illustrated by the development of a "one belt and one road" (*yidai yilu* 一带一路) strategy of developing new land and sea links with vital Western European markets via Eurasia and Russia. Central to these new links would be the "Silk Road Economic Belt" (*sichouzhilu jingjidai* 丝绸之路经济带), which would stretch across Central Asia and the Caucasus and Bosporus regions, with one link to Moscow and another to Western Europe. In addition to trade, the creation of the "belt" would also entail increased bilateral cooperation between Beijing and Central Asian and Caucasus states along with Russia.

These overland routes, which harken back to the trade routes between Imperial China and Europe first established during the Han Dynasty more than two millennia ago, would be accompanied by a "Maritime Silk Road" (*haishang sichouzhilu* 海上丝绸之路) or MSR. This route would traverse the Indian Ocean with ports in Bangladesh, India, Sri Lanka and Eastern Africa, and also involve the countries of the Association of Southeast Asian Nations (ASEAN). Like its landlocked counterparts, the Maritime Silk Road also has a historical precedent in the form of Indian Ocean sea routes traversed by Chinese vessels during the Tang Dynasty (618–907 CE) which linked the Imperial Tang Empire with the Byzantine Empire in south-eastern Europe and the Caliphates of southwest Asia, as well as eastern Africa and the Indian subcontinent.[11] The development of the MSR, which would greatly enhance China as a maritime power in Asia after many long decades of being seen as primarily a "continental" power with a primary focus on securing land borders,[12] was the result of several successful diplomatic initiatives including a South Asia tour by President Xi in mid-2014, as well as diplomatic initiatives which Chinese officials undertook in Southeast Asia during that year.[13] The MSR initiatives, in addition to their potential economic importance, suggest that Beijing has become more open to the idea of an "Indo-Pacific" sphere which was developing as East and South Asian financial and strategic interests begin to converge.[14]

China's growing diplomatic and "structural" power, meaning the ability to accrue what it wants through skilful engagement of organisations and norms internationally, means that it is not only better equipped to successfully join international organisations to benefit its foreign policy, but it is now able to shape their development in some cases, such as the AIIB and SCO, and to play a central role within them. During the Cold War, China under Mao was categorised as a "norm shaker", meaning that it often directly challenged the norms and policies set down by Western powers. However, after the Cold War Beijing was far more open to being a "norm taker", accepting and even welcoming participation with international, including Western, regimes and institutions. As China continues to develop as a great power, the country has become much more willing to be a "norm shaper", developing new structures and ideas which may run counter to those of the West.

Finally, China's "bigness" has also extended into health and environmental issues. Its large population is still attempting to address modern health care, and shortcomings in the system were graphically magnified as a result of the severe acute respiratory syndrome (SARS, known in China as *feidian* 非典) crisis in 2002–3. Initially, Beijing was strongly criticised for its lack of a rapid response to the crisis and the country later undertook a massive campaign to eradicate the disease. China is also seen as being highly susceptible to avian influenza which could potentially affect humans, and has participated in international endeavours to combat such an outbreak. Beijing also gratefully accepted international aid in May 2008 in the wake of a devastating earthquake which resulted in more than 700,000 casualties in Wenchuan County, in Sichuan province in central China, even requesting satellite information on affected areas from the United States. Analysts noted the contrast between Beijing's openness about the Wenchuan disaster and its conduct during the last major quake in Tangshan in 1976, when all offers of foreign assistance were rebuffed in the name of state secrecy.[15] China has also assisted with aid programmes elsewhere in the world, including disaster relief to South and Southeast Asia after the December 2004 Indian Ocean tsunami and to the United States after Hurricane Katrina in August 2005. However, Beijing was initially criticised for its tepid response to the massive damage caused by Typhoon Haiyan in the Philippines in November 2013, before later sending further funds and a relief team.

Box 1.3 Structural power

"Scholars focusing on institutional power usually define institutions and structure in almost interchangeable terms, as sets of rules, procedures, and norms that constrain the action of already-constituted actors with fixed preferences. Scholars focusing on structural power conceive structure as an internal relation – that is, a direct constitutive relation such that the structural position, A, exists only by virtue of its relation to structural position, B."

– Michael Barnett and Raymond Duvall, "Power in International Politics", *International Organisation* 59 (Winter 2005): 53.

The environment is another problem in China which is more visibly affecting the international system. The state contains some of the most polluted cities in the world, and has surpassed the United States to become the largest single contributor of carbon and pollution emissions. These problems, affecting land, water and air quality, are beginning to produce residual effects well beyond China itself, including sandstorms, smog and potential contributions to global warming. Although China is a signatory to the 1997 Kyoto Protocol which seeks to reduce global greenhouse gasses, China's legal designation as a developing state has exempted it from many of the agreement's provisions. As Beijing prepared for the Olympic Games in August 2008, much local and global pressure prompted the Chinese government to think more in terms of how much of the country's income, in areas including health and infrastructure, could be lost due to environmental damage.[16] In March 2014, Chinese premier Li Keqiang called for a "war on pollution" in the wake of record low air quality in Chinese cities during previous winters. Nonetheless, China demonstrated wariness about being asked to contribute too much to global environmental initiatives, as evidenced when American and Chinese representatives at the Copenhagen climate conference in late 2010 sharply disagreed on the provisions of the final accord. The Xi government did agree to stronger action on climate change during the Chinese leader's visit to Washington in September 2015.

Beijing is now growing increasingly conscious of its international status as it continues to assume the rights and responsibilities of a great power. Thus, in sharp contrast to the Maoist era, China is much more sensitive to the manner in which its identity and its foreign policies are perceived abroad, especially considering that no previous great power had ever "grown up" in an international milieu saturated with so many norms, organisations, regimes and information flows. What has also changed is that China now has access to many more tools in the international system which it can use to promote the idea that the country is returning to the great power status which it enjoyed centuries ago.

Box 1.4 China's quiet diplomacy?

"China must be the most self-aware rising power in history."
      – Mark Leonard, *What Does China Think?* (London: Fourth Estate, 2008), 84.

"China has come a long way in its diplomatic dealings with the world, but it remains a cautious diplomatic actor – and one which uses diplomacy largely in pursuit of its priority goal of economic modernisation as well as offsetting threats to its national security."
      – David Shambaugh, *China Goes Global: The Partial Power* (Oxford and New York: Oxford University Press, 2013), 120.

"China has participated in many of the prestige aspects of the nineteenth and twentieth century Western orders: hosting the Olympics; addresses by its presidents before the United Nations; reciprical visits with heads of state and governments from leading countries around the world. By any standard, China has regained the stature by which it was known in the centuries of its most far-reaching influence. The question now is how it will relate to the contemporary search for world order, particularity in its relations with the United States."
      – Henry Kissinger, *World Order* (New York: Penguin Press, 2014), 225–6.

Great power diplomacy

In the past, the rise of a great power often involved the displacing of another great power, sometimes violently. This was especially the case when a challenger great power felt that it was not being well served by the current global order, a central theme in power transition theory within international relations studies. This practice has become much more risky in the modern era of nuclear weapons which have served to deter great power conflict. However, the ascent of China to the realm of modern great powers, especially in such a swift and comprehensive fashion, calls into question how other great powers in the modern international system will accept China's arrival. As the centenary of the start of the First World War in 1914 approached, many international relations scholars, including in East Asia, debated whether the current conditions between China, the United States, and other East Asian nations were creating similar conditions to the fractious politics in Europe, including great power posturing amongst Austria-Hungary, Germany, Russia and the United Kingdom, which touched off WWI.[17]

One of the most significant changes in China's international relations is the fact that Beijing has become much more comfortable in its dealings with great powers than was the case during the first decades of the People's Republic when Mao was focused on the two superpowers and possibly even a "total war" between them. After Chinese relations with the USSR soured, more attention was paid to non-great powers including developing states. However, with China's power growth the question of how Beijing has and should relate to great powers has again assumed a priority for the country's foreign policy, with the primary focus now on the United States, especially in the wake of growing debates over whether American power is eroding in relation to the rest of the world.

Relations with the United States remain of considerable concern to Beijing, and since the end of the Cold War, these relations have been on a virtual roller-coaster. In the 1990s, China was unhappy with the idea of a "new world order" with the United States as the single superpower and repeatedly called for a more multilateral world system with many great powers, including China, having a say in major global issues. The Sino-American relationship took another turn after the terrorist attacks in the United States in September 2001 and the subsequent onset of the global war on terror (GWoT). After naming China as a "strategic competitor" upon taking office, President George W. Bush sought Chinese assistance in combating international terrorism, a campaign Beijing, also concerned about terrorism and extremism both domestically and internationally, agreed to join. However, the two countries have differed on occasion as to the definition of a terrorist threat.

Critics of current Chinese foreign policy in the West, especially "hard" or "offensive" realists, argued that Sino-American relations during the GWoT were more of a marriage of convenience than a long-term partnership, and that great power competition between the two sides will inevitably restart especially as Chinese interests begin to brush up against American ones with more frequency. In many cases, China was content to "bandwagon" with the United States on a number of foreign policy issues, including security matters and trade. For example, the Chinese press reacted negatively to an August 2014 *New York Times* interview with US President Obama in which he suggested that China was a "free rider" on American policies in the Middle East, and had been so for decades. However, there is the realist argument that as Beijing grows in power, it may seek to balance the power of the United States instead. These views have increased in intensity within Western policy circles under the Xi presidency, especially as the Chinese leader began to make reference early in his administration to Sino-American relations as being categorised as "a new type of great power relations" (*xinxing daguo guanxi* 新型大国关系). The message within this statement was clear. While Hu Jintao saw China as "peacefully developing" towards great power status, Xi began to see China as having attained that rank.

Even so, comparing potential balancing behaviour of China with that of the USSR is problematic, since unlike the Soviet Union, China has no sphere of influence *à la* Eastern Europe in the twentieth century and has neither the power nor the immediate desire to create one, especially given Chinese concerns that such actions would spark a more overt balance of power game in Asia between China and the West. Another major difference between China and the Soviet Union was that the latter had no degree of economic interdependence with the United States. By contrast, the economic ties between Beijing and Washington have grown so strong that one prominent China specialist referred to the relationship as a "symbiosis".[18] Since 2009, American and Chinese officials meet biannually in a "Strategic and Economic Dialogue" (S&ED) to discuss economic and political issues affecting both sides. Despite differences between China and the United States over security issues, including in the Asia-Pacific, the two states remain firmly linked by trade and mutual economic concerns.

China's relations with Russia have also warmed considerably since the end of the Cold War. The two countries have proclaimed a partnership and have shared information on issues related to regional security as well as joint international interests. It was widely noticed that Xi's first trip as Chinese leader was to Moscow. The Sino-Soviet border hostilities which marked the latter half of the Cold War were later settled via extensive negotiations, and in June 2008 the last of the two states' border disputes were settled with 174 km² of disputed land to be returned to Chinese sovereignty.[19] Economically, the two states began to move closer together, especially in the area of energy cooperation, culminating in a May 2014 natural gas deal worth US$400 billion. Despite some concerns in the West about a possible new alliance between the two large powers, the Sino-Russian relationship has been based primarily on partnership building, regional security concerns and increasingly on trade. The precarious state of the Russian economy after 2014 in the wake of Western sanctions against Moscow over the Crimean and Donbas conflicts in Ukraine has meant that Beijing has been wary of getting too close to its large neighbour. The 2014 Ukraine conflicts placed China in a difficult position, since while Beijing has frequently been critical of great power intervention in the other state's affairs, China was also unwilling to criticise Russian actions directly, noting that "historical prerequisites" existed between Russia and Ukraine.

Diplomacy across regions

A majority of the most significant foreign policy initiatives during the Chinese government of Jiang Zemin in the 1990s tended to focus on the great powers, especially the United States and Russia, as well as improving relations with other Asian states, including former adversaries such as South Korea, Vietnam, India and Singapore. Jiang was very interested in setting up a stable periphery for China in order to prevent the border conflicts which plagued both the Mao and Deng governments. Beijing was very successful in its "peripheral" (*zhuobian* 周边) diplomacy and many Cold War era border conflicts were resolved, while China began to develop as an active member of many Asia-Pacific initiatives including APEC and the ASEAN Regional Forum (ARF). When Jiang was succeeded by Hu Jintao in 2003, many outside observers were unsure of the new leader's foreign policy priorities as he had travelled little and his background in international affairs was a mystery to analysts.

Not long after taking office, however, using as a foundation Beijing's diplomatic successes in Asia, Hu began to build a policy of "cross-regional diplomacy", seeking to expand Chinese diplomatic ties with regions beyond the Asia-Pacific, including Europe as previously noted, but also in the developing states of Africa, the Middle East, Latin America and the South Pacific. Much Chinese diplomacy in these regions has been trade driven, as China has sought deals for regional commodities and in some cases energy. At the same time Beijing began to develop its role as an alternative to the West in these regions, and has been increasingly interested in developing different types of diplomatic and economic initiatives to better cement partnerships.

To give one example, Sino-European relations have been transformed in the past decade, with many European governments seeing Beijing as an alternative "pole" to the United States as well as a promising multifaceted trade partner. The recession hit many Western European economies hard, followed by the post-2011 eurozone crises which saw many European Union (EU) members suffer financial shocks, especially Greece but also Ireland, Italy, Spain and Portugal. Beijing was seen as a potential lifeline for increasingly insolvent parts of the Union. Before the recession, China had been criticised by the EU for unfair trade practices, an undervalued currency, and high trade deficits. Although free trade had been discussed between the EU and China, there is thus far little agreement among the membership as to how to proceed, and instead Beijing sought bilateral free trade agreements with non-EU members with mixed success. As well, at the beginning of the decade, some EU states, such as France and Germany, began to quietly promote the lifting of an arms embargo against Beijing, implemented since the Tiananmen Incident in June 1989. However, after much internal dissent, changes in government in Europe, as well as pressure from the United States, the European Union tabled that debate. China has also been pushing for the EU to formally recognise it as a "market economy", a move which had been resisted by some European policymakers. Despite these political differences, China has become an increasing foreign policy priority for European states, especially Germany, which was placed in the difficult position of being an island of stability of European economy under the leadership of Angela Merkel.

In another example, in Africa, Beijing has been making many diplomatic inroads via trade and cooperation agreements, and a watershed in the relationship was reached with the development of regular Sino-African summits.[20] China is now widely viewed as an important diplomatic and economic partner, including a major source of loans, for sub-Saharan Africa, but the relationship has not been without its problems. Beijing came under Western criticism for its Africa policies, which have stressed non-interference in government affairs, in both Sudan, whose government had fought a civil conflict in the country's Darfur province, and Zimbabwe, with a regime which had become an international pariah due to its oppressive rule. When oil-rich South Sudan achieved independence from Sudan in 2011, Beijing had to play a delicate diplomatic game to ensure stable relations with both sides. Despite setbacks, China has argued that its distinct approach to developing state diplomacy will increase mutual trade and combat poverty and underdevelopment. There is the question, however, of whether a rivalry between China and Western states will develop over trade deals with the developing regions and emerging markets. In short, China's cross-regional diplomacy has further underscored Beijing's increasing confidence in developing its foreign policy well beyond its original "comfort zone" for the Asia-Pacific region. This has marked a major step in China's development from a regional power to one which is more comfortable in engaging the international system.

Domestic actors in Chinese foreign policy

The number of issues which Chinese foreign policy must examine has directly impacted the domestic actors responsible for foreign policymaking in the country. As with domestic politics, foreign policymaking in China is dominated by the CCP. Yet as with Chinese domestic politics, there have been many changes, since Maoist times, in determining who plays a part in China's international relations. During the time of Mao Zedong, foreign policy was the responsibility of a closed elite, with much of the population having little say or even knowledge of China's international affairs. This changed with the coming to power in the late 1970s of Deng Xiaoping, who required greater foreign policy and especially trade expertise from his government. Deng's immediate successors, Jiang Zemin and Hu Jintao, insisted on even greater professionalism and education in the foreign policy arena. This policy has continued under Xi Jinping and Premier Li Keqiang. The era of closed foreign policymaking in China has diminished, and today no single actor has the ability to make unilateral decisions on international affairs. One question, however, is how the diversification of agents and structures will affect Beijing's still-evolving foreign policy thinking. The process of foreign policymaking in China is still very opaque compared with that of Western states and it is often difficult for outside observers to determine how particular decisions are made.

Although most foreign policy influence remains within the government and the CCP, non-governmental actors are slowly but surely gaining a voice as well. In China's larger cities, think-tanks dedicated to foreign policy are growing along with academic departments dedicated to looking at comparative foreign policy and international relations theory. Many of these institutions have been given more leeway to discuss foreign policy issues but some "red lines" remain. It was not long ago that the government was the sole source of foreign policy information, but as China has globalised, the number of information outlets has grown, including a more diverse news media, although critics have argued that even more transparency is needed. There is also rapidly increasing internet use in the country, with China now having the largest number of internet users in the world (668 million as of June 2015). The use of micro-blogs (*weibo* 微博) and messaging services like WeChat (*Weixin* 微信) in China has also exploded in popularity as the number of mobile internet users in China rose to 594 million by mid-2015. Information about foreign affairs issues, and online debates about China's foreign policy, have proliferated. However, internet censorship in China remains a source of international debate, as some Western news services, social media and video-streaming sites continue to be blocked in China. In January 2015, the Xi government began to crack down on virtual private networks (VPNs), which allowed some Chinese internet users to "climb the wall" and evade censors, as well as webmail sites such as Gmail.

Each Chinese leader has endeavoured to place a distinct stamp on Chinese foreign policy, and Xi Jinping has not been an exception. In addition to the idea of a Chinese and

---

Box 1.5　Xi Jinping and Li Keqiang

Xi Jinping (习近平) was born in 1953 and was a native of Fuping in Shaanxi Province. He received his degree in chemical engineering at Tsinghua University in Beijing in 1979 and joined the Communist Party in 1974. After assuming CCP positions in Hebei, Fujian, Zhejiang, he was appointed Party head in Shanghai after the ousting of Chen Liangyu in 2007. Shortly afterwards, he was appointed to the Politburo Standing Committee and made Vice President of China in 2008.

Asia-Pacific dream, the Chinese president has been upbeat about the development of "big diplomacy with Chinese characteristics" (*Zhongguo tese de daguo weijiao* 中国特色的大国外交) and expanded relations on the international level as well as in the Asia-Pacific region.

In a speech to the Australian parliament in Canberra in November 2014, President Xi noted that China was taking on the persona of a "big guy in the crowd" (*yige dajia huo zai renqun zhong* 一个大家伙在人群中), suggesting that "others will naturally wonder how the big guy will move and act, and be concerned that the big guy may push them around, stand in their way or take up their place". However, in the same remarks, Xi stressed that China wanted to develop in cooperation with the international community, and that the country's own history demonstrated that warlike states, regardless of their size, were consistently doomed to eventually fail. In late 2014, Xi published a compilation of his domestic and foreign policy statements in several languages. The work, entitled *Xi Jinping: The Governance of China* (*Xi Jinping tan zhiguolizheng* 习近平谈治国理政), addressed a wide variety of topics including the role of the Party, the "Chinese Dream", economic development, the environment, security issues, law, culture, and regional and international relations. Compared with his immediate predecessors, Xi appeared to be much more comfortable placing a personal stamp on Chinese foreign policy.

The greater foreign policy confidence expressed by Xi Jinping is an interesting contrast to the more cautious approach taken by his predecessor, Hu Jintao. Two major foreign policy concepts which had dominated Hu's foreign policy were "peaceful rise" (*heping jueqi* 和平崛起) or "peaceful development" (*heping fazhan* 和平发展) and "harmonious world" (*hexie shijie* 和谐世界). The first ideas referred to the fact that although China was a growing power, it would not grow along the same lines as other great powers of the past, namely not by military force and material acquisition. Scholars frequently debated the validity of this policy, and even in China some officials worried that using the word "rise" was also too confrontational, preferring the term "peaceful development" instead. "Harmonious world" referred to Hu's preference for global peace and stability through cooperation and communities rather than alliances and overt use of force.

Both Hu and Premier Wen Jiabao made multiple trips to many parts of the world, including to many developing regions, to promote mutual cooperation, trade and dialogue. This diplomacy, which has been called China's "charm offensive", made considerable inroads in Chinese foreign policy and stood in marked contrast to much American diplomacy, which was often focused specifically on security and counter-terrorism. China has also been seeking to better educate foreign actors about Chinese history and culture. Since 2004, there has been the proliferation of Confucius Institutes (*Kongzi xueyuan* 孔子学院) designed to promote Chinese language and culture abroad.

Some of China's charm offensive policy began to show strains in parts of Asia after 2008, when Beijing began to more overtly press its maritime claims in the Asia-Pacific and experienced diplomatic clashes with some of its neighbours, including Japan and Southeast

---

Box 1.6 China dreams

"The Chinese Dream is a desire for happiness, similar to the dreams of people in other countries. The people can attain happiness only when their country and nation thrive. China will thrive only when the world prospers."

– Xi Jinping, "The Rejuvenation of the Chinese Nation is a Dream Shared by
All Chinese", 6 June 2014.

Asia. However, the Hu government maintained its stance that China will develop as a status quo power and an international partner. During the first few years of the Xi presidency, high levels of summit diplomacy in Asia and beyond continued, but a greater degree of confidence was demonstrated in Chinese foreign policy. Expanded international relations interests and calls by the Xi government for a "great rejuvenation of the Chinese nation" (*Zhonghua minzu weida fuxing* 中华民族伟大复兴) left little doubt that China was ready to better assume its role as a great power.

Outline of the book

This book will examine how China's foreign policy interests have expanded and deepened in recent times and the effect of these changes on the modern international system. This will be undertaken through specific case studies as well as by broader analysis of developments, trends and ideas in Beijing's international relations. The key ideas expressed in this work will be that not only are Chinese foreign policy interests being expanded domestically and internationally, but that China's foreign policy itself is currently in a process of reconstruction to better fit both a changed international system as well as China's rising power within it. Chapter 2 will examine the question of who is now responsible for developing China's foreign policy interests, and how the study of international relations can explain some processes of Chinese foreign policy decision-making. The answer to who makes Chinese foreign policy is still very opaque, but as a result of the country's expanding foreign concerns and interests, the number of persons and institutions both within government and also without involved in China's foreign policy processes is growing. Although in many cases there is still much about the decision-making process which remains centralised, a "diversification" of actors involved in the process can now be studied.

Chapter 3 will examine the effects of China's growing economic power on its foreign policy thinking and how trade and globalisation are now playing a much more prominent role in international relations, a remarkable change from the closed economics of the Maoist era. China as a trading power is affecting many states in both the developed and developing world, and there is now the question of whether China's history of rapid development could serve as a model to other states. As well, after either shunning or being shut out of the various global endeavours to liberalise trade throughout the Cold War, China is now participating in large- and small-scale initiatives to improve international markets. Chapter 4 picks up on the theme of China's ongoing search for greater inclusion in the international arena by exploring its changed approaches to international institutions. During the early decades of the Cold War, Beijing's policy reflected a deep suspicion of international organisations which added to its isolationism after the Sino-Soviet Split (*Zhongsu jiaoe* 中苏交恶) of the early 1960s. Today, however, China is an enthusiastic joiner of many different types of institutions and is now confident enough in its abilities to pursue "goods" including material gains, political power and greater prestige, through the selective engagement of international institutions as well as the creation and development of new ones outside of Western practices. As well, China's evolving approaches to various areas of international law will be examined.

China's security concerns have in some ways decreased, as it is no longer as concerned about border conflicts or military clashes with great powers. However, in addition to the ongoing Taiwan question there are a number of newer security concerns which are considered less traditional, including terrorism, international crime, the safety of trade and shipping, cybersecurity, and increased participation in global UN peacekeeping and war-to-peace transitions. As well, Beijing remains concerned about the long-term strategy of the United

States towards China, as the gaps between American and Chinese power levels narrow. China has responded to these challenges by seeking to modernise and better fund its military, making it more capable of projecting power further abroad, including via growing sea power, and simultaneously searching for ways to improve security via international cooperation and confidence-building. Chapter 5 will thus be based on Beijing's developing strategic thinking and the role played by the military in modern Chinese international relations.

Chapter 6 will look at the importance of one specific state-to-state relationship, that between China and the United States. From a myriad number of viewpoints, ranging from diplomatic to economic to strategic, the Sino-American relationship is now seen as not only crucial for both states but also one of the most watched relationships in the modern international system. The chapter will trace the relationship from its beginnings through the Cold War and on to the present situation of partnership in some areas but also of "ambiguity". The United States and China today are neither friends nor enemies but lie somewhere in between, and the future of the relationship will have effects on the international system well beyond the two actors.

The following two chapters will track China's international interests after the start of the reform era from the regional to cross-regional level. Chapter 7 will examine Beijing's warming relations with countries in East, South and Southeast Asia as well as Oceania, since its peripheral diplomacy policies of the 1990s, as well as two regional cases of Japan and the Korean Peninsula, both of which have challenged China's regional policy and remain important concerns for Beijing. A major change in Asian foreign policy since the 1990s is that China's rise has entrenched the country as the political and economic centre of the Pacific Rim. Many East Asian states are therefore wondering how the relationship between China and the United States will play itself out in the region, in light of both the US "pivot / rebalancing" policies and China's developing plans to deepen its regional diplomacy and establish stronger Asian institutions which may more overtly rival those of the West.

Chapter 8 will then examine the more recent phenomenon of Beijing's cross-regional diplomacy, tracing the government's tentative and then more confident steps to engage regions beyond Asia, including Europe, Russia, South Asia, the Middle East and increasingly Africa, Latin America, and the Polar Regions for political, economic and strategic gains. Within a very short period of time, China has made its diplomatic presence felt in countries well beyond the Pacific Rim, challenging traditional ideas of "hegemony" and "spheres of influence" and underscoring that China as an actor is increasingly comfortable with international roles. The book will conclude by discussing the challenges ahead as China continues the process of expanding and reconstructing its foreign policy to better accommodate its domestic concerns and its goals within the ever-evolving international system.

Discussion questions

- Can China now be called a "great power"? If so, how does China differ from previous great powers?
- How does China's size in terms of its geography and its population affect its role in the international system?
- What are China's main priorities in its foreign policy today?
- What does Xi Jinping mean by the need for "big diplomacy with Chinese characteristics"?
- How did the post-2008 global financial crisis create shifts in Chinese power *vis-à-vis* other states?

Recommended reading

Callaghan, William A. and Elena Barabantseva (eds) *China Orders the World: Normative Soft Power and Foreign Policy* (Washington DC: Woodrow Wilson Centre Press, 2011).

Christensen, Thomas J. *The China Challenge: Shaping the Choices of a Rising Power* (New York: W.W. Norton, 2015).

Fenby, Jonathan. *Will China Dominate the 21st Century?* (Cambridge and Malden, MA: Polity Press, 2014).

Heilmann, Sebastian and Dirk H. Schmidt (eds) *China's Foreign Political and Economic Relations: An Unconventional Global Power* (Lanham and Boulder: Rowman & Littlefield, 2014).

Hunt, Michael E., *The Genesis of Chinese Communist Foreign Policy* (New York: Columbia University Press, 1996).

Kissinger, Henry. *On China* (New York: Penguin, 2011).

Li Lanqing. *Breaking Through: The Birth of China's Opening-Up Policy* (Oxford and New York: Oxford University Press, 2009).

Nathan, Andrew J. and Robert S. Ross, *The Great Wall and the Empty Fortress: China's Search for Security* (New York and London: W.W. Norton, 1997).

Rosecrance, Richard and Steven E. Miller (eds) *The Next Great War? The Roots of World War I and the Risk of US–China Conflict* (Cambridge: MIT Press, 2015).

Roy, Denny. *Return of the Dragon: Rising China and Regional Security* (New York: Columbia University Press, 2013).

Shambaugh, David. *China Goes Global: The Partial Power* (Oxford and New York: Oxford University Press, 2013).

Vogel, Ezra F. *Deng Xiaoping and the Transformation of China* (Cambridge and London: Belknap Press / Harvard University Press, 2011).

Yahuda, Michael. *China's Foreign Policy after Mao: Towards the End of Isolationism* (London and Basingstoke: Macmillan, 1983).

Yan Xuetong, *Ancient Chinese Thought: Modern Chinese Power* (Princeton and Oxford: Princeton University Press, 2011).

Zhu Zhiqun, *China's New Diplomacy: Rationale, Strategies and Significance* (Farnham, England and Burlington, VT: Ashgate, 2010).

Notes

1 Alexander E. Wendt, "The Agent-Structure Problem in International Relations Theory," *International Organisation* 41(3) (Summer 1987): 335–70; Walter Carlsnaes, "The Agency-Structure Problem in Foreign Policy Analysis," *International Studies Quarterly* 36(3) (September 1992): 245–70.

2 Harold K. Jacobsen and Robert D. Putnam (eds), *Double-Edged Diplomacy: International Bargaining and Domestic Politics* (Berkeley: University of California Press, 1993).

3 Keith Fray, "China's Leap Forward: Overtaking the US as World's Biggest Economy," *Financial Times*, 8 October 2014.

4 Remarks by President Obama and President Xi Jinping of the People's Republic of China Before Bilateral Meeting, Sunnylands Retreat, Palm Springs, California, *The White House, Office of the Press Secretary*, 7 June 2013, < http://www.whitehouse.gov/the-press-office/2013/06/07/remarks-president-obama-and-president-xi-jinping-peoples-republic-china->.

5 Peter J. Katzenstein, "Introduction: Domestic and International Forces and Strategies of Foreign Economic Policy," *International Organisation* 31(4) (Autumn 1977): 588.

6 Gabriel Wildau, "China's Large Forex Reserves Constitute Both a Blessing and a Curse," *Financial Times*, 30 September 2014.

7 Randall Peerenboom, *China Modernises: Threat to the West or Model for the Rest?* (Oxford and New York: Oxford University Press, 2007): 1–25.

8 David Shambaugh, "Learning from Abroad to Reinvent Itself: External Influences on Internal CCP Reforms," *China's Changing Political Landscape: Prospects for Democracy*, ed. Cheng

Li (Washington DC: Brookings, 2008): 292; Joseph Kahn, "China's Leader, Ex-Rival at Side, Solidifies Power," *The New York Times*, 24 September 2005.

9 Ralph A. Cossa, "US–Japan–China Relations: Can Three-Part Harmony be Sustained?" *The Brown Journal of International Affairs* 6(2) (Summer / Fall 1999): 89.

10 Xi Jinping, "Strengthen the Foundation for Pursuing Peaceful Development," *The Governance of China* (Beijing: Foreign Languages Press 2014), 271.

11 Li Qingxin, *Maritime Silk Road* (Beijing: China Intercontinental Press, 2006), 40–2.

12 Robert S. Ross, "The Geography of the Peace: East Asia in the Twenty-First Century," *International Security* 23(4) (Spring 1999): 103–8.

13 "China Accelerates Planning to Re-Connect Maritime Silk Road," *Xinhua*, 16 April 2014, < http:// news.xinhuanet.com/english/china/2014-04/16/c_133267903.htm>; "China Ready to Strengthen Maritime Cooperation with ASEAN," *Xinhua*, 16 September 2014; "Work Together to Build a 21st Century Maritime Silk Road," *Xi Jinping: On Governance* (Beijing: Foreign Languages Press, 2014), 320–4.

14 Liu Zhongyi, "New Delhi-Beijing Cooperation Key to Building an 'Indo-Pacific Era'," *Global Times / People's Daily*, 1 December 2014, <http://en.people.cn/n/2014/1201/c90780-8816244. html>.

15 Jake Hooker, "Quake Revealed Deficiencies of Chinese Military," *The New York Times*, 2 July 2008.

16 Elizabeth C. Economy and Adam Segal, "China's Olympic Nightmare," *Foreign Affairs* 87(4) (July / August 2008): 47–56.

17 Rosemary Foot, "Constraints on Conflict in the Asia-Pacific: Balancing 'The War Ledger'," *Political Science* 66(2) (December 2014): 119–42.

18 Susan L. Shirk, *China: Fragile Superpower* (Oxford and New York: Oxford University Press, 2007), 25.

19 Li Xiaokun, "China, Russia Sign Border Agreement," *China Daily*, 22 July 2008.

20 Horace Campbell, "China in Africa: Challenging US Global Hegemony," *Third World Quarterly* 29(1) (February 2008): 89–105.

2 Who (and what) makes Chinese foreign policy today?

People and policies

The decision-making processes guiding the development of Chinese foreign policy have traditionally been difficult to observe, especially from outside of the country. An attempt to examine the people and agencies responsible for the country's foreign policy development often provides only partial explanations or insights into Beijing's current or future policies. However, what can be argued is that the current perception of China's international relations as being decided by a very centralised and cloistered elite in Beijing is no longer as valid as it was previously, even under the government of Xi Jinping, as he has taken on a more direct role in both domestic and international affairs in China compared with recent previous leaders. The number of actors who participate in the formation of the country's foreign policy has grown both within the Chinese government as well as increasingly outside of it, and this trend is certain to continue as China's international interests grow and diversify. This chapter will examine the principal governmental actors and organisations responsible for crafting Chinese foreign policy today, beginning with the upper tier of the Chinese government and working towards lower-level government actors and others with much looser ties to the CCP.

To understand the role of domestic politics behind the evolution of China's international relations, one must begin by looking at the theories and ideas being used in China and elsewhere, including traditional theories of international relations and the growing role of different types of nationalism. Crafting an effective foreign policy while maintaining domestic affairs presents a challenge for any state as the line between the two continues to blur in the modern globalised world. However, in the case of China there is also the challenge of developing a foreign policy for a rising great power, while at the same time ensuring that Chinese domestic reforms, begun over 30 years ago, remain in place. In answering the question of who (and what) makes today's Chinese foreign policy, there are many different directions in which to look.

China's foreign policies at Cold War's end

The first two leaders of the People's Republic of China, Mao Zedong and Deng Xiaoping, had consolidated power to the point where they were central to much decision-making in both domestic and international relations policies. Under the governments of their successors, Jiang Zemin and Hu Jintao, Chinese foreign policymaking became more decentralised, as part of a greater focus on developing economic links and improved relations with the country's periphery and increasingly with other regions of the world. Greater emphasis was placed on the question of how Chinese foreign policy could help bring the country the stability it required in order to continue pursuing a complex series of domestic reforms designed to develop the country while keeping intact the paramount role of the Chinese Communist Party. At the same time, the number of actors involved in developing China's foreign policy grew considerably since the time of Mao and Deng, with more governmental and non-governmental actors having an actual or potential voice in the process.

Jiang Zemin left office having made significant progress in developing China's international relations, including opening up contacts both with the Pacific Rim region and with other parts of the world, including developing states. Jiang was also able to return China to its international status, including that of a rising economic power, after the trauma of Tiananmen in 1989, and oversaw the peaceful returns of Hong Kong and Macao to Chinese sovereignty in July 1997 and December 1999 respectively. China was also able to weather the Asian Financial Crisis in 1997–8 which saw the country ringed by economic crashes in East Asia, Southeast Asia and Russia. Foreign policy under the Jiang government also formed part of the separation process between policy and ideology, and unlike Mao and Deng, Jiang required a wider base of expertise for his administration to craft and implement new post-Cold War international relations. One summary of his foreign policy ideas reflected a pragmatic and more impartial (*bupianxie* 不偏斜) approach along with the need for Beijing to learn from global actors as well as the overall international system. He noted that China's foreign policy should encompass "making cool observations, dealing with situations calmly, grasping opportunities and making the best use of the situation".[1] This was a far cry from doctrines of the Mao era which stressed exporting of the socialist revolution as well as direct policy alignment against the West and later the Soviet Union and its allies.

At the same time, Jiang began to slowly but steadily depart from Dengist foreign policy which had stressed concealing China's capabilities, biding its time (*taoguang yanghui* 韬光养晦) in favour of more frequent experiments with "great power diplomacy" (*daguo weijiao* 大国外交).[2] Starting with China's immediate neighbours, Jiang sought rapprochement and improved relations based upon mutual benefits rather than ideology. It was under Jiang that China sought a policy of bilateral "partnerships" (*huoban* 伙伴), as well as increased multilateral cooperation through international organisations, which stressed political and often economic cooperation. As well, Jiang was comfortable with the foreign policy of summitry, attending high-level governmental meetings with other state leaders to develop partnerships and other deals. The establishment of many government-level organisations during Jiang's term in office, including the Asia-Pacific Economic Cooperation Forum (APEC) and the Shanghai Cooperation Organisation (SCO), provided many new opportunities for direct leader-to-leader talks.

Box 2.1 China's "partnership" agreements in the 1990s
1996 – Russia
1997 – ASEAN, Canada, France, India, Mexico, United States
1998 – European Union, Japan, Pakistan, United Kingdom
1999 – Egypt, Saudi Arabia, South Africa
 – Joseph Y.S. Cheng and Zhang Wankun, "Patterns and Dynamics of China's International Strategic Behaviour". *Chinese Foreign Policy: Pragmatism and Strategic Behaviour*, ed. Suisheng Zhao (Armonk, NY and London: M.E. Sharpe, 2004), 181.

Foreign policy expansion under Hu Jintao

In 2003, a leadership transition was completed between Jiang and his former vice-president, Hu Jintao. Unlike Jiang, Hu had less foreign policy exposure before assuming the presidency, and before coming to power had largely refrained from sharing his views on foreign relations. This transition marked the first time that such a transfer of power was made peacefully and as planned, and it was hoped that the Hu era would bring even more stability to both domestic and foreign policy in China. Like Jiang and many of China's current policymakers, Hu hailed from a scientific and technocratic background, studying hydroelectric engineering and barely escaping the Cultural Revolution with a degree in the mid-1960s before universities were forcibly shut down in the midst of the political chaos gripping the country.[3] Just as Deng Xiaoping chose Jiang to succeed him in the 1990s, Deng also chose Hu to succeed Jiang.

Hu's early political career in the CCP was spent in some of China's most remote areas of the interior, including Gansu and Tibet, which analysts have argued, explained his keen interest in fighting poverty and promoting economic equality. These interests were later transferred to foreign policymaking, especially the support for greater fairness in the international financial system. This was particularly obvious after the post-2008 global recession deepened and with more of a focus on global aid, assistance and peacebuilding. Initially, Jiang's ideas formed the basis for much of Hu's foreign policy, including his support for further trade development and the potential benefits from increased globalisation. Hu, like Jiang, was also critical of what he considered lingering Cold War thinking in the West and expressed his support for international multilateralism in different forms. His experience with the United States was especially limited, only visiting the country for the first time in 2002. Although Hu favoured ongoing American engagement, he nevertheless expressed concerns about potential US strategic "containment" policies directed towards Beijing in the post-Cold War era.

China's international interests under Hu Jintao were in many ways similar to Jiang's. There was a great deal of emphasis on the protection of the international status quo and a high concentration on developing trade and cooperation while enriching China's people and economy. Both leaders had been quick to criticise "old thinking" in other states, for example the persistence of alliances (such as NATO), in the West and concerns over establishing hegemony. However, while Jiang concentrated his diplomacy both on surrounding Asian states as well as big powers such as the United States and Russia, diplomacy under Hu became much more cross-regional, expanding in Africa, Europe, Latin America and Oceania/South Pacific. This process, as will be explained subsequently, has been accelerated under Xi Jinping. The maintenance of positive relations with China's many neighbours was seen as essential to both leaders, and China remained committed both to bilateral partnerships and increasingly to the United Nations and other international regimes.

Another similarity between the Jiang and Hu governments is that while both regarded China as a rising power in the international system, under Hu this idea was given much more prominence in policy speeches, with an emphasis on China's "peaceful development" and aversion to challenging the international system, as was a common practice by the Soviet Union and its satellite states. China's international thinking shifted considerably from that of a medium power seeking to overturn the status quo via revolution to a state seeking stability but also greater prestige and rights associated with being a great power. Beijing's claim to great power status is based on its growing market power and its increasing military capabilities, as well as its higher visibility in international regimes and its willingness and ability to promote its own interests further abroad.

A look at the individual level of analysis in foreign policy, as opposed to the state and international levels, also provides clues to the conservative views of foreign policy in the Chinese leadership. The individual level of analysis in international relations focuses on the role of leaders and policymakers. Although there are many agencies in China responsible for contributing to foreign policy, with many having much more influence than during the Maoist era, much of the overall decision-making power over both domestic and foreign affairs rests with the CCP Politburo Standing Committee, which includes the president, premier and other high-level officials. Many analysts seeking to gauge foreign and domestic policy directions often do so by examining the composition of the Standing Committee as it changes every five years. The "fourth generation" (*disidai* 第四代) of leaders in Beijing, including Hu and Premier Wen Jiabao, mainly came of age in the 1960s during the trauma of both the Cultural Revolution and the Sino-Soviet split, and historians suggest that this generation has a greater respect for maintaining international stability and order. Jiang was considered to be the political representative of the third generation of Chinese leadership, while Mao Zedong and Deng Xiaoping were considered to be the leaders of the first and second, respectively.[4]

As the head of the fourth generation, Hu Jintao's foreign policy sought to take advantage of China's improved standing in the international system, and Hu advocated a "theory of opportunity" (*jiyulun* 机遇论), stressing that Beijing should improve its security and its strategic policies by continuing its good-neighbour policies while expanding them beyond Asia. While Jiang's diplomacy was focused more on China's immediate periphery, including Southeast Asia, Russia and East Asia, the Hu government was much more comfortable in pursuing cross-regional diplomacy via a mix of economic and diplomatic initiatives. Upon taking office, Hu called for diplomacy and a foreign policy which stressed putting "people first" (*yiren weiben* 以人为本) and matched words with deeds by promoting greater transparency between foreign policymakers, especially the Ministry of Foreign Affairs and the people. An example of this was the anti-Japan protests in early 2005. At the same time, however, Hu, like Jiang, was sensitive to any policies of containment (*weidu zhengce* 围堵政策) emanating from the United States in the name of weakening or restricting Chinese power abroad.[5] Although American foreign policy shifted emphasis under the George W. Bush administration (2001–9) from great power politics to counter-terrorism and an international relations agenda dominated by Middle Eastern affairs, the tone shifted back, to a degree, under Barack Obama after 2009. With the withdrawal of American forces in Iraq in 2011 following almost a decade of operations and US disengagement from Afghanistan completed in 2014, the Asia-Pacific again assumed a more prominent role in American strategic planning and plans were established for American strategic "pivot" or "rebalancing" of US forces in the Pacific Rim. This move was viewed by China as a means of checking its own strategic expansion in the region. However, by President Obama's second term, terrorism in the form of the ISIL movement as well as conflicts in Eastern Europe and the Middle East would adversely affect US plans to place more strategic focus on the Pacific Rim.

The *disidai* was also the first generation which matured during the time of Deng's open-door economic policy and associated political and socio-economic benefits. As such, the current generation is considerably less attached to the original ideas of Maoist ideology foreign policy and the need for socialist revolution. This has been noteworthy in the case of North Korea, when Beijing in the 2000s adopted a much more pragmatic stance with the governments of Kim Jong-il and his son, Kim Jong-un, and their nuclear weapons development policies despite the two states' long-shared history. As well, unlike previous generations, the roster of policymakers in China during the Hu era had considerably more experience abroad and were able to observe international activities more directly and through a wider array of "Track I" (government) and "Track II" (sub-governmental) means. Although Hu's foreign policy and travel experience were comparatively limited in his role as Jiang's vice-president,[6] he more than compensated for it with numerous trips around the world for bilateral and multilateral meetings, including several to Europe, Latin America and Africa. Premier Wen Jiabao also made several high-profile trips to many parts of the world during his tenure.

Xi Jinping and the "fifth generation"

As Hu completed his term in office, more scrutiny was given to the political generation which would take power after the current president. Representatives of the "fifth generation" (*diwudai* 第五代) of Chinese leaders, born in or around the 1950s, were added to the CCP Politburo Standing Committee after 2007. The *diwudai* has been distinguished by an even greater exposure to the international system and higher education levels, with this generation better placed than its predecessors to appreciate the economic benefits of the Dengist reforms.[7] Following the October 2007 CCP Congress, two potential successors to Hu Jintao were elevated in rank, namely Xi Jinping as vice-president and Li Keqiang as vice-premier. Subsequently, Xi and Li were acknowledged as the next president and premier, respectively, after the 18th Party Congress in late 2012.

Xi, the first Chinese leader born after the revolution, joined the CCP in 1974, after multiple attempts, and later studied chemical engineering at Tsinghua University in Beijing. Xi was a leading Party representative in the wealthy province of Fujian before transferring to Zhejiang province and then being rapidly promoted to Party head in Shanghai after the ousting of Chen Liangyu following corruption charges in 2006. Jiang Zemin had also been leader of the Party in Shanghai in 1987–9 before being chosen as Deng Xiaoping's successor. Xi is also seen as being a member of the "princeling" group (*taizidang* 太子党) within the CCP, as his father was communist guerrilla leader Xi Zhongxun, who participated in the Long March in northern China during the Chinese Civil War in the 1930s, surviving a subsequent purge from the Party before being rehabilitated, thus giving Xi Jinping much ideological support within the CCP. During his career, Xi was also able to develop many international ties before assuming the presidency.

Li, a longstanding political ally of Hu Jintao, was based in two interior industrial provinces, Henan and Liaoning, earlier in his career and had a somewhat less defined international record. He was also distinguished by his educational background, which was in economics rather than the hard sciences like many "technocrats" in the Party's upper echelons during the Jiang and Hu eras. Before 2007, it was widely assumed that he was in the best position to succeed Hu Jintao as president, but he was seemingly outflanked politically by Xi, and instead was given the post of Premier.

However, beyond those posts there remained much uncertainty regarding which other policymakers would assume high positions and posts on the Standing Committee. In March 2012, Bo Xilai, CCP head of the municipality of Chongqing, was dismissed for "disciplinary violations" and later arrested amid accusations of corruption, abuse of power and possible involvement along with his wife, Gu Kailai, in the death of a British businessman. Bo, also a member of the "princeling" faction and well known for his populist, neo-leftist politics and enthusiasm for introducing traditional communist culture into his policies, was widely believed to be a viable candidate for Politburo Standing Committee membership after 2012 and was seen as openly campaigning for the position. His ousting, which garnered massive global attention, raised many uncomfortable questions about unity within the Party and brought into stark relief the problem of corruption within the party-state.

One of the most prominent domestic policies introduced by Xi since taking office was a widespread campaign against corruption within the ranks of the CCP. Although anti-corruption policies were not uncommon under previous Chinese governments, the width and depth of Xi's campaign has been unprecedented. The Xi government announced that it was not only targeting "tigers" (*laohu* 老虎), meaning high-ranking Party officials engaged in graft, but also "flies" (*cangying* 苍蝇), meaning low-ranked, local-level CCP members, and "foxes" (*hu* 狐), Party officials who sought to move massive amounts of wealth abroad, and often to escape China themselves, to avoid arrest. Several taboos, including not targeting high-ranking military personnel and former members of the CCP Politburo, were also broken, as high-level officials, or "tigers" were caught in corruption probes, including Ling Jihua, a former aide to Hu Jintao, and Xu Caihou, a General in the People's Liberation Army. By far the most visible "catch" however has been former Politburo member Zhou Yongkang, former head of the Central Political and Legal Affairs Commission of the Party, whose position was long considered unassailable even in retirement. In June 2015, Zhou was convicted of bribe-taking, abuse of power and leaking state secrets, and given a life sentence.

Concerns about the erosion of Party power have appeared in other political areas under Xi, including more visible efforts to prevent the proliferation of Western ideas of constitutional democracy and unchecked civil society which Chinese policymakers had traditionally maintained were incompatible with either Chinese governance or ongoing reforms. These concerns were addressed in a 2013 leaked internal Party memo entitled "Concerning the Situation in the Ideological Sphere", popularly known as "Document 9", which outlined apprehensions about the growth of Western values in the country, including media independence, neo-liberal economics, Western constitutional democracy and universal human rights. As with his predecessors, Xi expressed support for economic opening while retaining the paramount role of the CCP. In a January 2015 speech, Xi borrowed from Maoist terminology when he suggested that the "knife handle" (*daobazi* 刀把子) should remain in the hands of the Party and the people of China.

In addition to the anti-corruption campaign, Xi also used his first few years in office to unveil other concepts and ideas, including the "Chinese Dream" (*Zhongguo meng* 中国梦), which borrowed heavily from the "American Dream" ideas of the twentieth century and represented a strong signal that Beijing was demonstrating greater confidence in its economic capabilities despite the uncertain state of the global financial system. Central to the Chinese Dream concept was that China was in a process not only of growth but also of rejuvenation on the international level. This lofty idea was followed up in early 2015 with the unveiling of the "Four Comprehensives" (*sige quanmian* 四个全面) policies, namely Chinese leaders would comprehensively build a moderately prosperous society, deepen reform, govern the nation according to law, and strictly govern the Party. As with previous governments, the Xi administration wanted to ensure the longevity of the Party while guarding against the erosion of bonds between Party and people.

In the short period after Xi Jinping's taking office, Chinese domestic and international politics have become more personalised, but at the same time the diversification of China's foreign policy interests has continued apace. There has been a greater blurring of the lines between local and international affairs, and the number of policy actors within China responsible or influential in developing Chinese foreign relations continues to grow.

China's governing structure and foreign policy

Attempting to determine the domestic sources of Chinese foreign policy has in some ways become easier, but in others the question of who and what creates the policies which govern the country's international relations remains complex. Looking at foreign policy through agents and structures, it can be assumed that, unlike in Western states, information can often be incomplete or misleading. On the one hand, the era of single leaders in China dominating foreign policy decisions is over, despite current discussion about the stronger individual role taken by Xi Jinping in Chinese governance, especially compared with his predecessors. Instead, most decisions on the international level must be made through ministerial and bureaucratic consultation. As well, non- or semi-governmental actors, including businesses, NGOs and lobby groups, have been transformed from peripheral actors to much stronger players in Chinese foreign policy. Economic globalisation has forced some areas of foreign policy to become more transparent, and Beijing's expanded participation in international institutions has also assisted with providing more windows into the decision-making processes. Beijing's strong "neo-Westphalian" policy stance, stressing the sanctity of state sovereignty, has caused it to be extremely wary of foreign influence on its international relations decision-making processes. In short, the CCP still commands foreign policy, but the circle of decision-makers has become more diversified. As the Chinese state continues its economic and bureaucratic reforms, changes have begun to be observed at both the international and the domestic level.

Although the Chinese Communist Party has undergone a variety of changes since its inception, many of its institutions and much political thinking are left over from its revolutionary days, as can be seen in the Chinese constitution, the structure of the CCP, and its governing institutions. China today remains a "party-state", meaning that there is negligible separation between the apparatus of government and the structure of the CCP. Despite several moves away from Maoist philosophies, especially in the area of economics, the Party maintains its right to remain as the paramount political actor within the country as well as the right to maintain so-called *democratic centralism*, meaning that an individual is subordinate to the whole within the Party structure. Although there have been sporadic attempts, especially under Deng Xiaoping, to more clearly separate Party and government, the two remain inexorably linked. The democratic centralist idea has meant that the governing structure of China is that of a sharply defined pyramid, with local CCP organisations and work units on the bottom, working its way upward to the county, city and provincial levels and eventually to the upper echelons of the Party based in Beijing.

At the same time, another guiding principle in Chinese politics has been the idea of *collective leadership* within the Party, making it impossible for the government to return to one-person rule and the cult of personality which Mao enjoyed. Mao was able to exercise power even during times when he was not a formal member of the government, and Deng Xiaoping, despite having formally retired in the early 1990s, was also able to influence many aspects of Chinese governance until his death in 1997. Personality cults after that time were strongly discouraged under CCP codes of conduct. Jiang, for example, may have made an attempt to retain some degree of formal role within the Party in 2003 as he was planning his own retirement, but if so, did not succeed. Upon retirement, he remained an elder statesman within the Party with a great deal of influence both personally and via his subordinates, but not to the same degree as Deng. Hu was even less visible after his retirement, and critics argued that despite the impressive economic gains China saw under his government, he missed other opportunities for further reform and that in some ways his tenure was even a "lost decade".

Xi Jinping, by contrast, has been willing to play a more personal role in Chinese government affairs, and as a result the degree of collective policymaking has become less visible. His more personable style has resulted in an online nickname, "Uncle Xi" (*Xi Dada* 习大大) with cartoons and videos released which have highlighted his day-to-day work as well as campaigns such as that against corruption. One popular viral video, released on the Chinese website Youku in late 2013, compared the American and British leadership systems with China's, noting the differences in how a leader gets chosen and highlighting the process of "trials and tests" in the appointment of a Chinese president. The clip concluded with the assertion that while different countries have differing political systems, "as long as the people are satisfied, and the country develops and progresses as a result, it's working". As well, Xi's wife, Peng Liyuan, has had much greater public visibility compared with previous presidential spouses. Peng is famous in her own right, being one of China's most famous opera and folk singers, and was also an entertainer with the PLA. It remains to be seen, however, whether the trend towards greater decentralisation of policymaking power has actually slowed despite Xi's more direct approaches.

Since the 1990s, the upper tiers of power within the CCP have become much more decentralised, with both the Jiang and the Hu governments prevented from creating laws and policies without a great deal of support and information from various ministries. At the same time, the CCP itself has shown signs of developing specific factions based on political background, age, geography, and political connections. The need for consensus-building, largely buried under Mao, slowly returned and remains a crucial part of day-to-day governance in China, and one which has extended into foreign policy in several ways.

Another component of governance in China today is the increasing acceptance of differing opinions within the CCP, as long as they are dealt with within the Party structure using Party norms. This has been apparent through various anti-corruption programmes undertaken by both the Jiang and Hu regimes, as well as Jiang's attempts to widen the membership of the CCP and make it more diverse. The CCP claimed a membership of over 86 million people as of 2014, and one important change from the Maoist era was that the prerequisites for membership have been significantly loosened. Many younger Party members have considerable experience abroad and can often make use of international ideas and models. Not only are workers and peasants invited to join, but also those in the private sector and even entrepreneurs are welcomed, thanks to reforms implemented by the Jiang government at the turn of the century.

In looking at the structure of the party-state, it is important to separate the implied versus actual distribution of power within the government mechanism. In theory, the highest body in power in China is the National People's Congress (NPC), which meets annually to determine policy and debate new laws. However, the size of the NPC, which varies between 2000 and 3000 members, requires limits be placed on the number of topics which can be discussed. When the NPC is not in session, the Central Committee (CC) acts in its stead, but it too is a relatively large group, with a membership of about 350 persons, including alternates. The CC originally acted as an approving body for the Chinese leadership, and even today despite more open debates, especially in CC plenums which take place annually, much of the CC's work is codified by the Party's upper echelons. Despite the NPC and CC's apparent power, a majority of the true governing power in China has shifted to three bodies, the Secretariat, the Politburo and at the very top the CCP Standing Committee.

The small Secretariat of the Central Committee, composed of approximately ten people, was responsible for the daily bureaucratic decisions of the government, and under Mao and Deng the group saw its power increase considerably until it was decided by then-

Premier Zhao Ziyang in the 1990s that its power be downgraded in favour of the Politburo. Nevertheless, the Chinese president also holds the title of General Secretary of the CCP and head of the Secretariat. The Politburo of the Central Committee acts as the leadership body of the CC and normally has approximately 20 to 25 members. Various political factions, those that are strong enough, will find their highest representatives based there.[8] As a result, the Politburo is over-represented by members from the richest and/or most populous regions in China, despite complaints that this group needs to be more sensitive to the requirements of the Chinese interior.

The top rung of the CCP leadership is the Politburo Standing Committee, which includes the President, the Premier, the head of the NPC and the head of the Chinese People's Political Consultative Committee (CPPCC). The latter group serves as an internal think-tank for the Party, seeking new policy development and directions. Rounding out the Standing Committee is a handful of senior officials acting as a layer of policymaking between the leaders and the midlevel of the organisation. Appointment to the Standing Committee always involves months and even years of intense lobbying by various Party factions and interests. Membership in the Standing Committee normally indicates that one has the patronage of the president, or belongs to a faction so strong that it cannot be excluded from the Party's upper echelons.

Moving in and out of the Committee is seen as an indicator of political standing, and the current Standing Committee reflects major changes in power distribution at the top of the CCP. For example, the 2002 and 2007 Standing Committees comprised nine people, up from seven in the Committee from 1997 to 2002. This indicated a need to further decentralise power at the top, the need to represent a more diverse set of factions, or some combination thereof. During the transition only Hu Jintao was carried over from the previous Committee group. This upper echelon determines not only domestic policy but also the state of foreign policy. However, unlike during the time of Mao and Deng, the Committee often has to examine information and advice from various ministries also charged with foreign policy development, including the Ministry of Foreign Affairs, the Ministry of Commerce, and the People's Liberation Army. In 2012, the Standing Committee was returned to seven persons, with members representing a mixture of different educational and professional backgrounds. To give two examples, Wang Qishan, with an educational background in history and a career in finance, was named as Secretary for Central Commission for Discipline Inspection, the group which has spearheaded anti-corruption efforts in the Xi government, and Zhang Dejiang is a graduate of Kim Il-sung University in Pyongyang, where he received a degree in economics.

The Ministry of Foreign Affairs or MoFA (*Weijiaobu* 外交部) is China's leading foreign policy body, and has been charged with interpreting and often substantiating policy decisions made by the country's leadership. Yang Jiechi served as Foreign Minister during the later years of the Hu Jintao government, and was succeeded by Wang Yi in March 2013. The MoFA has become increasingly important as an information source to Chinese policymakers as the country's foreign policy deepens and diversifies. While the central decision-makers in the CCP often create and promote policy for engaging states of importance to Beijing, including the United States, Russia, the European Union and Japan, as well as China's immediate neighbours, the MoFA oversees more routine, low-level decision-making including policies towards smaller states. As part of the Dengist reforms, in 1982 the MoFA began to hold regular press conferences, which later became a weekly event due to the country's increasing foreign relations commitments.[9]

There is also a less-formal mechanism within the Chinese government which acts as a supra-ministerial policy actor coordinating foreign policy development. The Foreign

Affairs Leading Group (*zhongyang waishi gongzuo lingdao xiaozu* 中央外事工作领导小组) or FALG, was formed in the early 1980s. Xi Jinping assumed the leadership of the FALG in 2012, with Vice-President Li Yuanchao acting as deputy, and among the high-profile members is PLA General Chang Wanquan, who became China's Defence Minister in 2013. The FALG often brings together several agencies to discuss areas of foreign policy development, cutting through bureaucratic barriers and allowing specialists from different policy backgrounds to more effectively communicate. The group also allows for more direct contacts between foreign policy specialists and the top leadership.[10]

Adding to the various Party mechanisms which at times influence foreign relations are those specifically under the aegis of the government structure. The Premier of China acts as the head of government and also of the State Council of China, which is the main administrative body of the government charged with overseeing the Constitution, as well as the state budget and various laws and regulations designed to be submitted to the NPC. The exact amount of policy independence of the State Council *vis-à-vis* the Party is an open question, as in practice the two sides are very strongly linked. Also in the administrative section are various ministries and departments overseeing major sectors, such as foreign policy and defence. Various ministries are often lumped informally into larger groups, known as governing "systems" (*xitong* 系统) which often have complementary interests. Among the major *xitong* are organisation, party affairs, education, economics and military.[11] The ministerial structure within China underwent a considerable change in the 1990s, thanks largely to reform policies of then-Premier Zhu Rongji. Soon after achieving that position, Zhu acted to reduce the level of bureaucracy and government overlap not only to improve domestic governance but also to better prepare the country for increased engagement with the international economic system, including the World Trade Organisation.

It was this latter reason that Zhu used as justification for his sweeping reforms of the ministerial system in 1997. The number of ministries was reduced from 40 to 27, with some ministries absorbed into the newly-created State Economic and Trade Commission (SETC), modelled in part after the now-defunct Ministry of International Trade and Industry (MITI) in Japan. The SETC thus became a "super-ministry" designed to be more responsible and

---

Box 2.2 On the role of the Ministry of Foreign Affairs

"The growth of China has been accompanied by the extension of its national interests beyond its neighborhood. This is a trend of history that is both natural and unstoppable. This process brings to the region and the world, first and foremost, opportunities for cooperation and dividends of development. Even so, due to conventional thinking, some friends tend to worry that China might repeat the path of previous major powers and put the development space of others under constraint. Let me reaffirm here that as a participant of and contributor to the global and regional order, a growing China would only mean greater strength for peace and more positive energy in the world. We are determined to break the so-called law of history that draws a simplistic equation between power and attempts to seek hegemony."

– Speech at the Luncheon of the Fourth World Peace Forum by Chinese Foreign Minister Wang Yi, 27 June 2015.<http://www.fmprc.gov.cn/mfa_eng/zxxx_662805/t1276595.shtml>.

reactive to international challenges. In 2003, the SETC was broken up with pieces merged with the Ministry of Foreign Trade to become the Ministry of Commerce (MOFCOM, *Shangwubu* 商务部), an even larger and more powerful group.[12] However, the ministries and committees were being streamlined in the 1990s and later experienced a wave of staff reductions, a move bitterly disputed by some ministries which complained that such proposed cuts would greatly diminish their abilities. As well, the Ministries of Foreign Affairs and State Security argued that, if anything, their staff levels should be increased due to their rising importance. To soften the blow of so many job losses, some employees were given lateral promotions to other sections, others were transferred to universities for teaching and administrative jobs, and still others were transferred to the industrial sector. Despite these changes, the problem of overstaffed bureaucracies remains a complicated and politically sensitive area of China's reform process.

As a result of government centralisation processes in the late 1990s, other large centres of bureaucratic power were created, including the Ministry of Information Industry or MII, which was formed from various ministries including post, electronics and telecommunications. However, not only did the MII oversee these forms of communication but it also played a strong role in media oversight, including regulation of the internet, which is kept under tight government control and subject to restrictions on content perceived to be potentially damaging to the country. The MII was also viewed as a gatekeeper for foreign corporations interested in expanding high-technology markets in China, and has had to walk the line between encouraging international investments in China's growing information technology industries while ensuring that content rules are maintained. As a result of ministerial reforms after the 2007 Party Congress, the MII was merged with smaller related departments and re-named the Ministry of Industry and Information Technology (MIIT, *Gongye he Xinxihuabu* 工业和信息化部) in June 2008.[13]

An important actor in the Chinese government and in its international relations remains the People's Liberation Army (*Zhongguo Renmin Jiefangjun* 中国人民解放军), due to both its history and its numbers (about 2.33 million as of 2014). Both Mao and Deng, in addition to being survivors of the military struggle against both Imperial Japan and the Nationalists, were guerrilla leaders who were often willing to incorporate military thinking into their political views. Both were seen as "soldier politicians" who believed that the Party should have direct control over the gun. As such, there was a strong degree of CCP–PLA symbiosis until Deng's passing, but there was also a low-level power struggle between both sides, with Mao and Deng often taking steps to prevent the armed forces from dominating the political system. As well, the process of paring down the military was a constant issue, but could not be extensively undertaken until Mao's death. Deng, citing the need to fight limited conflicts under modern conditions rather than a grand "people's war" (*renmin zhanzheng* 人民战争) which was a strategic focus under Mao, accelerated the process of paring down the PLA and retiring elder members of the officers' corps while modernising both technology and strategic thinking. The PLA retains a central role in modern Chinese politics and foreign policymaking and has increased its visibility internationally during the later years of the Hu government and the opening years of the Xi administration for its abilities to operate more frequently out of territory (see Chapter 5). Compared with Hu, Xi has more personal contacts with the PLA which has also been a factor in the closer political relationship between party and military in his government.

Beyond the centre: Other actors in Chinese foreign policy

As China increased its role as a great power in the international system, the number of non-governmental actors, including individuals and groups who are involved with, influence, or are knowledgeable of foreign policy has continued to grow under Xi Jinping. Sources of foreign policy information which are accessed by the MoFA and other international relations actors within the government are now more frequently used by non-governmental actors, including academics, research institutes, and consultants, many of which have links with counterparts abroad.[14] As well, foreign policy issues are more widely discussed and debated in visual and print media as well as online. Increases in tourism and the number of Chinese students studying abroad have also contributed to a higher level of international relations awareness in the country.

It was not long ago that the government was the sole source of foreign policy information, but as China globalised, the number of information outlets has grown, including a more diverse news media and rapidly increasing internet use. By mid-2015, figures from the Chinese Internet Network Information Centre (known by its English acronym CNNIC), Beijing's leading internet authority, revealed that China had reached 668 million internet (*hulianwang* 互联网) users, the largest online population, with the United States being second. Limitations were also maintained on some websites, including those which covered sensitive political topics such as Taiwan, Tibet, and the banned *Falungong* spiritual movement, through a government filtering system colloquially referred to as "the Great Firewall" (*fanghuo changcheng* 防火长城). Also blocked were many foreign-owned social media websites including Facebook, Instagram and Twitter, video-sharing sites such as YouTube and blog-hosting sites such as Blogspot and Tumblr. Some Western news sites have also been subject to interdiction, with one notable case being the online version of the *New York Times*, which was blocked in China in the wake of government criticism of an October 2012 investigative report into the large financial holdings of outgoing Chinese premier Wen Jiabao. As noted in the previous chapter, the Xi government has been curtailing use of virtual private network (VPN) options, used for circumventing internet controls, since early 2015.

However, the spread of Chinese online news organisations, blogs (*boke* 博客) and "microblogs" (*weibo* 微博) similar to Twitter, in China have proliferated and some social media sites such as WeChat (*Weixin* 微信), QZone and Sina Weibo have tens of millions of subscribers. It has become commonplace to refer to the largest of China's internet firms as "BAT" (Beidu, Alibaba and Tencent), with Baidu being the most popular search engine in China, especially after Google China moved operations to Hong Kong in 2010, Alibaba being a hub for e-commerce in China, and Tencent (*Tengxun* 腾讯) being an internet

---

Box 2.3 Internet memes in China

As in many other parts of the world, Chinese internet slang and "memes" have occasionally gained international attention, including phrases like "APEC blue", a reference to the unusually pollution-free skies over Beijing during the APEC Summit in the capital in November 2014, and "no *zuo* no die" (*buzuo busi* 不作不死), meaning not taking risks leading to less chance of harm, and *tuhao* (土豪), a reference to the "new rich" in China. Also, a music video called "Little Apple" (*xiao pingguo* 小苹果) by a Chinese singing duo Chopstick Brothers was touted in 2014 as China's answer to the viral South Korean hit "Gangnam Style".

Box 2.4 What is China's "peaceful rise?"

"We term this path towards modernisation 'a development path of peaceful rise' because in contrast to some other emerging powers in modern history, who plundered other countries of their resources through invasion, expansion or even large-scale wars of aggression, China will acquire the capital, technology and resources needed for its modernisation by peaceful means."

– Zheng Bijian, *Bo'ao Forum for Asia and China Reform Forum Roundtable Meeting*, 18 April 2004.

---

company providing social networking and instant message among other services. Many of these Chinese services have directly or indirectly provided many new sources of foreign policy information and discourse for Chinese citizens.

Since the 1990s, Chinese policymakers have been more receptive to recommendations from beyond the central party apparatus, including from research institutes with varying levels of connections to the CCP. Many think-tanks of various sizes exist today in China which focus on international relations, including multi-functional ones such as the Chinese Academy of Social Sciences (CASS) as well as the China Institute of International Studies (CIIS) and the China Institutes of Contemporary International Relations (CICIR) in Beijing, and the Shanghai Institute of International Studies (SIIS). These groups and others have increased their visibility and maintain contacts both with Beijing and with international actors, acting as data centres, research centres, consultants and producers of policy publications for the public and for internal documents (*neibu wenjian* 内部文件).[15]

Another foreign policy tool of Beijing, outside of the central government, has been the rapid proliferation of Confucius Institutes (*Kongzi Xueyuan* 孔子学院) abroad. These institutes, created to promote Chinese language and culture via classes and instructional tools, along similar lines as the British Council, the *Alliance Français* (France), and the *Goethe-Institut* (Germany), have grown to more than 200 in number since the first Institute opened in Seoul in 2004. However, in some Western universities there was a backlash against the Institutes due to concerns about their closeness to the Chinese government and institutional conflicts over their curricula. Despite the growth of Chinese political and economic power, debates over the development of the country's "soft power" capabilities have persisted. The term, developed by Joseph Nye, is defined as the ability to get other actors to do what one wants via attraction, such as through agreeable institutions, rather than coercion via force or reward.

The roles of Hong Kong and Taiwan

The return of Hong Kong to Chinese sovereignty was a major event in the administration of Jiang Zemin, receiving much international attention and leading many to question what the eventual status of Taiwan would be. Since 1949, Taiwan has been viewed by the Chinese government as a part of China, and its status has also been the subject of global scrutiny. Under Jiang, Taiwan was warned by Beijing in 2000 that any attempt to stall reunification talks indefinitely would raise the risk of armed force being used. Jiang was especially unhappy with the ascent to power of President Chen Shui-bian in 2000 and his pro-sovereignty Democratic Progressive Party (DPP). Although Beijing was no supporter of the *Kuomintang* (KMT, Nationalists), which governed Taiwan without interruption from 1949 until 2000, Jiang was even less pleased with the prospect of a pro-independence party in power, the possibility of greater moves towards independence, and the possible response of other states, especially the West, to these events. Although the United States recognised the People's Republic in 1979, Washington retained low-level relations with Taipei and remained ambiguous about whether the US would assist Taiwan in a military crisis. One deviation took place in April 2001 when President George W. Bush stated that his country would do "whatever it took" to defend Taiwan. Since that time, the US has resumed attempts to avoid a definitive stance on assisting Taipei militarily, while maintaining its "One China" policy.

Chen, in his eight years in office, attempted to avoid making overtly provocative moves towards declaring outright secession but attempted some changes to the Taiwanese constitution and to passports through the use of referenda. Hu Jintao had no better luck in dealing with the DPP government on the island and had, at best, a brittle relationship with Taiwanese policymakers. Beijing's impatience was demonstrated in March 2005 when the Chinese parliament, the National People's Congress (NPC), passed an Anti-Secession Law which was designed to protect Chinese territorial integrity. Especially problematic for Taiwan and the international community was Article VIII, which states that should Taiwanese separatist forces attempt to engineer secession of the island, Beijing would employ "non-peaceful means" (*feiheping fangshi* 非和平方式) in order "to protect China's sovereignty and territorial integrity". It was not until the 2008 elections, which saw the KMT returned to office under Ma Ying-jeou, that cross-Strait relations would warm and allow for more points of contact and improved economic relations, including a free trade agreement struck in 2010, direct flights, and a diplomatic truce which paused the practice by both sides of seeking to accumulate allies in a zero-sum game. Since the People's Republic was founded in 1949, no country could officially recognise Beijing and Taipei at the same time.

Beijing has been willing since the Dengist era to allow for the same "one country, two systems" (*yiguo liangzhi* 一国两制) model in Taiwan which was offered for Hong Kong, meaning that Taiwan would receive a high level of autonomy in exchange for unification. However, differences related to political rights, freedom of the press and government accountability raised concerns in Taiwan that the integrity of their governmental system would be adversely influenced by accepting CCP sovereignty. The "two systems" policy was first articulated by Beijing in 1981, and stated that talks between the CCP and the then-governing Kuomintang should be carried out on a reciprocal basis. Both sides would increase exchanges of goods, mail and persons across the strait, and Taiwan should be allowed to retain a high level of autonomy and keep its own armed forces, a significant concession compared with the Mao era. Taiwanese persons would be allowed to serve in the PRC government and allowed to invest on the mainland with no discrimination. As well, Taiwan's economic system would be legally protected. While Hu had taken a more conservative approach to the Taiwan question, no government or leader in Beijing can afford to be seen as "losing" Taiwan, and Hu and his government have also been highly critical of any "Taiwan independence" (*Taidu* 台独) elements or movements on the island. The diplomatic balance between Beijing and Taipei had become more precarious under Jiang and Hu because as China expanded its diplomatic interests and its economic power, many more states were unwilling to recognise Taiwan and consequently pay the price of being shut out of the Chinese market.

After 2008, however, cross-Strait relations became considerably more cordial with a focus on economic cooperation and a downplaying of political differences. Direct air links were established and the number of business contacts grew after Ma took office. As well, talk of a potential military crisis in the Taiwan Straits faded quickly after the change in government in Taipei. The warming process continued after Ma won a second term in early

2012, but the core question of Taiwan's future political status remains unresolved, and there is also the possibility of the DPP returning to power after the next elections on the island, to be held in early 2016. The sensitivity of some Taiwanese citizens to developing a too-close economic relationship with Beijing was illustrated during April–May 2014 protests against an endeavour by the Ma government to pass a Cross-Strait Service Trade Agreement which would have added free trade in services to the existing ECFA agreement. Protestors, primarily members of the Sunflower Student Movement (*taiyanghua xueyun* 太阳花学运), occupied government buildings and prompted a delay in the services agreement's passing.

As well, the durability of the "one country, two systems" concept was sorely tested after protests and street occupations broke out in Hong Kong in September 2014. Nicknamed the "Umbrella Movement" or "Umbrella Revolution" (*yusan yundong* 雨伞运动 or *zheda geming* 遮打革命), due to the umbrellas used by the protestors to ward off pepper spray as well as rain and high heat, the demonstrations were the most serious in Hong Kong since the former British colony's return to Chinese authority in 1997. The protests broke out over plans by the Chinese government to allow for universal suffrage (one person, one vote), for the choice of Hong Kong's chief executive, but on the condition that potential candidates had to be approved by Beijing. Before the proposed reforms began to be circulated, the Chief Executive was elected by a 1200-member committee of individuals and groups as outlined in the Basic Law which detailed the structure of the Hong Kong government after the transfer of power from Britain to China. Pro-democracy groups in Hong Kong had expressed the desire for further moves towards a more liberal democracy by the time of the next Hong Kong election in 2017.

The demonstrators included members of student organisations as well as pro-democracy groups under the aegis of a campaign called "Occupy Central with Love and Peace" (*rangai yu heping zhanling Zhonghuan* 让爱与和平占领中环). Use of tear gas during the early stages of the protests swelled demonstrator numbers, and in the following weeks sections of Hong Kong were blocked off as the protestors called for true universal suffrage as well the resignation of the city's unpopular chief executive, Leung Chun-ying. Despite the negative publicity, leaders in Beijing opted to allow the protests to run their course, and by December 2014 the protestors had dispersed with few political gains made and Leung still in office. However, the demonstrations illustrated the still-considerable socio-political divides between Hong Kong and the rest of China, and sparked debate in Taiwan over whether reunification would be in the island's interests for the foreseeable future.

China and "great power" foreign policy

According to many schools of international relations theory, China's international behaviour is developing largely in keeping with a growing great power. It has been argued that many decades of instability in the country, created by international conflict, civil war and socio-political upheaval have prompted the current conformist approach in Chinese foreign policy thinking. This would also be in keeping with neo-realist ideas suggesting great powers are concerned about maintaining their place in an international hierarchy, as well as the defensive realist idea that Beijing would avoid seeking to gain more power unless absolutely necessary for self-preservation. As well, China seems to be proving Kenneth Waltz's idea of the "*sameness effect*" among great powers, meaning that once states reach the status of great power they tend to behave in a similar fashion to other states of similar "rank". This is because rising states tend to look at the successes of existing great powers and attempt to emulate their strategies and foreign policies hoping for the same good results.[16] The weakening of any state may be and has been traumatic but as history has repeatedly demonstrated, the weakening of a great power can produce aftershocks well beyond the state itself.

However, to claim that China has achieved superpower (*chaoji daguo* 超级大国) status would be very premature, as international relations theorists noted that to be considered a "super" or global power one must not only have the ability to project power throughout the world, an ability China still lacks, but also be able to manipulate and construct international systems on a global level. At present, only the United States is capable of this level of "system-determining" power and China has neither the desire nor the capability to create alternative international rules and norms. Instead, Beijing since the 1990s was content to operate within a Western-dominated international system of laws and norms, in keeping with a policy of conservatism and "norm-taking". Only under Xi Jinping has China been more willing to directly challenge Western ideas of governance, and to propose both new institutions and new concepts ("norm-making"). Moreover, China is the first great power to develop within the modern era of globalisation, which means that it has many sets of eyes upon it, while at the same time enjoying access to much more information about other states, big and small, powerful and not, than great powers of the past. As well, since China has been rising under a great deal of international scrutiny, Beijing has paid much attention, to an unusual degree compared with previous great powers, to its international image. This makes for an interesting contrast with Russia under President Vladimir Putin, which demonstrated much less sensitivity over its global identity in the wake of its 2014 annexation of Crimea and intervention in eastern Ukraine since that year, despite Western protests.

There have been, however, some differences between Chinese governments in terms of their approaches to China's international relations while a developing great power. The first difference is the greater level of foreign policy confidence which the Xi and Hu governments created and maintained. Both Hu and Premier Wen Jiabao engaged in many varieties of summit diplomacy as well as increased participation in international organisations, not only in the Asia-Pacific but in many other parts of the world. This was termed China's "charm offensive" (*meili gongshi* 魅力攻势) and it accomplished much since 2002 in cementing Beijing's ties with many parts of the world, sometimes even at the expense of American diplomacy, especially during the George W. Bush presidency. By 2010, however, some aspects of the charm offensive in Asia had begun to erode in the wake of more assertive Chinese policies in its surrounding waters, causing some concerns among the country's neighbours.

While the Xi government continued to put forward the idea of China as an international partner, its actions in East and South China Sea maritime disputes suggested that Beijing was more willing to promote its unilateral strategic interests even at the cost of diplomatic goodwill with its neighbours, including Japan and Southeast Asia. In the 1990s, some China sceptics noted that without the trappings of soft power Beijing was doomed to remain in the ranks of the medium powers.[17] However, as a result of China's more varied diplomacy and growing abilities, there is the argument that Chinese soft power, while remaining less visible than that of the United States, is significant and growing.

Before leaving office, Hu Jintao was determined to place his own stamp on China's foreign policy based on the ideas of "peaceful rise" (*heping jueqi* 和平崛起) and "harmonious world" (*hexie shijie* 和谐世界). The first concept, which began to appear in government policy circles as Hu was assuming office in 2002–3, was in reference to the idea that China is a rising power but it cannot and will not rise as other great powers did in the past, namely through force and material acquisition. Instead, peaceful rise assumes that China will grow within the status quo and within international norms rather than seek to create a "new world order" to use the American term. He argued that China's issues related to development must be tempered with the idea that there is still a great deal of work to do on the domestic level. Since China cannot become isolationist in the name of concentrating full-time on domestic problems, it must instead temper its foreign policy and rise peacefully. This idea gained much currency in some foreign policy circles in China around the time of the leadership transfer between Jiang and Hu, but others within the CCP argued that even using the term "rise" suggested a potentially combative stance. Instead, the term *"peaceful development"* (*heping fazhan* 和平发展) began to be used more commonly by Hu and his government since the middle of the decade.

As opposed to its stance in the 1990s, China has become more accepting of its status as a rising power, but the Hu government has insisted that it is interested in building what has been termed "comprehensive national power" (*zonghe guoli* 综合国力) via a peaceful rise.[18] Linking domestic and international interests, Beijing has stated its goal of improving its economic and political capabilities in order to create a more peaceful world in which China will grow. Beijing has frequently expressed a willingness to develop a multipolar world where many great powers can check each other, which partially explained China's interest in diversifying its foreign policy interests and pursuing improved relations with Russia and the European Union. For example, Hu and Wen were especially interested in improving EU ties in the early 2000s, and both noted that except for differences over human rights, many international approaches between the two were similar. Until the recession and the "eurozone" crisis which swept across many European economies after 2011, China had been optimistic about Europe's potential both as a trade partner and as an alternative pole in a preferred multipolar system. The Xi government, however, is more comfortable with the idea of direct great power interaction with the United States, cognisant that a multipolar system is likely to happen with other power centres, such as the European Union and Russia, experiencing internal turmoil.

"Harmonious world" had been developed more personally by Hu and has been used to explain his government's foreign policy preferences.[19] This idea rests on the need for harmony and justice in international affairs, the democratisation of the international system which also respects the sovereignty of large and small states, the rejection of alliances and instead the building of security communities which reflect post-Cold War issues, and respect for international law and institutions such as the UN. The Hu government respected globalisation and had paid more attention to the phenomenon than Jiang did, but at the same time "harmonious world" refers to greater fairness in the international trade system, including a greater focus on ending poverty and greater attention paid to ensuring that international trade agreements are made more fair to developing states. The theory draws a much stronger link between economic prosperity and peace and security. The idea also

---

Box 2.5 Deng Xiaoping on hegemony

"The question is whether or not China will practise hegemony when it becomes more developed in the future. My friends, you are younger than I, so you will be able to see for yourselves what happens at that time. If it remains a socialist country, China will not practise hegemony and it will still belong to the Third World. Should China become arrogant, however, act like an overlord and give orders to the world, it would no longer be considered a Third World country. Indeed, it would cease to be a socialist country."

– Deng Xiaoping, 7 May 1978.

originates from the traditional Dengist-era view that China would "never seek hegemony" (*baquan* 霸权),[20] and at present the only sovereign territorial claims which China is making, specifically Taiwan and islets in the East and South China Seas, are sought because they are viewed in Beijing as inalienable components of China's territory. For example, during 2010, there was much global concern expressed when the South China Sea, which contains islands disputed between China and other countries, was referred to as a "core national interest" (*guojia hexin liyi* 国家核心利益) by some Chinese officials.

There are many other interpretations of why China's foreign policy since the 1990s was notably more conservative and cautious towards the use of force or coercion despite the country's rising power status. First, there is the nuclear weapons factor, making great power conflict unacceptably risky. China came very close to a nuclear conflict during border skirmishes with the USSR in 1969, and has little desire to provoke such a conflict again. Unlike great powers of the past, China cannot challenge other such states without being cognisant of the risk of nuclear conflict. In contrast to Mao, who frequently took a radical approach to the power of nuclear weapons, Deng and his successors became increasingly sensitive to the problems of proliferation and the importance of disarmament regimes. In two modern cases of non-nuclear states seeking to develop nuclear weapons, namely North Korea and Iran, Beijing continuously pressed for a diplomatic solution and was critical of force being a policy option.

Second, in much of its foreign policy, China has avoided overt "balance of power" behaviour with the United States, and in many areas has actually "bandwagoned" (meaning aligning one's foreign policy with a strong state in the system in the hopes of gaining benefits) with Washington and other large powers instead. These include issues such as the post-2001 global war on terror (GWoT), the stability of the international trading and lending system, the importance of the United Nations in international law, and combating trans-national crime. China, unlike the Soviet Union, was not in a position to construct alliances and organisations similar to the now-defunct Soviet-era Warsaw Pact using coercion or strength, without unacceptable levels of political and economic suffering. However, there is also the alternative viewpoint that China in some areas is not so much bandwagoning but is in fact "free-riding", receiving the benefits of cooperation without contributing enough to the cooperating group.[21] For example, while China's direct participation in the global war on terror was limited compared with that of the West, it benefited much from the removal of the Taliban regime in Afghanistan and the comparatively calmer security climate in Central Asia. Economically, the US government under both George W. Bush and Barack Obama had been critical of China's perceived manipulation of its large market status and weak currency to further develop using largely Western trade rules and norms, yet both China and the United States continuously sought to avoid a trade war through the use of protectionist policies.

The international relations theory of liberal institutionalism also provides much insight into China's current conservative foreign policy. This is because China is the first rising power to develop within an international system characterised by what can be called "regime saturation". Since 1945, the number of international organisations and regimes has increased considerably, even more so since the end of the Cold War. Since the 1980s, Beijing has accelerated its engagement of many different types of regimes. This affects China's foreign policy in two ways. First, membership in organisations can be seen as restraining potentially revisionist behaviour on the part of China, since the country becomes committed to following many rules and norms in order to continue to receive the benefits of membership. Second, China has been gaining much information, goods, capital and prestige from regime membership, in theory reducing the requirement for China to use coercion to get what it wants.[22] Unlike small powers, Beijing receives much attention in all of the organisations to which it belongs, and has been an enthusiastic supporter, especially since the Hu era, of many different types of organisations. Under Xi, it can be seen that China is more comfortable developing regimes of its own, at least in the economic realm, such as the Asia Infrastructure Investment Bank (AIIB) which was designed to be an alternative to the Western-dominated IMF and World Bank institutions.

Another factor is the "two-level game" issue,[23] stressing the connections between China's domestic and foreign interests as the country engages in international negotiations. At present, Beijing has a long list of domestic problems which need to be resolved in the short term in order for the country to keep its development levels stable and rising. These include relieving poverty levels in the interior and better distributing wealth there, improving governance and the country's legal system, addressing social security and welfare, dealing with environmental problems and weeding out corruption. Any of these issues could conceivably grow to cause great harm to the country, the party, and economic growth. Although China, as an authoritarian state, is less directly accountable to the people for foreign policy decisions, the diversification of foreign policy actors in China and the growing awareness in Chinese citizens of international events have resulted in the need for the policymaking elite to pay greater attention to the growing number of links between domestic issues and foreign policy decisions. Beijing is well aware that faulty foreign policy, especially as the country becomes further immersed in international networks and norms as well as globalisation, can often lead to internal chaos, a scenario which both party and government seek to avoid.

It has also been argued through the international relations theory of "offensive realism" that rising states often experience periods of instability which may prompt them to seek to change the status quo, as demonstrated, for example, by Imperial Japan and Bismarckian Germany.[24] Thus, there is the concern that as China continues to grow it may be more tempted to discard a conservative approach to its foreign policy and unilaterally begin to challenge international norms, a concern commonly voiced by "China Threat" scholars. As well, as neo-realist political theorists have pointed out, rising powers achieving a certain level of power may seek to consolidate their gains, possibly even by changing the international system to one more favourable to their position.

Rising powers often find themselves becoming even more ambitious, which may fuel a desire to exercise more control over their international environment. China's confidence in its foreign policy has grown considerably since the Maoist and Dengist eras. Under Deng, China approached some international actors with much trepidation, mainly out of concern that they would suffer high transaction costs due to incomplete information and the tendency for other states to take advantage of weaker powers. However, these concerns have been largely removed under Jiang, Hu and Xi, and it remains to be seen whether China will seek to make changes in the international system because of it. Neo-realist great power theory has noted that great powers inevitably have a larger number of international interests and commitments, and often seek to better protect their new interests through a more assertive foreign policy.[25] It has been a very short time since China's foreign policy interests have been globalised to the degree that they have, and so it remains an open question whether Beijing will respond to its growing global commitments in a similar fashion as did the United States and great powers of the past.

As China becomes further integrated into the international system and the globalisation process, there is the possibility that Beijing will seek to increase its diplomatic, economic and perhaps even strategic presence in more parts of the world, and then possibly engage in more balancing behaviour against the West. These are the concerns which have been expressed

---

Box 2.6 How alike are great powers?

"Great powers are similar because they are not, and cannot be, functionally differentiated. This is not to say that great powers are identical. They may adopt different strategies and approaches; however, ultimately they all must be able to perform satisfactorily the same security-related tasks necessary to survive and succeed in the competitive realm of international politics."

– Christopher Layne, "The Unipolar Illusion: Why New Great Powers Will Rise", *International Security* 17(4) (Spring 1993): 16.

---

by the "China Threat" School in the West, primarily in the United States. The argument is that once China reaches a threshold level of power, it will begin to act more in keeping with great powers of the past and become less willing to accept the Western-dominated norms of the international system. There is also the argument from this school that as China grows it may eventually begin to challenge the United States politically and perhaps even militarily. Events such as the 1999 Chinese embassy bombing in Belgrade, the 2001 spy-plane incident near Hainan Island, the challenging of the American surveillance vessel *USNS Impeccable* in the South China Sea in 2009, the development of the American "pivot" policy after 2011, and various bilateral economic disputes were seen by this school as signs that Chinese and Western international perceptions are beginning to diverge. Although China's military is still smaller than that of the United States, as Beijing adds more funds to its annual security budget, the country's ability to project its power further away from the home state may continue to grow. This is why American views on how best to address a rising China have been split between the theory of containing Chinese power and engaging Beijing in the hope that it will become a responsible global citizen.

The role(s) of nationalism

Another wild card in the study of Chinese foreign policy is the question of nationalism. It has been argued that as Maoism and the traditional ideas of Marxism-Leninism which defined the Maoist era become increasingly dated, the CCP is turning to nationalism as a way of augmenting both its domestic and its international credentials. There have been many examples of this, ranging from benign to potentially problematic for Beijing's regional and international interests. On one side of the spectrum, there has been the integration of Jiang's "Three Represents" (*sange daibao* 三个代表) theory into both the Chinese constitution and current political thinking. Although the exact meaning is obscure, the idea was that the CCP would "always represent the requirements of the development of China's advanced productive forces, the orientation of the development of China's advanced culture, and the fundamental interests of the overwhelming majority of the people in China".[26] The idea of the CCP as the only guarantor of the safety and prosperity of the Chinese state has continued under Hu and Xi, and on occasion this view has spilled over into foreign policy issues.

The idea of China's restoration (*fuxing* 复兴) of its previous greatness before the last century of the Imperial era has manifested itself in many ways, including much celebration and attention paid to Beijing being awarded the 2008 Summer Olympic Games, Shanghai's hosting of the 2010 World Expo, and the successful Chinese campaign to host the 2022 Winter Olympic Games in Beijing and the city of Zhangjiakou. Under Hu

Jintao, there were also concerns within the Chinese government and even in the country's press that China should cease its habit of mentioning its perceived previous exploitation by international powers during the Imperial Era, including references to the pre-1949 "century of humiliation" (*bainian guochi* 百年国耻). In recent years, some Chinese scholars and analysts have increasingly denigrated this practice as a "victim mentality" in modern Chinese foreign policy. Instead, more scholars and analysts in China now argue that more attention should be paid to moving beyond such perceptions and managing the country as a rising power with many potential contributions to the international system.[27] This stance has become more apparent under Xi Jinping, but there still have been cases, for example in Beijing's political dealings with Japan, where Chinese history as a weaker state subject to foreign pressure is still widely promoted.

Seeking to define Chinese nationalism has resulted in many interpretations. These have included the idea of "pragmatic nationalism", which relies heavily on selective interpretations of history and is frequently modified to suit the needs of leaders and policymakers.[28] This type of nationalism relies less on ideology and more along the lines of loyalty to the state and the need for stability to promote prosperity and continued development. The Chinese Communist Party has staked its ongoing legitimacy on its ability not only to provide benefits on the domestic level but also to ensure that Chinese interests are best served in the international arena. Various concepts and models are borrowed from other states and subtly altered to match Chinese realities, such as the economic liberalisation programme which has been described as market socialism. Another Chinese foreign policy specialist has suggested a variation on this idea in the form of "techno-nationalism" which suggests that since so many of China's current leaders have scientific and engineering backgrounds, they tend to take a scientific approach to both domestic and foreign policy.[29]

However, there are concerns that Chinese nationalism could adversely colour its foreign policy thinking. Both the Belgrade and Hainan Incidents resulted in mass outpourings of anti-American sentiment and street protests which were tacitly supported by the government. In March–April 2005, anger at Japanese history textbooks, which Beijing claimed glossed over war crimes committed by Imperial Japan during the Second World War, as well as opposition to Japanese attempts to secure a permanent seat on the UN Security Council, resulted in street protests in major Chinese cities and was accompanied by vandalism of Japanese businesses and interests. A similar set of anti-Japan protests took place in Chinese cities in August and September of 2012 as Sino-Japanese tensions over the status of the Senkaku/Diaoyu Islands boiled over, with Japanese stores, businesses and even cars being targeted by rioters. In these cases, the Chinese government did not immediately intervene to curtail these incidents.[30] All of these events suggested to some that Beijing was willing to tolerate such demonstrations as a way of deflecting public attention from local issues, but at the same time, concerns have been expressed that permitting such displays of "hyper-nationalism" could have a backlash effect on Chinese domestic politics and damage China's attempts to develop a good-neighbour policy in Asia and the world.

Growing numbers of voices in China's international relations?

The Chinese Communist Party has consistently maintained that it is the only body capable of overseeing the country's increasingly complex domestic and international policies. However, changes are under way in terms of who contributes to China's international policies. Under Mao, foreign policymaking was the privilege of a select few within the upper echelons of the Party, but since Deng, the number of actors both from within the Chinese government, and even from outside, which routinely contribute to modern foreign policymaking has increased considerably. Newly active players from various ministries, the armed forces, the country's growing business sectors, academics and even fledgling non-governmental organisations have appeared on the scene, making the international relations process considerably more multifaceted. Chinese foreign policy is now less reactive, responding to international challenges as they occur, and much more active, openly seeking to improve its international status through unilateral and multilateral approaches. This leads to the question of how the CCP can adapt to these new participants and challenges and maintain its ability to continue to develop a cohesive foreign policy.

Discussion questions

- Has Chinese foreign policymaking become more decentralised since the time of Mao Zedong? Why or why not?
- How have the foreign policy priorities of Xi Jinping differed from that of his predecessors, Jiang Zemin and Hu Jintao?
- Which ministries are now seen as important sources of information and expertise on foreign affairs in China?
- Which international relations theories, in your view, are best suited to explaining Beijing's international relations development?
- Are non-governmental actors taking a more active role in Chinese foreign policy? In what way?
- Will China be able to continue its policies of "peaceful rise / development"?

Recommended reading

Austin, Greg. *Cyber Policy in China* (Cambridge and Malden, MA: Policy Press, 2014).

Beardson, Timothy. *Stumbling Giant: The Threats to China's Future* (New Haven and London: Yale University Press, 2013).

Brown, Kerry. *The New Emperors: Power and the Princelings in China* (London and New York: I.B. Tauris, 2014).

deLisle, Jacques and Avery Goldstein. *China's Challenges* (Philadelphia: University of Pennsylvania Press, 2015).

Deng, Yong. *China's Struggle for Status: The Realignment of International Relations* (Cambridge: Cambridge University Press, 2008).

Fewsmith, Joseph. *The Logic and Limits to Political Reform in China* (Cambridge and New York: Cambridge University Press, 2013).

Hunt, Michael H. *The Genesis of Chinese Communist Foreign Policy* (New York: Columbia University Press, 1996).

Lampton, David M. *Following the Leader: Ruling China from Deng Xiaoping to Xi Jinping* (Berkeley, Los Angeles and London: University of California Press, 2014).

Lynch, Daniel C. *China's Futures: PRC Elites Debate Economics, Politics and Foreign Policy* (Stanford: Stanford University Press, 2015).

Shambaugh, David. *China Goes Global: The Partial Power* (Oxford and New York: Oxford University Press, 2013).

Wang Hui, *China from Empire to Nation-State* (Cambridge, MA and London: Harvard University Press, 2014).

Notes

1　Simon Shen and Mong Cheung, "Reshaping Nationalism: Chinese Intellectual Response towards Sino-American and Sino-Japanese relations in the Twenty-First Century," *The Pacific Review* 20(4) (December 2007): 483.

2　Lowell Dittmer, "Leadership Change and Chinese Political Development," *China Quarterly* 176 (December 2003): 918.

3　Richard Daniel Ewing, "Hu Jintao: The Making of Chinese General Secretary," *The China Quarterly* 173 (March 2003): 19.

4　See Cheng Li, *China's Leaders: The New Generation* (Lanham and Boulder: Rowman & Littlefield, 2001).

5　Will Wo-lap Lam, *Chinese Politics in the Hu Jintao Era: New Leaders, New Challenges* (Armonk, NY and London: M.E. Sharpe, 2006), 165–76.

6　Andrew J. Nathan and Bruce Gilley, *China's New Rulers: The Secret Files* (New York: New York Review Books, 2003), 231–5.

7　"China – The Rising Stars," *The Straits Times*, 5 October 2007.

8　Tony Saich, *Governance and Politics of China* (2nd edn) (Basingstoke, UK and New York: Palgrave, 2004), 121–33.

9　Lu Ning, "The Central Leadership, Supraministry Coordinating Bodies, State Council and Party Departments," *The Making of Chinese Foreign and Domestic Policy in the Era of Reform*, ed. David M. Lampton (Stanford, CA: Stanford University Press, 2001), 50–2; Qian Qichen, *Ten Episodes in China's Diplomacy* (New York: Harper Collins, 2005), 1–4.

10　Cary Huang, "How Leading Small Groups help Xi Jinping and other Party Leaders Exert Power," *South China Morning Post*, 20 January 2014.

11　Kenneth Leiberthal, *Governing China: From Revolution Through Reform* (2nd edn) (New York and London: W.W. Norton, 2004), 218–33.

12　Dali L. Yang, *Remaking the Chinese Leviathan: Market Transition and the Politics of Governance in China* (Stanford: Stanford University Press, 2004), 58–63.

13　"The MII Renamed as the Ministry of Industry and Information Technology," *China Business Newswire*, 30 June 2008.

14　M. Taylor Fravel and Even S. Medeiros, "China's New Diplomacy," *Chinese Foreign Policy in Transition* (New York: Walter de Gruyter, 2004), 393–5.

15　David Shambaugh, "China's International Relations Think Tanks: Evolving Structure and Process," *The China Quarterly* (2002): 575–96.

16　Kenneth N. Waltz, *Theory of International Politics* (Reading, MA: Addison-Wesley, 1979), 128.

17　For example, see Gerald Segal, "Does China Matter?" *Foreign Affairs* 78(5) (September / October 1999): 24–36.

18　Yan Xuetong, "The Rise of China and Its Power Status," *China Journal of International Politics* 1 (2006): 5–33.

19　Yu Bin, "China's Harmonious World: Beyond Cultural Interpretations," *Journal of Chinese Political Science* 13(2) (August 2008): 119–41.

20　Andrew Scobell, *China's Use of Military Force: Beyond the Great Wall and the Long March* (Cambridge and New York: Cambridge University Press, 2003), 30–1.

21　Avery Goldstein, *Rising to the Challenge: China's Grand Strategy and International Security* (Stanford: Stanford University Press, 2005), 34–5; Janyong Yue, "China's Peaceful Rise: Myth or Reality?" *International Politics* 45(4) (July 2008): 439–56.

22　Marc Lanteigne, *China and International Institutions: Alternate Paths to Global Power* (New York and London: Routledge, 2005): 12–30.

23　Robert Putnam, "The Logic of Two-Level Games," *International Organisation* 2(3) (Summer 1988): 427–60.

24　John J. Mearsheimer, *The Tragedy of Great Power Politics* (New York: W. W. Norton, 2001), 168–233.

25　Christopher Layne, "The Unipolar Illusion: Why New Great Powers Will Rise," *The Perils of Anarchy: Contemporary Realism and International Security*, ed. Michael E. Brown, Sean M. Lynn-Jones and Steven E. Miller (Cambridge, MA and London: MIT Press, 1995), 136; Robert Gilpin, *War and Change in World Politics* (Cambridge: Cambridge University Press, 1981), 94–5.

26 "The 'Three Represents' Are the Foundation for Building the Party, The Cornerstone for its Exercise of State Power and a Source of its Strength," *Jiang Zemin: On the 'Three Represents'* (Beijing: Foreign Languages Press, 2003), 14–37.
27 Yong Deng, *China's Struggle for Status: The Realignment of International Relations* (Cambridge: Cambridge University Press, 2008), 51–4.
28 Suisheng Zhao, *A Nation-State by Construction: Dynamics of Modern Chinese Nationalism* (Stanford: Stanford University Press, 2004), 29–36.
29 Christopher R. Hughes, *Chinese Nationalism in the Global Era* (London and New York: Routledge, 2006), 34–49.
30 Peter Hayes Gries, *China's New Nationalism: Pride, Politics and Diplomacy* (Berkeley, Los Angeles and London: University of California Press, 2004), 1–29; Sow Keat Tok, "Neither Friends Nor Foes: China's Dilemmas in Managing Its Japan Policy," *China: An International Journal* 3(2) (September 2005): 292–300.

3   China in the world economy

Introduction: China as number one?

China's rise as an economic and trading power has been impressive on many levels, and the development of the Chinese economy and its remarkable transformation from having a minimal effect on the global economy to actively shaping it will be examined in this chapter. There is currently much debate over the development of what has generally been referred to as "China Inc.",[1] including the effect of Chinese economic growth on its foreign policy development. Following the initial economic reforms of the late 1970s and especially after joining the World Trade Organisation at the turn of this century, China's effect on the global economy has been staggering, and both scholars and economists have noted the growing percentage of global trade coming from the country, its increasing stockpiles of foreign exchange, and the gradual development of Chinese brands for sale internationally. In 2011, China officially overtook Japan as the second-largest economy in the world after the United States, and there was much speculation as to when, not if, the Chinese economy would become the biggest. Figures released by the International Monetary Fund (IMF) in October 2014 indicated that China had surpassed the United States as the largest economy, at least in terms of purchasing power parity (PPP). However, it is important to remember that in many ways China's economy remains very much in a state of reform and transition, with important obstacles to overcome both on the domestic and the global levels. This chapter will discuss how and why the country has made the transition from a closed command economy directly controlled and often restrained by the state to a more modern, but still reforming, economic and trading system.

Some side-effects of China's economic power have included frictions between China and the West over Beijing's trade policies, the value of China's currency, the growing levels of pollution emitted from Chinese factories, and the country's expanded economic interests in the developing world. The 2008 "credit crunch", and the global recession in the years

---

Box 3.1 Economic progress and the "blue sky"

"But just thirty years ago, before we took that leap, we saw no high-rises, apart from one or two in big cities like Beijing and Shanghai; we had no concept of expressways or advertisements; we had very few stores, and very little to buy in the stores we did have. We seemed to have nothing then, but we did have a blue sky."

– Yu Hua, *China in Ten Words* (New York: Pantheon Books, 2012), 147.

following, further demonstrated China's increasing economic influence in global affairs as the country was widely seen as an oasis of stability, especially in comparison with the United States, Europe and Japan. This chapter will also examine China's approach to economic globalisation, as on the one hand Beijing is very anxious to continue to immerse itself in global trade, but at the same time the country worries about negative influences entering the country through trade as well as via the internet economy. Moreover, China's economic powerhouse requires ever-increasing amounts of resources, raw materials and energy, creating concern in the West about competition with Beijing over international oil and gas supplies.

In the area of international relations, it is difficult to avoid discussion and speculation on the rise of China and its development as a political and economic power. What has recently changed, however, is the fact that China's economic reach has expanded beyond the Pacific Rim and into both the developed and developing world in a great number of ways. Since the global recession began, China's economic growth has also moderated and the country has had to quickly adjust to slowdowns in manufacturing as well as increased competition from other emerging markets. However, the fact that Beijing has achieved this economic success so quickly, often ignoring Western-based rules and norms for developing states, has made China the recipient of much attention from both developed and developing states.

China's economic rise and international responses

The results of Beijing's economic opening over the past quarter-century have been remarkable by any standards. Between 1979 and 2013, China's total GDP jumped from US$177 billion to more than US$9 trillion, while at the same time the country's international trade levels increased from negligible to becoming the largest trading power in early 2013, surpassing the United States. By 2014, China's GDP was estimated to be at approximately US$10.4 trillion, or possibly as high as US$17 trillion using PPP measurements. Assuming Chinese growth remains constant, despite doubts raised by the global recession, the country remains on track to exceed American economic output somewhere near the year 2020, according to various economic estimates. China also became the world's largest manufacturer of goods (about 22 per cent of global output as of early 2014) at the end of 2010, edging out the United States and underscoring the ongoing importance of the manufacturing sector to China's new economy. In 1990, China's share of global output of manufactured goods stood at only 3 per cent.[2] At the same time, China continues to develop its service and high-technology sectors, a far cry from the agriculture-dominated economy which existed in China under Mao Zedong.

By September 2015, China held approximately US$3.5 trillion in foreign exchange reserves, the largest amount of funds managed by a single state, as an insurance policy against domestic or international economic crises. When China's economy did begin to slow in mid-2015, some of these funds were pressed into service to help stabilize the Chinese currency. A majority of these reserves are believed to be in American dollars, and this has been viewed as a major component of what has been called China's increasingly visible "symbiosis" with the American economy, meaning that successes or failures on one side would greatly affect the other.[3] The depth of China's integration into the global economy was well illustrated in February 2008 when the Shanghai stock market dropped nearly 9 per cent in value on a single day, affecting other markets throughout East Asia, the United States and Europe. When the global economic downturn became more acute, the health of the Chinese economy became an even greater international concern. As well, China's trade surplus, meaning the difference in the amount that it buys from and sells to the world, remains a sensitive political issue with the United States and Europe. However, due to the recession and lower demand for Chinese goods, the surplus began to decrease in value, from US$296 billion in 2008 to US$155 billion three years later.[4]

These numbers are beginning to generate concerns in both the United States and the European Union, both of which have trade deficits with China of over US$100 billion, and have resulted in numerous debates over the fairness of Chinese trade. For example, China's dominance in the textile trade has created concerns in both developed and developing states about unfair competition. There has also been the question of how fair China's policies are in dealing with the method of conversion of its currency, known formally as the *renminbi* (RMB, translating as "people's currency"); the unit of currency is the *yuan* and uses the symbols "¥" or "元". Critics in the United States and Europe have argued that the ongoing government control of currency rates as well as the fact that the value of the *renminbi* is undervalued provides Beijing with an unfair trading advantage. Starting in the 1990s, China maintained a *de facto* "peg" of its currency at 8.28 *yuan* to the American dollar. A currency peg is a policy whereby the value of a country's currency is fixed ("pegged") to a specific value of another country's currency, usually the American dollar. This practice is commonly used among developing economies to avoid rapid and often destabilising changes to the value of their money overseas. However, critics of China's peg argued that Beijing's economy had matured to the point where the policy was unnecessary and called instead for the *renminbi* to "float", meaning to rise and fall in value more in keeping with global market conditions rather than Chinese internal politics.

In July 2005, under international pressure, Beijing agreed to a change in foreign exchange policy and instead pegged the *renminbi* to a group (or "basket") of currencies including the US dollar, the British pound, the euro, the Japanese yen and others, and also indicated that the value of the RMB would better reflect market conditions.[5] The value of the *renminbi* has increased slowly since then, but as the recession began to take hold after 2009 Beijing became more wary of allowing the *yuan* to appreciate too quickly. These policies have not been enough to satisfy some international critics who continued to claim that the *yuan* was still artificially low on global markets. Beijing has insisted that it will consider further currency liberalising, but only at its own pace, as China was well aware of the difficulties encountered by Thailand and other Southeast Asian economies when they attempted to float their currencies too fast in the late 1990s, namely the Asian Financial Crisis (AFC) which saw economic slowdowns throughout East and Southeast Asia in 1997–8. After the recession began, Beijing expressed concerns that allowing the *yuan* to rise in value too quickly would choke off the country's already vulnerable export markets. Nonetheless, since the start of the global financial crisis, the value of the *yuan*, in relation to the American dollar, rose at a steady pace, from about 7.28 *yuan* per dollar in January 2008 to 6.22 by the start of 2015. However, in August 2015, Beijing implemented currency policies which saw the value of the yuan drop 3% in value against the US dollar. The result was a small devaluation, but the decision nonetheless raised global concerns about an economic slowdown in the country. The rationale given by Beijing for the decision was that it was seeking to reform the yuan to become more of an international currency by allowing market forces to better determine its value.

Even before the downturn, Western companies and governments were routinely hearing about the so-called "China price", referring to the cost of a good or service which can be provided by China, a price normally far lower than can be found in the West.[6] However, unlike the United States and other large economies China's GDP *per capita* using purchasing power parity remains comparatively low, at about $US8400 at the end of 2010, although different studies have suggested higher and lower figures using different methods of measurement.[7] Moreover, these numbers do not reflect the wide gaps in living standards between China's coastal cities and populations in the interior, as well as differing urban and rural figures. The recession did have an effect on GDP growth, as figures dropped from a rate of 14.2 per cent in 2007 to 9.6 per cent a year later. In March 2012, then-Premier Wen Jiabao stated that in light of ongoing economic uncertainties China should only expect an economic growth rate of 7.5 per cent,[8] below the traditional "floor" of 8 per cent which the country has traditionally sought to maintain in order to keep its economic reforms on track. Under Xi Jinping, the preferred "floor" was adjusted to 7 per cent amid talk that a "new normal" (*xin changtai* 新常态) was required, with greater austerity measures and a stronger focus on stimulating the Chinese domestic economy by encouraging more consumption within the country. Nonetheless, Chinese growth remained impressive in relation to the economic slowdown in the United States and the "double-dip" recessions which many European economies have been facing since 2012.

Before the international economic downturn, Beijing sought to slow its economic growth rate in the hope of avoiding runaway inflation, a problem which almost derailed the Chinese economy in 1994 due to rapidly escalating prices for goods and services. China's inflation rate rose to about 6 per cent in 2008, pushed upward by high global prices for food and fuel and leading to price hikes in China on commodities including foodstuffs, but the economy dipped a year later producing price deflation before rebounding in the following two years.[9] Although saving rates in China remain high compared with those of Western countries, consumption rates are increasing more rapidly as more people are able to afford both necessities and luxury goods. Although talk of classes is still politically sensitive, the size of China's middle class continues to grow, estimated to have surpassed 300 million people in 2012. More specific figures can be difficult to obtain given differences in measuring tools. A 2013 report by the consulting firm McKinsey suggested that of 256 million urban households in China in 2012, 54 per cent could be classified as "mass middle class" (meaning having 60,000 to 106,000 *renminbi* in disposable income per year) while another 14 per cent were categorised as upper middle class (106,000 to 229,000 RMB in disposable income *per annum*). The report added that by 2022, the number of urban households would jump to 357 million, with 54 per cent being of upper middle class level and 22 per cent being mass middle class based on the measurements of disposable income.[10] A commentary in the Chinese news service *People's Daily* in February 2015 noted the great size of China's middle class but argued that such a trend would not lead to stresses on the CCP. Rather, the group would "only support the legitimacy" of the Party.[11]

Looking at the Chinese economy today, it is sometimes easy to forget that before the reforms began almost 40 years ago, the country had a solid command economic system, meaning that all industry was state-owned and heavy industry was favoured by the government. Wages and prices were under central governmental control and services sectors and private industry were discouraged. Foreign trade was kept at a minimum, international investment was prohibited and China's currency could not be converted to other currencies overseas.[12] Needless to say, these restrictions are no longer in place and the shape of Chinese trade has been altered considerably since the 1980s as Beijing placed a high priority on acquiring hard capital through trade. At first, only a few sectors were well represented. For example, until 1985 China's largest export was petroleum, accounting for 20 per cent of total Chinese exports, yet in 1993 China began to import petroleum.

Following the introduction of the Coastal Development Strategy during the 1980s, however, exports became more numerous and more diverse. Another spike in export growth was recorded after 2002 when China joined the WTO, and much of these exports are composed of machinery, electronics and clothing. The country is being especially scrutinised for its growing share of exports of computers and other high-technology. The economic reforms under Deng Xiaoping were credited for developing high savings rates and government investment as well as a large and educated labour force. The growing middle class (*zhongchan jieji* 中产阶级), with some Chinese studies using the less politically-sensitive term "middle stratum" (*zhong jiceng* 中基层),[13] has proven eager to purchase consumer goods from China and increasingly from abroad. As well, many more Chinese are in a position to travel and study abroad. Beijing maintains a list of "approved destination status" (ADS) states with bilateral tourism agreements, with over 100 countries and territories striking ADS deals with China. As well, the post-2008 upgrading of cross-Strait relations has provided tourists from China with greater opportunities to visit Taiwan.

Much of China's growth can also be attributed to the development, since the 1970s, of a "Greater China" economy, encompassing those of Hong Kong, Macau, Taiwan and overseas Chinese business communities in Southeast Asia (such as in Singapore), and beyond. Since 1997, China has become increasingly linked with Hong Kong, which still acts as a primary port, and Taiwan which, despite ongoing political differences, is becoming increasingly tied to the Beijing economy. Both Taiwan and Hong Kong have lost manufacturing jobs to China, especially to the country's south-eastern provinces of Guangdong, Fujian and Zhejiang, since the 1980s, and as a result Taiwan and Hong Kong have begun to switch their economic focus to services and higher-technology areas. An increase in Taiwan's economic ties with the mainland has been a source of some worry in Taipei, however, as politicians are concerned that too much economic interdependence would give Beijing an increasing political influence over the island. These concerns increased in some political quarters within Taiwan with the 2010 signing of the Economic Cooperation Framework Agreement (ECFA) between

---

Box 3.2 To get rich (and richer) in China

"Two factors, however, have been particularly instrumental in increasing the public awareness of and scholarly interest in China's middle class. The first is the Chinese business community's drive to promote the image of Chinese consumers as potentially the 'world's largest middle class market'; the second is the Chinese government's decision to 'enlarge the size of the middle income group'."

– Cheng Li, "Introduction: The Rise of the Middle Class in the Middle Kingdom", *China's Emerging Middle Class: Beyond Economic Transformation*, ed. Cheng Li (Washington, DC: Brookings, 2010), 8.

"China's new rich are certainly a consequence of globalisation, as that country has become not simply integrated with the world economy, but in many ways the focus of every other country's globalisation."

– David S.G. Goodman and Xiaowei Zang, "Introduction: The New Rich in China: The Dimensions of Social Change", *The New Rich in China: Future Rulers, Present Lives*, ed. David S.G. Goodman (London and New York: Routledge, 2008), 1.

"Once the Got Rich First crowd had the trappings of fortune – a child in the Ivy League, a reading team to stay up on new books – they wanted the habits of mind. The men and women who had struggled to reach the top of China's Industrial Revolution craved the chance to extend their exercise of choice to a wider world, to matters of taste, art and the good life – to see, at last, what they had been missing."

– Evan Osnos, *Age of Ambition: Chasing Fortune, Truth and Faith in the New China* (London: Bodley Head, 2014), 95.

Beijing and Taiwan which cut tariffs on goods traded between the two economies.[14] The Taiwanese government of Ma Ying-jeou praised ECFA for producing many new economic opportunities for both sides and potentially allowing Taiwan to seek new free trade deals of its own, with New Zealand and Singapore completing free trade agreements with Taiwan in 2013, despite neither country recognising Taipei. With improved cross-Strait relations, the idea of a "Greater China" (China, Taiwan, Hong Kong and Macau) is being looked at more seriously as an economic power within Asia as well as internationally.

China as an economic model?

As China continues to expand its economic interests beyond the Asia-Pacific region, affecting more and more of the developing world, the term "Beijing Consensus" (*Beijing Gongshi* 北京共识) has evolved from a theoretical idea to one which is increasingly taken more seriously both in analyses of China's foreign policy and as its growing economic footprint on a global level.[15] Many developing states are considering emulating China's economic success by using some of the same policies. This concept, first coined in a 2004 paper by Joshua Cooper Ramo of the Foreign Policy Centre in London, suggested an alternative theory of development to the standard Washington Consensus model which was omnipresent in the 1990s and formed the cornerstone of loan and capital assistance policies issued by international financial regimes such as the World Bank and the International Monetary Fund (IMF), as well as the United States in its financial dealings with the developing world.

The Washington Consensus, first articulated by economist John Williamson in 1989, stressed "neo-liberal" economic policies including a reduction of the public sector, openness to foreign economic competition, fiscal discipline, the sale of state enterprises, and liberalised trade. Under this view, the state was to intervene as little as possible in favour of allowing trickle-down economics both within states and among them. These ideas were routinely used by developed world states and regions in their financial engagement of developing states in the name of improving the economic status of the latter.[16] However, this approach soon came under harsh criticism in developing states, especially in the wake of economic crises in Mexico, Argentina, Russia and East and Southeast Asia during the 1990s, for perpetuating neo-mercantilism and entrenching divides between rich and poor both within developing states and between the developing and developed countries.

The backlash against the neo-liberal policies of the Washington Consensus has been keenly felt in Latin America, where leftist or left-leaning governments in Venezuela, Brazil and Bolivia increased the role of the state in economic development. Russia under Vladimir Putin also carefully noted the Chinese growth model in maintaining a high level of state control over economic development. In the case of China, the state remains omnipresent in domestic economic affairs, but in a much different way than under Mao. Until the late 1970s, the Chinese economy was both heavily regulated and largely shielded from Western-dominated international markets. Today, China is open to both inward and outward investment, but much economic strategy remains the exclusive purview of the state and there is now the perception that China is seeking to develop a form of "state capitalism" which cements the role of the state in the country's modernisation process.

The Beijing Consensus rejects many aspects of the neo-liberalism model as well as the uniform approach to helping countries develop and prosper in the international economy. According to Ramo's study, "China is in the process of building the largest asymmetric superpower in history", one which thus far has not been built upon Western concepts of hard power and rigid policy ideas but rather upon developing alternative development ideas and adhering to a strong Westphalian view of the primacy of state sovereignty. It can therefore be argued that although it is now more generally agreed that China does matter as a great power and that questions over whether China will continue to dominate international discourse for the longer term have largely been answered, China as a great power is considerably different from like powers of the past.

The "Consensus" itself rested on three assumptions. First, innovation is the key to economic growth, and the old model of starting with simpler technologies and then working one's way to more complex ones should not be taken as a given. Certainly, China's growth has upended the traditional "flying geese" model of Asian economic growth, whereby the lead goose, Japan, transfers older technologies to geese further back, such as South Korea, Singapore and Taiwan, and then further on to Southeast Asia, as it becomes richer and develops newer industries based on higher technologies, such as from textiles to computer chips. Using this model, other Asian states also develop more modern economies but the lead goose retains its central role.[17] However, the centre of economic gravity in Asia has begun what seems to be an inexorable move from Tokyo to Beijing. The pivotal event which caused this switch has been widely acknowledged as being the Asian Financial Crisis, which saw China largely immune from its effects due to the fact that its currency was still tightly government controlled.

However, Beijing was affected peripherally as the Hong Kong stock market dropped suddenly in October 1997; and as surrounding states experienced currency crashes, Beijing resisted intense pressure to devalue the *yuan* to remain competitive. However, China further aided its reputation by offering a total of US$4 billion in bailout packages to Thailand, South Korea and Indonesia. These events, plus the growing reputation of the Chinese economy being categorised by conservatism and rationalism, created the impression of the PRC as a safe haven in Asia among the economic chaos.[18] Beijing promoted its new status as a regional "white knight" by supporting regional organisations like the ASEAN-plus-three (APT) and later the East Asian Summit (EAS) to prevent further economic meltdowns in the Asia-Pacific and to encourage Asian economic cooperation separate from that of North America. By contrast, the Asia-Pacific Economic Cooperation (APEC) forum, which encompasses nearly all the Pacific Rim economies, was greatly discredited after not succeeding in reaching a joint agreement on how best to address the financial crisis.

As well, Beijing's policies and behaviour during the crisis also served to convince its neighbours that its rise as an economic power was not a regional threat but rather an advantage to the region. China was favourably contrasted with Japan, which was rocked by its own economic problems throughout much of the 1990s and was perceived as less effective in combating the regional crisis. As the beneficiary of much political capital as a result of its actions during the crisis, Beijing has been encouraged to propose increased economic interdependence in the region, especially with East and Southeast Asia.

However, innovation remains an area in which China is perceived as lacking. A major priority for the current Chinese economy has been the development of global brands which can successfully compete with international counterparts. After two decades of developing a policy of "inviting in" (*qingjin* 请进), meaning encouraging foreign firms to invest in China and develop joint ventures with domestic corporations, the catchphrase in China now is "going out" (*zouchuqu* 走出去). This policy calls upon Chinese firms, once they have developed global products and gained the necessary expertise, to venture out into international markets.[19] So far, results have been mixed. Although many products sold around the world are made in China, the number of truly international brands developed in China is very low compared with those of the United States, Europe and Japan. Some exceptions include Lenovo, a Chinese computer firm which bought IBM's personal computer division in 2005;[20] Haier, which markets white goods and made an attempt to purchase the American firm Maytag that same year; telecommunications firms Huawei and ZTE; TCL, an electronics company and television-maker; and Xiaomi, a producer of mobile phones. However, as China faces more economic competition in Asia and domestically, the pressure is strong for more global brands to be developed, and the 2008 Beijing Olympics was seen as an ideal opportunity for large Chinese companies to obtain more global exposure.

The second assumption put forward by the Beijing Consensus is that chaos is a constant in economic development. However, this chaos can be minimised by adding measurements of economic progress beyond traditional ones such as *per capita* GDP, including quality of life statistics as well as sustainability and equality. Chaos management, therefore, becomes of paramount concern during the development process. The idea that a single economic reform approach can solve every developing country's ills is rejected, as well as the idea of shock therapy to push a given economy from command to liberal economics. Beijing has been critical of such approaches by the West, especially during the 1997–8 Asian Crisis. By contrast, China has strongly favoured a gradualist approach to economic reform to minimise potential disruptions. As well, the gradualist method has been interpreted by some observers as a rejection of rapid democratisation, which Beijing has stated increases the possibility for chaos which can, in turn, hamper economic goals. These ideas began to attract more attention in the West. For example, an article in *The Australian* in August 2005 commented that China's growth proved that economic freedom and political freedom did not necessarily have to be linked, and that the post-Cold War "end of history" arguments that liberal democracy has been hailed as the only viable model of governance were looking increasingly shaky.[21]

However, critiques of China's slow pace of economic reform, including Pei's *China's Trapped Transition* (2008), Breznitz and McMurphree's *Run of the Red Queen* (2011) and Beardson's *Stumbling Giant* (2013), expressed concerns that allowing the state to have too great a role in economic management created risks to the long-term viability of the reform process.[22] Christensen, in his book *The China Challenge* (2015), notes that although there has been much hype regarding the eventual surpassing of the American economy by China's, citing China's large currency reserves, its reluctance to allow the *renminbi* to float more in accordance with market forces, and disputes over Chinese protectionist policies signal a high degree of economic insecurity rather than strength. In a critical editorial published in the *Wall Street Journal* in March 2015, noted China specialist David Shambaugh also sounded a discordant note about China's economic future under Xi Jinping, pointing to the high number of wealthy Chinese and Party officials who were sending money abroad, as well as the large number of CCP officials who have children studying abroad. He also noted that the ambitious economic reforms which were unveiled at the Party's Third Plenum in November 2013 had yet to be implemented, and suggested that bureaucratic pressures were acting as a brace against overdue economic restructuring.[23]

In February 2012, the World Bank published a report, in conjunction with the Development Research Centre of the State Council in China, entitled *China 2030*.[24] The report, which caused some consternation within the Chinese government, called for further market liberalisation and reforms of state-owned enterprises to prevent a longer-term slowdown of the Chinese economy and reduce the risk of falling into a "middle income trap" (*zhongdeng shouru xianjing* 中等收入陷阱) due to a lack of productivity and innovation.

Despite China's impressive economic growth, it can readily be argued that Beijing still faces many challenges which, if not properly addressed, could dramatically slow or even reverse the country's economic gains. Near the top of the list are the environment and the question of sustainable development. China is facing serious environmental problems as an unwanted side-effect of its unchecked economic growth, and it has affected the country's air, land and water quality while causing great concern among China's neighbours. Health problems and other damage caused by pollution are on the rise in China. Air pollution has become more chronic as a result not only of the heavy reliance upon coal-burning as a primary source of energy but also the burgeoning "car culture" and the accompanying pollution in many Chinese cities.

This problem was illustrated in Beijing in the weeks leading up to the 2008 Olympics, when driving restrictions were implemented in the capital in an attempt to reduce the level of exhaust fumes. City air quality has also been affected by the country's urban construction boom. Industrial pollution has had a detrimental effect on land, lakes and rivers, placing strains on fresh water supplies in the country. Popular discontent in China about worsening air quality became more acute in the wake of a string of severe smog alerts in many Chinese cities, including the winters of 2013 and 2014 when air quality levels reached new lows, including high concentrations of "PM 2.5", particulate matter so small that it can enter the lungs and bloodstream, sparking online discussion of an "airpocalypse" in Chinese coastal regions. The US Embassy in Beijing raised much ire in the Chinese government when it began to send smog alerts via Twitter after 2008, information which often contradicted official Chinese figures, and was increasingly accessible to people in China through various firewall-circumventing applications. In 2013, Beijing relented and began to establish its own air quality monitoring stations.[25] In early 2014, Premier Li Keqiang publically called for a "war on pollution".

As well, the Gobi Desert in Western China is growing in size, fed by soil erosion, and leading to an increasing frequency of sandstorms which now routinely plague Chinese coastal cities in the spring. These issues do not stop at the Chinese border, as many of these problems have also affected nearby states as well as Hong Kong, and it was suggested in 2007 that China had surpassed the United States as the single largest emitter of carbon dioxide into the atmosphere, contributing significantly to global warming threats.[26] There have also been highly publicised examples of pollution crises, including an incident when tonnes of the highly toxic chemical benzene were accidentally spilled into the Songhua River in November 2005, not only leaving the north-eastern Chinese city of Harbin without drinking water for days but also threatening fresh water supplies in Siberia. In March 2013, thousands of pig carcasses were found to be floating in the Huangpu River near Shanghai, resulting in much public outcry throughout China.

The growing pressure to address China's worsening pollution problems has regularly been addressed by the Chinese government and also by non-state actors. Days before the

---

Box 3.3 Maintaining economic harmony

"As a key stakeholder in the global economy, China must remain pro-active in resuscitating the stalled Doha multilateral trade negotiations, advocate 'open regionalism' as a feature of regional trading arrangements, and support a multilateral agreement on investment flows. Integrating the Chinese financial sector with the global financial system, which will involve opening the capital account (among other things), will need to be undertaken steadily and with considerable care, but it will be a key step toward internationalizing the renminbi as a global reserve currency."

– World Bank, *China 2030: Building a Modern, Harmonious, and Creative High-Income Society* (2013) <http://www.worldbank.org/content/dam/ Worldbank/document/China-2030-complete.pdf>.

start of the CCP's annual National People's Congress full session in March 2015, a video documentary entitled *Investigating China's Smog: Under the Dome* (*wumai diaocha: qiongding zhixia* 雾霾调查: 穹顶之下) began to circulate online. The documentary, produced and hosted by Chai Jing, a former journalist with China Central Television (CCTV), examined the growing problems of pollution in the country and its socio-economic costs. The production received many positive responses in China and was compared to the 1962 book *Silent Spring* by Rachel Carson, which touched off an environmental movement in the United States, as well as the 2006 environmental documentary *An Inconvenient Truth* by former American vice president Al Gore which used a similar visual style as *Under the Dome*. During the Asia-Pacific Economic Cooperation (APEC) summit in November 2014 in Beijing, strict anti-pollution measures cleared the skies around the capital, leading to the internet phrase "APEC blue", which further illustrated the problem of keeping air pollution in check on the days when important international conferences were *not* taking place.

Beijing is a signatory of the 1997 Kyoto Protocol, an international agreement which calls upon members to reduce emissions of greenhouse gasses contributing to climate change, and began to observe its guidelines in 2005. The country has also participated in the Intergovernmental Panel on Climate Change and has acknowledged the potential severity of these issues.[27] However, its status under Kyoto as a developing country exempted it from the emission limits placed on developed states, which has caused some international disapproval, and concerns remain about the rising percentage of such gasses being generated in China. A follow-up environmental conference in Copenhagen in 2009 was marked by sharp differences between the United States and China over reductions of carbon emissions, but Beijing and Washington agreed to a bilateral deal to cut carbon emissions in November 2014, underscoring the idea that any significant environmental accords on the global level will require the acceptance of both great powers.

Although Beijing has generally been more accepting of the concept of the "Green GDP", meaning the total GDP minus losses incurred due to environmental damage, its implementation has proven far more difficult. Both urban and rural centres have been resistant to centrally-organised "green" policies. At the same time, while there are signs

---

Box 3.4 "Green" pressures in China

"China's leaders have resisted widespread tough economic policies, such as raising prices for natural resources or closing polluting factories, that might engender social unrest. By promoting the growth of environmental NGOs and media coverage of environmental issues, the Chinese leadership hopes to fill the gap between its desire to improve the country's environment and its ability to do so."

> – Elizabeth Economy, *The River Runs Black: The Environmental Challenge to China's Future* (2nd edn) (Ithaca and London: Cornell University Press, 2011), 135–6.

"In both media and academic discussions, optimism and scepticism, acclaim and blame seem to coexist regarding China's potential in global environmental mitigation. China is protrayed simultaneously as a reckless polluter and an emerging leader."

> – Joy Y. Zhang and Michael Barr, *Green Politics in China: Environmental Governance and State–Society Relations* (London: Pluto Press, 2013).

of a growing green movement in China, it differs from environmental non-governmental organisations (NGOs) in other countries as NGOs in China are usually more closely tied to the state.[28] While it was hoped the Beijing Olympics would prompt more serious governmental and non-governmental efforts towards an environmental clean-up, it remains to be seen whether the country's pollution problems will begin to have an effect on both economic growth and the health of the population.

The third component of the Beijing Consensus argued there is the need for states to develop using their own methods, free from unwelcome international interference. Self-determination should be a right of all states in the development process, a direct swing at Washington Consensus ideas of great power intrusion and an extension of China's traditionally strong Westphalian (state-centric) view of sovereignty. These views were first elucidated in the late 1950s with the development of the "Five Principles of Peaceful Coexistence", tenets which would become the focus of Chinese foreign policy thinking until well after the Maoist era. The principles, which borrowed heavily from Westphalian views of state supremacy and sovereignty, were the mutual respect for territory and sovereignty, mutual non-aggression, mutual non-interference in other states' domestic affairs, the equality of states and mutually beneficial exchanges, and peaceful co-existence. These principles have been folded into China's current economic thinking, which tends to view all states as equal and deserving of non-interference.

The Beijing Consensus has now evolved from an abstract idea to a policy concept frequently debated in the developing world, especially as Beijing increases its economic presence in Latin America, sub-Saharan Africa, Central Asia and Oceania. After developing a strong and stable periphery policy in the 1990s, China expanded its international priorities to these areas of the world, culminating in a "charm offensive" (*meili gongshi* 魅力攻势) of diplomatic visits by Chinese leaders around the world, seeking to distinguish Chinese foreign policy, stressing multilateralism and a mix of political and economic cooperation, from American policy which was viewed as too one-dimensionally fixated on security and anti-terrorism during the Bush administration. Although Chinese investment in many developing states is not at Western levels, the fact that China is seeking to diversify its imports to satisfy growing Chinese consumer demand and is serious about increasing investment abroad, has received the attention of many developing states and regions.

This has led to the question of whether China is capable of wielding "soft power" (*ruan shili* 软实力), meaning power gained through attraction rather than coercion or force and first proposed by the American scholar Joseph Nye, and if so, where the soft power is coming from. Not only has China gained much in terms of wealth and political prestige from its trade policies, but it is also argued that China gains security by convincing other states that its rise is not harmful but rather beneficial internationally.[29] While this stance has eroded in terms of China's relations with its immediate neighbours in East and Southeast Asia, Beijing maintains a high degree of partnership diplomacy in many parts of the world, from Africa to the Middle East to the South Pacific. China's evolving international trade policies can be defined as a consolidation of Beijing's soft power, as well as an alternative model of economic growth uncoupled from established Western norms on how states should develop. However, in Nye's 2015 book *Is the American Century Over?* he explains that while Beijing had taken steps to increase its soft power in East Asia and globally, the Chinese government was still experiencing problems mixing hard and soft power into "smart power", partially because unlike in the United States, where much soft power is derived from civil society, in the case of China it is the government which seeks to become the main source of Chinese soft power, with mixed results.[30]

Box 3.5 Hard and soft power

"Hard power is the ability to get others to do what they otherwise would not do through threats or rewards. Whether by economic carrots or military sticks, the ability to coax or coerce has long been the central element of power.

   Soft power, on the other hand, is the ability to get desired outcomes because others want what you want. It is the ability to achieve goals through attraction rather than coercion. It works by convincing others to follow or getting them to agree to norms and institutions that produce the desired behaviour."

   – Robert O. Keohane and Joseph S. Nye, Jr., "Power and Interdependence in the Information Age", *Foreign Affairs* 77(5) (September–October 1998): 86.

One oft-cited example of Chinese soft power has been its economic model which, since the 1990s, has demonstrated great durability despite a number of internal and external shocks. However, there is the question of how well China's model of economic development can be successfully exported to other developing states. China is in a distinct position due mainly to its size and the strength of its market, features not seen in many other reforming states except for the other four "BRICS" nations, Brazil, Russia, India and South Africa, which along with China are seen as the largest emerging markets. The BRICS group (*Jinzhuan Guojia* 金砖国家) began organising their own summits in 2009 with much talk focused upon the precarious global economy. In addition, much Chinese growth has not been led by research and development but rather by emulation of other economic models, including Western, and a strong focus on maintaining economic stability. The announcement of a BRICS financial institution, the New Development Bank or NDB, in 2014 was further evidence of China's growing willingness to support non-Western development practices.

The Chinese growth model also must contend with a still-underdeveloped welfare state coupled with an ageing population, governmental accountability, negative issues such as pollution, and issues of corruption which continue to affect both domestic economics and international investment. Another example is the stubborn problem of income inequality within China, an issue which has also affected other large developing economies. As the country's domestic economic reforms got underway, Deng Xiaoping stated during a 1985 speech that "some areas and some people can get rich first, lead and help other regions and people, and gradually achieve common prosperity". However, China's GINI co-efficient, which measures on a scale of zero to one how equitably wealth is distributed within a country, was last published in China in 2000 (0.412), and since then Beijing has been unwilling to publicise annual figures. As economist Thomas Piketty noted in his book *Capital in the Twenty-First Century* (2014), at the start of the reforms the level of Chinese income inequality was very low, comparable to that of northern Europe, but once the reforms commenced inequality grew rapidly, though not to the same degree as in other emerging economies such as Argentina or South Africa.[31]

It has been assumed that as China's economy continued to grow in the following decade, and as was stated by Chongqing CCP leader Bo Xilai before his ousting, inequality in China by early 2012 had become excessively high and GINI figures had reached 0.46.[32] Any figure above 0.4 is commonly seen as sufficient to create an enhanced risk of social disorder. Since the Dengist reforms began, CCP leaders have struggled with the question of how best to reduce inequality and create economic opportunities for poorer areas in China, especially in the interior of the country.

Changing attitudes on trade and globalisation

China's method of growth as a developing state has been very distinct, both because of the size of its market and the speed by which it has implemented market reforms. Not long after economic globalisation (*quanqiuhua* 全球化) was accepted into Chinese policy statements under President Jiang Zemin in the early 1990s, its identification as a source of both economic "goods" and potential risks was acknowledged by the CCP. In comparison with the West, the ideas of globalisation were somewhat slower in being introduced in Chinese policymaking and academic discourse, only appearing in the mid-1990s and even then in a very halting fashion. At the start of the Dengist economic reforms, there was the acknowledgement that China could ill-afford to continue to stay out of the modernising global economic system, despite its domination by Western markets, and that China had neither the means nor the desire to set up a separate system to better suit its needs, as the USSR had attempted to do when it established the Council for Mutual Economic Assistance (COMECON) organisation during the Cold War with its Eastern European and Asian socialist satellite states.[33] Although China is facing the same questions about globalisation as other states, including how best to take advantage of its social and economic potential while avoiding an unacceptable erosion of state power, Beijing has nevertheless approached some aspects of globalisation differently than has the West.

On one side, globalisation in China's view could be seen as a primary method of enriching the state and sweeping aside archaic and ineffectual Maoist economic relics, such as state-owned enterprises (SOEs) incapable of standing up to international competition and often acting as a drain on state resources. However, to gain the benefits of globalisation, tight governmental control of the Chinese economy required loosening to adjust to the unpredictability of the market, raising fears not only of "peaceful evolution" (*heping yanbian* 和平演变), namely that the Chinese party-state would be eroded due to Western pressures caused by globalisation, but also concerns for the social impact for the many workers forced to leave SOEs in search of other work due to foreign competition. This was a dilemma reminiscent of one of Deng Xiaoping's quotes during the start of the economic reform era, namely that when one opens a window, some flies will get in. It was partially because of these concerns that Jiang tended to view globalisation as being linked with comprehensive security and the links between poverty and conflict.

The adjustment of the Chinese economy to globalisation today takes place under the twin problems of what Zheng Bijian, author of the initial views on the concept of China's "peaceful rise" in the international system, termed the "mathematical propositions". First, any socio-economic issue related to development, no matter how minor, has the potential to be multiplied exponentially by China's population of 1.3 billion. Second, the country's financial and material resources must be viewed as divided among the said great population.[34] The level of economic distortion caused by the population factor raises the country's sensitivity and vulnerability to the potential problems of globalisation to great heights in proportion to other emerging markets. At the same time, the population factor both underscores and helps to explain the cautious approach the Chinese government has taken toward maximising the benefits of its international opening while seeking to minimise the risks. In his 2012 book *The China Wave*, Zhang Weiwei explained that when speaking of the Chinese economy it was useful to view the country as a collection of different economies, including emerging ones and developed ones, but that China would benefit overall from the interactions between these two groups, producing what he called a "1 + 1 > 2" effect.[35]

It was with these concerns in mind that Beijing under Deng, looking closely in the 1980s at the growing "tiger" economies of East Asia such as Japan and the "Newly

Industrialising Economies" (NIEs) of Hong Kong, Singapore, South Korea and Taiwan, opted to develop a modified "developmental" economy as it emerged from the no-longer-viable Maoist command system. The post-1978 opening of the Chinese economy has been described as implementing export-oriented policies designed to take advantage of China's strong position in both labour and manufacturing, while still retaining degrees of import substitution industrialisation (ISI) left over from the late Maoist/transition period (1972–8). An ISI system involves the widespread blocking of imported industrial goods into a country, thus favouring and protecting domestic companies and strongly encouraging consumers to "buy local". This was a common practice among newly independent developing states in the last century, especially in Latin America, as a means of protecting infant industries. In order for China to open to international markets and be accepted into the WTO, however, its ISI system had to be scaled back to permit foreign goods and services to be offered to Chinese consumers, and Chinese companies had to prepare for competition or run the risk of bankruptcy.

Yet, in looking at both Chinese economic strategies and policies during the initial stages of economic reform, an argument can be made that the economic system being created was not solely a mix of import substitution and export-guided policies but rather a modified developmental system designed to expand China's economic presence while maintaining its economic mechanisms under a threshold degree of party-state control. The question here, however, is whether developmentalism will be a second stage in the country's shift from a closed economy to a liberalised one, or will the political and social pressures of globalisation assist in the perpetuation of developmental economics for the near term?

"Developmental" states have been rare in the international economic system, and the debate concerning the degree of developmentalism contributing to the rise of Asia as a strong economic region remains a subject of continued analysis. The Asian developmental model, used in Japan in the 1970s and later by NIEs such as Singapore, South Korea and Taiwan, is defined by its observance and respect for market economics and private property, as well as the role of competition in international markets, with growth being seen as the primary goal. However, markets in this system are largely guided by a small group of highly skilled and educated elites. There are commonly strong links between government and major economic actors (firms, factories and unions, for example), which allow for mutual consensus-building on the direction development should take, combined with much information sharing. The state bureaucracy has a commanding role in overseeing development, and often there is a "pilot agency", such as the former Ministry of International Trade and Industry (MITI) in Japan, to coordinate policymaking and the implementation of new schemes.[36]

China does not have an equivalent agency, and its model of developmentalism is also different from those seen elsewhere in East Asia given its larger size and much greater agricultural and manufacturing sectors. Nonetheless, China has been open to borrowing developmental concepts from other Asian economies. For example, Singapore was often viewed during the Dengist reform era in China as an intriguing model, given the success of Singapore's first post-independence leader, Lee Kwan Yew, in transforming the country from underdeveloped status to a global financial hub in a matter of decades. When Lee passed away in March 2015, he was highly praised by the Chinese media for his economic accomplishments under a one-party dominant system of government in Singapore.[37]

In China, the line between state-owned and non-state-owned industries is far less defined in comparison with other East Asian economies, and there is more emphasis on "bottom-up development", encouraging the development of small businesses at very local levels as well as larger firms, but with more risk of corruption and gaps between rich and poor.[38] The developmental model for developing states was studied as an alternative to the neo-liberal model of economic modernisation and market engagement. As well, those states using this model, as well as China today, largely liberalised their economies before developing democracy, a fact which has not gone un-noticed by current authoritarian states facing twin pressures to democratise and liberalise, often simultaneously.

China's views on liberalised trade agreements have become much more favourable as the country grows in economic power. Beijing remains an enthusiastic supporter of both the WTO and the post-2001 Doha Round of global trade talks, while at the same time often siding with those demanding more equitable treatment of developing states. However, support for the WTO and indeed Beijing's approach to globalisation has not been uniformly accepted by either policymakers or other economic specialists, including academics. The latter stages of the WTO negotiations in the 1990s were very difficult, especially the direct negotiations with Washington, and as a result two separate schools of thought on these subjects emerged. On one side are liberalists who have supported greater economic opening, and on the other is the so-called "New Left Movement" (*xinzuopai* 新左派) which has been highly critical of Beijing's rush to join Western-dominated economic institutions. Their argument, which has manifested itself in articles and commentaries, was that China's rush to join international economic institutions and rapidly liberalise the Chinese economy has been inherently destabilising and has resulted in an overabundance of Western control over China's development.[39] Wang Hui, a professor at Tsinghua University in Beijing, has been one of the most prominent figures associated with the New Left and has written extensively on its ideas.

The degree to which the Chinese economy should continue to liberalise became a subject of increased debate as the Hu Jintao regime came to a close and the severity of the global financial crisis became more apparent. For example, a cornerstone of a proposed "Chongqing model" of Chinese development, spearheaded by Bo Xilai before his 2012 dismissal and subsequent imprisonment, included rejuvenation of state-owned enterprises and the promotion of greater income equality and shared prosperity, coupled with the idea of singing "red" (patriotic) songs and smashing "black" or corrupt practices (*changhong dahei* 唱红打黑).[40] This model began to be compared, even within China, with an alternative "Guangdong model" of economic liberalisation coupled with greater political openness, and became associated with that province's Party chief, Wang Yang. Increasing incidents of worker unrest in southern China, including strikes and work shutdowns which plagued the region in 2011 and included a wildcat strike at a Honda car parts plant in Foshan in May of that year, were viewed as a partial motivator for greater governmental responsibility. This debate between economic liberalists and "new leftists" further underlines how the domestic and international economies in China have become increasingly blurred. Frustration with Western foreign and economic policies also manifested itself in a controversial book released in China in 2009 called *Unhappy China* (*Zhongguo bu gaoxing* 中国不高兴) which criticised Western influences and called for a more assertive China in the international system.

China, although not adapting all aspects of the developmental model, has created a modified version to account for the still-embryonic private property laws, a very large agricultural sector, and a considerable percentage of the Chinese economy which remains directly state-owned. The number of SOEs, along with their financial contribution to the Chinese economy, has been dropping since the accelerated reforms of the 1990s, but many remain in business through government and bank support. Then there is the simple fact that China is much larger, geographically and demographically, than the other developmental states of the past, presenting a different set of governance concerns for the party-state and accentuating the need to avoid economic chaos which could spark domestic crises. China today is on a much different economic footing from the East Asian developmental states of the 1960s and 70s, when they first adapted such policies.

Nevertheless, there are many points of comparison between Asian developmentalism and the modified Chinese version which continues to take shape. As with previous developmental systems, the Chinese state was insulated to a sufficient degree to enable it to implement developmental policies without facing strong domestic opposition and it also had the ability to make changes or repairs during the process, again without significant barriers. Also, the dominant role of the Chinese Communist Party in government allowed for the implementation of developmentalist policies as well as the "capture" of emerging economic actors, especially business sectors, using economic incentives, a process commonly associated with what is studied in comparative politics theory as "state corporatism".[41] In the case of China, the often-complicated division between SOEs and private and semi-private industries, as well as between Chinese enterprises and the government, further permitted state oversight of major economic "players" and the sharing of information.

It has been argued that developmental states are not only rare but also appear in very specific cases, namely when state leaders perceive distinct and potentially very harmful challenges to governance, namely the process of "systemic vulnerability". A state may seek developmentalist policies if it is facing the threat of economic instability precipitating mass unrest (such as in Indonesia when the Suharto government was toppled in May 1998 in the wake of economic protests during the AFC, or economic downturns in the Middle East and North Africa which fed into protests which toppled governments in Tunisia and Egypt in 2011), an increased need for foreign exchange and the wherewithal to fight wars based on national-level insecurity and constraints on budgets caused by a lack of easily-accessible sources of revenue.[42] It can certainly be argued that China falls into these three categories to varying degrees, and this would explain why Beijing would wish to retain developmental features even under globalisation pressures. As well, the Chinese party-state is painfully aware of the country's long history of peasant revolts during the imperial eras, conflicts which often led to the removal of dynasties and, in the case of the fall of the Qing Dynasty in 1911, warlordism and state balkanisation. An economic slowdown would magnify these problems and directly challenge the legitimacy of the party-state. However, unlike during the pre-communist era in China, a serious economic crisis in the country would now create considerable global aftershocks.

As China's economy continues to modernise, its level of engagement with the global economy has also, by necessity, expanded. The country's first few steps into the global market were tentative, but as a member of the WTO and as a recognised large emerging market, China is demonstrating more confidence in its dealings with outside economic actors, even giants like the United States, the European Union and Japan. However, as China further adapts to globalisation, an area which China only started to consider seriously under Jiang in the early 1990s, many new questions about economic maturation have appeared. One of these questions is how the country will adjust to its increasing need for raw materials, and especially energy, to fuel its ongoing growth. As well, there is the question of whether the international community will be able to adjust to a China with increasing international requirements for commodities. Will the future see cooperation with other great powers or increased and potentially dangerous competition?

Since the Asian Financial Crisis of the late 1990s, Beijing has been promoting the greater liberalisation of trade on a regional and increasingly on a cross-regional basis as a way of protecting and developing its trade interests should the Doha Round of the WTO talks, which are already behind schedule and wracked with differences both between the US and the EU as well as developed and developing states, ultimately fail. Since joining the WTO, China has been increasingly proactive in its stance on trade rights for itself and other emerging markets. However there have been criticisms of some Chinese trade practices, including government subsidies on environmental technologies such as solar panels and wind turbines. In US President Barack Obama's January 2012 State of the Union speech, China was singled out for condoning unfair trading practices, and a US "trade enforcement unit" was proposed in order to monitor any improper activity. Such declarations have resulted in a cooling of Sino-American trade relations, exacerbated by the uncertain global financial climate.

Also, since the turn of the century, Beijing has become more interested in diversifying its trade beyond the WTO as a hedge against future problems within the organisation. Subsequently, China reversed its long-held suspicion of preferential trade agreements (PTAs), actively supporting them with selected states and regional regimes. This process was begun within the greater Asia-Pacific region, and bilateral PTAs were completed with Chile, Costa Rica, Hong Kong, Macau, Pakistan, Peru and Singapore, as well as the ECFA with Taiwan. China also began to negotiate free trade with more developed economies belonging to the OECD, completing agreements with New Zealand (2008), Iceland and Switzerland (2013) and Australia (2014), with a South Korea agreement completed in early 2015.

The Gulf Cooperation Council (GCC) in the Middle East, India and states in Latin America and Central Asia as well as the Southern African Customs Union (SACU) have also been cited as potential free trade partners with Beijing.[43] This ASEAN–China Free Trade Agreement (ACFTA) was first proposed by then-Premier Zhu Rongji in 2000, and was considered at the time to be not only a dramatic policy shift but also the strongest indicator that Beijing was serious about developing regional preferential trade despite its previous misgivings. The ACFTA came into force in early 2010 and is the largest such agreement in terms of population. Not only have these deals and negotiations cemented Beijing's reputation as a strong supporter of bilateral liberalised trade, but also its activities have prompted two of its neighbours which had been sceptical of freer trade deals, namely Japan and South Korea, to reconsider their own liberalised trade policies.

China's new-found enthusiasm for free trade has become a major element of another new dimension of Chinese foreign policy, namely "commercial diplomacy" (*shangwu waijiao* 商务外交). This idea has two components. First, commercial diplomacy signifies the use of negotiations designed to influence government policy in the areas of trade and investment. Second, commercial diplomacy uses economic power to influence non-commercial decisions in the political or even strategic realm. If successful, the results are positive-sum rather than zero-sum, meaning that when two sides negotiate an economic or political deal, both sides make gains rather than only one side benefiting.[44] China's large market (actual and potential) with its accompanying power has enabled it to engage in commercial diplomacy, and this is another area in which Western economies increasingly worry about Chinese competition. What is significant about China's approach to commercial diplomacy and PTAs is that it has been willing to enter into negotiations with states with much smaller economies and fewer economic sectors, both in the name of gaining more information about the PTA process and also in some cases to gain economic footholds in key regions.

For example, there are many economic differences between China and the European Union which have prevented all but the very basic steps towards developing freer trade, and therefore China began to seek agreements with Iceland, Norway and Switzerland, which were not EU members and thus could negotiate as single actors.[45] All three states have very small economies in comparison with China's, but there was the anticipation that PTAs with these states would provide Beijing with a useful window into the often-complicated European

Box 3.6 China's preferential trade agreements
ASEAN
Australia
Chile
Costa Rica
Hong Kong SAR
Iceland
Macau SAR
New Zealand
Pakistan
Peru
Singapore
South Korea
Switzerland
Taiwan (via the ECFA)
Thailand

Free trade agreements under negotiation (as of mid-2015)
Gulf Cooperation Council (GCC)
Norway (*suspended since 2010*)
Regional Comprehensive Economic Partnership (RCEP)
Southern African Customs Union (SACU)
Sri Lanka

market system. However, after Iceland fell into a deep recession following its banking crisis in late 2008 and considered joining the EU, the PTA talks were temporarily suspended, and negotiations between China and Norway were abruptly severed in late 2010 after the Nobel Peace Prize that year was awarded to jailed Chinese dissident Liu Xiaobo, despite Beijing's protests. With global trade talks still at an impasse, the Xi government has expressed ongoing interest in developing new bilateral and sub-regional free trade agreements in Asia and beyond. Putting these ideas into practice, China's free trade agreements with Iceland and Switzerland were completed in 2013, and in the following year free trade deals with larger economies, Australia and South Korea, were also finalised.

Going big: China develops new economic institutions

On a regional and global level, China's economic confidence under the Xi government could be viewed from a variety of angles, but one noteworthy illustration has been Beijing's growing interest in developing alternative economic and financial institutions to traditional Western-backed regimes. One example has been Chinese plans for an Asian Infrastructure Investment Bank (*Yazhou jichusheshi touzi yinhang* 亚洲基础设施投资银行) or AIIB, which coalesced in 2014 and began to develop into a greater international body in early 2015 when several Western governments, including friends and allies of the United States, agreed to become members. The AIIB, first proposed by the government of Xi Jinping in 2013, was to have an initial value of US$50 billion with Beijing providing the greatest proportion of the initial start-up funding. The initiative was in part a response to Chinese frustration over what it considered the slow pace of infrastructure development in Asia and the domination of Western interests within the IMF and World Bank, despite China's rise as an economic power. The AIIB was designed by Beijing to address these issues, and when the initial memorandum of understanding was signed between China and 20 other governments in October 2014, President Xi noted that, "to build fortune, roads should be built first", an idea in keeping with an "Asia-Pacific Dream" of regional economic development which he described during the Asia-Pacific Economic Cooperation (APEC) forum meeting in Beijing in November 2014.[46]

Shortly after the inception of the AIIB, the United States expressed its misgivings about the new bank due to concerns about Beijing's growing diplomatic power as well as whether the bank would uphold "international standards of governance and transparency". Washington also appeared to be tacitly discouraging its partners and allies from signing on to the AIIB. The original signatories to the AIIB project were governments from East, South and Southeast Asia, although New Zealand, which has a long history of independent foreign policymaking *vis-à-vis* the United States, did agree to sign on. Other American partners in the Asia-Pacific region such as the Philippines and Singapore also agreed to join, but others such as Australia, Japan and South Korea originally opted to steer clear, mainly due to US concerns. Despite Beijing's call for AIIB partners from all around the world, during the opening months of 2015 it appeared that the new bank would be strictly regional in scope.

However, in March 2015 the situation changed dramatically when one of the United States' closest allies, the United Kingdom, agreed to become a partner in the AIIB. In an unusually sharp rebuke by Washington, especially in light of the "special relationship" between Britain and the United States, the UK government was accused of making the decision without consulting its American partner. As one US official noted, "We are wary about a trend toward constant accommodation of China, which is not the best way to engage a rising power."[47] London counter-argued that British economic interests would be well served by AIIB membership and greater financial cooperation with Beijing. Days after London's decision to join the AIIB, statements were released by the governments of France, Germany and Italy confirming that the three countries would also seek membership in the AIIB, further isolating Washington's views on the new bank.[48]

In the space of a very short time, the bank was transformed into the object of a tug-of-war between two great powers which the United States soundly appeared to lose. Other European economies, including those of Belgium, Denmark, Finland, Norway, Spain and Switzerland also expressed an interest to join. Even Australia and South Korea, which originally had been wary of the new bank and nervous about going against American policy, agreed to sign on days before the deadline for "founding member status" passed, with Japan and the United States standing largely alone. Even Taiwan applied to join, potentially under a different name such as "Chinese Taipei" to avoid enflaming the "one China" question. However, in April 2015 it was announced that Taiwan would not be able to apply as a founding AIIB member due to a disagreement over a proper name. Of all the applications to the AIIB, only one state was rejected outright by Beijing for having insufficient credentials: North Korea.

These events have suggested that much has changed both in regard to the shape of the global economy but also in the area of Chinese foreign policy. The development of the AIIB, as well as the creation of the New Development Bank by Beijing and the other BRICS, add further weight to the idea of shifting global economic power further towards Asia. As well, the development of the AIIB suggested that China is becoming more comfortable with developing new economic organisations which do not necessarily include the West. Decades ago, when China began launching its economic reforms, Beijing was pleased to engage with Western financial institutions including the IMF/World Bank, and Beijing was willing to negotiate for 15 years before finally joining the World Trade Organisation in 2001. However, China's growing economic power and ongoing concerns about being marginalised by the United States as a result, have changed these views in Beijing. China now holds the largest reserves of foreign currency by a single actor, and has expressed interest in developing greater commercial diplomacy, meaning the ability of transforming wealth into diplomatic power.

In addition to the AIIB plans, at the landmark summit of the Asia-Pacific Economic Cooperation (APEC) forum in Beijing in November 2014, President Xi promoted the revival of a Free Trade Area of the Asia-Pacific (FTAAP), which would jump-start the long-delayed process of developing a free trade zone to encompass the entire Pacific Rim and, if successful, would become the largest such free trade zone in the world. It was at the same APEC summit that Xi suggested the "Asia-Pacific Dream" for the region to match the "China Dream", which the president began to promote shortly after taking office. The FTAAP could also be an alternative to the US-led Trans-Pacific Partnership (TPP), which China was not invited to join but does include several American partners, including Australia, Canada, Japan, New Zealand and Vietnam. Beijing, however, is a participant in another proposed cross-Pacific free trade regime, namely the Regional Comprehensive Economic Partnership (RCEP), launched in 2012, which also includes Australia, India, Japan, South Korea and several Southeast Asian economies.

Finally, the Xi government has also been describing the creation of new "Silk Roads" in Eurasia and the Indian Ocean which would further enhance east–west trade between Europe and China and promote economic development in the countries along the way. President Xi's proposals comprise a "one belt and one road" (*yidai yilu* 一带一路) strategy of developing new land and sea links with vital Western European markets. Central to these new links is the "Silk Road Economic Belt" (*sichouzhilu jingjidai* 丝绸之路经济带), which would stretch across Central Asia and the Caucasus and Bosporus regions, with links to Moscow and others to ports in Northern Europe. In addition to trade, the creation of the "belt" would involve increased bilateral cooperation between Beijing and Central Asian and Caucasus states along with Russia, and stronger institutional engagement between the Shanghai Cooperation Organisation (SCO), a regional security regime which includes Russia, China and Central Asian states, and the Eurasian Economic Community (EurAsEC) which was succeeded in January 2015 by the Eurasian Economic Union (EEU).

These overland routes, similar to the trade routes between Imperial China and Europe first established during the Han Dynasty more than two millennia ago, would be accompanied by a "Maritime Silk Road" (*haishang sichouzhilu* 海上丝绸之路) or MSR. This route would traverse the Indian Ocean with ports in Bangladesh, India, Sri Lanka and Eastern Africa, and also involve the countries of the Association of Southeast Asian Nations (ASEAN). Like its landlocked counterparts, the Maritime Silk Road has a historical precedent in the form of Indian Ocean sea routes traversed by Chinese vessels during the Tang Dynasty (618–907 CE) which linked the Imperial Tang Empire with the Byzantine Empire in south-eastern Europe and the Caliphates (Rashidun, Umayyad and Abbasid) in southwest Asia, as well as eastern Africa and the Indian subcontinent.[49] Although critics in the West referred to the Silk Road proposals as a modified Marshall Plan to build Chinese economic and political power in Eurasia, Xi Jinping has referred to the one belt and one road plan as a way of bringing together Chinese and Eurasian economic and development interests in the name of mutual benefit. The question, however, is whether an increased Chinese role in Eurasia, Southeast and South Asia, as well as in eastern Africa, will result in greater regional cooperation or in power rivalries between Beijing and other major players, notably Russia and India, as well as American interests in these regions.

"Resource diplomacy" and its effects

China's external trade and economic policies have gained much political capital in the developing world, notably in Africa, Latin America, Southeast Asia and the South Pacific. States from all of these developing regions are contemplating expanded trade and even the possibility of free trade agreements with Beijing. The Chinese economic magnet continues to affect economies well outside of the Asia-Pacific region, and has contributed much to the rising of commodity prices as well as a spike in south–south trade. China's economy is dependent upon a steady stream of raw materials, including base and precious metals, construction materials, wood and foodstuffs, and many of these resources are being imported from developing states.[50] Unlike other economic booms in Asia, much current investment in Chinese infrastructure is domestic and supported by the country's very high savings rates compared with those of other emerging markets.

As well, China's approach to economic assistance includes the premise that reforms in developing countries should be overseen by the countries themselves, meaning that Beijing does not require as many preconditions on aid or overseas development assistance, making China an increasingly popular option for developing states seeking international assistance. Maintaining such a strong division between politics and economics, say critics, has at times offered solace to authoritarian regimes. China maintains that its approach is more pragmatic and ultimately more effective at alleviating poverty. Yet there is concern about a backlash against Beijing's resource diplomacy within its newest trading partners. For the present, however, China's economic visibility in developing regions continues to grow.

China is in need of many raw materials, but it is in the area of fossil fuels, oil and gas, where its resource diplomacy is being most keenly felt internationally. Beijing is fast becoming a large energy consumer, affecting how its foreign policy is conducted, especially with resource-rich states. The country, as previously noted, has a heavy reliance upon coal for the majority of its energy needs (about 69 per cent), with oil second, accounting for about 22 per cent and natural gas only 3 per cent.[51] After a long history of self-sufficiency in oil, China became a net importer of oil products in 1993 and of petroleum itself in 1996, and has seen its dependency rise steadily since then, with approximately 55 per cent of its oil now coming from international sources as of 2014. China is now the world's largest petroleum consumer, with the country importing 308 million tonnes of crude oil in 2014, compared with only 22.8 million tonnes in 1996. In 2014, the percentage of oil imported by China broke the 60% mark for the first time.[52] Global oil prices fell at the beginning of 2015 to under US$50 per barrel, down from over US$100 at the start of 2014, due to a market glut, shale oil development in the United States, and weakening demand from China due to its economic slowdown. However, China appeared to be a major potential beneficiary of falling energy prices given its increasing reliance on imported petroleum supplies.

Domestic oil supplies are no longer sufficient to satisfy China's economic demands, as the need for both industrial and consumer goods continues to rise. The country now finds itself in the same situation as other great powers including the United States and Europe. China's primary oil field at Daqing, in the country's northeast province of Heilongjiang, reached peak production of one million barrels per day in 1975–2003, but production has been steadily dropping since that time,[53] while the Tarim Basin, located in China's far-Western territory of Xinjiang, and the Bohai Gulf in north-east China might also act as indigenous energy sources. However, it is unlikely that those sources will be enough to satisfy China's increasing thirst for oil and gas. Beijing has responded to the concerns about domestic supplies and unstable international prices by establishing strategic petroleum reserve sites as a first phase of an oil stockpiling initiative. These concerns about access to energy have meant that China is now joining the international game of seeking out global oil and gas supplies while making optimum use of its indigenous resources. Beijing had been criticised in the West for signing gas and oil deals with states such as Iran and Sudan, and later South Sudan when the country became independent in 2011. As well, part of the escalating tensions between China and Japan over demarcation of the East China Sea and difficult Chinese relations with the Philippines and Vietnam over the South China Sea after 2010 involved the question of whether there were substantial oil and gas deposits in the disputed zones.

President Hu Jintao, in his October 2007 keynote policy speech at the 17th National Congress of the Chinese Communist Party, noted that the building of a more effective energy policy for the country was directly linked with environmental responsibility and the need for sustainable development.[54] Beijing released its first policy White Paper on Energy in 2007 which included calls for joint energy exploration with other states, encouraging foreign investment in power plants, improving the transfer of energy technology from other countries, maintaining stable political relations with energy producing states and preventing energy trade from being adversely affected by international politics.[55] A follow-up White Paper in 2012 added the importance of developing renewable resources and promoting more efficient energy usage.

However, there are several challenges facing Beijing as it seeks to maintain a steady energy supply. This has led to critical re-thinking in China about the issues and problems of energy security (*nengyuan anquan* 能源安全), defined as the need to obtain sufficient and stable supplies of energy at prices which are suitable and under conditions which do not endanger "national values and objectives".[56] Energy security has been a concern of other large energy consuming states, including the United States and Europe, at least as far back as the energy shocks in the Middle East in the 1970s, but China now has to look at the same policy choices within an international milieu which is much more susceptible to energy competition. Adding to these issues is the fact that China remains a relative newcomer to the politics of international energy trade and often has to engage regions, especially the Middle East and the Persian Gulf, which have been heavily dominated by Western interests and firms.

The Gulf Region in the Middle East, including Saudi Arabia, is providing a majority of China's imported oil and gas, but China since the 1990s has also been striking deals with Central Asia (especially the Caspian Sea region), Latin America, sub-Saharan Africa and Canada for joint oil and gas development. While Beijing has been willing to make use of its expanding economic resources to secure foreign oil and gas supplies, it has been wary of Western powers expressing concerns about how China's need for imported fossil fuels affects

---

Box 3.7 China's energy policies

"As the largest developing country in the world, China is faced with the daunting tasks of developing its economy, improving its people's livelihood, and building a moderately prosperous society. It is an important strategic task of the Chinese government to maintain long-term, stable and sustainable use of energy resources. China's energy development must follow a path featuring high-tech content, low consumption of resources, less environmental pollution, satisfactory economic returns, as well as security. It is moving towards the objective of economical, clean and secure development."

– *China's White Paper on Energy*, 2012.

global prices and access to these resources. Those who look at international energy policies will be asking whether heightened international competition for oil and gas may occur as a result of Beijing's entrance into global energy markets. Much will also depend on whether fossil fuel prices rebound in the short term from their rapid drop after 2014, and whether Beijing is able to take advantage of lower oil and gas prices to more fully promote energy diversification and clean energy initiatives.

Conclusions

As an editorial in the *Financial Times* suggested in July 2005, from an economic viewpoint "if the rest of the world doesn't know where China is going, neither does China".[57] Even though Beijing is still experimenting with models of economic growth and faces a myriad of obstacles, its economic growth and increasing effect on the developing world has opened a whole new area of power which China can wield in the international system. The country is in the difficult position of continuing to open up to international markets while simultaneously undertaking complex and risky domestic economic reforms designed to further remove the old vestiges of the Maoist command system. Beijing is now re-focusing on its economic priorities in the wake of the post-2008 recession and the "new normal" of China's slowing economic growth. Debates included how to maintain economic growth rates through domestic growth, which prompted the decision by Beijing, rather than relying on exports, to quickly implement an economic stimulus package in November 2008 worth about US$586 billion. As the Chinese government has tied much of its legitimacy to being able to continue the economic reform process in the country and further improve the living standards of its citizens, its ongoing ability to engage international markets, improve trade and economic cooperation and build an identity as a responsible and helpful partner in the globalising world will continue to be tested. During the summer of 2015, China's two stock markets experienced great instability, and concerns over falling demand for Chinese goods may have contributed to Beijing's decision to allow for a minor drop in the value of the country's currency. These events, coupled with a major industrial accident in the port city of Tianjin in August 2015, added to questions about China's short-term economic situation.

China is now an indispensable part of the global economy, and its economic policies will reverberate well beyond its borders or even the frontiers of the Pacific Rim. Although many have suggested that the country is on track to become the largest economic power in the world, it being merely a question of when, much will depend not only on Beijing's ability to maintain stable and effective economic growth under uncertain conditions but also on how other countries seek to address China's economic rise. Under Xi Jinping, China has begun to face the possibility of more "normal" development with slower growth rates, perhaps 5–7%, yet the role of China in the global economy continues to widen and deepen. Those examining the ongoing phenomenon of economic globalisation will increasingly need to look not only at how the West has developed within it, but also how China has responded to it.

Discussion questions

- How have China's views on economic globalisation differed from those of the West?
- What have been the successes and problems of China's expanding trade policies?
- How has the global recession affected China's economic power?
- How has China's economic growth affected economies in the developing world, emerging markets and developed economies?

- Will there be a greater international competition between China and the West for resources, especially energy?
- Can the Chinese experience with state-led economic growth act as a model for other developing states?

Recommended reading

Cardenal, Juan Pablo and Heriberto Araújo. *China's Silent Army: The Pioneers, Traders, Fixers and Workers Who Are Remaking the World in Beijing's Image* (London: Allen Lane, 2013).

Dyer, Geoff. *The Contest of the Century: The New Era of Competition with China* (London and New York: Allen Lane, 2013).

Economy, Elizabeth C. and Michael Levi. *By All Means Necessary: How China's Resource Quest is Changing the World* (Oxford and New York: Oxford University Press, 2014).

Halper, Stephan. *The Beijing Consensus: How China's Authoritarian Model will Dominate the Twenty-First Century* (New York: Basic Books, 2010).

Huang, Yasheng. *Capitalism with Chinese Characteristics: Entrepreneurship and the State* (Cambridge: Cambridge University Press, 2008).

Kurlantzick, Joshua. *Charm Offensive: How China's Soft Power is Transforming the World* (New Haven and London: Yale University Press, 2007).

Lardy, Nicholas R. *Sustaining China's Economic Growth after the Global Financial Crisis* (Washington DC: Peterson Institute for International Economics, 2011).

Li, Cheng (ed.) *China's Emerging Middle Class: Beyond Economic Transformation* (Washington DC: Brookings, 2010).

Lin, Justin Yifu. *Demystifying the Chinese Economy* (Cambridge: Cambridge University Press, 2012).

Moyo, Dambisa. *Winner Take All: China's Race for Resources and What it Means for the World* (New York: Basic Books, 2012).

Naughton, Barry. *The Chinese Economy: Transitions and Growth* (Cambridge, MA and London: MIT Press, 2007).

Nolan, Peter. *Is China Buying the World?* (Cambridge and Malden, MA: Polity Press, 2012).

Osnos, Evan. *Age of Ambition: Chasing Fortune, Truth and Faith in the New China* (London: Bodley Head, 2014).

Shapiro, Judith. *China's Environmental Challenges* (Cambridge and Malden, MA: Polity Press, 2012).

Simons, Craig. *The Devouring Dragon: How China's Rise Threatens Our Natural World* (New York: St. Martin's Press, 2013).

Song, Ligang and Wing Thye Woo (eds). *China's Dilemma: Economic Growth, the Environment and Climate Change* (Washington DC: Brookings, 2008).

Walter, Carl E. and Fraser J.T. Howie (2nd edn). *Red Capitalism: The Fragile Financial Foundation of China's Extraordinary Rise* (Singapore: John Wiley and Sons, 2012).

Wang, Hui. *China's Twentieth Century: Revolution, Retreat, and the Road to Equality* (London and New York: Verso Books, 2015).

Zeng, Ka and Joshua Eastin. *Greening China: The Benefits of Trade and Foreign Direct Investment* (Ann Arbor: University of Michigan Press, 2011).

Zhang, Joy Y. and Michael Barr. *Green Politics in China: Environmental Governance and State–Society Relations* (London: Pluto Press, 2013).

Notes

1 Ted C. Fishman, *China Inc.: How the Rise of the Next Superpower Challenges America and the World* (New York: Scribner, 2005).
2 Peter Marsh, "China to Overtake US as Largest Manufacturer," *Financial Times*, 10 August 2008.

3 Shirk, Susan, *China: Fragile Superpower* (Oxford and New York: Oxford University Press, 2007), 25–8.
4 Nick Edwards, "China Surprises with Export-led Trade Surplus," *Reuters*, 10 April 2012.
5 Barry Eichengreen, "China's New Exchange Rate Regime," *Current History* (September 2005): 263–5.
6 Alexandra Hartney, *The China Price: The True Cost of Chinese Competitive Advantage* (New York: Penguin Press, 2008), 1–17.
7 Neil Reynolds, "China Far Poorer than World Thinks," *The Globe and Mail*, 12 December 2007, B2.
8 "China Cuts GDP Growth Rate to 7.5% for Quality Development," Xinhua, 5 March 2012.
9 "China's GDP Growth Hits 11.4 Pct Year-on-Year in 2007," *China Business Newswire*, 24 January 2008; "China Inflation about 7 Pct This Year – Think Tank," *Reuters*, 2 July 2008.
10 Dominic Barton, Yougang Chen and Amy Jin, "Mapping China's Middle Class: Generational Change and the Rising Prosperity of Inland Cities Will Power Consumption for Years to Come," *McKinsey Quarterly*, June 2013 < http://www.mckinsey.com/insights/consumer_and_retail/mapping_chinas_middle_class>.
11 Nectar Gan, "Rise of China's Middle Class Will Not Challenge Communist Party: State Media," *South China Morning Post*, 27 February 2015.
12 Susan Shirk, *The Political Logic of Economic Reform in China* (Berkeley, Los Angeles and London: University of California Press, 1993), 24–5.
13 Yingjie Guo, "Class, Stratum and Group: The Politics of Description and Prescription," *The New Rich in China: Future Rulers, Present Lives*, ed. David S.G. Goodman (London and New York: Routledge, 2008), 38–52.
14 http://www.mac.gov.tw/public/data/051116322071.pdf.
15 Joshua Cooper Ramo, *The Beijing Consensus* (London: Foreign Policy Centre, 2004) <http://fpc.org.uk/fsblob/244.pdf>.
16 Randall Peerenboom, *China Modernizes: Threat to the West or Model for the Rest?* (Oxford and New York: Oxford University Press, 2007), 1–25.
17 Mitchell Bernard and John Ravenhill, "Beyond Product Cycles and Flying Geese: Regionalization, Hierarchy and the Industrialization of East Asia," *World Politics* 47(2) (January 1995): 171–209.
18 Thomas G. Moore and Dixia Yang, "Empowered and Restrained: Chinese Foreign Policy in the Age of Economic Interdependence," *The Making of Chinese Foreign and Security Policy in the Era of Reform*, ed. David M. Lampton (Stanford: Stanford University Press, 2001), 191–229.
19 Eunsuk Hong and Laixiang Sun, "Dynamics of Internationalisation and Outward Investment: Chinese Corporations' Strategies," *The China Quarterly* 187 (September 2006): 610–34.
20 James Kynge, *China Shakes the World: The Rise of a Hungry Nation* (London: Weidenfeld and Nicolson, 2006), 163–74.
21 Greg Sheridan, "Chinese Model Passes the West," *The Australian*, 25 August 2005, 10.
22 Minxin Pei, *China's Trapped Transition: The Limits of Developmental Autocracy* (Harvard: Harvard University Press, 2008); Dan Breznitz and Michael Murphree, *Run of the Red Queen: Government, Innovation, Globalization, and Economic Growth in China* (New Haven and London: Yale University Press, 2011).
23 David Shambaugh, "The Coming Chinese Crackup," *Wall Street Journal*, 6 March 2015.
24 The World Bank, *China 2030: Building a Modern, Harmonious, and Creative High-Income Society* http://www.worldbank.org/content/dam/Worldbank/document/china-2030-complete.pdf.
25 David Roberts, "How the US Embassy Tweeted to Clear Beijing's Air," *Wired*, 6 March 2015.
26 Elizabeth C. Economy, "The Costs of China's Environmental Crisis," *Foreign Affairs* 86(5) (September / October 2007): 38–59.
27 Ning Zeng, Yihui Ding, Jiahua Pan, Huijun Wang and Jay Gregg, "Climate Change – The Chinese Challenge," *Science* 319(5864) (8 February 2008): 730–1.
28 Phillip Stalley and Dongning Yang, "An Emerging Environmental Movement in China?" *The China Quarterly* 186 (June 2006): 333–56.
29 Joshua Kurlantzick, *Charm Offensive: How China's Soft Power is Transforming the World* (New Haven and London: Yale University Press, 2007), 86–91; Bates Gill and Yanzhong Huang, "Sources and Limits of Chinese 'Soft Power'" *Survival* 48(2) (Summer 2006): 23.
30 Joseph S. Nye Jr. *Is the American Century Over?* (Cambridge and Malden, MA: Polity Press, 2015), 59–62.

31 Thomas Piketty, *Capital in the Twenty-First Century* (Cambridge and London: Belknap Press, 2014), 326–7.

32 Michael Wines, "An Ambitious Chinese Party Chief Admits His Failure to Oversee an Aide," *The New York Times*, 10 March 2012.

33 Samuel S. Kim, "Chinese Foreign Policy Faces Globalisation Challenges," *New Directions in the Study of Chinese Foreign Policy*, ed. Alastair Iain Johnston and Robert S. Ross (Stanford: Stanford University Press, 2006), 279–84.

34 Zheng Bijian, *China's Peaceful Rise: Speeches of Zheng Bijian* (Washington DC, Brookings, 2005), 38.

35 Zhang Weiwei, *The China Wave: Rise of a Civilisational State* (Shanghai: World Century Publishing, 2012), 29–51.

36 Chalmers Johnston, *MITI and the Japanese Miracle: The Growth of Industrial Policy, 1925–1975* (Stanford: Stanford University Press, 1982).

37 Chris Buckley, "In Lee Kuan Yew, China Saw a Leader to Emulate," *The New York Times*, 23 March 2015.

38 Alvin J. So, "Introduction," *China's Developmental Miracle: Origins, Transformations and Challenges*, ed. Alvin Y. So (Armonk, NY and London, M.E. Sharpe, 2003), 18–19.

39 Joseph Fewsmith, *China Since Tiananmen* (2nd edn) (Cambridge and New York: Cambridge University Press 2008), 221–4.

40 Goh Sui Noi, "Don't Let Politics Discredit Chongqing's Growth Model," *Straits Times*, 13 March 2012.

41 Philippe C. Schmitter, "Still the Century of Corporatism?" *The Review of Politics* 36(1) (January 1974): 82–131.

42 Richard F. Doner, Bryan K. Ritchie and Dan Slater, "Systemic Vulnerability and the Origins of Developmental States: Northeast and Southeast Asia in Comparative Perspective," *International Organization* 59 (Spring 2005): 327–61.

43 Yanying Zhang, Gaiyan Zhang and Hung-Gay Fung, "The Prospects for China's Free Trade Agreements," *The Chinese Economy* 40(2) (March–April 2007): 7.

44 Ellen L. Frost, "China's Commercial Diplomacy in Asia: Promise or Threat?" *China's Rise and the Balance of Power in Asia*, ed. William W. Keller and Thomas G. Rawski (Pittsburgh, University of Pittsburgh Press, 2007), 96–9.

45 Marc Lanteigne, "The Falcon and the Dragon: Commercial Diplomacy and the Sino-Icelandic Free Trade Negotiations," *Centre for Small State Studies Working Paper* 2 (May 2008): 4–17.

46 "China Promotes 'Asia-Pacific Dream' to Counter U.S. 'Pivot'," *Washington Post*, 11 November 2013.

47 Geoff Dyer and George Parker, "US Attacks UK's 'Constant Accommodation' with China," *Financial Times*, 12 March 2015.

48 Andrew Higgins and David E. Sanger, "3 European Powers Say They Will Join China-Led Bank," *The New York Times*, 17 March 2015.

49 Li Qingxin, *Maritime Silk Road* (Beijing: China International Press, 2006), 23–30.

50 "A Ravenous Dragon," *The Economist*, 15 March 2008, Special Report 3–5.

51 Barry Naughton, *The Chinese Economy: Transitions and Growth* (Cambridge, MA and London: MIT Press, 2007), 336.

52 Record Oil Imports Take China Closest Ever to Passing US, *Bloomberg Business*, 14 January 2015 <http://www.bloomberg.com/news/articles/2015-01-14/record-oil-imports-take-china-closest-ever-to-passing-u-s-1->.

53 Andrew Neff, "CNPC Says Oil Production at China's Biggest Field down 4% in 2007," *Global Insight Daily Analysis / Factiva*, 3 January 2008.

54 Hu Jintao, "Hold High the Great Banner of Socialism with Chinese Characteristics and Strive for New Victories in Building a Moderately Prosperous Society in All Respects: Report to the Seventeenth National Congress of the Communist Party on October 15th, 2007," *Documents of the 17th National Congress of the Communist Party of China* (Beijing: Foreign Languages Press, 2007), 29–30.

55 China's Energy Conditions and Policies, *Information Office of the State Council*, Beijing, December 2007 <http://www.china.org.cn/english/whitepaper/energy/237089.htm>.

56 Daniel Yergin, "Energy Security in the 1990s," *Foreign Affairs* 67(1) (Fall 1988): 111.

57 Mark Leonard, "The Road Obscured," *Financial Times*, 9 July 2005, 16.

4 Multilateralism and international institutions

China reconsiders multilateralism

One of the most visible changes in China's foreign policy since the Dengist reforms has been in the country's approach to multilateralism and international regimes and organisations. As the country's global interests have expanded, China has optimised its engagement of various types of organisations in order to gain more "goods" and information from the international system. Moreover, as China's power grows, it has developed a greater ability to help shape the policies and directions of political, economic and security organisations, and as a result has seen its structural power rise. Structural power, as described for example in the work by Barnett and Duvall, is a concept broadly described as the ability to influence rules, norms and the "structure" of relationship patterns within the international system, sometimes through formal organisations but also occasionally through more subtle social relationships between state and non-state actors, such as businesses, academia and non-governmental organisations.[1] This type of power is also based on the ability and capacity of an actor to "socialise" with other actors in foreign relations to gain either material resources or political goods such as prestige and diplomatic power.

The idea of structural power stands in contrast to, but also sometimes complements, the more discernible and observable "coercive power", namely the ability to use force or other pressures to prompt an actor to do something they would not normally do.[2] For example, a superpower such as the United States often makes use of both types of power in its international policies, and there is the growing question about whether, as China develops as a great power, that country will develop those same capabilities on a regional and global level. The People's Republic of China, during its first few decades, possessed structural power levels which were, at best, negligible under Mao given the country's initial position as a member of the pro-Soviet collective and then as an isolated actor after the Sino-Soviet Split. Following the Dengist reforms, and especially during the expansion of Chinese foreign policy interests under Jiang and Hu, growing structural power was demonstrated by Beijing's recent behaviour towards a growing variety of institutions ranging from the international (the United Nations, including the UN Security Council) to the regional (such as the Asia-Pacific Economic Cooperation forum, the East Asian Summit and the Shanghai Cooperation Organisation).

As the number of international organisations continues to grow in the post-Cold War system, China is embedding itself more intensively with greater agility and confidence in global networks. Under Xi Jinping, China has begun to take the next step in advocating and creating new organisations such as the Asian Infrastructure Investment Bank, the New

Development Bank (NDB, also colloquially known as the "Bank of BRICS"), and the "one belt and one road" initiative. Beijing has also been at the forefront of new regimes which link China with regions further afield of the Asia-Pacific, including for example the Forum on China–Africa Cooperation (FOCAC), created in 2000, and the Strategic and Economic Dialogue between China and the United States, begun in 2009 following an agreement between Hu Jintao and US President Barack Obama. China has also joined regional organisations as an observer, examples being the Organisation of American States (OAS) in 2004, the South Asian Association for Regional Cooperation (SAARC) as of 2006, and the Arctic Council since 2013. The effect of this deep engagement on modern Chinese foreign policymaking is a question worthy of further study.

The transformation of China's views of international organisations is especially remarkable when one considers its past history with them. Imperial China experienced a very harsh introduction to international regimes, including the perceived negligence of the League of Nations and the harsh conditions of the 1919 Treaty of Versailles, when the Republican Chinese government signed the agreement which transferred the German-occupied Shandong region not to China proper but to Japan. The transfer took place in the wake of the Siege of Tsingtao (Qingdao) in late 1914, when German and Austro-Hungarian occupiers were routed by a joint Anglo-Japanese taskforce in the only major battle of the First World War to take place in Asia. Public anger over what it saw as capitulation to foreign pressure would spark the anti-imperialist 1919 May Fourth Movement.[3] After 1949, Maoist China was shut out of the United Nations, with the UN recognising only the Nationalist government on Taiwan, and then fought directly with American-backed UN forces on behalf of North Korea under Kim Il-sung during the 1950–3 Korean War. It was only under the reformist governments of Deng Xiaoping and Jiang Zemin that China's views on multilateral institutions became increasingly favourable.

Today, China has in many cases switched its policies towards existing regimes from primarily "reactive", meaning the engagement of an organisation with a primary focus on observing and collecting information from within the said regime, to a more active stance by openly proposing policies and reforms, seeking to manoeuvre regimes in new directions, and more frequently proposing new institutions to better serve Chinese interests. To use the classic international relations terminology put forward by Keohane, China is making the transition from being a "system-influencing" state, one which can sway the nature of a given international system either alone or with others (a common trait of a medium power such as Australia, Brazil, Canada, Indonesia and South Korea), towards more of a "system-determining" state which can unilaterally shape an international order, along the lines of the United States today and great powers of the past.[4] Although China remains far from having the same institution-building and moulding capabilities demonstrated by the United States, which has created and guided numerous political, economic and security organisations since the Second World War, Beijing's confidence in putting forward its own ideas and agendas in the global community is nonetheless growing.

So, China's rise has been matched by an increasing confidence in engaging international institutions. Yet the country retains concerns about being subject to "containment" via security alliances, and has expressed apprehension about unilateral great power intervention in the strategic affairs of other states, including US intervention in the Kosovo conflict in 1999, the decision by the US to invade Iraq in 2003, the conflict between Russia and Georgia in 2008, and the Russian annexation of the Crimea region from Ukraine in 2014 and Moscow's subsequent support for separatist rebels in the Donbas region of eastern Ukraine. Beijing was also critical of Western intervention in the 2011 Libyan conflict and has been opposed to potential US military actions in Syria, a country which descended into full civil war in early 2011. Closer to home, China has been sensitive to American strategic support of allies such as Japan and the Philippines, which have opposed Beijing over disputed maritime regions, and greater American support for other Chinese neighbours such as India and Vietnam.

This wariness has meant that China has often considered the United Nations, as well as more informal security communities as opposed to alliances, as better vehicles by which to address international problems too large or complex for Beijing, or any single state, to solve alone. While China continues to follow its longstanding practice of establishing one-to-one partnerships with selected states, including seeking partnerships with medium and great powers, the country has also become more open to engagement with smaller actors. Moreover, China has not followed the lead of the Soviet Union, which was often a revisionist great power, in attempting to develop regimes to overtly counter or balance the West along the lines of the old Warsaw Pact. Instead, China has sought to work within the existing global network of organisations to better develop its interests, and has frequently eschewed even the appearance of power balancing, in keeping with the identity of a "status quo" power. However, Beijing is nonetheless signalling that it will no longer remain as passive within the institutions that it joins, as it has in the past.

One of the most distinct features of a rising China is that it is developing into a great and potentially global power within an international system now dominated by institutions, regimes, organisations, laws and norms, a considerably different situation faced by other rising powers, such as Britain, the United States and the Soviet Union, which ascended to the highest ranks of states in a world considerably less multilateral in its global relations. The process of the "institutionalisation" of international relations is seen as both entrenched and still developing.[5] As well, unlike in previous cases of great power development, China is able to make more extensive use of organisations to seek power and goods rather than constantly having to resort to hard power. Membership in international institutions does entail a loss of sovereignty, since it requires a given degree of cooperation and transparency. Joining any institution can also carry risks, including the possibility of some members *defecting* (leaving an organisation, thus likely weakening it), *cheating* (breaking set rules) or *free-riding* (benefiting from a regime without properly contributing to it). Yet, institutions have continued to grow in number and it has been suggested that the overall level of compliance in inter-state organisations is high, to the benefit of their memberships.[6] Therefore, the current international system is very conducive for a state, especially a large one with developing actual and dormant power, to more deeply engage them.

Thus, China's approaches to multilateralism (*duobian weijiao* 多边外交) have matured considerably, becoming a major component of its foreign policy, despite much emphasis on bilateral foreign policy in Chinese diplomacy. A greater confidence level in approaching multilateralism is especially important in today's climate of increasing ties between China and ever-growing numbers of regions, sub-regions and state actors well beyond Asia. There is also the question of whether the international system may become multipolar with the relative decline of American power versus the rise of emerging powers, including China. However, Beijing's approach to multilateralism continues to evolve and in some cases, especially in defence matters, there remain some lingering concerns about the potential loss of Chinese sovereignty as a result of deeper regime cooperation and participation. The current state of China's international engagement, especially since the coming to power of Xi Jinping, is remarkable given the short amount of time which passed between the era of distrust and separation from the global system during the Republican era as well as under the PRC's first leader, Mao Zedong, and the current period of deep engagement.

Isolation and suspicion under Mao

Much of Mao's Zedong's thinking was influenced by international events which soured him and the Communist movement as a whole on the process of international treaties and rules. The "unequal treaties" (*buping dengtiaoyue* 不平等条约) since the mid-nineteenth century which China had to sign with Western colonial powers and Japan demonstrated that international legal processes were not guaranteed to be fair. Instead, international rules were frequently perceived as a means of establishing sovereignty of the strong over the weak. This animosity would bubble over most visibly during the 1899–1900 Yihetuan Movement (*yihetuan yundong* 义和团运动), more commonly known in the West as the Boxer Rebellion, which resulted in a wave of violence against foreigners including Christian missionaries, as well as Chinese who were branded as collaborators or turncoats. The rebellion was suppressed only after an Eight-Nation Alliance comprising Austria-Hungary, France, Germany, Italy, Japan, Russia, the United Kingdom and the United States, staged an armed intervention.[7] The aftermath of the crisis included the Boxer Protocol in 1901 which forced the Qing government to pay reparations to the Alliance, further weakening the already moribund Qing leadership and doing nothing to halt rancour towards the foreign powers among the Chinese citizenry.

During the entire period of Republican China between 1911 and 1949, China was broken up into competing fiefdoms under the partial control of a variety of foreign powers, thus preventing China from engaging the international system as a unified state. As previously noted, the May Fourth Movement of 1919 was largely prompted by public anger at both the Chinese government and foreign powers following the signing of the Versailles Treaty. This was seen by many radicals as the final straw after decades of "open door" policies which saw Europe and Imperial Japan carve up huge territories within Imperial and Republican China, often using treaties as legal cover.[8]

After 1949, throughout most of the Maoist era, Beijing was openly hostile to the growing web of international regimes and laws, viewing them as imperialist and Western dominated, designed to hamper the development of international socialism. As a result, as US-led post-war organisations developed, China remained outside of those processes. Mao's "leaning to one side" (*yibiandao* 一边倒) strategy thus was based on adherence to the Soviet Union which, as Mao described it, was the side of equality and the benefits of Marxism-Leninism for China, and a stand against "foreign reactionaries" and "imperialists and their running dogs".[9] China was left out of the rapidly developing set of post-Second World War regimes, including the General Agreement on Tariffs and Trade (GATT) and the International Monetary Fund (IMF) which assisted other states in recovering from the conflict. However, Beijing's negative views on regimes would later extend to many of the USSR's own institutions, such as the Warsaw Pact, the Soviet Bloc's strategic alliance, and COMECON, the Soviet-overseen Council for Mutual Economic Assistance. As Sino-Soviet relations worsened, China withdrew from its observer role in the Warsaw pact in 1961 and stopped responding to invitations from COMECON in 1966. With the development of the "Brezhnev Doctrine" (named after the Soviet leader who devised it), in the 1970s, which sought to consolidate the socialist world under the aegis of the USSR, Beijing viewed Soviet-backed organisations as little better than the Western ones, and began to deride hegemonic behaviour not only on the part of Washington but also increasingly of Moscow.[10]

After the Second World War, the United Nations, despite Soviet objections, opted to recognise the *Kuomintang* (Nationalist) government in exile on Taiwan as the sole governmental representative of the entire Chinese state. The 1950–3 Korean War, a United Nations-backed operation spearheaded by the United States, reconfirmed Mao's negative opinion of the UN Organisation's impartiality. Finally, attempts to create a Western alliance in Asia to defend against communism and further American interests suggested to Mao that institutions were being created merely to contain the spread of socialism and further weaken Chinese interests. Mao was also highly critical of military alliances, and bristled when plans were put into place by Washington to copy the model of the North Atlantic Treaty Organisation (NATO) in Europe in order to create the Southeast Asian Treaty Organisation (SEATO) among US allies in the Pacific Rim in 1954.

Mao denounced SEATO, referring to it as running "counter to the trend of history", while the United States sought to make the organisation a bastion against Beijing's influence in the region, a move which dismayed other members who preferred a more non-aligned approach.[11] SEATO was eventually proven a failure, falling into dormancy in the 1970s,[12] but its very existence had further increased China's suspicion of multilateral cooperation and institutions. As well, even though the creation of a NATO-like structure failed, the US did succeed in developing a "San Francisco System" of hub-and-spoke treaties with Japan, South Korea and the Philippines, as well as maintaining strategic ties with other Asian states including Thailand and Singapore.

Strong Westphalian views on the primacy of the state and its absolute sovereignty in Chinese foreign policy under Maoism also explains why China was initially reluctant to engage (non-Soviet) post-war economic or strategic regimes, or even those developing international laws, until the Dengist reforms. The legacies of colonialism and foreign intervention during the Qing and Republican eras were very much present in Mao's foreign policy thinking in the early years of the PRC. Participation in any international regimes, regardless of their size or function, entails both a loss of sovereignty and a requisite transfer of information to the other members, costs which Beijing was quite unwilling to assume in the 1950s and 60s. China's weaknesses, as well as its lack of strong links with the international system, made Beijing acutely aware of the "prisoners' dilemma" of dangers based on cooperation without sufficient information. The Sino-Soviet Split further isolated China from both Western and Eastern institutions, forcing Beijing to rely on limited bilateral ties. Self-reliance, along with Mao's views of that time that China was "poor and blank" (*yi qiong er bai* 一 穷二白),[13] became cornerstones of China's international thinking and further isolated the country from the ongoing development, primarily in the West, of international regimes.

Thus, Chinese views on international institutions until Mao's death were very much in keeping, albeit to an extreme extent, with traditional realist views of interdependence, namely that it created an atmosphere of both sensitivity and vulnerability to international actors and events which China, as a weak state recovering from years of civil and regional conflict, believed it could not withstand. This cost/benefit equation changed in Beijing's view after

---

Box 4.1 Members of SEATO (1954–77)

Australia
France
New Zealand
Pakistan (including then-East Pakistan / Bangladesh)
Philippines
Thailand
United Kingdom
United States

Deng came to power, and realised China needed both hard capital and information about global norms and practices in order to pull itself out of its isolation and economic despair. In the 1970s, a popular backlash against the Gang of Four, who believed any increased international contact would be harmful to China, also assisted Deng in changing opinions about multilateralism. Under Deng's "cats' theory" (the colour of the cat is irrelevant as long as the mice are caught), China's rapprochement to both the West and its now-advanced network of rules and norms was seen as necessary, providing potential beneficial to Chinese interests.

Before Mao's death, some of the framework for what would become China's multilateralist policy was being constructed by Mao in the form of his "Three Worlds Theory" (*sange shijie* 三个世界) in the late 1960s. Departing from his traditional views that the world was largely divided into only two camps (capitalist and socialist), Mao later began to speak of a "Third World" (*disan shijie* 第三世界) outside of the rivalry between the superpowers, the US and the USSR, which he considered to be of the First World and the Second World which included "Europe, Japan, Australia and Canada", according to one set of remarks.[14] The Third World, of which China was a leading member, included states in Africa, Asia and Latin America which were emerging from colonialism by the middle of the twentieth century.

Through various diplomatic initiatives to developing states in the 1950s and 60s, Mao sought to develop a Chinese identity as a large developing state but stopped short of directly engaging in many new institutions representing developing state interests. For example, China became an observer in the Non-Aligned Movement (NAM), a group dedicated to avoidance of great power politics, in the 1960s but declined full membership. Beijing also declined membership in the Group of 77, an organisation composed of developing states and former colonies lobbying for greater economic rights, and Beijing only tangentially supported the New International Economic Order (NIEO) when it was conceived in the early 1970s by developing states seeking greater economic fairness from the Group of Seven (G-7) most advanced economies.[15]

During the later Maoist period, China was seeking to walk a line between being viewed internationally as a "developing state" but also as a potentially important player in global affairs. At the start of China's opening to international regimes, Deng's approach to such organisations suggested that this policy was part of his larger doctrine of "not taking the lead" (*bu daitou* 不带头) and avoiding hegemonic behaviour in international affairs. The need for China to develop a stronger knowledge base of global politics, international organisations and the comparative foreign policies of other states meant that in many organisations recently joined by China, its representatives would adapt a watch, learn and wait approach to gatherings and meetings.

This philosophy, for example, was demonstrated when China received its United Nations seat in 1971. Until that time, the PRC was largely against the idea of the UN, just as it was highly critical of its predecessor, the League of Nations, in the 1930s. All of these views changed by the 1970s, and instead China began to develop as one of the UN's strongest supporters, adopting what has been called a "system-maintaining" stance.[16] China has praised the UN's views on security-building and more recently on disarmament,[17] and during the 1990s took a more conciliatory view on United Nations peacekeeping and humanitarian intervention. China would later match words with deeds by the turn of the century by contributing more personnel for UN peacekeeping missions than any of the other permanent five Security Council members.[18] Despite fears by some Western states that Beijing would attempt to hamstring the UN, taking advantage of its veto power, Chinese voting behaviour has been for the most part conservative, rarely using the veto option compared with its use by the two superpowers during the Cold War.

Regimes re-evaluated: Deng and after

In the Dengist reform era, China's approach to international organisations had to be quickly and effectively redesigned. In the late 1970s, China was approaching each institution from a weakened position, as years of isolation had greatly reduced both Chinese diplomatic capabilities and the available information about the preferences and strengths of other actors. As liberalist theories of international organisation have frequently noted, this lack of data can often lead to problems including mistrust, suspicion, and abnormally high "transaction costs" in terms of lost capital, goods or prestige.[19] As well, China's pre-communist history arguably increased its sensitivity to the issues of cheating. Finally, China's initial approach to international regimes was very much in keeping with Waltzian or "hard" realism, namely that institutions and regimes were primarily extensions of great power foreign policy.[20] It was only when the period of détente with the United States began to gain momentum in the late 1970s that Deng believed engaging many Western-dominated institutions would not leave Beijing vulnerable to American manipulation.

There were strong motivations for China to begin the process of developing a multilateral strategy and engage international regimes. In addition to practical matters such as the requirement for hard capital, the international community required convincing that Maoist doctrine in China was becoming more accepting of the international system. From a constructivist viewpoint, Deng's reforms demonstrated shifts in China's identity, both in terms of how it saw itself and how other governments should view it. Engaging institutions provided Beijing with many new forums to demonstrate its determination to be redefined as a status quo power rather than a revisionist one. To use Wendt's Social Theory, China was seeking sweeping changes in the equation of its foreign policies and its perception by the international system.[21]

With the decline of the zero-sum thinking which had previously dominated Maoist international policy, Deng was better able to consider international organisations in terms of positive-sum. China could cooperate and gain benefits along with the other players. This is in keeping with the liberalist theory of *"shadow of the future"*, meaning that many international interactions, especially activities within regimes, are often repeated and that states which choose not to cooperate in the short term can be persuaded to change their minds if a series of potential long-term gains are effectively demonstrated.[22] It has been argued that the political legacy of the Cultural Revolution and the late Maoist period has resulted in post-Maoist governments being highly sensitive to being labelled obstructionist or isolationist, and as China develops as a great power, international organisations are seen as essential for Beijing to further refine its foreign policy interests.

China also had significant advantage in the form of its size, and more specifically its market power, which many advanced economies, including America, Europe and Japan made little secret of their desire to develop. This gave Beijing much additional leverage as well as bargaining power in its relations with organisations while selectively allowing or withdrawing market access based on the actions of potential partners. China's size also allowed the country to potentially utilise what has been called a "grim trigger" strategy, namely that if Actor A defects or acts in a harmful manner, Actor B can punish it and continue to punish it even if Actor A behaves perfectly well afterwards.[23] China's growing potential during the 1980s and 90s as a large emerging market has been considered a major bargaining chip in its relations with international regimes and especially economic organisations during this period. As China's economic power continues to grow, the country has the ability to use a grim trigger approach both to encourage cooperation from other states (and markets) as well as to influence the development of economic regimes and to a lesser degree, other types of organisations.

Deng was very much in favour of a gradualist approach in Beijing's initial overtures to international regimes, a method he often categorised as "crossing a river by feeling the stones". His preference was to start slowly and engage with international lending organisations such as the IMF and World Bank in the early 1980s and then join the Multi-Fibre Agreement (MFA) in 1983 so that China could have a stronger influence on the textile trade, which was and remains a major component of the country's reforming economy. These lending organisations granted China access to essential hard capital needed for rebuilding its economy, and in convincing other potential donors, especially Japan, that China could handle the loan processes and behave as a responsible debtor. Ultimately, the influx of external capital contributed much to Deng's plans to lift the country out of widespread poverty. In 1979, Beijing reversed its opposition to receiving overseas development assistance, or ODA, and instead encouraged investment from Japan and Western Europe as well as Commonwealth members such as Canada and Australia.[24] In addition to improving China's solvency, the country's initial contacts with these lending institutions can be viewed as the country's first lessons on successful multilateral behaviour.

Economic regimes continued to be considered by Beijing to be less risk-prone than strategic ones during the expansion of Beijing's institutional engagement in the 1990s.[25] Economic agreements are normally more transparent, and members who engage in "cheating" or "free-riding" are easier to identify and, if necessary, penalise. In the case of cheating or defection within an economic regime, while the financial damage might be considerable to the whole, it would not place other members at great risk. In the case of security organisations, by contrast, defection or cheating can directly threaten the core interests or even the survival of the other states within the agreement. Moreover, China was assuming, correctly, that as a large market, other members of economic regimes would treat it with respect in exchange for ready future access to China's substantial consumer base (as in the old adage, "trade follows aid"). As a fringe benefit, engagement with economic regimes also provided China with information on international markets and trade practices imperative to the country's "reform and opening up" processes.

For example, in 1986, despite the fact that much of its economy had yet to be liberalised, Beijing announced it wished to join the General Agreement on Tariffs and Trade (GATT) as a full member. The announcement was met with much scepticism by the West, especially in the United States, given that China still had a long road to travel in its economic reform policies. Beijing first attempted to claim immediate membership on the grounds that the Nationalist government, which later decamped to Taiwan, was granted GATT status but withdrew from it, illegally, in Beijing's view, in 1950. Therefore, China sought to claim retroactive membership. However, the GATT rejected this claim and as a result China began 15 complicated and sometimes politically divisive years of negotiations in an effort to become a member of that trade body. Beijing had to deal with multiple political obstacles during the talks, along with concerns its economic system was too immature and closed to withstand global liberalised trade.

First, talks were put on hold after the 1989 Tiananmen incident, and it was not until the early 1990s that the talks could be effectively restarted. Second, the break-up of the Soviet Union and the reforms in Eastern Europe meant that China had to wait in a much longer line. Third, a year after the completion of the Uruguay Round of the GATT in 1994, the World Trade Organisation was created and China wished to join the WTO as a founding member, but ran into strong opposition from the United States. Finally, pressure began to be applied to China after Taiwan announced that it wanted to join the GATT/WTO as a customs union, and the Chinese government maintained that under no conditions would it allow Taipei to enter the agreement before Beijing.[26]

The most important obstacle to China's WTO ambitions was undoubtedly the United States, which was concerned about both Beijing's lack of free market history and the potential damage to the American economy which might occur as a result of accepting such a large and still greatly unregulated market into the organisation. As per membership rules, Beijing was required to conclude liberalised trade agreements with all major markets before being allowed in and the United States proved to be the most complicated negotiation partner. Washington initially attempted to cite the Jackson–Vanik Amendment of the 1974 US Trade Act which disallowed most-favoured nation trade status with a "non-market economy", meaning a communist state, unless the president requested permission to do so every year.[27] Even with that provision waived, the US also insisted that China join the WTO as a developed economy, forcing it to accept more stringent trade rules than as a member deemed a developing state. China protested against this provision, dragging out negotiations throughout the entire Clinton administration. US law-makers cited numerous concerns over Chinese labour rights, the continued existence of state-owned enterprises, lack of intellectual property rights and an erratic taxation system as reasons to delay American support for membership.

China responded to the US and other critics by implementing further trade reforms, slashing taxes on a variety of goods and standardising others, and in the late 1990s greatly streamlining government ministries in charge of trade and economic reform. At the same time, China also began to remove so-called "non-tariff barriers" (NTBs, rules or laws which impede trade outside of actual tariffs).[28] Although the long process created much dissatisfaction from some Chinese political actors both towards the United States and towards the Jiang government for its eagerness to cut deals, including emerging "New Left" (*xinzuopai* 新左派) academics and intellectuals concerned about China's too-enthusiastic embrace of globalisation, Beijing insisted that membership was necessary to achieve the next step in the development process. The deadlock was finally broken in 2001 and China joined the WTO in December of that year, with Taipei signing on a month later under the unwieldy name of "Separate Customs Territory of Taiwan, Penghu, Kinmen and Matsu (Chinese Taipei)". WTO membership or not, elements of the New Left in Chinese academic circles has continued to act as a critic of Chinese globalisation.

Despite American concerns that China would seek to disrupt the WTO process upon gaining membership, China's relations with the organisation have so far been largely non-confrontational. Since becoming a member, the number of disputes Beijing became involved in with other WTO members slowly increased between 2006 and 2011, with China more often the respondent rather than the complainant, and a majority of disputes involved the United States. These included a case Beijing brought against Washington in 2009 over tariffs implemented by the Obama government on Chinese tyres, and complaints filed by the US and the European Union in 2012 over China's export restrictions of "rare earths" including tungsten and molybdenum which are essential for electronics and other high-technology equipment. In 2014, China and the US also sparred within the organisation over American accusations that Beijing was supporting the sale of solar panels below cost, a process known as "dumping", while Beijing made a case against the United States that countervailing duty measures Washington had placed on Chinese goods were retaliation and against WTO protocols.[29]

There was considerable interest as to why Beijing was willing to wait so long and make a considerable number of concessions in order to enter the WTO despite significant internal opposition. As the international relations theory of "club goods" notes, states will often incur high initial costs to join organisations out of strong fears of being left out of an exclusive body.[30] China at this stage was already seen as an indispensable economic player, an impression which would not have changed had Beijing remained out of the WTO. However, with China in, the country now has the ability to greatly influence the regime's direction as well as participate in the development of new trade rules. The Doha Round of trade negotiations in the WTO, begun in 2001, has been beset by delays and disputes, with considerable splits between developed and developing economies which were further exacerbated by the onset of the global recession after 2008.[31]

When the schism between emerging market states and advanced actors such as the United States and the European Union grew during the Doha Round, China participated in the loose coalition known as the Group of Twenty Plus (or G-20 Plus), advanced developing states which called for a final trade deal more equitable to developing economy interests. However, unlike the more outspoken members of the G-20 Plus coalition, such as Brazil and India, Beijing was viewed as more of a mediator between the two sides by avoiding aligning itself with the more critical members of the group.[32] Not only was this an example of China's new-found ability to operate effectively within informal groups, but it also illustrated China's determination to present itself as a large developing state with growing international diplomatic capabilities.

This view was further reinforced when China with other large developing states (Brazil, Russia and India) formed the "BRIC" group in June 2009 at a meeting in Yekaterinburg, Russia, and began to hold annual summits on economic affairs. South Africa would join in 2010, thus creating the "BRICS" group representing close to three billion persons and the most rapidly growing economies in the world. In July 2014, at the BRICS Leadership Summit in Fortaleza, Brazil, the five governments signed a protocol to create the BRICS Development Bank worth initially US$100 billion, later named the New Development Bank, and to create a reserve currency pool worth over US$100 billion. Considering that the idea of the BRICS had its start as part of a (previously) nondescript 2001 economic policy paper from the consultancy firm Goldman Sachs,[33] the swift evolution of the organisation from abstract concept to formal institutions remains striking.

Another economic regime which China would court, and be courted by, was the Asia-Pacific Economic Cooperation Forum. APEC was founded in 1989 with the primary goal of developing a free trade zone in the Pacific Rim. Australia, Japan, and later the United States, Canada and Singapore would be APEC's early advocates, motivated both by growing regionalism in Asia and by deepening concerns about the development of other large international trading blocks. In North America, the Canada–US Free Trade agreement was being finalised, with Mexico to be added later, to form NAFTA, while the European Community, languishing in the early 1980s, received a push towards a single market with the signing of the Single European Act in 1985. Many Asia-Pacific states were concerned about being left outside of these exclusive arrangements and desired a trade regime of their own. APEC planners initially wanted China to be added as a founding member, but the diplomatic fallout from Tiananmen in 1989 and questions over how to include the economic powers of Hong Kong and Taiwan along with China stalled the admission process during the first stages of APEC's development.

In 1991, a deal was brokered by South Korea that permitted China, Taiwan and Hong Kong to enter under specific conditions and titles. APEC members would be formally referred to as "economies" rather than states, and Taiwan was to accept the title "Chinese Taipei" and Hong Kong, the "Hong Kong Special Autonomous Region" (SAR).[34] APEC currently has 21 member economies including the US, Russia, China and Japan, as well as most of Southeast Asia. China has been a supporter of APEC because it is considered an "anarchic" regime, meaning that every member has veto power and therefore equal say over rule-making processes,[35] and therefore overt bloc voting is not possible. As well, APEC's informal structure gave Beijing the ability to test its own trade liberalisation policies on a smaller group before bringing them up to the international level and to the GATT/WTO.

Moreover, APEC as an institution was also defined by its adherence to "open regionalism", meaning that APEC would be willing to extend club benefits to non-club members, and "voluntarism", the idea that decisions would be made by consensus and members would not be pressured into accepting rules with which they disagree.[36] The development of both concepts within APEC did much to convince Beijing that it would not be bound to a formal, rules-based regime. Thus, China took advantage of its membership by dropping tariffs within the organisation as a means of demonstrating to the WTO that it was committed to trade liberalisation.[37] China also found itself one of the few APEC economies largely unaffected by the Asian Financial Crisis of 1997–8, but at the same time the crisis did much to slow down APEC's progress. Although APEC has promised the development of a complete free trade zone in the region by 2020 at the latest, there remain many obstacles to be overcome and momentum within APEC slowed considerably by the turn of the century in favour of more Asia-specific economic regimes. Despite the slowdown of APEC's forward momentum, Beijing demonstrated its ongoing commitment to the process when Xi Jinping hosted the November 2014 APEC Leadership Summit in Beijing. During the meetings, Xi not only called for an "Asia-Pacific Dream" more accurately reflecting the economic milieu of the region, but also for a revival of a Free Trade Area of the Asia-Pacific (FTAAP) which has been discussed in APEC policy circles in some form since the 1990s.

Box 4.2 Members of APEC

Australia
Brunei
Canada
Chile
China, People's Republic
Chinese Taipei (Taiwan)
Hong Kong SAR
Indonesia
Japan
Malaysia
Mexico
New Zealand
Papua New Guinea
Peru
Philippines
Russia
Singapore
South Korea
Thailand
United States
Vietnam

Expansion of multilateral relations

Following Deng's passing, China's interest in organisations beyond economic ones increased. Although Beijing remained concerned about maintaining sovereignty, the governments of Jiang Zemin and Hu Jintao were considerably more confident of their foreign policy capabilities and far less fearful of being victimised by security organisations in relation to China's views on UN peacekeeping. Nevertheless, China approached the expansion of multilateralism very cautiously, and even today is much more critical of some of its forms, notably in the area of security cooperation.

Under Jiang in the 1990s, China sought to pursue multilateralism in security via the development of partnerships with select states. The first partnership of note was with the Russian Federation under Boris Yeltsin in the 1990s, formally burying the years of Sino-Soviet enmity. Throughout much of the late 1990s, other partnership agreements of varying width and depth were adopted including those with the United States, Great Britain, France, Pakistan, South Africa, Mexico and India.[38] These partnerships would form the backbone of Beijing's developing multilateral policy, enabling it to familiarise itself with issues beyond the immediate Asia-Pacific. By the turn of the century, China under Hu Jintao continued to place much importance on the partnership model, while simultaneously increasing its comfort level with multilateral strategic institutions.

China also began to mend fences in the 1990s with organisations previously seen as overtly hostile. For example, after a very difficult relationship with the Association of Southeast Asian Nations, or ASEAN, during the 1960s and 70s, Beijing in the 1990s began to meet more regularly with ASEAN members about a wider variety of topics. In October 2003, Beijing agreed to sign ASEAN's 1976 Treaty of Amity and Cooperation (TAC), which discouraged the use of force in the settlement of regional disputes and upheld the sovereignty of signatory states. Following the Asian Financial Crisis, Beijing proposed formal meetings with ASEAN, which by 1999 would develop into the ASEAN-Plus-Three (APT) grouping bringing together all ten ASEAN members with Japan, China and South Korea. China also held direct bilateral talks between itself and ASEAN (ASEAN-plus-one).

In November 2000 at an APT summit, then-Chinese Premier Zhu Rongji advocated a free trade agreement between China and ASEAN. Since then, both sides have developed a free trade area between them, with the ASEAN–China Free Trade Agreement (ACFTA) being formally launched in 2010.[39] Although trade between the two actors accelerated following the ACFTA, the issue of sovereignty over the South China Sea and its various islets still divides the two sides, especially in the case of the Philippines and Vietnam, even though China and Southeast Asia agreed in 2003 to settle the matter via diplomacy and to avoid any military posturing, especially over the Spratly Islands. After 2010, China began to again press its claims to the islands and to a significant portion of the South China Sea as defined by the "nine-dashed line", and by 2015 reports surfaced indicating China was building up land on some of disputed islets, creating further alarm and policy divisions within ASEAN despite Beijing's assertions that its activities were within the bounds of international law.

China is also seen as first among equals at the annual East Asian Summit, which originated in December 2005 and was an extension of previous annual meetings between China, Japan and South Korea with the ten ASEAN states. The EAS was designed to act as a forum to discuss primarily Asian regional issues, and China was one of the major backers of the initiative, arguing that a forum specifically dedicated to Asian affairs would greatly assist political and economic cooperation. The United States was not invited and the European Union announced in April 2006 that it wished to be included as an observer. Australia,

India and New Zealand were given last-minute invitations to the first EAS meeting despite Chinese objections, suggesting not only that Beijing's influence over the regime does have limits but also that other EAS members were concerned that China would take a dominant role in EAS decision-making.[40] The shape of the EAS was radically altered after 2011 when both the United States and Russia attended the annual summit as full members. Despite its short lifespan, the 18-member-strong EAS already appears to be dealing with an internal dispute over its identity.

The desire by China to play a greater part in regional organisations began to be tested after 2010 when the Trans-Pacific Strategic Economic Partnership (TPP), originally a small and limited free trade agreement, acquired other interested parties, including the United States. Created in 2005, the TPP brought together four small economies in the Pacific with long histories of liberalised trade, namely Brunei, Chile, New Zealand and Singapore. However, after 2009 the success of the group led to other states including Australia, Canada, Japan, Malaysia, Mexico, Peru, the United States and Vietnam seeking and gaining admission to the talks, with others such as the Philippines, South Korea and Taiwan also expressing interest in joining future negotiations. The TPP talks since 2010 aimed to create a much deeper free trade agreement than what APEC had achieved, but the fact that China was not included in the initial expansion of the TPP, despite China's huge economy, raised concerns in Beijing that a form of economic containment was being attempted, especially since the expansion of the TPP took place at the same time as the American "pivot to Asia" strategic initiatives. Although no Partnership member has overtly sought to exclude China from future talks, there is the question of whether the TPP, and especially the US role within it, was seeking to curtail China's economic power in the region, either through politics or by setting the admission criteria beyond what Beijing is willing to accept.

In short, multilateralism has developed into a cornerstone in China's foreign and strategic thinking, a product of both late Cold War frustrations with the bipolar system and current concerns over American unipolarity. As the United States began to be viewed as the lone superpower in the 1990s, Beijing made little secret of its preference for a multipolar world, and has often approached multilateralism with this view. Chinese foreign affairs literature frequently downplayed the idea of the post-Cold War system as being unipolar, and often made reference to "one superpower, four great powers" (*yi chao si qiang* 一超四强), namely the United States with China, Russia, Europe and Japan.[41] Since the global recession, however, the question of multipolarity has changed given economic problems in the United States as well as considerable internal disputes within the EU since its post-2010 debt crises, the volatile political and economic situation in Russia since the 2014 Ukraine crisis, and the question of Japan's economic health since the 2011 Tohoku earthquake and tsunami, and attempts by the government of Shinzo Abe to press forward politically divisive economic reforms. Rather than an emerging multipolar system, China might instead be facing what one study suggested would be a "G-zero" world, where no country or organisation has the power to unilaterally shape the emerging global policy agenda.[42]

Much has been written about the role of "socialisation" of states which engage in multilateralism, namely the increased acceptance of rules and norms of the international system by progressive embedding in inter-state rules, norms and networks. As a result of Beijing's growing acceptance of international regimes and norms both regionally and increasingly internationally, the socialisation process in China's case has been seen as proceeding effectively.[43] China's socialisation, however, has also been viewed as a two-way street. Chinese foreign policy under Hu Jintao and especially Xi Jinping has reflected fewer concerns over lack of information and potential victimisation, accepting that it can gain many "goods" on its path to great power status through ongoing reciprocity and cooperation. At the same time, Beijing is hopeful other nations can be "socialised" in accepting the idea of China as a great power, one which is experiencing a "peaceful rise".

Critics of China's multilateralism policy have suggested Beijing's embrace of international regimes and norms, while developing, remains in many cases very shallow or conditional. The era of deep engagement in international institutions, it has been argued, only began in the mid-1990s and Beijing still exercises great caution within regimes, occasionally tending to be passive or even free-riding. One approach explained by Shambaugh was that China's interest in Asian regional institutions grew partially with the realisation that the United States was not necessarily dominating many of them, such as APEC or the EAS, and that the "open" nature of many emerging Pacific Rim institutions presented an opportunity for Beijing to promote its own views on informal and non-hierarchical strategic cooperation.[44] Not only was China not at risk of being marginalised within these regimes, including by the United States, but they also offered Beijing opportunities to further underscore its regional cooperation policies.

Other analysts have described China's policy towards international regimes as being inherently self-interested and following what Kim termed a "*maxi-mini*" principle, namely that China will only engage them if they can gain the maximum number of goods for the minimum costs.[45] However, it can certainly be argued that all states and notably great powers seek this outcome when engaging all sorts of institutions. Great powers, being dominant, are in a much better position to choose which regimes they want to cooperate with and which goods they hope to gain from them.

Small steps: China and international law

As with economic regimes such as the WTO, China had to overcome much hostility and suspicion over other types of international legal organisations, especially considering that these regimes, too, were created when China was still largely outside of emerging post-war global networks. The role of the "unequal treaties" signed under duress during the dying decades of the Qing Dynasty, and the later exclusion of the People's Republic from the United Nations until 1971, did little to help develop more positive views in China of international law-making until the Dengist reforms. During the Maoist era, the very concept of human rights was denigrated as a "bourgeois slogan" (*zichanjieji kouhao* 资产阶级口号). Yet, as the process of opening up the international system intensified, Beijing began to take a more open approach to international legal institutions, while being more receptive to international legal ideas as potential models from China's own ongoing legal reforms. Beijing's engagement of the international system comes at a time when the country is also wrestling with the complex political process of developing stronger "rule of law" (*fazhi* 法治) and greater independence of legal structures without diminishing the role of the Communist Party in Chinese governance. On an international level, China has been approaching legal regimes with greater interest while ensuring that these structures do not undermine what Beijing sees as its core interests in addition to its sovereignty.

One example of this evolution has been in the area of human rights law, which has been the subject of much political delicacy in Beijing especially since China remains sensitive to international, and especially American, criticism of its human rights record. Despite Chinese objections, the question of the country's human rights was further internationalised after the Tiananmen incident, as well as attempts by the United States in the 1990s to link Sino-American trade reform with Beijing's human rights record. Since 1991, China has begun publishing government white papers on human rights, detailing the country's progress in various areas including individual and minority rights. The most recent white paper, the eleventh such document on human rights, was released in June 2015, describing rights in relation to development, the environment, culture and economics. From a broader international viewpoint, China affirmed its support for the United Nations Charter and Universal Declaration of Human Rights when it re-joined the UN in 1971, and also joined the 1993 Bangkok Declaration on Human Rights as well as more issue-specific agreements such as the International Covenant on Economic, Social and Cultural Rights (ICESCR) in 2001 and the International Covenant on Civil and Political Rights (ICCPR), signed in 1998 but yet to be ratified due to domestic-level disputes.[46] However, Beijing in 1998 voted against the Rome Statute of the International Criminal Court (ICC), a move which suggested that the Court, which entered into operation in 2002, was not seen by Beijing as compatible with Chinese views on sovereignty and regime security.[47] The ICC was created with the jurisdiction to investigate and prosecute, in conjunction with state judicial systems, individuals for the international crimes of genocide, crimes against humanity, and war crimes, and current cases have included accused human rights violations in the Central African Republic, Libya, Mali and Sudan. China has not signed the Rome Statute, along with other sizeable states such as India, Indonesia, Pakistan and Turkey, while Egypt, Iran, Russia and the United States are among countries which signed but have yet to ratify the statute.

In the area of international environmental law, China's views have also adapted to changing domestic and international conditions. As previously noted, Beijing has begun to respond more directly to the political and socio-economic impacts of the country's pollution crises. China is now a major player in global solar and wind technology, and since 2008 the country has been the world's largest producer of solar panels, with the top two manufacturers, Trina Solar and Yingli Green Energy, based in China.

Part of China's change in "green thinking" has also been greater engagement of environmental agreements and protocols. Examples include the Kyoto Protocol on reducing greenhouse gasses which was created in 1997 and entered into force in 2005. China signed the protocol in June 1998 and ratified it in mid-2002, but there were differences between China and the United States (which signed but has yet to ratify Kyoto) over carbon reduction targets. These differences spilled over during a follow-up conference in Copenhagen in December 2009 when only a tepid agreement could be signed between the American and Chinese governments in the wake of Chinese concerns that it, along with other developing economies, was being held to the same standards as the West.[48] The situation improved greatly, however, in November 2014 when a bilateral agreement between US President Obama and Chinese President Xi included pledges by the United States to cut carbon dioxide emissions more sharply by 2025, and that China would work to ensure that its own CO_2 emissions would peak by approximately 2030.

A third illustrative example of evolving views by Beijing on international law has been China's response to the maritime law, including the United Nations Convention on the Law of the Sea (UNCLOS). Beijing signed the UNCLOS agreement in 1982 and ratified it in 1996. However, while China has been supportive of the regulations under UNCLOS which allow for a 200 nautical mile (370.4 km) exclusive economic zone (EEZ) for coastal states, there have been differences between China and other countries, including the United States, which has not signed UNCLOS, and Japan over the legality of military activities within a given EEZ. Incidents which have taken place in both the East and South China Seas involving China, its neighbours, and at times the United States, have reflected this ambiguity. The South China Sea (SCS) and the competing maritime claims to it have been a serious acid test for UNCLOS, especially in regards to the above-water features within the region.

Under the terms of UNCLOS, an island can generate both an EEZ of 200 nautical miles (370.4 km) and a territorial sea up to 12 nautical miles (22.2 km), while a rock (or sandbar or reef), above the sea line, which cannot sustain human habitation, only generates the 12 nm territorial sea, and nothing else. This distinction has led to rancorous debates involving China and other SCS claimants, especially the Philippines and Vietnam, over the definition of an island versus a rock in the region.[49] Adding to the complications, reports surfaced in early 2015 that China was seeking to "upgrade" reefs under its administration by adding sand to elevate them to island status, thus forcing an EEZ (Vietnam was also accused in May 2015 of engaging in land reclamation of reefs in the SCS). Once information about China's land reclamation policies in the SCS came to light, American officials accused Beijing of seeking to create "new facts on the water" and engaging in "lawfare", meaning use of the law for specific strategic ends. The Chinese government stressed that these activities were well within the boundaries of international law and that the US should not include itself in the debates. As well, in January 2013, the government of the Philippines presented a call for legal proceedings over competing SCS claims with Beijing to the international Permanent Court of Arbitration, under the guidelines of Annex VII of UNCLOS, which allows for such arbitration. The move was dismissed by Beijing as without merit, as China considered the issue to be one which could best be solved via bilateral diplomacy with other disputants.

Cooperation with security regimes

In comparison with economic and political organisations, China's engagement with security regimes has been more selective and has consistently reflected a strong post-Cold War aversion to alliances. Since the 1990s, Beijing has argued that the need for alliances has faded with the demise of the Soviet Union and any requirements to protect against other state-based security threats. Instead, the post-bipolar international system was viewed as more congenial to the creation of "positive-sum" international regimes which encouraged mutual security and confidence-building.[50] China's engagement policies have been focused on the creation of, and engagement with, security communities which concentrate on mutual security and cooperation rather than alignment and hierarchical power structures.

China's activities within the United Nations have also become much more unilateral since the 1990s, further reflecting greater comfort in working within the organisation. For example, Beijing made use of the veto in the UN Security Council (UNSC) to block two peacekeeping initiatives, one for Guatemala in 1997 and one for Macedonia in 1999. In both cases the states at that time were recognising Taiwan.[51] Beijing, along with Russia, vetoed a January 2007 UN resolution criticising Myanmar (Burma) for its human rights violations, and both states implemented a similar UNSC veto in July 2008 which would have punished the government of Robert Mugabe in Zimbabwe. On both occasions, China was working to protect allies from what it saw as excessive international intrusion in domestic security affairs. China has also been accused of being wary of using the UN's enforcement mechanisms to place stronger pressure on Iran to curtail its possible development of nuclear weapons and on the Sudanese government for its complicity in the civil conflict in that country's Darfur province.[52]

Beijing also incurred much criticism from the United States and the United Kingdom after China and Russia both vetoed a February 2012 resolution which would have called for the president of Syria, Bashar Assad, to step down as part of a potential peace deal between the Syrian government and rebels seeking regime change since violence erupted in the country in March 2011. Both Beijing and Moscow expressed concerns that the resolution would have violated Syrian sovereignty and instead called for negotiations with the Assad government. That would be the first of four "double vetoes" which were issued by China and Russia on matters related to the Syrian conflict, with the fourth taking place in May 2014 when the UNSC voted on a France-backed resolution to refer the specifics of the conflict to the International Criminal Court (which neither China nor Russia recognise, and that the United States has also not signed on to). However, when a March 2014 UNSC resolution which criticised the secession referendum in Ukraine's Crimea region was brought to a vote, Russia predictably issued a veto, but China opted instead to abstain, reflecting not only Beijing's concerns about Russian-backed military activities in Crimea and eastern Ukraine but also that China was seeking to avoid the appearance of directly opposing Moscow's actions.

China issued its first veto in 1972 shortly after successfully obtaining its UNSC seat from the Republic of China (Taiwan) the previous year, and the reason for the veto was opposition to the new country of Bangladesh receiving UN membership, a reflection of the close relationship between China and Pakistan, which also opposed what was then East Pakistan becoming a separate state. Since that time, China's early uses of the UNSC veto (eight times between 1972 and early 2012) have been far less frequent than those of the other four permanent members of the UNSC. As well, Beijing has occasionally offered suggestions as to how the United Nations Security Council could be reformed to better reflect the post-Cold War system. While Beijing had offered support for the possible inclusion of Brazil and Germany as permanent UNSC members, regional political rivalries in Asia are seen to have influenced the lack of Chinese support for either India or Japan getting such status.[53] Beijing currently appears to be translating its increased foreign policy interests into a much more activist position in the United Nations, including in the areas of peacekeeping and addressing civil conflicts.

From a regional viewpoint, while Beijing has long accepted the idea that some security issues are better addressed on a multilateral level, China like other states in the Asia-Pacific has had to approach security problems in a region with still-underdeveloped strategic regimes. There is no equivalent of a NATO or an Organisation for Security and Cooperation in Europe (OSCE) in the Pacific Rim, and there is little sign that such a configuration will come about given political differences between the two largest states in the region, China and Japan, and concerns among many other Asian governments about acceding to a security agreement with the same level of formality as a NATO-type grouping. Hopes during the 1990s that the end of the Cold War and the removal of various ideological camps in the region would spark a greater push for formal security organisations have so far proven unfounded.[54] Although APEC has addressed strategic issues, including transnational crime and mutual support against terrorism, there is little sign that the forum will be in a position to develop into a security regime. Those security organisations which do exist in the region are for the most part informal and lack strong policymaking powers. The ASEAN Regional Forum (ARF) is a good example of this.

China agreed to join the ARF when it was created under ASEAN's auspices in 1994. The ARF is a large-scale security community (with 27 members), which addresses regional strategic problems. However, unlike NATO, it lacks an enforcement mechanism and remains largely a consultative body rather than a defence pact. As its name suggests, ARF was created by the ASEAN states in order to address regional security issues and it was decided early in the organisation's development that China, along with the United States and Japan, needed to be included in order to strengthen the regime and maintain its physical and policy coherency.[55] Although it has been argued that the ARF has been beneficial in engaging China on the subject of improving regional security, critics argue there are issues which Beijing has successfully kept out of the ARF dialogue, specifically Taiwan, which is not a member of the forum.

As well, Beijing has kept issues such as cross-Taiwan Strait security, the disputed status of the islands in the East China Sea and maritime sovereignty issues in the South China Sea largely off the ARF agenda, and did not participate in the initial meetings of the forum's informal "Track II" (sub-governmental) advisory body, the Council of Security and Cooperation in the Asia-Pacific (CSCAP), founded in 1993. China's initial wariness was due to concerns that Taiwan would be given too visible a role there. Only after a tacit agreement was made to strictly limit Taiwanese participation to individual experts from the island did China begin to participate in CSCAP.[56] Since that time, Chinese representatives have been active in a variety of different CSCAP working groups including Northeast Asian security.

With these caveats in place, however, China grew much more comfortable with the ARF's development as it became evident the group was not seeking to develop into a formal alliance. Its consensus-based method of decision-making meant that China did not have to worry about norms and rules being forced upon it, thus presenting it with an "exit vs. voice" problem; in other words, leaving the group or attempting to wield influence to change its rules or structure.[57] Moreover, in the eyes of other ARF members, the Forum could be used to channel China's growth as a strategic actor in more congenial directions, and allow for Beijing to become more comfortable with an Asia-Pacific security dialogue.[58] As well, despite the limitations of the ARF, the group's informality has prevented the development of great power politics and may have forestalled, for now, the development of a more formal, NATO-like Western alliance agreement in the Pacific Rim which could be used to encircle China.

These concerns were further illustrated when the United States began announcing its Asia-Pacific "pivot" or "rebalancing" strategies in late 2011 which saw US security relationships with many regional friends and allies, including Australia, Japan, the Philippines and Singapore, upgraded with the promise of a strong American security presence in the region. The security relationship between Washington and Tokyo and its upgrading since the end of the Cold War has been of special concern to Chinese policymakers, especially given differences between China and Japan over the sovereignty of the Senkaku/Diaoyu islands and surrounding waters in the East China Sea. In April 2015, the US–Japan Security Treaty was further upgraded, allowing Japanese forces to engage in "collective self-defence", meaning that Japan could aid a third party country under attack. The question of whether the US would assist Japan in a conflict in the East China Sea remains a complex one. For example, in April 2014, US President Barack Obama asserted publically that the disputed islands would fall under the aegis of the Security Treaty.

North Korea remains another challenge to China's regional security cooperation, given the longstanding strategic links between Beijing and Pyongyang. The Six-Party Talks (SPT)

Box 4.3 Track II dialogues in Asia

"Advocates of Track 2 security dialogues reject the notion that state officials should monopolise consideration of security matters. They seek to engage participation of leaders from the academic, financial social and political sectors of society in order to bring expertise and new ideas to the table and, more important, to foster transnational understanding and confidence-building."

– Brian Job, "Track 2 Diplomacy: Ideational Contribution to the Evolving Asian Security Order", *Asian Security Order: Instrumental and Normative Features*, ed. Muthiah Alagappa (Stanford: Stanford University Press, 2003), 247.

which had taken place sporadically since 2003 provided another example of China's growing willingness to take the lead in a regional security dialogue. While the SPT was not a formal regime, it nevertheless has developed into an important foreign policy tool for Beijing in developing its views on multilateral security. China, along with South Korea, Japan, the United States and Russia, has expressed interest in addressing the crisis surrounding North Korea's development and testing of nuclear weapons.

Since the inauguration of the SPT, Beijing has been the driver of the process, often using shuttle diplomacy to promote and at times revive the talks. As one of the few states with direct access to the Pyongyang government, Chinese negotiators have attempted to keep North Korea at the table despite various setbacks.[59] These attempts became more difficult after North Korea conducted two nuclear tests in 2006 and 2009 and then entered into a change of regime when leader Kim Jong-il died in December 2011 to be replaced by his son Kim Jong-un. Even before the elder Kim's death, Pyongyang had expressed frustration with the SPT and walked away from talks in 2009. It remains to be seen whether the SPT can be revived despite Beijing's support for the process, let alone whether the talks will be successful in ultimately de-nuclearising the peninsula. Should a permanent deal be reached, the SPT could ideally develop into a Northeast Asian security organisation, but the still-cold relations between North Korea and Washington, which worsened when the Kim Jong-un government conducted a third nuclear weapons test in February 2013, have made that scenario quixotic at best in the near term.

China's foreign policy confidence over the past decade has translated into assuming a more active role, both by participating in existing regimes and also by attempting to create new ones which better fit Chinese foreign policy priorities. The best example of this thinking has been the Shanghai Cooperation Organisation (SCO), a security regime, which represents the largest regime created primarily by Beijing's initiative. The SCO was created with much Chinese influence in June 2001, bringing together China, Russia, and most of the former Soviet Central Asia states into a security community. It evolved from more informal meetings beginning in 1996 between Beijing, Moscow, and bordering Central Asian governments (Kazakhstan, Kyrgyzstan and Tajikistan) in order to oversee border demarcation issues left over from the Sino-Soviet split as well as to promote mutual security. The group, which came to be known as the "Shanghai Five" began regular meetings on improving frontier security. The group was re-named the SCO after the inclusion of Uzbekistan in 2001.[60] Following the resolution of all outstanding border issues between Beijing and the bordering post-Soviet states, by the turn of the new century, the SCO's focus shifted to combating what it termed "three evil forces" (*sangu shili* 三股势力) of terrorism, secessionism and extremism in Eurasia. A former Chinese diplomat, Zhang Deguang, was appointed in 2004 as the SCO's first Secretary General, further underscoring Beijing's guiding role in the SCO's evolution. As of January 2013, the SCO has been chaired by Dmitry F. Mezentsev from Russia, who was to hold the position until the end of 2015.

The organisation's official charter was unveiled at its second conference in St. Petersburg in June 2002. The document upheld the SCO's mandate to build "mutual trust, friendship and good neighbourliness" and to encourage "comprehensive cooperation". Other key elements of the document included the confirmation that a Regional Anti-Terrorism Structure (RATS) would be created to act as an information nexus for regional security and that decisions would be based on mutual consensus. To demonstrate inclusiveness beyond regional concerns, the charter also gave support to other peace-building initiatives in the Asia-Pacific region, including the ARF and multilateral initiatives on security and cooperation on the Korean Peninsula and South Asia. The SCO Charter specified the organisation was not to be established as an alliance but rather would be based on respect for mutual interests and common approaches to dealing with regional and international problems, rather than uniting against an outside adversary.[61]

SCO members routinely share security information and have participated in joint military manoeuvres since 2002, and the RATS centre was opened in Tashkent in January 2004. The SCO has maintained that it is a security community interested in cooperating with other organisations such as NATO and ASEAN in the international war on terrorism (*fankong zhanzheng* 反恐战争), with no intention of developing into an anti-Western alliance, despite Western criticism. The increased visibility of the SCO has attracted potential new members, with Afghanistan, Belarus, India, Iran, Mongolia and Pakistan having official observer status, although in July 2015 it was agreed that India and Pakistan would be promoted to full member status. Armenia, Azerbaijan, Cambodia, Nepal, Sri Lanka and Turkey have been given the status of SCO "dialogue partners". Although the SCO is a consensus-based body, and lacks a strong central governing agency, it nevertheless is playing a stronger role in regional Eurasian security policy and Beijing remains the primary driver of the organisation.[62]

The SCO has also endeavoured to coordinate joint military operations designed to further boost confidence among members and to develop a coordinated military policy against potential threats. The first round of war games took place between China and Kyrgyzstan in October 2002, and an expanded set of exercises which featured all members except Uzbekistan was held in Kazakhstan and Xinjiang, China, in August 2003. In August 2005, the SCO's great powers, China and Russia, staged their own military exercises with the other SCO members and with Iran, India and Pakistan sending observers. Dubbed "Operation Peace Mission 2005", the exercise took place near Vladivostok, Russia, and Weifang, in China's Shandong Province, and involved joint strategic planning followed by a mock offshore blockade, amphibious landing and airborne assault. The Peace Mission manoeuvres in August 2014 were noteworthy both because of their location (near Zhurihe in Inner Mongolia) and their scope, with a record 7000 personnel participating, and use of advanced Chinese and Russian weaponry, including Chinese CAIC Z-10 and Harbin Z-19 attack helicopters.[63]

Despite the apparent hard security dimensions of the simulation, it was nonetheless officially described afterwards as a non-traditional security, anti-terror exercise.[64] Semantics aside, the ongoing development of joint security operations under the SCO's guidance is strong evidence of the organisation's growing confidence, especially as it continues to seek a balance between various methods of security management as well as other forms of political cooperation. Peace Missions have been held at irregular intervals among SCO armed forces since then. Despite its relative infancy, the SCO has developed into both a strong strategic actor in the Eurasian region and a barometer of China's evolving policies on regional security cooperation.

Norm-making: The curious case of the AIIB

Among the cornerstones of Xi Jinping's foreign policy during the early years of his presidency was the development of stronger regional relations between China and its Asian partners and neighbours, but the depth of that commitment, as well as Beijing's growing regional and international power, were thrown into sharp relief as a new financial institution, the Asia Infrastructure Investment Bank or AIIB, was put together by China. Like the New Development Bank developed by the BRICS nations, the AIIB was designed to be a lending institution to developing states, but with a stronger focus on Asia and on infrastructure projects. The announcement was widely interpreted, especially in the West, as an attempt to build an alternative to the Western-dominated IMF and the World Bank as well as to the Asian Development Bank (ADB) in which Japan played a prominent role.

The AIIB was first proposed by the government of Xi Jinping in 2013 and was to have an initial value of US$50 billion. The initiative was partly a response to Chinese frustration over what it saw was the slow pace of infrastructure development in Asia and the domination of Western interests within the IMF and the World Bank, despite China's rise as an economic power. Ben Bernanke, the former chair of the US Federal Reserve, even went on record in June 2015 in saying that the American Congress was partially responsible for the creation of the AIIB, given its refusal to support legislation which would have allowed for a greater voting share within the IMF for emerging economies.[65] The AIIB was designed by Beijing to create a more Asia-specific financial institution and when the initial memorandum of understanding was signed between China and 20 other governments in October 2014, President Xi noted that, "to build fortune, roads should be built first", an idea in keeping with an "Asia-Pacific Dream" of regional economic development.

Shortly after Beijing's announcement of the AIIB, the United States expressed its misgivings about the new bank, due to concerns about Beijing's growing diplomatic power as well as whether the bank would uphold "international standards of governance and transparency". Washington also appeared to be tacitly discouraging its partners and allies from signing on to the AIIB. The original signatories to the AIIB project were governments from East, South and Southeast Asia, although New Zealand, which has a long history of independent foreign policymaking *vis-à-vis* the United States, did agree to becoming a founding member of the institution. Other American partners in the Asia-Pacific region such as the Philippines and Singapore also agreed to join, but Japan and South Korea opted to abstain. Despite Beijing's call for AIIB partners from all around the world, during the first few months of 2015 it appeared that the new bank would be strictly regional in scope.

However, in early March 2015, the United Kingdom agreed to become a partner in the AIIB, triggering much surprise and dismay from the United States. In an unusually sharp rebuke by Washington given the "special relationship" between Britain and the United States, London was accused of making the decision without consulting its American partner. As one US official reportedly noted, "We are wary about a trend toward constant accommodation of China, which is not the best way to engage a rising power." London counter-argued that it is in British interests to better engage the growing commercial power of China.

Days after London's decision to join the AIIB, statements were released by the governments of France, Germany and Italy confirming that the three Western European countries would also seek membership in the AIIB, further isolating Washington's views on the new bank. In an editorial released by *Xinhua*, an official Chinese news agency, the decision by the four EU members to join the bank was praised while Washington was accused of being "petulant" and "holding sour grapes" over the issue. The AIIB question had suddenly transformed from one of economics to one of geopolitics, as well as a test of American and Chinese diplomatic persuasive power.

In the weeks leading up to the deadline of April 2015 for countries to apply to become founding members of the AIIB, other European states including Austria, Denmark, Iceland, the Netherlands, Norway, Spain, Sweden, Switzerland and Portugal all applied to join. In the Asia-Pacific region, Australia and South Korea reversed their initial stances and also applied, and fellow BRICS nations Brazil, Russia and South Africa also did so. Taiwan submitted an application that was declined, reportedly over disagreements over what name it would be allowed to join under, but Taipei was given the option of re-applying. In an odd development, North Korea was also rejected as a potential member, seemingly due to Pyongyang's unwillingness to provide the necessary economic information to the bank under the terms of membership. By April 2015, 57 states had been accepted as founding members of the AIIB, a number which likely surprised even Beijing policymakers, and the US found itself on the sidelines with only Canada and Japan as major allies which also declined to submit an application. In June of that year, the AIIB released its "Articles of Agreement", which included a description of the institution.

> The purpose of the Bank shall be to: (i) foster sustainable economic development, create wealth and improve infrastructure connectivity in Asia by investing in infrastructure and other productive sectors; and (ii) promote regional cooperation and partnership in addressing development challenges by working in close collaboration with other multilateral and bilateral development institutions.[66]

These events suggested that much has changed both in regard to the shape of the global economy but also in the area of Chinese foreign policy. The development of the AIIB, as well as the creation of the New Development Bank by emerging economic powers including China and India, adds further weight to the idea of shifting global economic power further towards Asia. As well, the development of the AIIB further suggested that Beijing was becoming more comfortable with developing new economic organisations which do not necessarily include the West. China's growing economic power and ongoing concerns about being marginalised by the United States as a result, including for example over the TPP, have changed these views in Beijing. With China now holding the largest reserves of foreign currency, about US$3.5 billion, its ability to wage "commercial diplomacy", meaning the ability of transforming wealth into diplomatic power, has greatly increased. While Beijing has argued that it wishes to continue to work with economic organisations of many shapes and sizes as it seeks to further internationalise its economy, and that it is not interested in seeing the AIIB become an overt rival of other financial organisations, the new bank is the strongest proof to date that China is now much more confident about putting forward its own economic ideas and institutions on a global scale.

China: The engaging state?

The past 30 years will be remembered as a period of transformation in Chinese foreign policy for a variety of reasons, but one of the most important for the country as well as the international system has been Beijing's reversal from avoidance to embracing multilateralism and international organisations. The Chinese case has been a distinct one for a variety of reasons. China is a large state, albeit still developing in many ways, and a rising power which is developing within a global order, one becoming increasingly dominated by international agreements, rules and regimes. Moreover, China must overcome much suspicion of the motives of other states and actors while seeking to reverse its Maoist-era isolation. As was noted, despite the fact that China as a state is quite old, it suffered from being a comparative "novice" in the policies of international organisations, and often had to address considerable information deficits.

Moreover, Beijing had to collect information about regimes and their membership in short time periods, to avoid being taken advantage of, to avoid transaction costs, and to allow for Beijing to attain the best possible benefits from engaging a given regime. Since the 1990s, China has become an enthusiastic joiner of various organisations and attained a

Box 4.4 The diplomatic seesaw over the AIIB

"The initial success of AIIB is a diplomatic victory for China. The U.S. diplomatic response has not been adroit, playing into the narrative of U.S. decline in the Asia-Pacific. But that perception could change quickly. Infrastructure is the 'hardware' of economic integration, which is certainly necessary. But trade agreements such as the Trans-Pacific Partnership are the 'software.' If the U.S. and its partners can negotiate and implement this agreement for deeper integration, that will provide a large boost for the members and reestablish U.S. importance to the Asia-Pacific economy."

– David Dollar, "Lessons for the AIIB from the Experience of the World Bank", *Brookings*, 27 April 2015.

participation rate well above global averages.[67] This has provided Beijing with a variety of benefits ranging from the tangible, such as improved trade, access to new markets, security guarantees and improved cross-regional diplomacy, to the less quantifiable, including foreign policy confidence, prestige and soft power.

At the same time, China has shown an increased willingness to engage many institutions which are Western-dominated rather than seek alternative structures as the USSR sought to do.[68] Chinese power, both coercive and structural, has therefore developed very effectively within the framework of many regimes which were established by the United States and other Western actors. As has been argued, China is making selective and strategic use of international organisations through engagement, in order to advance its power and capabilities in the international system, develop an identity as a "responsible stakeholder" in the international system, and move towards developing as a great and perhaps global power. The development of the SCO and China's support of the East Asia Summit were early signs that Beijing was also becoming more comfortable with organisations which do not include Western members or norms. However, Beijing is now much more willing and able to develop and support newer institutions which may counter traditional Western ones, such as the NDB and the AIIB. There is the possibility that China may be more tempted in future to develop or support other organisations as a means of balancing Western power, but such actions would be risky. China has accrued many goods from working within the current system of organisations and has arguably used them to augment not only its power but also its sought-after "international status".[69]

China is now a vital part of the growing farrago of international organisations and is unlikely to reverse this element of its foreign policy development despite its ongoing power rise. The next questions however will concern the transformation of China's role within them, the country's interests in developing new organisations, and how other states within international regimes will view these events. These questions are now inevitably tied to the larger question of what kind of great power China will be.

Discussion questions

- What were Mao Zedong's motivations for limiting China's exposure to international organisations and how did that decision affect China's foreign policy thinking during his regime?
- How was engagement with international organisations tied to Deng's greater policy of "reform and opening up" to the international system?

- Why did Beijing place a high priority on engaging economic organisations? Why was its drive to join the GATT and the WTO difficult and lengthy?
- Is China distinct in its ability to obtain what it wants from different types of international organisations? If so, how?
- Is China developing a more independent policy stance within the United Nations?
- Does the development of the Shanghai Cooperation Organisation and the Asia Infrastructure Investment Bank signal a shift in Chinese views on international institutions and/or a departure from Western views on multilateralism?

Recommended reading

Callaghan, William A. and Elena Barabantseva, *China Orders the World: Normative Soft Power and Foreign Policy* (Washington DC: Woodrow Wilson Centre Press, 2011).

Deng, Yong and Fei-ling Wang (eds), *China Rising: Power and Motivation in Chinese Foreign Policy* (Lanham and Boulder: Rowman and Littlefield, 2005).

Dessein, Bart (ed.), *Interpreting China as a Regional and Global Power* (Basingstoke, UK: Palgrave Macmillan, 2014).

Jacobson, Harold K. and Michel Oksenberg, *China's Participation in the IMF, the World Bank, and GATT: Toward a Global Economic Order* (Ann Arbor: University of Michigan Press, 1990).

Johnston, Alastair Ian, *Social States: China and International Institutions, 1980–2000* (Princeton and Oxford: Princeton University Press, 2007).

Kent, Ann, *Beyond Compliance: China, International Organizations, and Global Security* (Stanford: Stanford University Press, 2007).

Lanteigne, Marc, *China and International Institutions: Alternate Paths to Global Power* (Milton Park, UK and New York: Routledge, 2005).

Odgaard, Lisette, *China and Coexistence: Beijing's National Security Strategy for the Twenty-First Century* (Washington: Woodrow Wilson Centre Press, 2012).

Potter, Pitman B, *China's Legal System* (Cambridge and Malden, MA: Polity Press, 2013).

Toohey, Lisa, Colin Parker and Jonathan Greenacre (eds), *China in the International Economic Order: New Directions and Changing Paradigms* (Cambridge: Cambridge University Press, 2015).

Notes

1 Michael Barnett and Raymond Duvall, "Power in Global Governance," *Power in Global Governance*, ed. Michael Barnett and Raymond Duvall (Cambridge and New York: Cambridge University Press, 2005), 16–18.
2 Thomas Volgy and Alison Bailin, *International Politics and State Strength* (Lynne Renner, 2002).
3 Peter Zarrow, *China in War and Revolution: 1895–1949* (London and New York: Routledge, 2005), 149–51; Jonathan Fenby, *The Siege of Tsingtao* (London: Penguin Books, 2014).
4 Robert O. Keohane, "Lilliputians' Dilemmas: Small States in International Politics," *International Organization* 23(2) (Spring 1968): 295–6.
5 Lisa L. Martin, "An Institutionalist View: International Institutions and State Strategies," *International Order and the Future of World Politics*, ed. T.V. Paul and John A. Hall (Cambridge and New York: Cambridge University Press, 1999), 78–9.
6 George W. Downs, David M. Rocke and Peter N. Barsoom, "Is the Good News about Compliance Good News about Cooperation?" *International Organisation* 50(3) (Summer 1996): 379–406.
7 Diana Preston, *A Brief History of the Boxer Rebellion: China's War on Foreigners, 1900* (London: Constable and Robinson, 2002).
8 Rana Mitter, *A Bitter Revolution: China's Struggle with the Modern World* (Oxford and New York: Oxford University Press, 2004), 3–40.

9   Mao Zedong, "Unite with Those Nations of the World which Treat us as Equals and with the Peoples of All Countries," and "Is It Right to 'Lean to One Side'?" Mao Zedong, *On Diplomacy* (Beijing: Foreign Languages Press, 1998), 72–4; 215–16.

10 James C. Hsiung, "Chinese Critique of the 'Socialist Commonwealth': Implications for Proletarian Internationalism and Peaceful Co-existence," *American Society of International Law Proceedings* 67(1973): 66.

11 W. Macmahon Ball, "A Political Re-examination of SEATO," *International Organisation* 12(1) (Winter 1958): 20–1; Mao Zedong, "On the Intermediate Zone, Peaceful Co-existence, Sino-British and Sino-US Relations," Mao Zedong, *On Diplomacy* (Beijing: Foreign Languages Press, 1998), 125.

12 Amitav Acharya, "Regional Institutions and Asian Security Order: Norms, Power and Prospects for Peaceful Change," *Asian Security Order: Instrumental and Normative Features*, ed. Muthiah Alagappa (Stanford: Stanford University Press, 2003), 218.

13 John Cranmer-Byng, "The Chinese View of Their Place in the World," *The China Quarterly* 52 (January 1973): 75–6.

14 "On the Question of the Differentiation of the Three Worlds," Mao Zedong, *On Diplomacy* (Beijing: Foreign Languages Press, 1998), 454.

15 Harold K. Jacobson and Michael Oksenberg, *China's Participation in the IMF, the World Bank and GATT* (Ann Arbor, MI: University of Michigan Press, 1990), 41–2.

16 Samuel S. Kim, "China and the United Nations," *China Joins the World: Progress and Prospects*, ed. Elizabeth Economy and Michael Oksenberg (New York: Council on Foreign Relations, 1999), 45–9.

17 Evan S. Medeiros, *Reluctant Restraint: The Evolution of China's Non-proliferation Policies and Practices, 1980–2004* (Stanford: Stanford University Press, 2007), 212–14.

18 Bates Gill and Yanzhong Huang, "Sources and Limits of Chinese 'Soft Power'," *Survival* 48(2) (June 2006): 22.

19 John Gerard Ruggie, "International Regimes, Transactions and Change: Embedded Liberalism in the Postwar Economic Order," *International Regimes*, ed. Stephen D. Krasner (Ithaca and London: Cornell University Press, 1983), 195–231; Katja Weber, "Hierarchy amidst Anarchy: A Transaction Costs Approach to International Security Cooperation," *International Studies Quarterly* 41(1997): 321–40.

20 Kenneth N. Waltz, "Structural Realism after the Cold War," *International Security* 25(1) (Summer 2000): 5–41.

21 Alexander Wendt, *Social Theory of International Politics* (Cambridge and New York: Cambridge University Press, 1999).

22 Michael Taylor, *Anarchy and Cooperation* (New York: John Wiley, 1976).

23 Bruce Bueno de Mesquita, *Principles of International Politics: People's Power, Preferences and Perceptions* (Washington DC: CQ Press, 2002), 143–4.

24 Lu Jianren, "China's Experience in Utilising ODA and APEC Development Cooperation," *APEC and Development Cooperation*, ed. Mohammed Ariff (Singapore: Institute of Southeast Asian Studies, 1998), 103–7.

25 Jianwei Wang, "Managing Conflict: Chinese Perspectives on Multilateral Diplomacy and Collective Security," *In the Eyes of the Dragon: China Views the World*, ed. Yong Deng and Fei-ling Wang (Lanham, MD and Oxford: Rowman and Littlefield, 1999), 86.

26 Lanteigne, *China and International Institutions*, 39.

27 Dabid M. Lampton, *Same Bed, Different Dreams: Managing US–China Relations, 1989–2000* (Berkeley and London: University of California Press, 2001), 117.

28 Elena Ianchovichina and Will Martin, "Trade Impacts of China's World Trade Organization Accession," *Asian Economic Policy Review* 1(2006): 46–50; Dali L. Yang, *Remaking the Chinese Leviathan: Market Transition and the Politics of Governance in China* (Stanford: Stanford University Press, 2004), 25–64.

29 Chi Minjiao, "China's Participation in WTO Dispute Settlement over the Past Decade: Experiences and Impacts," *Journal of International Economic Law* 15(1) (March 2012): 29–40; "World Trade Organization – Disputes by Country," *World Trade Organization* (2012) <http://www.wto.org/english/tratop_e/dispu_e/dispu_by_country_e.htm>. "Dispute Settlement: Dispute DS437, United States – Countervailing Duty Measures on Certain Products from China," World Trade Organisation, 16 January 2015, <https://www.wto.org/english/tratop_e/dispu_e/cases_e/ds437_e.htm>.

30 Lloyd Gruber, *Ruling the World: Power Politics and the Rise of Supernational Institutions* (Princeton: Princeton University Press, 2001).

31 Baldwin, Robert, "Political Economy of the Disappointing Doha Round of Trade Negotiations," *Pacific Economic Review* 12(3) (August 2007): 253–66.

32 Rosemary Foot, "Chinese Strategies in a US-Hegemonic Global Order: Accommodating and Hedging," *International Affairs* 82(1) (2006): 87–8.

33 Jim O'Neill, "Building Better Global Economic BRICs," *Global Economics Paper No. 66,* Goldman Sachs, 30 November 2001, <http://www.goldmansachs.com/our-thinking/archive/archive-pdfs/build-better-brics.pdf>.

34 Chen-pin Li, "Taiwan's Participation in Inter-Governmental Organizations: An Overview of Its Initiatives," *Asian Survey* 46(4) (July 2006): 597–614.

35 David A. Lake, "Beyond Anarchy: The Importance of Security Institutions," *International Security* 26(1) (September 2001): 130.

36 Vinod K. Aggarwal and Charles E. Morrison, "APEC as an International Institution," *Asia Pacific Economic Cooperation (APEC): Challenges and Tasks for the Twenty-first Century*, ed. Ippei Yamazawa (London and New York: Routledge, 2000), 304–5.

37 Lanteigne, *China and International Institutions*, 40; Nicholas R. Lardy, *Integrating China into the Global Economy* (Washington, DC: Brookings, 2002), 32–62.

38 Joseph Y.S. Cheng and Zhang Wenkun, "Patterns and Dynamics of China's International Strategic Behaviour," *Chinese Foreign Policy: Pragmatism and Strategic Behaviour*, ed. Suisheng Zhao (Armonk, NY and London: M.E. Sharpe, 2004), 179–206.

39 Markus Hund, "ASEAN Plus Three: Towards a New Age of Pan-Asian Regionalism: A Sceptic's Appraisal," *Pacific Review* 13(3) (September 2003): 394–5.

40 "Success for the EAS?" *Japan Times*, 17 January 2007; "US Official 'Concerned' over East Asian Summit," *Kyodo News Service / BBC Monitoring,* 30 November 2004.

41 Brantley Womack, "Asymmetry Theory and China's Concept of Multipolarity," *Journal of Contemporary China* 13(39) (May 2004): 356.

42 Ian Bremmer and Nouriel Roubini, "A G-Zero World: The New Economic Club Will Produce Conflict, Not Cooperation," *Foreign Affairs* 90(2) (March/April 2011). See also Charles A. Kupchan, *No One's World: The West, The Rising East, the Coming Global Turn* (Oxford: Oxford University Press, 2012).

43 Mark Beeson, "American Hegemony and Regionalism: The Rise of East Asia and the End of the Asia-Pacific," *Geopolitics* 11(4) (December 2006): 552.

44 David Shambaugh, "China Engages Asia: Reshaping the Regional Order," *International Security* 29(3) (Winter 2004/2005): 73–8.

45 Samuel S. Kim, "China's International Organisational Behaviour," *Chinese Foreign Policy: Theory and Practice*, ed. Thomas W. Robinson and David Shambaugh (Oxford, Clarendon Press, 1994), 423; Ann Kent, "China, Regional Organisations and Regimes: The ILO as a Case Study in Organisational Learning," *Pacific Affairs* 70(4) (Winter 1997–8): 520–1.

46 Yong Deng, *China's Struggle for Status: The Realignment of International Relations* (Cambridge and New York: Cambridge University Press, 2008), 82–9.

47 Jing Tao, "China's Socialization in the International Human Rights Regime: why did China reject the Rome Statute of the International Criminal Court?" *Journal of Contemporary China* (2015): 1–19.

48 Joy Y. Zhang and Michael Barr, *Green Politics in China: Environmental Governance and State–Society Relations* (London: Pluto Press, 2013), 124–5.

49 Bill Hayton, *The South China Sea: The Struggle for Power in Asia* (New Haven and London: Yale University Press, 2014), 112–13.

50 David M. Finkelstein, "China's 'New Concept' of Security," *The People's Liberation Army and China in Transition*, ed. Stephen J. Flanagan and Michael A. Marti (Washington: National Defence University Press, 2003), 197–209; David Shambaugh, "China Engages Asia: Reshaping the Regional Order," *International Security* 29(5) (Winter 2004/05): 70.

51 Wu Xinbo, "Four Contradictions Constraining China's Foreign Policy Behaviour," *Journal of Contemporary China* 10(27) (May 2001): 298.

52 "East Asia and the Pacific: Shaping China's Global Choices through Diplomacy: Thomas J. Christensen, Deputy Assistant Secretary for East Asian and Pacific Affairs, Statement Before the US–China Economic and Security Review Commission, Washington, DC, March 18, 2008," *US*

State Department Press Releases and Documents, 18 March 2008; "China, Russia Embolden Myanmar to Snub Pressure: Analysts," *Agence France-Presse*, 26 May 2007.

53 J. Mohan Malik, "Security Council Reform: China Signals Its Veto," *World Policy Journal* 21(1) (Spring 2005): 19–29.

54 John Duffield, "Why is there no APTO? Why is there no OSCAP? Asia-Pacific Security Institutions in Comparative Perspective," *Contemporary Security Policy* 22(2) (August 2001): 69–95.

55 Rolf Emmers, *Cooperative Security and the Balance of Power in ASEAN and the ARF* (London and New York: Routledge Curzon, 2003), 31.

56 Nicholas Khoo and Michael L.R. Smith, "Correspondence: China Engages Asia? Caveat Lector," *International Security* 30(1) (Summer 2005): 204.

57 Albert. O. Hirschman, *Exit, Voice and Loyalty: Responses to Decline in Firms, Organisations and States* (Harvard: Harvard University Press, 1970).

58 Rosemary Foot, "China in the ASEAN Regional Forum: Organisational Processes and Domestic Modes of Thought," *Asian Survey* 38(5) (May 1998): 425–40.

59 Anne Wu, "What China Whispers to North Korea," *Washington Quarterly* 28(2) (Spring 2005): 35–48.

60 Chien-peng Chung, "The Shanghai Cooperation Organisation: China's Changing Influence in Central Asia," *China Quarterly* (2004): 990–1.

61 "Charter of Shanghai Cooperation Organization," *Shanghai Cooperation Organization* <http://www.sectsco.org/news_detail.asp?id=96&LanguageID=2>.

62 Marc Lanteigne, "*In Medias Res*: The Development of the Shanghai Cooperation Organisation as a Security Community," *Pacific Affairs* 79(4) (Winter 2006/2007): 605–22.

63 Shannon Tiezzi, "China Hosts SCO's Largest-Ever Military Drills," *The Diplomat*, 29 August 2014.

64 Yong Deng, "Remoulding Great Power Politics: China's Strategic Partnerships with Russia, the European Union, and India," *Journal of Strategic Studies* 30(4–5) (August–October 2005): 873–4.

65 David Pilling and Josh Noble, "US Congress Pushed China into Launching AIIB, Says Bernanke," *Financial Times*, 2 June 2015.

66 "Articles of Agreement: Asian Infrastucture Investment Bank," *Ministry of Foreign Affairs of the People's Republic of China*, 29 June 2015. <http://www.mof.gov.cn/zhengwuxinxi/caizhengxinwen/201506/P020150629360882722541.pdf>.

67 Alastair Ian Johnston, *Social States: China and International Institutions, 1980–2000* (Princeton and Oxford: Princeton University Press, 2007), 32–9.

68 G. John Ikenberry, "The Rise of China and the Future of the West," *Foreign Affairs* 87(1) (January / February 2008): 31–2.

69 Yong Deng, "Better than Power: 'International Status' in Chinese Foreign Policy," *China Rising: Power and Motivation in Chinese Foreign Policy* (Lanham, MD: Rowman and Littlefield, 2005), 51–72.

5 Strategic thinking and the roles of the military

The People's Liberation Army as a foreign policy actor

The past two decades saw rapid changes in China's strategic thinking, for two significant reasons. First, the end of the Cold War in the 1990s reduced the possibility of direct state-to-state conflict with Beijing's then-rivals, including the Soviet Union, with which it had severed all political ties in the 1960s. As well, Beijing was in a better position immediately following the Cold War to address lingering border disputes, including with the former USSR, Vietnam and to a degree with South Asia. During this period, Beijing suddenly found itself the beneficiary of a "peace dividend" permitting it to focus on mending relations with many of its neighbours in the former Soviet regions as well as in East, Southeast and South Asia. By the late 1970s China had already begun to lose interest in exporting its revolutionary thinking abroad, a policy frequently attempted under Mao Zedong, and by the 1990s Beijing was in a stronger position to redefine itself as a partner in Asia as opposed to a potential hegemon.

Second, China's security concerns have moved well beyond the traditional, becoming much more multifaceted and now include issues such as border and maritime security. They now encompass terrorism, protection of economic goods, health, trade security, access to resources and energy, and trans-national crime. At the same time, the Taiwan question, despite its often being considered by the Chinese government as a domestic issue, retains many international dimensions given the ambiguous role of the United States in determining Taiwan security concerns. Therefore, Beijing recognised the requirement to review its grand strategy to better fit a post-Cold War security system.

Despite the increasing professionalism of the PLA, its role in crafting foreign policy in China does not appear to have diminished significantly, despite the difficulty for outside actors to judge this, even though many other foreign policy actors have appeared in Beijing in recent decades on governmental and sub-governmental levels. The current Chinese military is still in the process of moving beyond its limited, ideologically-based ideas of "people's war" of the Maoist period. It is focusing on modernisation and adaptation to modern strategic issues in an increasingly wider arena, and addressing issues which extend well beyond East Asia. It has been frequently demonstrated that potential great powers often experience an increase in their security concerns as they "grow" within the international system. In the case of China, the country aspires to develop peacefully within the international system while remaining aware of various security issues which could curtail its domestic reforms. Under the Xi Jinping government, stronger links have been made between domestic and international security concerns faced by China. This was the basis for the founding in November 2013 of a National Security Commission (*Zhongyang Guojia'anquan Weiyuanhui* 中央国家安全委员会) designed to support other security agencies within China and to better coordinate their activities. The Commission, chaired by President Xi himself, held its founding meeting in Beijing in April 2014, amid calls from the Chinese government for a security apparatus to address various traditional and non-traditional strategic concerns on both local and global levels.

At the same time, there exists the potential for friction both with some of China's neighbours as well as with other great power actors such as the United States, as China continues to transform from a regional power to an international one. Reaction to this situation, it has been argued, has taken two forms. China has sought international partnerships and greater engagement with security organisations in order to underline its new status as an "indispensable" partner in security areas. Examples include a more robust participation in the United Nations Security Council as well as with regional organisations such as the Shanghai Cooperation Organisation (SCO) and the Conference on Interaction and Confidence Building in Asia (CICA). Also, Beijing has attempted to promote itself as a "responsible great power" (*fuzeren daguo* 负责任大国), stressing its disinterest in overturning the strategic status quo and in refraining from provoking other countries to align in tandem against rising Chinese power.[1]

Nonetheless, as China's military power grows and the country is better able to project its power further beyond its borders, the question of whether the country will seek to challenge international norms persists. As well, China's growing military capabilities have coincided with a revival of longstanding territorial differences between China and some of its immediate neighbours, especially in the cases of the East and South China Seas. In both of these cases, China is developing the military capability to better defend what the country sees as its historical waters, as well as island groups such as the Spratly and Paracel Islands in the South China Sea and the Diaoyu (known in Japan as the Senkaku) Islands in the East China Sea. As well, since 2011 the United States has sought to deepen its strategic commitment to the Asia-Pacific region with its "pivot" or "rebalancing" strategies, which have included improving partnerships with several American friends and allies in the region, and the introduction in April 2015 of new guidelines for US–Japan defence coordination which would allow for greater Japanese military operations in the name of "collective self-defence", meaning that Tokyo would be able to assist militarily should an ally such as the United States come under attack.[2] Thus, the question of the type of role China will play in future international security will depend not only upon China, but also on others' interpretation and reaction to its ongoing "rise".

China's military forces and capabilities

The Chinese People's Liberation Army (*Zhongguo renmin jiefangjun* 中国人民解放军) was created in 1927 in the wake of the first major clash between communist and Nationalist forces during the Nanchang Uprising. In addition to Mao Zedong, other revolutionary leaders such as Zhu De, He Long and Zhou Enlai also participated in shaping the communist armed forces' structure and ideology.[3] Following the end of the Second World War and the Japanese withdrawal from Chinese territory in 1945, a brittle truce between the Communists and the Nationalist Party (*Guomindang* 国民党) led by Chiang Kai-shek completely broke down and after June 1946 the Red Army under Mao was renamed the People's Liberation Army, reflecting a grander purpose in defeating the Nationalists and re-unifying China. Through various conflicts such as the Korean War (1950–3), and subsequent border conflicts with

India (1962), the Soviet Union (1969) and Vietnam (1979), the Chinese military maintained a strong political role both in Chinese governance and foreign policymaking as well as in defence matters. Although China's borders became largely peaceful with the dissolution of the USSR, and the PLA has not been involved in direct conflicts since the end of the Cold War, it remains an important political actor in China's government and continues to contribute a significant voice in the country's foreign relations.

In examining the political power of the PLA, it is useful to take note of its size and scope. Although PLA numbers have dropped from a high of approximately 5 million in the 1950s when the fusion between Party and army was at its highest, total PLA forces are currently estimated at approximately 2.33 million in 2015 (including army, navy, air force, missile forces and paramilitary forces), with reserve forces standing at approximately 510,000. China is in possession of one of the largest armed forces in the world and the largest when measuring active personnel. The actual "army" forces of the PLA, also known as the PLA Ground Forces, or PLAGF (*renmin jiefangjun lujun* 人民解放军陆军), total 1.6 million, the majority of China's total PLA personnel.[4] However, since the turn of the century China has increasingly focused upon reducing its ground forces and modernising both the PLA Air Force, or PLAAF (*renmin jiefangjun kongjun* 人民解放军空军), which numbers approximately 398,000, and the PLA Navy or PLAN (*renmin jifangjun haijun* 人民解放军海军) which comprises approximately 235,000 personnel. Another key component of the Chinese military has been the strategic missile forces division, which employs 100,000 and is often referred to as the "Second Artillery" Corps (*di'er paobing* 第二炮兵), overseeing China's conventional and nuclear missile arsenals. In addition to reducing personnel, since the mid-1990s a campaign has been underway to transform the PLA from a labour-intensive force to one which stresses technical prowess, education and professionalism.[5] These changes have resulted in more emphasis being placed on training and education and producing a greater comfort level with modern technology, in marked contrast to the Maoist "people first" views which stressed the power of numbers and an emphasis on continental power and ground forces. At the same time, the PLA continues to play a key role in domestic security, including disaster relief such as provided during the July 2007 floods in central China and the May 2008 Wenchuan earthquake in Sichuan province.[6]

China also retains a People's Armed Police force (*renmin wuzhuang jingcha budui* 人民武装警察部队), technically a civilian body with a membership of approximately 660,000. Established as a non-military police force in 1949–50 to augment security forces within the country, it was renamed the PAP in 1982. Many personnel who retire from the PLA often joined PAP units. There has on occasion, however, been a blurring of its role *vis-à-vis* the Chinese armed forces. For example, until 2003, the PAP was responsible for overseeing the Chinese border with North Korea, but after that year the role was assumed by units of the PLA as bilateral relations between Beijing and Pyongyang began to cool and take on a more pragmatic nature. As well, various localities host People's Militia forces (*minbing* 民兵), designed to uphold law and order on a local level. Also assisting with domestic security is the Ministry of Public Security or MPS (*gong'anbu* 公安部), which addresses public domestic security matters, and the Ministry of State Security or MSS (*guojia anquan bu* 国家安全部), a civilian organisation which investigates threats to internal security, monitors foreign activity on Chinese soil and protects against external influences and domestic espionage.[7]

The PLA in Chinese politics

The influence of the PLA, and China's overall security apparatus, in the creation of current Chinese foreign policy remains difficult to measure. Strength of numbers, and the PLA's historical legacy under Mao has ensured that the Chinese military has retained a role in shaping foreign policy but its degree of influence has waxed and waned in the decades after Mao's passing. The relationship between Party and Army was strained during the advent of the Dengist reforms, as Deng Xiaoping was unhappy with what he saw as a bloated, overly politicised military which was still seeped in outmoded Maoist strategies and becoming increasingly ineffective against modern security threats. The costly Chinese invasion of northern Vietnam in early 1979 gave Deng the political clout required to introduce sweeping budget cuts and re-allocation of military funds into various economic and educational sectors, as well as retiring and removing PLA leadership personnel and making cuts to the military's budget. These reforms continued well into the early 1990s as Deng wished to ensure that the PLA would not be in a position to challenge his successor as leader, Jiang Zemin, who himself lacked substantial military experience.

While defence became one of Deng's "four modernisations", it was fourth in priority, behind agriculture, industry, and science and technology. During the 1980s, the PLA's overall numbers also continued to be reduced.[8] However, after the Tiananmen incident in June 1989, it was necessary for both Deng and later Jiang Zemin to placate PLA leaders in the wake of strained Party–Army relations after the confrontation. Military budgets began to swell again in the 1990s as Jiang began to more fully oversee military affairs,[9] and during the 1990s some American policymakers and scholars, noting China's growing military budget, began to raise alarms about a potential Chinese military challenge. Although adherents to the "China Threat theory" (*Zhongguo weixie lun* 中国威胁论) school suggested that growth in military spending during the decade demonstrated China's development as a potentially belligerent power, in reality there were other reasons for these increases. One important factor was concern about the China threat idea becoming a vicious cycle, with the United States and China becoming locked in, not an arms race, but an arms build-up nonetheless.

For example, the rise in Chinese military spending can be seen as a natural outcome of China's overall economic growth and the accompanying requirement to maintain modern armed forces. Both American-led Middle East Gulf Wars (Iraq/Kuwait, 1991 and Iraq, 2003–12) and the NATO intervention in Kosovo (1999) were viewed as strong signals by Beijing that more attention needed to be paid to "C_4I" systems (command, control, communications, computers and intelligence) and the need to develop greater power projection skills.[10] It was noted that the situation in Taiwan, during which the administrations of Lee Teng-hui and Chen Shui-bian were flirting more openly with the idea of autonomy and even independence, was also a catalyst for increased military spending since the 1990s. The embarrassment of the 1996 Taiwan Straits crisis, when China was unable to effectively respond to the deployment of two American aircraft carrier groups near Taiwan, illustrated the limits of China's near-abroad military power, thus necessitating increased military development and arms purchases.[11] At the same time, day-to-day increases in expenses, including salary increases for the still-large numbers of military personnel, as well as modernisation of equipment and facilities, also require consideration when examining military budget increases.

Increases in military salaries were required in order to offset the losses incurred when Jiang Zemin ordered the PLA to divest itself of its business holdings in July 1998. When the Dengist reforms were announced 20 years earlier, members of the PLA had eagerly begun to purchase businesses ranging from small shops to large factories and even corporations, as military personnel were in an excellent position to take advantage of the economic liberalisation policies due to their entrenchment within the CCP structure and their exclusive access to financial information. However, both Jiang and Premier Zhu Rongji were growing increasingly frustrated with the fact that PLA-owned businesses were both a distraction from military development and an invitation for corruption.[12] Jiang called upon all members of the PLA to either sell off their business holdings or retire from the armed forces. Despite dire predictions that the PLA would resist the order, the divestiture was for the most part carried out, although some exemptions were negotiated.[13]

As well, under Jiang Zemin and Hu Jintao, as China's international interests began to move beyond the regional milieu to more international interests, including the Indian Ocean, Africa and the Middle East, Beijing recognised the need to develop technologies which would allow its military to operate further away from Chinese territory. These issues included greater participation in peacekeeping, protection of international economic assets, combating terrorism and extremism, and joint cooperation with other states.

Beijing has repeatedly denied that spending increases have been designed to create a more offensive-minded military, yet the United States and others have called for greater transparency in Beijing's strategic policymaking.[14] China has released White Papers on Defence since the late 1990s, but critics argue that China is not being sufficiently candid in terms of its defence spending or its strategic development. In China's White Paper, entitled "The Diversified Employment of China's Armed Forces", published in April 2013, Beijing's assessment of the international security situation was pointed:

> Since the beginning of the new century, profound and complex changes have taken place in the world, but peace and development remain the underlying trends of our times. The global trends toward economic globalization and multi-polarity are intensifying, cultural diversity is increasing, and an information society is fast emerging. The balance of international forces is shifting in favour of maintaining world peace, and on the whole the international situation remains peaceful and stable. Meanwhile, however, the world is still far from being tranquil. There are signs of increasing hegemonism, power politics and neo-interventionism.[15]

A follow-up document, "China's Military Strategy", released in May 2015,[16] further articulated Beijing's growing security concerns, including the impacts of the US rebalancing policy, the overhaul of Japan's military capabilities and strategies, and the actions of "some external countries" which were "meddling" in the South China Sea, the majority of which Beijing views as its home waters. Other potential threats included instability on the Korean Peninsula, the problem of "Taiwan independence" (*Taidu* 台独) despite the warming of cross-Strait relations since 2008, and the instigation of "colour revolutions" (*yanse geming* 颜色革命), similar to those which took place in the former Soviet Union, by foreign actors.

The paper also addressed two major strategic goals of building China as a "moderately prosperous society" by 2021, the centenary of the founding of the CCP, and then creating a "modern socialist country that is prosperous, strong, democratic, culturally advanced and harmonious by 2049", the hundredth anniversary of the People's Republic. Policy statements from the Maoist era were also reintroduced in the paper, including "We will not attack unless we are attacked, but we will surely counterattack if attacked", and the need for "preparation for military struggle" (*junshi douzheng zhunbi de jidian* 军事斗争准备的基点). There was also a reference to the greater role which information would play in future Chinese strategy, as the document stressed the need for the PLA to be prepared for "winning informationised local wars" (*daying xinxihua jubu zhanzheng* 打赢信息化局部战争). Four "critical security domains" (*sige zhongda anquan lingyu* 四个重大安全领域) for Chinese security interests were also identified, namely the oceans, space, cyberspace and nuclear weapons.

China's military budget has also grown at a steady pace in recent years despite the country's slowing economy. In 2015, China's defence budget was officially set by Beijing at approximately US$145 billion, a 10 per cent increase from the previous year. However, in comparison with American military spending, which was approved in early 2015 to be set at US$585 billion for that year, the Chinese defence budget remained low. The gap in military spending between the two states has been steadily narrowing since the turn of the century, but any kind of parity in spending continued to be viewed as unlikely in the near future.[17] Beijing has responded by noting that their overall military spending lags well behind that of the United States, and that defence generally only makes up (officially) about 2 per cent of Chinese GDP compared with approximately 4 per cent in the United States as of 2013 according to the World Bank.[18] Moreover, Washington began to face growing domestic pressure in the run-up to the elections of 2016 to increase its military spending, not only because of the Asia pivot policy but also due to the need to protect US allies in Eastern Europe in the wake of Russia's actions in Ukraine, and to protect Middle Eastern interests against the virulent ISIL/Islamic State movement. Even assuming, as some Western commentators suggest, that Beijing may have been under-reporting its military budget, Chinese military spending patterns are such that a direct China–US arms race would not be in Beijing's favour.

American and Western interest in China as a stronger military power continues to grow, especially as Beijing has begun to press its maritime interests in the surrounding East and South China Seas as well as sending naval vessels further from Chinese waters. Also, China's economic interests in many other areas of the world added to policy debates over whether China's military power would start to become more visible on a global scale.

China as a nuclear power

With the testing of China's first nuclear weapon in the remote Lop Nur region in Xinjiang on 16 October 1964, undertaken under the codename "596",[19] the country became the fifth nuclear power and the last of the "legal" nuclear powers under the international Nuclear Non-Proliferation Treaty (NPT) of 1968. Beijing, however, would not sign that Treaty until 1992 as the country remained suspicious of superpower attempts to hamper Chinese security interests.[20] China also became the first "developing" state to deploy a nuclear weapon, and would retain that distinction until India tested its first nuclear weapon in 1974. China conducted its last atmospheric nuclear test in 1980, and its last underground nuclear test was completed in July 1996 as China began to more closely adhere to international non-proliferation and testing protocols.[21] Since the 1990s, China has become a much stronger advocate of nuclear non-proliferation, citing its wariness of a potential nuclear competition between India and Pakistan after 1998, opposition, albeit muted, to the three nuclear tests conducted by North Korea since 2006, and increasing discomfort over Iran's potential for developing a nuclear weapon despite denials from Teheran. However, China has not appreciably reduced its own arsenal, and has instead sought to modernise its current nuclear capabilities while supporting global nuclear disarmament efforts.

Mao Zedong's views on nuclear weapons until the Lop Nur test were at times very contradictory. He remarked that such weapons were "paper tigers" (*zhilaohu* 纸老虎) of limited use in modern warfare, and that China because of its relative lack of development

---

Box 5.1 The world's nuclear powers

Recognised by the Nuclear Non-Proliferation Treaty (NPT)
China
France
Russia
United Kingdom
United States

Outside of the NPT
India
Israel
North Korea
Pakistan

---

could not hope to match the stockpiles of either superpower. Mao noted to a visiting British official in 1961 that the best China could hope for would be a limited nuclear stockpile, or "one finger" as opposed to the "ten fingers" which the United States possessed.[22] Despite these public views he was insistent that China develop nuclear weapons even in the face of rising opposition from the Khrushchev regime in Moscow. Since developing nuclear weapons, China has not attempted to match either the United States or Russia in terms of inventory size, and has pledged that it would not be the first to use a nuclear weapon ("no first use" or NFU) during a conflict, that it would maintain an arsenal sufficient to deter an attack but not to overwhelm an adversary, a concept known as *"force de frappe".*[23] China's views on nuclear weapons became increasingly conservative during the latter stages of the Cold War and after, but nuclear politics remain an important area of modern Chinese international relations.

By the late 1950s, Mao was dedicated, even in the face of mounting Soviet opposition, to obtain a bomb to deter a potential attack by the United States or its allies, to increase its stature both in the communist world and in Asia specifically, and to bolster its power in supporting various wars of national liberation in the developing world.[24] The prospect of a Chinese bomb greatly alarmed Washington, to the point where it was revealed in the late 1990s via declassified documents that the Kennedy administration was seriously considering a pre-emptive strike on the Lop Nur base in order to prevent a Chinese test, and was even contemplating joint action with Moscow to achieve this. However, as the test became more imminent it was decided that the risks and political damage from such actions would be too great, and in the end the US did not interfere.[25] In 2014, China was estimated to possess approximately 250 nuclear weapons, a much smaller stockpile than the United States or the Russian Federation, both of which were in possession of over 7000 warheads each.[26] Moreover, a majority of China's nuclear weapons was estimated to be at fixed sites, but there has been reportedly some debate within the PLA to develop more mobile warheads via the construction of nuclear submarines and submarine-launched ballistic missiles (SLBMs) of the *Julang-1* and *-2* class. China's missile arsenal has also undergone much upgrading since the 1990s. The country possesses approximately 130 medium-range ballistic missiles and 250 short-range ballistic missiles, as well as approximately 66 inter-continental ballistic missiles (ICBMs).[27]

Although there have been international concerns about China's nuclear modernisation, Beijing's views on nuclear arms control and disarmament have shifted significantly since the end of the Cold War. Before that time, China harboured deep suspicions about international efforts to reduce nuclear arms and largely viewed such efforts as only relevant to the affairs of two superpowers. By the end of the 1990s, however, China had agreed to sign, or adhere to, several non-proliferation agreements, including the Nuclear Non-Proliferation Treaty (NPT) which it signed in 1992, the Missile Technology Control Regime (or MTCR, which controls the export of missile technology) and the Zangger Committee, whose members agree not to export fissionable material or related equipment to non-nuclear states. China also agreed to dramatically scale back nuclear weapons-related cooperation with its previous partners in this area, including Iran and Pakistan, by the beginning of the following decade.[28] China is also the only one of the five original nuclear powers which keeps its warheads separate from its missile arsenal. Beijing has been supportive of an international agreement which would allow US-led sanctions on Iran to be removed in exchange for a scaling back of Teheran's alleged nuclear development programme, and by 2015 China had partnered with the United States, as well as Britain, France, Germany and Russia, in reaching such an agreement with Iran in July of that year.

By the turn of the century, China had begun to argue for maintenance of the status quo on nuclear affairs, strongly criticising the American decision to withdraw from the Anti-Ballistic Missile (ABM) Treaty in 2002 and expressing concerns about US-led plans to develop missile defence technology which could theoretically negate China's comparatively small ICBM capability.[29] After many decades of being viewed by the West as a potential obstacle to global arms control, Beijing has now positioned itself as a great power detractor of international WMD (weapons of mass destruction) proliferation.

Strategic thinking

As suggested above, the PLA's voice in foreign affairs is seen to be rising, partially as a result of the diversification of the decision-making process in Beijing. Unlike Mao and Deng, current Chinese leaders cannot claim personal ties to the military, and therefore they must cultivate relations with the PLA in order to maintain their positions. Compared with Jiang Zemin and Hu Jintao, Xi Jinping has been more successful in this regard given his longer history of PLA relations, and the status of his late father, Xi Zhongxun, who served in the communist army and participated in the Long March and the subsequent Yan'an Soviet in the 1930s, before surviving a political purge and assuming leadership positions in the party, including as Secretary General of the State Council. As well, Xi's wife, Peng Liyuan, has had a longstanding career in the PLA, and holds the rank of Major-General due to her civilian service as a military entertainer, and is president of the People's Liberation Army Arts College.

The PLA has also been traditionally viewed in the West as a major element of nationalistic thinking in China, and can often influence decisions involving economics as well as foreign policy. At the same time, many military leaders have been seen as voices of conservatism, calling for restraint in areas of potential conflict. On occasion, however, some military leaders have made emphatic comments, such as in January 1996 during the Taiwan Straits Crisis when a PLA official, General Xiong Guankai, noted that the US would not dare intervene because it "cared more about Los Angeles than Taipei",[30] a quote which was often cited by those concerned about a possible "China threat" or military expansion.

For the most part, however, China's military policy has centred more on modernisation and defence issues, as well as the defence of Chinese interests abroad and multilateral cooperation in various forms including peacekeeping under the United Nations, than possibly provoking international actors. Moreover, China has been wary of taking any actions which might provoke a direct arms race with the West or the development of a pro-Western military alliance being created by the United States in order to balance or contain Chinese strategic interests. The late-2011 announcement by Washington of a "pivot to Asia" or a "rebalancing" of US forces in the Pacific as well as increased military ties with Australia, Japan, the Philippines, Singapore, South Korea and Vietnam was met with much consternation among Chinese leaders who expressed concerns about a *de facto* "containment" designed to limit Chinese power and encourage US allies, notably Japan, to challenge Beijing's regional security interests.

China's military strategy has also undergone a significant transformation since the Maoist era, both in terms of potential threats and methods of defence and offence. Under Mao, revolutionary strategies left over from the civil war era were prevalent in Chinese military thinking, especially embodied in the idea of "people's war" (*renmin zhanzheng* 人民战争). Mao believed in the supremacy of people over weapons, and that the best way of defeating an enemy was to lure threat forces deep into China's vast territory where they would be subdued by superior numbers, a remnant of Mao's experiences in guerrilla strategies during the Chinese Civil War and the war with Japan in the 1930s. Mao's 1937 text, *On Guerrilla Warfare* (*Lun youji zhan* 论游击战) remains one of the seminal works on that subject. The Chinese military under Mao also placed great emphasis on "red over expert", meaning that advancement would be based on fealty to the revolution rather than practical expertise. Another major component of "people's war" was the necessity of exporting the socialist revolution to other parts of the world through the support of armed insurgencies by communist forces, particularly in Southeast Asia.[31]

As well, Mao was a strong believer in so-called "total war" doctrine, meaning that the next war would be a great power conflict requiring all of China's resources, as well as the inevitability of a nuclear conflict, which partially motivated his desire to develop a nuclear weapons capability. Some of Mao's subordinates, notably his ill-fated defence minister and one-time heir, Lin Biao, also believed in the total war concept, but others in Mao's inner circle were less convinced about the usefulness of Maoist strategies. The Korean War, for example, was a limited conflict which saw Chinese forces participating outside of Chinese territory. However, it was not until Mao's death in 1976 that the idea of "people's war" could be challenged and replaced more formally with strategies related to "local war" (*jubu zhanzheng* 局部战争).[32]

Under Deng, the military began to change its strategic thinking in light of changed international conditions. The inevitability of nuclear war was downplayed, and more attention began to be paid to the naval and air capabilities instead of just the ground forces.[33] Debates began over the "red" versus "expert" idea and soon there was a greater emphasis on a military which would be both "red and expert" (*youhong youzhuan* 又红又专) and traditional Maoist ideas of guerrilla warfare were updated to reflect changing threats. The USSR had replaced the United States as the most likely adversary, and total war was deemed less likely to occur than limited war which would not require a complete mobilisation of resources. By the time of Jiang and Hu, many Maoist ideas on "people's war" had been completely transformed and upgraded.

The PLA today is expected to be more fully educated and be both red and expert as well as to be prepared to adjust to high-technology conditions, including modern border defence, protection of strategic assets, and the prevention of Taiwanese independence. The current phrase which embodies modern strategic thinking is "local war under modern high technology conditions" (*gaojishu jubu zhanzheng* 高技术局部战争) and the idea of fighting wars within "conditions of informationalisation" (*xinxihua tiaojianxia* 信息化条件) was first described in China's White Paper on Defence in 2004,[34] a theme which has continued to the present day given the growing importance of information warfare in Chinese strategic thinking.

After the fall of the Soviet Union, many PLA planners again considered the United States as the most likely adversary. Yet at present, China cannot hope to match the US in terms of overall military power as its power projection capabilities remain very limited despite post-2008 advances, reducing the PLA's effectiveness in out-of-home-theatre operations. Indigenous military research and development, while growing, remains small and underdeveloped which is why many branches of the Chinese military were dependent upon Russian arms purchases since the 1990s, including *Kilo*-class attack submarines and *Sovremenny*-class naval destroyers which carry SS-N-22 anti-ship missiles, also known as "Sunburns", which could be used against American vessels.[35]

After the turn of the century there were more examples of indigenous military development which may soon improve power projection. These included the development after 2010 of the *Dongfeng* (*East Wind*)-21D missile which reportedly has the capability of sinking an aircraft carrier, as well as a new generation of ICBMs, the *Dongfeng*-41 (DF-41), confirmed in August 2014 and reportedly tested in December of that year. The DF-41 was estimated to have a range of at least 12,000 km and MIRV (multiple independently targetable re-entry vehicle) capability. Also, in January 2011, a PLA Air Force J-20 stealth fighter was introduced with the estimated capability to counter the American F-22 *Raptor* jetfighter. In November 2014, a second class of Chinese stealth fighter, the J-31, nicknamed the *Snowy Owl* (*Xuexiao* 雪鸮), was demonstrated at an air show in Zhuhai, a potential response to the F-35 *Lightning II* stealth jetfighter being tested that year by the United States.[36] It is expected that China will make more use of domestic weaponry in the near future rather than rely on Russian hardware purchases. Indeed, Russia has been seen as a likely purchaser of future Chinese military technology given the warming security relationship between the two powers.

One major component missing from China's developing military power was finally addressed in 2011 with the deployment of the PLA Navy's first aircraft carrier in August of that year for sea trials. Until that time, Beijing was unable to build or purchase an aircraft carrier, an essential component of any maritime-theatre conflict. This deficiency was especially glaring given that Beijing was the only permanent member of the United Nations Security Council without carrier capabilities. By contrast, the United States has ten carriers deployed internationally, with an eleventh planned for 2016. In the late 1990s, Beijing arranged the purchase of an unfinished carrier from Ukraine which had been abandoned when the USSR dissolved, towed it to the Chinese port of Dalian, and spent the following decade completing and modernising the vessel. Well after the refurbishing was completed, however, the carrier lacked an official name and was often referred to by its previous moniker when it was still owned by Ukraine, the *Varyag*. In September 2012, the carrier, finally officially named the *Liaoning* (辽宁), was commissioned with sea trials commencing shortly afterwards. Although the vessel has been primarily used for training, its addition to the PLA Navy was nonetheless seen as further proof of Beijing's commitment to modernising and expanding its maritime power, and indigenous carriers are said to be under development for the PLAN.

It had been argued that China's previous deficiencies in power projection were a factor in restraining Beijing from directly pressing its claims both to Taiwan and to the South China Sea. An amphibious assault against Taiwan would incur many mainland casualties, and it is likely that should Beijing attempt to attack Taipei, methods might include a softening up of Taiwanese defences using missile strikes before an invasion, or possibly a blockade using mines and/or naval vessels.[37] Much would depend, however, upon whether the West would seek to directly intervene should such an invasion take place and the United States has maintained an opaque stance on whether it would intervene in a cross-Strait military conflict. However, after the election of Ma Ying-jeou in Taiwan in 2008 and the resulting cooling off of diplomatic tensions, assisted by strengthened trade, direct air links, and political visits, military tensions between the two sides diminished considerably, with more attention paid to improving economic and social links.

As for the South China Sea, Beijing was able to seize and hold the Paracel Islands (*Xisha Qundao* 西沙群岛) in that region during the 1980s despite countering claims by Vietnam, but the other major islet group in the Sea, the Spratly Islands (*Nansha Qundao* 南沙群岛), which are further to the south and claimed in whole or in part by other Southeast Asian states, including Brunei, Malaysia, the Philippines and Vietnam, as well as Taiwan, have been a more complex issue.[38] After the Second World War, Beijing began to assert a formal claim to the majority of the South China Sea as its territorial waters, based on historical claims from the Imperial eras. Chinese maps since the 1950s designated about 80 per cent of the Sea as Chinese waters extending well south of the Chinese coast, as indicated by a horseshoe-shaped "nine-dashed line" (*jiuduan xian* 九段线). However, until the turn of the century, the Chinese navy lacked the ability to establish a full military presence there. In November 2002, China agreed to sign the Declaration on the Conduct of Parties in the South China Sea with the Association of Southeast Asian Nations (ASEAN). The following year, Beijing signed the Treaty of Amity and Cooperation (TAC) with ASEAN, resulting in a cooling of tensions over the South China Sea.

Détente in the region began to falter after 2009 following a series of incidents which suggested that Beijing was again seeking to press its claims to the South China Sea. In March of that year, the American naval surveillance vessel *USNS Impeccable* was challenged by a PLAN vessel and Chinese civilian ships about 120 km south of Hainan Island, the first major military incident between the US and China since the "spy plane" affair in April 2001.[39] In May 2009, a similar incident took place involving the American vessel *USNS Victorious*. Finally, there was an incident in December 2013, when a Chinese navy amphibious dock ship, *Jianggang Shan* (井冈山), steered itself into the path of the US Navy cruiser *USS Cowpens* as it was operating close to the Chinese carrier *Liaoning*, forcing the *Cowpens* to change course in order to avoid a collision.

These events took place at a time when China's policies towards disputed waters also began to shift. In early 2010, Chinese officials were quoted as saying that Beijing considered the South China Sea to be part of the country's "core interests" (*hexin liyi* 核心利益), a term which had previously only been used to describe integral parts of the Chinese mainland plus Taiwan, suggesting a hardening of policy on the matter on Beijing's part. However, the top leadership in Beijing did not use the term, and the term remains ambiguous in Chinese foreign and security policy. The policy shift not only alarmed the government of the Philippines and Vietnam, but also prompted an American response in the form of a statement by then-US Secretary of State Hillary Clinton at a July 2010 ASEAN Regional Forum (ARF) meeting in Hanoi calling for an international body to oversee the disputed sea, and that it was in America's "national interest" to promote freedom of navigation and respect for international law in the waterway, assertions which were swiftly criticised in Beijing as US interference in Chinese sovereign affairs. Beijing maintains that the South China Sea is an internal issue not subject to international arbitration.

Other subsequent incidents raised concerns among China's neighbours about the country's evolving maritime security policy. China reacted with criticism of its southern neighbours when the governments of the Philippines and Vietnam submitted requests to the

UN in March 2009 calling for an extension of their territorial waters in the South China Sea which challenged Chinese claims. During the first half of 2012, incidents occurred between Chinese and Vietnamese vessels as well as ships from China and the Philippines, including a tense standoff between vessels from different Chinese maritime policing agencies and Philippine ships in the region of the Scarborough Shoal, known in China as Huangyan (黄岩) Island. Hanoi also accused Beijing of interfering with Vietnamese survey vessels, including an incident in December 2012 when Vietnam accused Chinese patrol ships of purposely cutting a seismic cable which was being towed by a Vietnamese survey ship in the disputed waters.[40] Hanoi was also furious at a June 2012 scheme, later rescinded, by the Chinese National Offshore Energy Corporation (CNOOC) to offer for sale nine fossil fuel blocks in waters also claimed by Vietnam. During the same month, the government of Vietnam released a revised maritime law which codified the country's legal rights to the Paracel and Spratly island groups, prompting a request from China's National People's Congress (NPC) that Hanoi correct what Beijing saw as an "erroneous" law.[41]

Then, in May–July 2014 China's CNOOC moved a petroleum drilling rig, the *Haiyang Shiyou 981* (海洋石油981), into waters also claimed by Vietnam close to the Paracel Islands. The move resulted in violent anti-China protests in Vietnam, and concerns expressed from the international community that Beijing was again seeking to gradually create a *fait accompli* in the South China Sea. The response from the Chinese Foreign Ministry in a June 2014 statement was that the rig was drilling in Chinese waters, and that it was Vietnam which was acting in a provocative fashion contrary to international laws and norms.

The South China Sea debate intensified again in early 2015, when reports appeared stating that China was reinforcing buildings and other structures on the reefs it held in the Spratlys, as well as adding sand to increase their overall area and to make it possible for other structures to be built on them. In February 2015, reports appeared of extensive Chinese construction at Hughes Reef, Gaven Reefs and Johnson South Reef, all occupied by China.[42] Less than two months later, similar reports appeared about the adding of infrastructure, including a runway approximately 3 km long, to Fiery Cross Reef (*Yongshu jiao* 永暑礁). These reports drew criticism from the United States, with the Commander of the US Pacific Fleet, Admiral Harry Harris Jr., stating that Beijing was "creating a great wall of sand" in the SCS, and noting that China had created an extra 4 km^2 in the Spratly region, using sand and concrete to shore up local reefs.[43] China maintained, however, that such construction was completely justified and well within international legal bounds.

The security situation in the East China Sea has also become more precarious as the positions between the main disputants, China and Japan, have become firmer. In September 2010, a Chinese fishing boat, the *Minjinyu 5179* (闽晋渔5179号), collided with two Japanese Coast Guard vessels in the East China Sea and was detained by Japanese authorities with the intention of trying the captain in local courts. Following intense diplomatic pressure from Beijing, the captain and crew were released before the end of that month.[44] The exact demarcation line between China and Japan in the East China Sea remains disputed, and includes the *Diaoyu dao* (钓鱼岛) island group (known as the Senkaku Islands in Japanese and the *Diaoyutai* 钓鱼台 in Taiwan), and is claimed by all three parties. In November 2013, China announced that an Air Defence Identification Zone (*fankong shibiequ* 防空识别区) or ADIZ, would be implemented in the East China Sea, including over the disputed Diaoyu / Senkaku area, which would overlap a similar Japanese ADIZ in the region put into place in 1969. Shortly after the announcement, which was strongly criticised by both Tokyo and Washington, speculation began over whether China would also seek a similar ADIZ in the South China Sea in the future, despite the much larger area which would need to be overseen.[45] Beijing maintains that both the East and South China Sea issues are internal in nature and therefore not subject to international arbitration, and remains wary of any direct American involvement, even under the aegis of mediation.

In the cases of both the East and South China Seas, in addition to territorial concerns there is also the question of potential fossil fuels, oil and gas, which may rest underneath those waters. Chinese claims to these islands would extend the country's exclusive economic zone (EEZ) far south of the mainland and directly overlap EEZs claimed by Southeast Asian states. With Chinese naval power continuing to develop, the country is in a much stronger position to test its claims, and in light of those events the United States began to express concerns that China was seeking an "anti-access / area denial" or A2/AD (*fanjieru / quyuzujue* 反介入 / 区域阻绝) strategy designed to hamper US military operations around Chinese waters, especially in the region between the Chinese coastline and the "first island chain" (*diyi daolian* 第一岛链) in the Pacific which includes Japan, Taiwan and the Philippines. Chinese policymakers have referred to such A2/AD strategies as "active strategic counterattacks on exterior lines" or ASCEL (*jiji de zhanlue waixian fanji zuozhan* 积极的战略外线反击作战).[46] There is a greater speculation that China is seeking to develop a more formal oversight role in the waters between its coast and the first island chain, discouraging American naval activity in that region. The widespread mid-2014 release of a new vertical map of China, which suggested continuous maritime holdings in both the East and South China Seas and also featured a tenth "dash" to the west of Taiwan, added to this view.

Despite many advances, China's navy is still more "green water", meaning designed for coastal defence, than "blue water", designed for use in the open seas, so Beijing began to seek ways of addressing this imbalance.[47] Such an opportunity appeared in late 2008 when the United Nations began to organise a naval response to the deteriorating security situation in the Gulf of Aden off the coast of Somalia, a country collapsed, beset not only by warring militias on land but also pervasive piracy off its coast. Several countries, including China, experienced the seizure of their civilian vessels by pirates seeking huge ransoms. In January 2009, Beijing agreed to send PLAN vessels to take part in an internal naval coalition designed to thwart pirate attacks, an event which marked the first time the country's vessels operated out of territory since modern China was founded 60 years earlier. From that date, a series of PLAN taskforces, usually comprising three vessels, served as part of the coalition to deter pirate attacks on civilian cargo ships, reflecting growing Chinese interests in protecting important sea lanes of communication (*haishang jiaotongxian* 海上交通线) or SLoCs, in the Middle East and greater Indian Ocean.

As well, in February 2011 a Chinese warship attached to the counter-piracy coalition, the missile frigate *Xuzhou* (徐州), was diverted through the Red Sea and into the Mediterranean to oversee the evacuation of over 35,000 Chinese nationals, primarily guest workers, from Libya as that country erupted in civil war between forces supporting and opposing the regime of Muammar Gaddafi. This was only the second time a Chinese military vessel had entered the Mediterranean Sea and the first time for a humanitarian mission. In March 2015, a similar event took place when two PLAN missile frigates operating off Somalia, the *Linyi* (临沂) and the *Weifang* (潍坊), participated in the evacuation of Chinese nationals from Yemen as that country's civil war intensified. All of these events suggested that in addition to concentrating on power projection, the Chinese navy was seeking to develop its capabilities with missions involving "Military Operations other than War" or MOOTW (*feizhanzheng xing junshi xingdong* 非战争性军事行动).

China's ability to engage in high-technology combat is also lacking, but there have been signs of improvement there. One component of China's thinking on asymmetrical conflict is the ability to deprive an adversary of needed communications abilities, which is why China has reportedly been seeking the ability to disable enemy communications both through dedicated denial-of-service attacks on digital communications as well as the use of anti-satellite (ASAT) technology to physically destroy an adversary's satellites. In January 2007, the PLA tested what appeared to be an ASAT projectile weapon on an aged *Fengyun* weather satellite.[48] The United States registered its displeasure at the test, noting that such actions were inconsistent with the need to prevent space from becoming an arena for international military competition. However, both the United States and the USSR had themselves tested ASAT weapons in the 1980s. Beijing responded to international criticism that it was not seeking to spark an arms race in space,[49] and has pressed the point that it does not want to instigate or engage in an arms race, in space or elsewhere.

From a strategic viewpoint, China's current defence concerns appear on the surface to be relatively minimal compared with various times in the past. Despite its large number of neighbours, Beijing was successfully able in the 1990s to conclude border agreements at various levels with several of them. Border disputes no longer plague Chinese relations with either Vietnam or the former Soviet Union, and those disputes which remain, including possession of the Aksai Chin (*Akesaiqin* 阿克赛钦) region, occupied by China but claimed by India after their conflict in 1962,[50] and a region of the Himalaya Mountains which India administers as part of its Arunachal Pradesh state but which China claims is part of Tibet and is referred to by Beijing as "South Tibet" (*Zangnan* 藏南), have been dormant. For the first time since 1949, Beijing does not have a direct great power adversary. Nevertheless, China remains concerned about both traditional and non-traditional security threats and has sought to modernise its strategic thinking to address these issues. Therefore, China's current strategic environment has seen a diversification of potential security threats, meaning that Beijing's planners are paying more attention to the issues of "comprehensive" (*quanmian* 全面) security rather than strictly military-based hard power considerations.

At present, there is no equivalent of a NATO or an OSCE in East Asia which would hypothetically create better security confidence-building and mediate regional disputes.[51] Those mechanisms which do exist, such as the ASEAN Regional Forum (ARF) and the East Asian Summit (EAS), are comparatively very weak and act mainly as debate forums. However, China has viewed the ARF as useful in developing non-alliance forms of regional security

---

Box 5.2 China's space programme

After 1992, Beijing began making preparations to send persons into space under the *Shenzhou* (神舟) programme (also originally called "Project 921"). The first test flight, *Shenzhou I*, was launched in November 1999. After three other test missions into space, China sent its first astronaut (or "taikonaut"), Yang Liwei, into space in October 2003 aboard *Shenzhou V*. Three other manned missions would follow, and in June 2012, Liu Yang of the PLA Air Force became the first Chinese woman in space as one of three crew members aboard *Shenzhou IX*. *Shenzhou X* was completed in June 2013, a mission which included docking with the experimental *Tiangong 1* (天宫一号) space station. Also that year, China's first robotic lander and automated rover landed on the Moon as part of a mission called *Chang'e 3* (嫦娥三号), named for the goddess of the Moon in Chinese mythology. These missions have been overseen by the China National Space Administration (国家航天局 *Guojia Hangtianju*), created in 1993.

cooperation.[52] Thus, there is concern that the region remains conflict-prone due to a lack of strong regional security mechanisms. For example, relations with Japan became increasingly strained by the turn of the century due to both historical grievances and regional security concerns.[53] North Korea has been transformed from an ally to a troublesome neighbour of China after Pyongyang tested its first nuclear weapon in October 2006, along with two subsequent tests, and concerns about longer-term American strategies for the Pacific Rim region also persist. It can be argued that the presence of a strong regional security organisation for Northeast Asia could be useful to, at the very least, provide a forum to address these problems.

China has also become more accepting of "Track II" diplomacy (*ergui weijiao* 二轨外交) in strategic matters, another area of traditional suspicion. Track II diplomacy has been increasingly used to address traditional and non-traditional security problems in regions where direct government-to-government contact is complicated. Rather than meetings between official state representatives or officials (or "Track I"), Track II meetings involve persons from academia, think-tanks and research centres, non-governmental organisations, businesses, and oftentimes government functionaries representing themselves *de facto* rather than their offices.[54] Politically difficult topics can be discussed more freely and often ideas can be circulated which would be too difficult to address at the governmental level. China has made increasing use of such Pacific Rim meetings, including the Council of Security Cooperation in the Asia-Pacific (CSCAP), the ASEAN Institutes for Strategic and International Studies (ASEAN-ISIS) and the Network of East Asian Think Tanks (NEAT), to discuss delicate issues relating to regional security.[55] Chinese representatives also participate in the annual Shangri-La Dialogue in Singapore, organised by the International Institute for Strategic Studies (IISS), which could be considered a "Track 1.5" meeting as the Dialogue includes representatives of both government and non-government groups. While Beijing has been wary of allowing certain topics, especially Taiwan and the South China Sea, onto the agendas of Track II meetings, other issues such as terrorism, trade security and maritime strategy are increasingly discussed by Chinese representatives.

Although China and the US remain allies combatting international terrorism, Beijing's suspicions of American power persist and there is concern by scholars in the US that the current partnership between Beijing and Washington is a marriage of convenience only. China appears uncomfortable with America's strengthening of traditional alliances, including the upgraded security link with Tokyo, ongoing hegemonic behaviour, its pursuit of democratisation around the world, which Beijing believes is a cover for a policy of weakening potential adversaries, its shaky adherence to international law and its selective intervention in domestic disputes under the guise of humanitarian intervention. As well, China is sensitive to the possibility that it may be the victim of so-called "neo-containment" or "encirclement" strategy by the United States, especially since Washington has a military presence in Central Asia, Southeast Asia, the North Pacific and Japan, and maintains forces on the Korean demilitarised zone.[56]

In a very short timeframe Beijing has had to re-visit many areas of its strategic thinking to take into account not only changing international conditions, including new types of threats but also new possibilities for strategic cooperation, as well as its own expanding size and influence in security areas well beyond its borders. The issues of so-called "non-traditional security" threats (*feichuantong anquan weixie* 非传统安全威胁) and the rise of the global war on terror at the beginning of the new century which has included non-state adversaries such as *Al-Qaeda* and more recently the Islamic State, best illustrate this new reality. It is within these security realms where China is also starting to make its presence felt, especially in its proposals involving alternative forms of cooperation to address non-state threats.

Non-traditional security and terrorism

From a non-traditional security viewpoint, China worries about trans-national crime, including smuggling and piracy, with terrorism becoming a primary strategic concern. Since 2001, Beijing has sought to share terrorism information with the United States, Russia and Europe and has called for anti-terror cooperation through organisations such as the Asia-Pacific Economic Cooperation forum (APEC).[57] While there was initial concern that Beijing would seek to link terrorism activities with "splittist" or secessionist (*fenlie zhuyi* 分裂主义) forces, which could be interpreted as including Taiwan, this never materialised and China, while not always in agreement with some Western policies on anti-terror, nevertheless has considered terrorism to be very much an international threat rather than strictly a regional one.[58]

China's responses to the war on terror (*fankong zhanzheng* 反恐战争) over the past decade have largely been in step with international debates and practices. After the events of September 11th, Beijing was among the first governments to pledge support for American-led efforts to combat terrorism internationally and agreed to support an anti-terror resolution in the United Nations Security Council (UNSC) in the hours after the tragedy.[59] China's post-Dengist foreign policy has shifted considerably from a concentration on traditional security, namely the aspects of state-to-state conflict, to more non-traditional strategic issues such as terrorism and international crime. While China has pledged support through both bilateral and multilateral talks in fighting terrorism, this has not meant that Chinese and Western views on this subject are completely compatible.

Much of China's concerns about terrorism stem from both its proximity to the former Soviet regions of Central Asia and from its own minority groups in the country's far west. There has been a common perception that China is a distinct entity from Central Asia, but an examination of the country's demographics and political history reveals much overlap between Western China and Central Asia in terms of peoples, politics and issues. Xinjiang and Tibet are China's westernmost territories with sizeable minority populations (Uyghurs in Xinjiang and Tibetans), and are isolated from the political centres of China. As a result, both areas have been designated "autonomous regions" and concerns remain in Beijing that both could fall victim to secessionist pressures.

Since 2001, Beijing attempted to illustrate the connection between political extremism in Central Asia and groups seeking to promote independence for the far-Western territory of Xinjiang. Beijing has accused the East Turkestan Independence Movement or ETIM (*Dongtu juesitan yisi lanyundong* 东突厥斯坦伊斯兰运动) and other splinter groups of seeking the violent separation of Xinjiang and linking up with cross-regional terrorist organisations including *Al-Qaeda*. China sought to bring international attention to ETIM and in 2002 the United States recognised the group as a terrorist organisation after much lobbying from Beijing.[60] In the months leading to the 2008 Beijing Olympics, the ETIM and a possibly-related group, the Turkestan Independence Party (TIP), were blamed by Beijing for a series of incidents including July explosions in Shanghai and Kunming and an attack on police officers using grenades and knives in the Xinjiang city of Kashgar in August which resulted in 16 casualties.[61] Concerns over security in Xinjiang were again raised after riots broke out in the territory's capital of Ürümqi in July 2009, which the Chinese government claimed were instigated by outside Uyghur organisations seeking to destabilise the region. Ürümqi was also the site of a terrorist attack in April 2014, which included a knife attack and a bombing.

After 9/11, Beijing recognised that the problem of terrorism was too great to be addressed unilaterally, and supported US-led attempts to dismantle both *Al-Qaeda* and the Taliban regime in Afghanistan. After military operations began in Afghanistan, its border with China was sealed and Beijing was instrumental in prodding the Musharraf government in Pakistan to support the West, as well as calling for Islamabad to sever its ties with the Taliban regime. Beijing also offered political and economic support to the Afghanistan government of Hamid Karzai while at the same time maintaining a much closer watch on the narrow Sino-Afghan border.[62]

Since the loss of three Chinese nationals at the World Trade Centre, Chinese citizens have also been victims of terrorist attacks in the Middle East, including in Israel and Iraq, as well as Central and Southeast Asia. One of the most devastating of these occurred in June 2004 when 11 Chinese guest construction workers in the northern Afghanistan province of Kunduz were killed.[63] There have also been increasing signs that although Beijing remains wary of a long-term American presence in Central Asia under the aegis of the war on terror, it also worries about the regional impact of terrorist organisations regrouping in the region. In April 2007, China for the first time noted that terrorist cells were operating on the soil of its longstanding ally, Pakistan, and that some were directly connected to separatist activities in Xinjiang. When Beijing released its December 2006 Defence White Paper, in addition to traditional concerns about territorial conflicts and hegemonism, it also recognised the ongoing problem of terrorism in the international community, drawing links between terrorism and separatism as well as uneven economic growth internationally.[64]

In contrast to the United States, however, Beijing has long preferred a multilateral approach to addressing terrorism in Asia, through regimes such as the Asia-Pacific Economic Cooperation Forum and the ASEAN Regional Forum. The most recent APEC meetings have seen expanded discussions on the threat of so-called economic terrorism, meaning attacks designed to directly damage Asia-Pacific trade. It was for this reason that China opted to sign the Container Security Initiative (CSI) in 2005 despite the project being dominated by the United States, and has also been a participant in the Japan-led Regional Cooperation Agreement on Combating Piracy and Armed Robbery against Ships in Asia (ReCAAP).[65] China has also been making use of governmental and sub-governmental meetings to discuss other issues of trans-national crime including drugs, piracy and money-laundering.

Beijing has also attempted to develop its own mechanisms to address the issue of regional terrorism, the most visible of these being the Shanghai Cooperation Organisation. The major impetus for the creation of the SCO came from China, as shortly after the Central Asian republics gained independence after 1992, Beijing engaged the region with an eye to resolving the border disputes it had inherited from the former USSR. Annual meetings between China, Russia and three Central Asian states (Kazakhstan, Kyrgyzstan and Tajikistan) took place to discuss joint security matters after 1996, and in 2001 with the joining of Uzbekistan the "Shanghai Five" became the SCO.[66] Since its founding, the SCO has added observer states (Afghanistan, India, Iran, Mongolia, Pakistan) and "dialogue partners" (Belarus, Sri Lanka and Turkey). After concentrating much of its policymaking efforts and assuring border security in Eurasia, the SCO began to focus much more closely, especially after 9/11, on combating the three evils of terrorism, extremism and separatism, creating both a secretariat in Beijing and a "regional anti-terrorism structure" (RATS) in Tashkent to coordinate security information.

After many years of taking a conservative approach toward security organisations, the steps leading to the SCO represented the genesis of multilateral security and anti-terrorism cooperation in Eurasia through information sharing and joint "anti-terrorism" military exercises.[67] Due to its proximity, Afghanistan has also been of great interest to the SCO and Afghanistani representatives have often attended SCO meetings. With the United States formally disengaging from Afghanistan at the end of 2014, and American relations with Pakistan becoming more fragile after the US military intervention which killed *Al-Qaeda* leader Osama bin Laden in the northern Pakistani city of Abbottabad in May 2011, the SCO appeared well placed to play a more prominent role the Afghanistan–Pakistan region.

Although China is not geographically vulnerable to blockade, a security issue which for example affected much strategic thinking in Imperial Japan in the late nineteenth and early twentieth centuries, Beijing is nonetheless concerned about the safety of its trade routes. The Chinese government has staked much of its current legitimacy on its ability to continue to provide improving standards of living for greater numbers of its citizens and therefore Beijing's sensitivity and vulnerability to potential trade disturbances continues to develop. One of the most visible signs of this new thinking has been in the area of maritime security and the protection of what China views as increasingly vital sea-trade routes.

As China is heavily dependent upon maritime trade for much of its consumer goods and raw materials, especially energy, from abroad, the question of "what if" these routes are blocked or subject to interference from outside actors, state-based or otherwise, is of growing concern to Beijing. The most visible manifestation of this thinking has been President Hu Jintao's enunciation of the so-called "Malacca Dilemma" (*Maliujia kunju* 马六甲困局), meaning that China has the potential to be greatly and adversely affected by blockages of key Asia-Pacific maritime trade routes, especially the narrow Malacca Straits in Southeast Asia, a lifeline for much Chinese international trade.[68] It was with these concerns that President Xi Jinping announced its "one belt and one road" (*yidai yilu* 一带一路) trade corridors which would connect China by land to Europe, Eurasia and Russia and by sea to Africa, South Asia and Northern Europe). Once in operation, these routes would not only more directly connect China to key markets but also add another layer of economic security for the country.

Cybersecurity and cyberwarfare

In recent years, the Chinese military has been active in establishing a cybersecurity presence, both in terms of collecting foreign information and by protecting against and reacting to information-based attacks. These mechanisms include a signals intelligence (SIGINT) capacity via the Third Department of the General Staff Headquarters, also known as 3/PLA (*zongcan sanbu* 总参三部), which monitors and collects information on foreign armed forces.

The United States began to view China as a potential source of "cyber-espionage" at least as far back as 2006 when the term "advanced persistent threat" began to circulate in American intelligence circles as a euphemism for hacking attempts traced back to China.[69] In February 2013, a report from the American computer security firm Mandiant was released regarding a dedicated PLA unit based in Pudong, Shanghai, designated "Unit 61398", responsible for targeted hacking attacks against foreign, including American, organisations.[70] The Chinese government traditionally maintained that it did not sponsor such activities, only reversing itself in March 2015 when an edition of *The Science of Military Strategy* (*Zhanlu xue* 战略学), published by the PLA's Academy of Military Science (AMS) that month, made the first official references to Chinese cyberwarfare units.[71]

Since that time, the issue of cyberwarfare in China has become a subject of international debate as well as a strain on Sino-American relations. For example, a report issued by the Munk School of Global Affairs, University of Toronto, in April 2015 suggested that China was developing a mechanism which could instigate a targeted dedicated denial of service (DDoS) attack on a foreign computer system, effectively disabling it. Information about the mechanism, which the report referred to as the "Great Cannon", appeared at the same time the

Chinese military began to step up warnings about the potential use of the internet by hostile foreign actors to destabilise Chinese security. A May 2015 article in the *People's Liberation Army Daily* suggested that the internet has evolved into an "ideological battlefield" and that steps needed to be taken in order to "protect ideological and political security" online. [72] These ideas had also been articulated when the World Internet Conference was held in Wuzhen, near Shanghai, in November 2014, where the main topics were cybersecurity and cyberterrorism, international globalisation and e-government. China has been critical of American charges of supporting espionage in cyberspace, and government representatives have frequently noted that Chinese organisations themselves have also been frequent targets of hacking attacks. In early 2015, the Chinese Ministry of Defence promised to develop a stronger "cyber force" to protect information security.

In June 2015, Washington accused China-based hackers of accessing protected information on American federal employees and US intelligence and military personnel. Beijing denied support for such operations, and noted that China has also been on the receiving end of foreign cyber attacks. The United States has been concerned about the growing capability of the PLA to potentially engage in "C_4ISTAR" activities, meaning command, control, communications, computers, intelligence, surveillance, target acquisition and reconnaissance, and in January 2011, US President Barack Obama made reference to the technological and economic rise of China representing a "Sputnik moment" for America. Beijing, however, has called upon the United States to practise what it preaches in terms of cybersecurity, especially in light of the 2013 Edward Snowden scandal. Snowden, a junior analyst from the American Central Intelligence Agency (CIA), flew to Hong Kong and revealed a wide scope of US surveillance activity on a domestic and global scale, sometimes in conjunction with the four other members of the "Five Eyes" (FVEY) intelligence coalition (Australia, Canada, New Zealand, United Kingdom), before travelling to Moscow. One February 2013 editorial in the *People's Daily* likened American policy to cybersecurity as "a thief crying 'stop thief'". [73] However, during the September 2015 summit between Obama and Xi, the two leaders pledged greater prevention of cyber attacks. The still-emerging area of cybersecurity appears to be emerging as another arena for Sino-American security rivalry.

The new security concept and future trends

The development of "new thinking" on security and cooperation on Beijing's part since the 1990s emanated from Chinese displeasure at the methods employed by other great powers, especially those in the West, to assure their security since the end of the Cold War. For example, a 1997 editorial in the *Beijing Review* noted that standard security practices among states included the creation of alliances designed to counter a mutual enemy, large powers protecting smaller ones, and weaker states deferring to stronger ones. [74] Moreover, the security of states and state cooperation was traditionally seen as being "incompatible" since measures taken by one country to better protect itself invariably created insecurities in others, a nod to the Western international relations concept of the "security dilemma". However, the piece argued that at the close of the twentieth century, states' security interests had become so intertwined that it was necessary to approach the ideas of security and cooperation from a different, more conciliatory standpoint. These concerns were expressed within Beijing's 1998 White Paper on Security, which specified that, "To obtain lasting peace, it is imperative to abandon the Cold War mentality, cultivate a new concept of security and seek a new way to safeguard peace." [75] This became the cornerstone of what came to be known as the "New Security Concept" or NSC (*xin anquan guandian* 新安全观点).

The NSC, which was first developed at the ARF summit in 1996 and later promoted by Jiang Zemin, draws heavily on the Five Principles of Peaceful Coexistence (mutual respect for sovereignty and territory, non-aggression, non-interference in internal affairs, equality and mutual benefit, and peaceful co-existence).[76] The Five Principles have their origins in talks between China, Burma and India in the 1950s as means were sought to promote peaceful interaction between states with different social systems in ways which discouraged alliances or bloc mindsets, which the states agreed often led to mistrust and conflict. Chinese Premier Zhou Enlai was credited with their incorporation into Chinese foreign policy doctrine in the mid-1950s. The Five Principles were also praised by China for their flexibility and resiliency, since they were adaptable to both Cold War and post-Cold War strategic interactions.[77]

Indeed, the Five Principles experienced a renaissance of sorts in the late 1980s and early 1990s as a result of international efforts led by the United States and the West towards humanitarian intervention, exemplified tacitly by the first Gulf War and more overtly by interventions in the former Yugoslavia, Somalia and Haiti during the 1990s. China's response to this international trend was that humanitarian intervention had the potential of damaging international law and giving a green light to strong countries wishing to impose their views on weaker ones. The Five Principles and later the NSC could therefore be seen as a firewall against such abuses.

A major facet of China's New Security Concept has been an obvious preference for security communities over alliances. Beijing has been increasingly hostile to the American preference for security alliances and has frequently noted that such cooperation is increasingly outmoded in the post-Cold War era.[78] Although relations between Beijing and NATO have improved somewhat, China's suspicion of this organisation has persisted since the accidental NATO bombing of the Chinese embassy in Belgrade in 1999, touching off widespread protests against the United States. China is also concerned about the possibility that American strategic partnerships with Japan, Australia, the Philippines, South Korea and Singapore might eventually lead to a more formal US-led security alliance in the Pacific,[79] concerns which resurfaced after the US "pivot" policy began to coalesce in 2011.

Instead, China has insisted that ideal regional strategic cooperation should be in the form of security communities. Unlike alliances, which are strongly hierarchical and designed to create alignment against an adversary, security communities are based on shared strategic interests, mutual cooperation and respect for sovereignty, joint development,

---

Box 5.3 The new security concept

"After the Cold War, the international situation has become characterized by relaxed international relations and growing world economy. Under the new historical conditions, the meaning of the security concept has evolved to be multifold with its contents extending from military and political to economic, science and technology, environment, culture and many other areas. The means to seek security are being diversified. Strengthening dialogue and cooperation is regarded as the fundamental approach to common security. The September 11 incident has glaringly demonstrated that security threats in today's world tend to be multi-faceted and global in scope. Countries share greater common security interests and are more interdependent on one another for security."

– *China's Position Paper on the New Security Concept*, 31 July 2002.

and nonalignment against a third party.[80] China has also called for security communities which incorporate other shared interests, such as economic and cultural cooperation, and which are "anarchic" in construction, meaning that every member has a *de facto* veto and decisions are made by consensus. Since the 1990s, China has sought to build security communities in Asia, making use of regimes like APEC and the East Asian Summit, and being the force behind the creation of the Shanghai Cooperation Organisation. In China's view, alliances turn security into a zero-sum game, while security communities using the NSC model create potential "positive-sum" outcomes, with all actors benefiting from peaceful discourse.

China has also softened its stance on the question of multilateral security and intervention, under specific conditions. During much of the Cold War as China was shut out of the UN, Beijing tended to view UN peacekeeping efforts as mere tools of the great powers, an impression not helped by the Korean War. However, with the growing recognition that many security issues, including terrorism and maritime security, are too large and complex for single states to address, Beijing has warmed to the idea that there are good and bad forms of multilateral security cooperation and intervention. China's views on current multilateral intervention are that such operations are best undertaken via the United Nations and within the boundaries of international law.[81] Both the NATO operations in Yugoslavia and the US-led Iraq intervention were criticised by China for going outside of UN mandates, and the country has been resistant to the use of force in both the Iran and the North Korea cases, and was highly critical of the NATO involvement in Libya during the civil war in 2011, which resulted in the fall of the Gaddafi regime but destabilised the country to the point where fighting erupted again in 2014.

However, China was supportive of the UN peacekeeping missions in Cambodia and East Timor (now Timor-Leste), even though both missions in theory set a precedent regarding interference in another state's internal security affairs. This view stood in marked contrast to Beijing's hostility over military intervention in Kosovo in 1999, which bypassed the UN and was conducted under the leadership of NATO.[82] China has also supplied observers and troops to UN peacekeeping missions including in the Democratic Republic of the Congo, Cambodia, Lebanon, Liberia, South Sudan, Sudan and Timor-Leste. China also supplied UN personnel to Haiti despite that country recognising Taiwan, and eight Chinese UN personnel lost their lives and were recognised as martyrs in the wake of a January 2010 earthquake. In June 2013, China took the additional step of agreeing to supply regular forces to assist with security as part of UN peacekeeping operations in Mali, although the preferred term from Chinese officials was "comprehensive security forces", and made a similar commitment to supply combat forces in South Sudan in December of that year.

As of May 2015, China had slightly more than 3000 personnel stationed abroad under the UN, the largest number of the UNSC's permanent five members. After many decades of uncertainty towards UN operations, under the Hu Jintao government China began to express great enthusiasm for the role of the UN in international security roles, including peacekeeping, a tradition which has continued under Xi Jinping, who in September 2015 committed another eight thousand Chinese personnel for peacekeeping missions during a speech at the UN. As well, Chinese participation in UN missions has allowed the country to diversify its strategic interests and demonstrate its support for non-traditional security cooperation, especially in the developing world.

China's evolving security policy has been one of pragmatism since the turn of the century and rests on several key ideas. These have included an expansion of China's strategic interests from the regional to the international, greater enthusiasm for cooperation with

---

Box 5.4 China's changed views on peacekeeping

"Since the end of the Cold War, Chinese participation in all UN debates and activities on peacekeeping issues has been more active. It has also tried to influence the process of decision-making regarding UN operations. The Chinese delegation to the UN has consistently affirmed the government's position that China attaches great importance to the success of peacekeeping operations."

– Pang Zhongying, "China's Changing Attitude to UN Peacekeeping,"
International Peacekeeping 12(1) (Spring 2005): 92.

"As China becomes more visible in peacekeeping, expectations grow for China to show dexterity in policy areas on which it was formerly mute or inflexible. Also, unlike states that have alternative security platforms to deploy peacekeepers, through NATO or the EU for instance, China remains committed to engaging the UN peacekeeping regime as its sole mechanism to bolster international peace and security."

– Courtney J. Richardson, "A Responsible Power? China and the UN
Peacekeeping Regime", *China's Evolving Approach to Peacekeeping*, ed. Marc
Lanteigne and Miwa Hirono (London and New York: Routledge, 2012), 44.

---

multilateral strategic regimes under select circumstances, creating bilateral and regional partnerships through strategic and non-strategic dialogues designed to promote trust and understanding, expanding regional economic linkages with the idea that mutual prosperity greatly contributes to peaceful development, and removing distrust while lessening the security dilemma with other states. However, as China's military spending increases and its capabilities and interest continue to expand further beyond East Asia, the question is whether Chinese strategic interests and those of other states, including the United States, will be complementary or competitive. The underlying question is whether China will retain a conservative, pro-status quo strategy as it continues to mature as a great power and addresses the current deficiencies in its military strength.

Discussion questions

- What are the major differences in China's security thinking between the Maoist era, the Dengist reforms, and the current post-Dengist era?
- How have China's views on nuclear weapons changed between the Cold War and post-Cold War periods?
- What role does the People's Liberation Army play in China's current foreign and defence policy?
- What accounts for Beijing's increasingly positive views on multilateral cooperation on security issues?
- How has "non-traditional security" affected China's current strategic thinking?
- How has China responded to more high-technology strategic threats?
- What are China's most crucial future security concerns?

Recommended reading

Austin, Greg. *Cyber Policy in China* (Cambridge, UK and Malden, MA: Polity Press, 2014).

Cheung, Tai Ming (ed.). *Forging China's Military Might: A New Framework for Assessing Innovation* (Baltimore: Johns Hopkins University Press, 2014).

Coker, Christopher. *The Improbable War: China, The United States, and the Origins of Great Power Conflict* (London: Hurst, 2015).

De Guttry, Andrea, Emanuele Sommario and Lijiang Zhu (eds). *China's and Italy's Participation in Peacekeeping Operations: Existing Models, Emerging Challenges* (Lanham and Boulder: Lexington Books, 2014).

Erickson, Andrew S., Lyle J. Goldstein and Nan Li (eds). *China, the United States and 21st-Century Sea Power* (Annapolis, MD: Naval Institute Press, 2010).

Fisher, Richard D., Jr. *China's Military Modernisation: Building for Regional and Global Reach* (Stanford: Stanford Security Studies, 2010).

Fravel, M. Taylor. *Strong Borders, Secure Nation: Cooperation and Conflict in China's Territorial Disputes* (Princeton and Oxford: Princeton University Press, 2008).

Goldstein, Lyle. *Meeting China Halfway: How to Defuse the Emerging US–China Rivalry* (Washington DC: Georgetown University Press, 2015).

Guo, Xuezhi. *China's Security State: Philosophy, Evolution and Politics* (New York: Cambridge University Press, 2014).

Haddick, Robert. *Fire on the Water: China, America and the Future of the Pacific* (Annapolis, MD: Naval Institute Press, 2014).

Lanteigne, Marc and Miwa Hirono (eds). *China's Evolving Approach to Peacekeeping* (London and New York: Routledge, 2012).

Lewis, Jeffrey. *The Minimum Means of Reprisal: China's Search for Security in the Nuclear Age* (Cambridge and London: MIT Press, 2007).

Lewis, John Wilson and Xue Litai. *Imagined Enemies: China Prepares for Uncertain War* (Stanford: Stanford University Press, 2006).

Lindsay, John R., Tai Ming Cheung and Derek S. Reveron (eds). *China and Cybersecurity: Espionage, Strategy and Politics in the Digital Domain* (Oxford and New York: Oxford University Press, 2015).

McReynolds, Joe (ed.). *China's Evolving Military Strategy* (Washington DC: Jamestown Foundation, 2015).

Nathan, Andrew J. and Andrew Scobell. *China's Search for Security* (New York and Chichester, UK: Columbia University Press, 2012).

Parello-Plesner, Jonas and Mathieu Duchâtel. *China's Strong Arm: Protecting Citizens and Assets Abroad* (London: IISS Routledge, 2015).

Rosecrance, Richard and Steven E. Miller (eds). *The Next Great War? The Roots of World War I and the Risk of U.S.–China Conflict* (Cambridge, MIT Press, 2014).

You, Ji. *China's Military Transformation* (London: Polity Press, 2015).

Yu, Yin. *Fighting for Peace: Narratives of Chinese Forces on UN Peacekeeping Missions' Frontlines* (Beijing: China Intercontinental Press, 2011).

Notes

1 Avery Goldstein, *Rising to the Challenge: China's Grand Strategy and International Security* (Stanford: Stanford University Press, 2005), 29–30.
2 "The Guidelines for U.S.–Japan Defense Cooperation April 27, 2015," United States Department of Defense, April 2015, <http://www.defense.gov/pubs/20150427_--_GUIDELINES_FOR_US–JAPAN_DEFENSE_COOPERATION.pdf>.
3 Peter Zarrow, *China in War and Revolution: 1895–1949* (Milton Park, UK and London: Routledge, 2005), 279.
4 "Asia," *The Military Balance 2015* 115(1) (March 2015): 237.
5 Xiaobing Li, *A History of the Modern Chinese Army* (Lexington: University Press of Kentucky, 2007), 2.

6 "Sophisticated Equipment Helps PLA to Fight Floods," *Xinhua*, 11 July 2007; "China Says 50,000 troops Mobilised for Quake Rescue Operation," *Xinhua / BBC Monitoring*. 14 May 2008.

7 Dennis J. Blasko, *The Chinese Army Today: Tradition and Transformation in the 21st Century* (Milton Park, UK and New York: Routledge, 2006), 16–30.

8 Richard Baum, *Burying Mao: Chinese Politics in the Age of Deng Xiaoping* (Princeton: Princeton University Press, 1994), 88; Andrew Scobell, *China's Use of Military Force: Beyond the Great Wall and the Long March* (Cambridge and New York: Cambridge University Press, 2003), 138–40.

9 Joseph Fewsmith, "China's Defence Budget: Is there Impending Friction between Defence and Civilian Needs?" *Civil–Military Relations in Today's China: Swimming in a New Sea*, ed. David M. Finkelstein and Kristen Gunness (Armonk, NY and London: M.E. Sharpe, 2007), 203–6.

10 David Shambaugh, *Modernising China's Military: Progress, Problems and Prospects* (Berkeley, Los Angeles and London: University of California Press, 2002), 69–89.

11 Susan Shirk, *China: Fragile Superpower* (Oxford and New York: Oxford University Press, 2007), 73–4.

12 Dali L. Yang, *Remaking the Chinese Leviathan: Market Transition and the Politics of Governance in China* (Stanford: Stanford University Press, 2004), 134–40.

13 James Mulvenon, "Soldiers of Fortune, Soldiers of Misfortune: Commercialisation and Divestiture of the Chinese Military–Business Complex, 1978–99," *Remaking the Chinese State: Strategies, Society and Security*, ed. Chien-min Chao and Bruce J. Dickson (London and New York: Routledge, 2001), 204–27.

14 For example, see "US Forces Chief in Japan Says China's Military Intent Unclear," *Agence France-Presse*, 14 April 2008.

15 "Full Text: The Diversified Employment of China's Armed Forces," *Xinhua*, 16 April 2013, < http://news.xinhuanet.com/english/china/2013-04/16/c_132312681.htm>.

16 "China's Military Strategy," *The State Council Information Office of the People's Republic of China*, May 2015, Beijing.

17 Edward Wong and Chris Buckley, "China's Military Budget Increasing 10% for 2015, Official Says," *The New York Times*, 4 March 2015.

18 "Military Expenditure (% of GDP)," *The World Bank*, June 2015, <http://data.worldbank.org/indicator/MS.MIL.XPND.GD.ZS>.

19 Lyle J. Goldstein, "When China was a 'Rogue State': The Impact of China's Nuclear Weapons Program on US–China Relations during the 1960s," *Journal of Contemporary China* 12(37) (November 3003): 746.

20 John Wilson Lewis and Xue Litai, *China Builds the Bomb* (Stanford: Stanford University Press, 1988), 186–9; Evan S. Medeiros, *Reluctant Restraint: The Evolution of China's Nonproliferation Policies and Practices, 1980–2004* (Stanford: Stanford University Press, 2007), 71.

21 Stockholm International Peace Research Institute (SIPRI), "Facts on International Relations and Security Trends – China," June 2012, <http://first.sipri.org/search?country=CHN&category=nuclear-explosions+nuclear-forces&dataset=nuclear-explosions&dataset=nuclear-forces>.

22 "Nuclear Weapons are to Scare People, Not to Use," *Mao Zedong On Diplomacy* (Beijing: Foreign Languages Press, 1998), 364–5.

23 George H. Quester, "The Continuing Debate on Minimal Deterrence," *The Absolute Weapon Revisited: Nuclear Arms and the Emerging International Order*, ed. T.V. Paul, Richard J. Harknett and James J. Wirtz (Ann Arbor: University of Michigan Press, 2000), 180–3.

24 Morton H. Halparin, "China and the Bomb – Chinese Nuclear Strategy," *China under Mao: Politics Takes Command*, ed. Roderick MacFarquar (Cambridge, MA and London, England: MIT Press, 1966), 449–61.

25 William Burr and Jeffrey T. Richelson, "Whether to 'Strangle the Baby in the Cradle': The United States and the Chinese Nuclear Program, 1960–64," *International Security* 25(30) (Winter 2000/01): 54–99.

26 "Nuclear Forces Reduced While Modernizations Continue, Says SIPRI," *Stockholm International Peace Research Institute*, 16 June 2014, <http://www.sipri.org/media/pressreleases/2014/nuclear_May_2014>.

27 "Asia," *The Military Balance 2015* 115(1) (2015): 237–8.

28 Evan S. Medeiros, *Reluctant Restraint*, 32.

29 Lanxin Xiang, "Washington's Misguided China Policy," *Survival* 43(3) (Autumn 2001): 15–16.
30 Andrew Scobell, "Show of Force: Chinese Soldiers, Statesmen, and the 1995–96 Taiwan Straits Crisis," *Political Science Quarterly* 115(2) (Summer 2000): 241.
31 Andrew Scobell, *China's Use of Military Force: Beyond the Great Wall and the Long March* (Cambridge and New York: Cambridge University Press, 2003), 46–9.
32 Shambaugh, *Modernizing China's Military*, 62–6.
33 John Wilson Lewis and Xue Litai, *Imagined Enemies: China Prepares for Uncertain War* (Stanford: Stanford University Press, 2006), 29–34.
34 Blasko, The Chinese Army Today, 12; Nan Li, "The PLA's Evolving Warfighting Doctrine: Strategy and Tactics, 1985–95: A Chinese Perspective," *The China Quarterly* 146 (June 1996): 443–63; "China's National Defence in 2004," Information Office of the State Council, of the People's Republic of China, Beijing, December 2004, <http://www.china.org.cn/e-white/20041227/III.htm#3>.
35 You Ji, *The Armed Forces of China* (London and New York: I.B. Tauris, 1999), 186–93; Leszek Buszynski, "Russia and Northeast Asia: Aspirations and Reality," *Pacific Review* 13(3) (August 2000): 406.
36 Greg Torode, "Carrier-Killer Missile May Give China Powerful Edge," *South China Morning Post*, 15 July 2011; Jeremy Page, "China's New Stealth Jet Reveals Itself on the Runway," *Wall Street Journal*, 5 January 2011; Dave Majumdar, "China vs. America in the Sky: A Stealth-Fighter Showdown Is Brewing," *The National Interest*, 14 November 2014, < http://nationalinterest.org/feature/china-vs-america-the-sky-stealth-fighter-showdown-brewing-11676>.
37 Michael O'Hanlon, "Why China Cannot Conquer Taiwan," *International Security* 25(2) (Fall 2000): 51–86.
38 Joshua P. Roawn, "The US–Japan Security Alliance, ASEAN, and the South China Sea Dispute," *Asian Survey* 45(3) (May / June 2005): 414–36.
39 Eric A. McVadon, "The Reckless and the Resolute: Confrontation in the South China Sea,' *China Security* 5(2) (Spring 2009): 1–15.
40 "Vietnam Urged to Stop Sovereignty Violation," *China Daily*, 6 June 2011; "Vietnam Condemns China's Sea Claims as 'Serious Violation'," *Reuters*, 4 December 2012; Emile Kok-Kheng Yoh, "Nationalism, Historical Consciousness and Regional Stability: Rising China as a Regional Power and Its New Assertiveness in the South China Sea," *Interpreting China as a Regional and Global Power*, ed. Bart Dessein (Basingstoke, UK and New York: Palgrave, 2014), 197–8.
41 Song Yen Ling and Dao Dang Toan, "Vietnam against CNOOC South China Sea Block Offer," *Platts Oilgram News*, 28 June 2012; "Vietnam Enacts Maritime Law as Tension High with China over So. China Sea," *Platts Commodity News*, 16 July 2012; "China Urges Vietnam to Correct Erroneous Maritime Law," *Xinhua*, 22 June 2012.
42 Sean O'Connor and James Hardy, "Imagery Shows Progress of Chinese Land Building Across Spratlys," *IHS Jane's*, 15 February 2015, < http://www.janes.com/article/48984/imagery-shows-progress-of-chinese-land-building-across-spratlys>; Jeremy Page and Julian E. Barnes, "China Expands Maritime 'Fortresses'," *Wall Street Journal*, 19 February 2015.
43 "Speech by Commander, U.S. Pacific Fleet Australian Strategic Policy Institute Canberra, Australia Admiral Harry B. Harris Jr.," 31 March 2015, *Commander, US Pacific Fleet*, <http://www.cpf.navy.mil/leaders/harry-harris/speeches/2015/03/ASPI-Australia.pdf>; James Hardy and Sean O'Connor, "China's First Runway in Spratlys under Construction," *IHS Jane's*, 16 April 2015, <http://www.janes.com/article/50714/china-s-first-runway-in-spratlys-under-construction>; "US Navy: Beijing Creating a 'Great Wall of Sand' in South China Sea," *The Guardian / Associated Press*, 31 March 2015, <http://www.theguardian.com/world/2015/mar/31/china-great-wall-sand-spratlys-us-navy>.
44 Yuka Hayashi and Jeremy Page, "Japan Prosecutors Release Chinese Boat Captain," *Wall Street Journal*, 25 September 2010; Thomas J. Christensen, "The Advantages of an Assertive China," *Foreign Affairs* Vol.90, No.2 (March/April 2011): 54–67.
45 Gabriel Dominguez, "How China is Transforming the South China Sea," *Deutsche Welle*, 20 February 2015, < http://www.dw.de/how-china-is-transforming-the-south-china-sea/a-18271485>.
46 International Crisis Group, "Stirring Up the South China Sea," *Asia Report* No. 223 (April 2012); Anton Lee Wishik II, "An Anti-Access Approximation: The PLA's Active Strategic Counterattacks on Exterior Lines," *China Security* 19(2011): 37–48.

47   James R. Holmes and Toshi Yoshihara, "The Influence of Mahan upon China's Maritime Strategy," *Comparative Strategy* 24(1) (January 2005): 23–51; Gordon Fairclough, "Surface Tensions: As China Grows, So Does Its Long-Neglected Navy," *Wall Street Journal*, 16 July 2007, A1.

48   Eric Talmadge, "Chinese Satellite Kill Challenges US Vow to Dominate Space," *Associated Press*, 13 April 2007.

49   William J. Broad and David E. Sanger, "Flexing Muscle, China Destroys Satellite in Test," *The New York Times*, 19 January 2007; Eric Hagt, "China's ASAT Test: Strategic Response," *China Security* (Winter 2007): 31–51. On costly signals, see Jeffrey W. Taliaferro, "Security Seeking under Anarchy: Defensive Realism Revisited," *International Security* 25(3) (Winter 2000/01): 146–7.

50   M. Taylor Fravel, "Power Shifts and Escalation: Explaining China's Use of Force in Territorial Disputes," *International Security* 32(3) (Winter 2007/2008): 68–9.

51   John Duffield, "Why is There No APTO? Why is There No OSCAP? Asia-Pacific Security Institutions in Comparative Perspective," *Contemporary Security Policy* 22(2) (August 2001): 69–95.

52   Marc Lanteigne, *China and International Institutions: Alternate Paths to Global Power* (London and New York: Routledge, 2005), 90–4; David Shambaugh, "China Engages Asia: Reshaping the Regional Order," *International Security* 29(3) (Winter 2004/2005): 87.

53   Tomohiko Taniguchi, "A Cold Peace: The Changing Security Equation in Northeast Asia," *Orbis* 49(3) (Summer 2005): 445–57.

54   Brian L. Job, "Track 2 Diplomacy: Ideational Contribution to the Evolving Asia Security Order," *Asian Security Order: Instrumental and Normative Features*, ed. Muthiah Alagappa (Stanford: Stanford University Press, 2003), 241–79.

55   Desmond Ball, Anthony Miller and Brendan Taylor, "Track 2 Security Dialogue in the Asia-Pacific: Reflections and Future Directions," *Asian Security* 2(3) (2006): 177.

56   Thomas J. Christensen, "Fostering Stability or Creating a Monster? The Rise of China and US Policy towards East Asia," *International Security* 31(1) (Summer 2006): 81–126; Christian Caryl, "America's Unsinkable Fleet," *Newsweek*, 5 November 2007.

57   "Chinese President Explains Views on Anti-Terrorism, APEC Financial Cooperation," *Xinhua*, 27 October 2002.

58   Denny Roy, "China and the War on Terrorism," *Orbis* 46(3) (Summer 2002): 511–21.

59   Andrew Scobell, "Terrorism and Chinese Foreign Policy," *China Rising: Power and Motivation in Chinese Foreign Policy*, ed. Yong Deng and Fei-ling Wang (Lanham and Boulder: Rowman & Littlefield, 2005), 305.

60   Andrew Scobell, "Terrorism and Chinese Foreign Policy", 317; Russell Ong, "China's Security Interests in Central Asia," *Central Asian Survey* 24(4) (December 2005): 429–30.

61   "Olympics: Facts on East Turkestan Islamic Movement," *Agence France-Presse,* 3 August 2008; "Chinese Media Says Banned ETIM Group 'Likely' Behind Attack," *Agence France-Presse*, 5 August 2008.

62   Bates Gill, *Rising Star: China's New Security Diplomacy* (Washington DC: Brookings, 2007), 129; Colin Mackerras, "Some Issues of Ethnic and Religious Identity among China's Islamic Peoples," *Asian Ethnicity* 6(1) (February 2005): 3–18; Nickolas Swanström, "China and Central Asia: A New Great Game or Traditional Vassal Relations?" *Journal of Contemporary China* 14(45) (November 2005): 573.

63   Gill, *Rising Star*, 124–32.

64   "China's National Defence in 2006," Information Office of the State Council of the People's Republic of China, Beijing, December 2006, <http://www.china.org.cn/english/features/book/194486.htm>.

65   "Keeping Cargo Safe: Container Security Initiative," *US Customs and Border Protection*, available at http://www.customs.treas.gov; Donna J. Nincic, "The Challenge of Maritime Terrorism: Threat Identification, WMD and Regime Response," *Journal of Strategic Studies* 28(4) (August 2005): 635; "US–China Counterterrorism Cooperation: Issues for US Policy," *CRS Report for Congress*, June 27, 2006, available at http://fpc.state.gov; Lanteigne, "China's Maritime Security", 156.

66   Chien-peng Chung, "China and the Institutionalisation of the Shanghai Cooperation Organisation," *Problems of Post-Communism* 53(5) (September / October 2006): 3.

67   Marc Lanteigne, "*In Medias Res*: The Development of the Shanghai Cooperation Organization as a Security Community," *Pacific Affairs* 79(4) (Winter 2006/2007): 605–22.

68 Marc Lanteigne, "China's Maritime Security and the 'Malacca Dilemma'," *Asian Security* 4(2) (May 2008): 143–61.

69 John R. Lindsay, "The Impact of China on Cybersecurity: Fiction and Friction," *International Security* 39(3) (Winter 2014/15): 7–47.

70 David E. Sanger, David Barboza and Nicole Perlroth, "Chinese Army Unit Is Seen as Tied to Hacking Against U.S.," *The New York Times*, 18 February 2013.

71 Shannon Tiezzi, "China (Finally) Admits to Hacking," *The Diplomat*, 18 March 2015, <http://thediplomat.com/2015/03/china-finally-admits-to-hacking/>.

72 Bill Marczak, Nicholas Weaver, Jakub Dalek, Roya Ensafi, David Fifield, Sarah McKune, Arn Rey, John Scott-Railton, Ronald Deibert and Vern Paxson, "China's Great Cannon", *CitizenLab, Munk Centre of Global Affairs, University of Toronto*, 10 April 2015, <https://citizenlab.org/2015/04/chinas-great-cannon/>; "PLA Daily Warns of Internet's Revolutionary Potential," *Xinhua*, 20 May 2015, <http://news.xinhuanet.com/english/2015-05/20/c_134254845.htm>.

73 Zhong Sheng, "The United States Bears Primary Responsibility for Stopping Cyber War," *People's Daily*, 7 February 2013; Patrick F. Walsh and Seumas Miller, "Rethinking 'Five Eyes' Security Intelligence Collection Policies and Practice Post Snowden," *Intelligence and National Security* (January 2015): 1–24.

74 A. Ying, "New Security Mechanism Needed for Asian-Pacific Region," *Beijing Review* (August 18–24, 1997): 6–7.

75 "China's National Defence" (White Paper), Information Office of the State Council, of the People's Republic of China, Beijing, July 1998, <http://www.china.org.cn/e-white/5/5.1.htm>.

76 Russell Ong, *China's Security Interests in the 21st Century* (London and New York: Routledge, 2007), 12–14.

77 "4–3 Excerpt from the Speech by Premier Zhou Enlai at the Plenary Session of the Asian–African Conference, April 19, 1955," *On the Five Principles of Peaceful Coexistence* (Beijing: China Institute of International Studies / World Affairs Press, 2004), 555–6.

78 David M. Finkelstein, "China's 'New Concept of Security'," *The People's Liberation Army and China in Transition*, ed. Stephen J. Flanagan and Michael E. Marti (Washington, DC: National Defence University Press, 2003), 197–209.

79 Bates Gill, "China's Evolving Regional Security Strategy," *Power Shift: China and Asia's New Dynamics*, ed. David Shambaugh (Berkeley, Los Angeles and London: University of California Press, 2005), 261–2.

80 Emanuel Adler and Michael Barnett, "Security Communities in Theoretical Perspective," *Security Communities*, ed. Emanuel Adler and Michael Barnett (Cambridge and New York: Cambridge University Press, 1998), 3–28.

81 Pang Zhongying, "China's Changing Attitude towards UN Peacekeeping," *International Peacekeeping* 12(1) (March 2005): 87–104; David Lampton, *The Three Faces of Chinese Power*, 62–4.

82 Bates Gill and James Reilly, "Sovereignty, Intervention and Peacekeeping: The View from Beijing," *Survival* 42(3) (Autumn 2000): 48–50.

6 The United States views China (and China views the United States)

"A new type of great power relations"

From the time of the Sino-American *rapprochement* between Mao Zedong and US President Richard Nixon in the early 1970s, and the United States' official recognition of the People's Republic in 1979, the Sino-American relationship between China and the United States has experienced a number of diplomatic highs and lows. While respecting each other's importance in the post-Cold War era, each of the two states is also concerned about the long-term foreign policy intentions of the other, especially as China continues to develop as a great power. Since the 1990s, China's rise has led to divisions within American policymaking and academic circles concerning how Washington should address the growth of Chinese power. Since Xi Jinping assumed power in 2012 and with the expansion of China's foreign policy interest during his first years in office, these divisions among China-watchers in the US have, if anything, grown wider.

In China, there have also been concerns expressed as to whether the United States can accept China as a great power, especially in light of the larger question of whether American power, at least in the Asia-Pacific region, is waning. For example, in a June 2015 editorial in China's *People's Daily*, written during a time of sharp policy differences between Beijing and Washington over the South China Sea sovereignty issue, it was argued that "the relationship between China and the US has, like the coin, an upside and a downside... Over the last few decades, Sino-US relations have even in the midst of complications gone forward, and even when fragile the relations have shown resilience." However, the piece added that, "one should never take this resilience for granted, since areas of weakness also play a major part in the relationship. The areas of weakness root from the hard-headedness of the US".[1] Just as the "China debate" has evolved in the US, so has the "America debate" within China. The two countries continue to enjoy a strong trading relationship, and share interests in a variety of areas related to diplomacy and strategy, and yet the question of these two states adjusting to the narrowing power gaps between them is becoming one of the most important in international relations.

Those who argue that the US–China relationship can, and should, remain stable point to the increasing dependence, politically and economically, each side has upon the other. This stands in contrast to the US–Soviet relationship in the twentieth century, where both sides faced off not only in the military sphere but also in the ideological and the institutional. At the same time, there is the argument that China will continue to find common ground with the United States on several issues. These issues include economic cooperation, improving the health of global markets since the post-2008 recession, international security issues such as the threat of global terrorism and trans-national crime, and the prevention of civil and interstate conflict in many parts of the world. Adherents to this thinking argue it would be in Beijing's interests as a great power to behave in a more conservative fashion with the United States, and vice versa, in order to better address mutual problems and threats. From a realist perspective, a great power conflict involving the United States and China would be unacceptably risky in the current nuclear era. Thus, the best option for Washington, it is argued, would be to encourage Chinese participation in global affairs and to seek common ground with Beijing in addressing them.

However, adherents to the "China Threat" theory school in the United States and elsewhere, namely those who argue for a high probability of Sino-American conflict as Chinese power grows, point to China's growing military budget, its increased confidence in the international arena, including in regions which were previously more exclusively linked to the West such as Africa and the Middle East, and China's potential to challenge American strategic interests, especially in the Asia-Pacific region. More recently, this school of thought has also highlighted Beijing's socio-political differences with Washington, pointing to nationalism concerns and differing views on individual rights, as well as growing economic differences based on American criticism of China's growing market power and the still-close relationship between the Chinese government and its large firms.[2] "China Threat" adherents also point to historical precedent, noting that states which rise towards great power status are often war-prone, as they seek a louder voice in international affairs and focus on protecting assets outside of their immediate territory.

There are also arguments that the policies of the United States and China differ widely on issues including human rights, democratisation, and intervention in the affairs of other states. At the same time, the realist theory of "power transition" is frequently cited to suggest a possible Chinese threat, arguing that there is a significant potential for violence when a rising dissatisfied power (China) challenges a satisfied great power (America). However, this theory is based upon the supposition that Beijing is sufficiently unhappy with the current international order to consider challenging, directly or indirectly, American power. This supposition is shaky at best, given that since the start of the country's reform era China has benefited greatly from the international system despite many institutions, rules and norms having been set down by the United States since the Second World War. Liberalist theories of international relations would suggest that the introduction of additional channels of communication between given states, both above and below the state level, increases the level of communication and reduces the possibility of misunderstandings and information gaps leading to conflict.

"China Threat" scholars have also pointed to the major diplomatic and economic gains which China has made in Africa, Latin America, Southeast Asia and Oceania, gains which have at times been made at the expense of American influence. Differences between the two states began to spill over into the economic realm even before the global recession began after 2008, as Washington began criticising Beijing for unfair trading practices benefiting Chinese manufacturers and also questioned the increasing amount of American currency which Beijing has purchased in recent years. However, the economic relationship between the two states has grown so close that it could be described not only as one of intense interdependence but even "symbiosis" as one publication suggested.[3] As well, there is a potential rivalry between the two big states over natural resources, including energy, as China increases its purchases of international supplies of oil and gas. "China Threat" adherents have often called for policies which attempt to limit Chinese growth as a great power, politically, economically and militarily, to avoid possible conflict with the US.

The theory of a potential power transition between the states, however, rests on zero-sum thinking in terms of how power is viewed in the modern international system, as well as the questionable idea that the only two options for the United States to deal with a rising China are to accept a power transition unconditionally or concentrate all efforts on preserving the status quo. However, a growing body of literature on the US–China relationship has explored the middle ground of accommodation and power sharing, especially in the Asia-Pacific region. *The China Choice* by Hugh White and *America's Challenge: Engaging a Rising China in the Twenty-first Century* by Michael Swaine are two examples. Another work, *Meeting China Halfway: How to Defuse the Emerging US–China Rivalry* by Lyle Goldstein, argues that many areas of Sino-American dispute, including the Taiwan question and East and Southeast Asian security, can be addressed through "cooperation spirals", a series of policies designed to develop greater confidence between the two parties and to reduce the risk of conflict. The idea of accommodation, while representing a middle path in the US–China debate, nonetheless raises its own questions about the degree and the areas in which the two countries are able and willing to share power.

This question became more pressing with the leadership of the Chinese government passing from Hu Jintao to Xi Jinping in 2012–3 and announcements made by the US government of Barack Obama in 2011–12 that America would be shifting a larger number of military assets to the Pacific region and promoting deeper engagement with US allies and partners in the Pacific Rim. So far, the results of this "pivot" or "rebalancing" policy have been uneven, largely due to pressure on the United States to address looming security concerns elsewhere, including in the Middle East (ISIL, civil conflicts in Libya, Syria and Yemen) and in Eastern Europe (the post-2014 Russia/Ukraine conflict and insecurity among US allies near the Russian frontier), as well as strains on the American military budget as a result of the country's economic troubles during the financial crisis. Nevertheless, the American commitment to "rebalancing" in the Asia-Pacific, and especially a stronger security commitment with Japan, have been interpreted in China and elsewhere to mean that Washington is interested in maintaining a strong strategic presence in Asia, possibly seeking to better balance Chinese power.

In June 2013, shortly after President Xi completed his transition into office, he met with President Obama at the Sunnylands Retreat in Palm Springs, California, where the two leaders held their first set of serious talks about the relationship as well as other pressing global affairs. In a press conference afterwards, President Xi noted that the Pacific Ocean has enough room for both China and the United States, suggesting that the two governments should work towards creating "a new type of great power relations" (*xinxing daguo guanxi* 新型大国关系).[4] This quote was especially indicative of the fact that unlike his predecessor, Xi Jinping was ready for, and comfortable with, expressing the Sino-American relationship as one among equals. As the United States began to move towards its pre-election season before the presidential vote in November 2016, China was already factoring into a great deal of foreign policy debate amongst the candidates.

This chapter will first analyse the course of the Sino-American relationship and then examine various interpretations of the relationship and possible outcomes accompanying China's rise. As will be demonstrated, although relations between China and the United States have greatly evolved since the days of complete isolation during the middle of the Cold War, the link between the two states continues to be defined by a series of diplomatic twists and turns. The growing confidence that Beijing has expressed as a great power under the Xi administration has only added to the overall complexity in the relationship.

Sino-US relations before the Cold War

The literal translation of the Chinese word for the United States, *Meiguo* (美国), is "beautiful country", and the term contributes much to illustrating the complicated relationship between the United States and China both before and after 1949. The first official contact between the United States and China occurred when the American vessel *Empress of China*, carrying a supply of ginseng from the US, arrived in the southern port of Canton (now Guangzhou), returning with Chinese black tea and initiating an expansion of American trade with Imperial China in 1784–5. Before achieving independence, the American colonies had been barred by Britain from direct trade with China, so the United States was anxious to make up for lost time. The result was a growing trade rivalry between Britain and her former colony in the region.[5]

After the First Opium War in 1842, the United States under President John Tyler was anxious to take advantage of the forced opening of Chinese ports and signed the 1844 Treaty of Wang-hsia, or Wangxia (*Wangxia tiaoyue* 望厦条约), the first Sino-American treaty, which permitted extensive use of five Chinese ports for American vessels, exclusive trading status, and groundbreaking special rights for American expatriates and traders. China was more than willing to make concessions, including permitting the construction of American hospitals and churches on Chinese soil, since the treaty was less "unequal" than treaties with European countries at the time, notably in comparison with the Treaty of Nanking (1842) and its supplementary document signed the following year, the Treaty of the Bogue (known in China as *Humen tiaoyue* 虎门条约), signed between the Qing Dynasty and the British Empire. The United States also accepted the view of the Qing government that opium trade should be declared illegal, and agreed that any Americans venturing outside of the treaty ports to engage in opium trade would be subject to Chinese imperial law.[6] However, as the 2015 book *The China Mirage* by James Bradley noted, profits from the opium trade could and did work their way into American businesses and institutions in the mid-eighteenth century. Nonetheless, for much of the nineteenth century the United States was seen as a more pragmatic friend to Chinese interests in comparison with the European great powers. As a former British colony, the US was largely viewed more sympathetically by Imperial China, and vice versa.

After the fall of the Qing Dynasty in 1911 and in the wake of China's subsequent descent into warlordism as well as growing Japanese occupation, the United States continued to treat China as a strategic ally. The US and Japan had originally found themselves on the same side in many Asian affairs during the First World War, supporting British and Japanese efforts to liberate German-held regions in China during the battles which later came to be known as the Siege of Tsingtao (Qingdao) in late 1914.[7] This was the only major battle of the First World War fought on Asian soil. Despite the success of the battles in uprooting German and Austro-Hungarian interests from China, Washington was growing increasingly concerned about the expansion of Japanese imperial power in the Asia-Pacific. After the Mukden (*Liutiaohu* 柳条湖) Incident in September 1931, involving a staged attack by Japanese armed forces in the northern Manchurian region of China, Imperial Japan had begun the process of establishing a permanent military presence in northern China, as well as a vassal state named Manchukuo.

After the start of the Sino-Japanese War in the wake of the Marco Polo / Lugou Bridge Incident in July 1937, and America's entry into the Pacific War against Japan after the Pearl Harbour attack in December 1941, Washington opted to ally itself specifically with the *Kuomintang* (Nationalists) under Chiang Kai-shek (Jiang Jieshi). This was despite periodic

American concerns about the ability of the Nationalists to successfully combat Japanese armed forces.[8] This decision further isolated the growing communist militants under Mao Zedong, who became convinced that the US was developing into an imperialist power little better than those in Europe.

In 1940, powerful American policymakers began to construct a pressure group advocating American support for Chiang, which later came to be known as the "China Lobby". This lobby group was made up of American officials and representatives who actively supported the policies of Chiang Kai-shek and the Kuomintang both before and after the Nationalists' decamping to Taiwan, as well as a peripheral, multifaceted group sympathetic to Chiang's policies.[9] Towards the end of the conflict, the United States attempted to promote a power-sharing agreement between Mao and Chiang, sending General George Marshall to China to mediate in January 1946. The talks were a complete failure, as neither side could be persuaded to trust the other. Nor were the Communists especially happy with the continuation of American arms shipments to the Nationalists under US President Harry Truman during the talks.[10] Mao insisted that he would be unable to initiate ties with the United States or other Western powers as long as they continued to support Chiang.

By 1949, Mao was directly attacking the perceived American policy of deceitful diplomacy designed to weaken the Communist movement and turn China into a US colony. Despite a last-ditch attempt, spearheaded by American diplomat Leighton Stuart, to reach some kind of accommodation with Mao allowing for recognition of the Communists, the differences could not be bridged and Mao began his policy of "leaning to one side", namely towards the Soviet camp. Thus began an era of a near-complete severing of direct communication between "Red China" and the United States, with each side relying on intermediaries for any information about the other. The China Lobby was furious at the KMT's fall in mainland China, and the addition of China into the pro-Soviet camp, and spearheaded an investigation into "Who lost China?" going as far as to suggest that pro-Communist supporters might be embedded in the American government, touching off a round of "red-baiting" political inquiries in the 1950s.[11] The first Taiwan Straits crises in the 1950s and the Korean War of 1950–3, which saw the US and China at direct military odds with each other, further intensified the diplomatic deep freeze.

Not only did the United States refuse to recognise the communist government in Beijing but it also strongly encouraged its allies in the West to do the same. There were however, some exceptions, as the United Kingdom, concerned about the safety of its colonies in Hong Kong and Southeast Asia and wanting to retain a communications link with Mainland China, opted to risk American displeasure and recognise the Maoist regime in January 1950.[12] Other Western European states who opted to recognise the People's Republic shortly after its founding included Denmark, Finland and Switzerland (1950) and Norway (1954). In 1964, another NATO ally, France, switched its recognition from the Nationalists to the Maoist government in China, and Canada and Italy did the same in 1970 before the People's Republic regained its seat at the United Nations the following year. It was only after the death of Soviet leader Joseph Stalin in 1953, and increasingly difficult Sino-Soviet relations with his successor, Nikita Khrushchev, that Mao began to consider pursuing warmer relations with the United States. Much of this decision was fuelled by political realism. In 1960, dismayed at Mao's launching of the radical Great Leap Forward policies, which the USSR saw as a twisting of communist ideals, Khrushchev began the process of withdrawing personnel and aid from China. The Maoist government found itself facing political isolation, and a difficult choice regarding whether to re-open the door to its old adversary in the West.

The path to Sino-American rapprochement

The decision taken in the early 1970s by US President Richard Nixon to re-open the door to the People's Republic was in many ways a result of *realpolitik* (practical political concerns; in Chinese the term is "realistic politics" or *xianshi zhengshi* 现实政治) rather than a matter of ideology. By the late 1960s the US had realised there was little chance of Moscow and Beijing mending fences, especially after China tested its first nuclear weapon in 1964, and that left China essentially isolated. As Nixon argued in his watershed 1967 *Foreign Affairs* article, it would be far more dangerous for the international community to continue to shun China and risk it turning into a revisionist power worse than the USSR, than to attempt to bring it back into the international community.[13] The idea did not sit well with many in his Republican party, especially the China Lobby, which was why the initial contacts with Mao in Beijing had to be undertaken covertly by Nixon and his National Security Advisor, Henry Kissinger. As Kissinger would note in his watershed 2011 book *On China*, Mao had also been laying the groundwork for a potential warming of US relations since the mid-1960s out of concern that isolation from both superpowers was an unacceptable security risk. Until 1968, the Chinese government continued to publically identify American imperialism as the "primary enemy" despite deteriorating relations with the USSR, with Moscow being referred to as the "secondary enemy". However, in the wake of the Soviet invasion of Czechoslovakia in August 1968 in order to halt the political liberalisation policies of the Alexander Dubček government, a process known in the West as the "Prague Spring", Chinese views on who should rightfully be considered the primary and secondary superpower enemies became less clear.[14]

Nixon was also hoping to defuse tensions over Taiwan and gain support for China's disengagement from the Vietnam conflict, a battle which at this point was growing deeply unpopular in the United States. The idea of America siding with China against the Soviet Union came to be known as playing the "China card", and Kissinger was initially widely credited, or blamed, for originating it. In his memoirs, Kissinger denies that he was the source of the idea, noting that his intention had been to improve relations with both communist giants. Instead, Michael Pillsbury, an analyst at Rand, a Washington-based strategic research institute, was seen as the source of the idea in the early 1970s.[15] There were high hopes in Washington that bringing Beijing closer to the United States would seriously compromise Soviet policy interests, especially in Asia.

There were, however, earlier signs of a thaw in Washington's China policy. For example, in December 1963, Roger Hilsman, a foreign policy advisor to both the Kennedy and Johnson administrations, made a speech which subtly advocated a strengthening of ties between the US and China. Although comparatively very tepid in its wording, it was subsequently viewed as the first public indication that Washington was open to the idea of breaking the diplomatic impasse between the two sides.[16] Other cracks in the wall between China and the United States appeared in less-traditional areas, including the "ping-pong diplomacy" (*pingpang waijiao* 乒乓外交) of the early 1970s which culminated in an American table-tennis team being invited to Beijing in 1971.[17]

The initial diplomatic breakthrough between Nixon and Mao, once the US president visited Beijing for the first time in February 1972, paved the way for gradually warming ties via the Shanghai Communiqué signed that year by Nixon and Chinese Premier Zhou Enlai. The document opposed the development of great power competition and the creation of spheres of influence in Asia. Most crucially for Beijing, the document included the American view that there was only one China and that Taiwan was a part of China, calling upon Beijing and Taipei to settle their differences peacefully. The visit and the communiqué were widely seen as further pulling China away from Soviet influence and dramatically changing the shape of the latter periods of the Cold War. Moreover, the fact that the visit was made by a US president who was renowned for his staunch opposition to communism further underscored the willingness of the United States to repair relations regardless of the political risks; hence the phrase, "only Nixon could go to China".

With the thawing of relations, China suddenly turned from an isolated country to a pivot state during the remainder of the Cold War. Despite the mistrust of Deng Xiaoping by Ronald Reagan in the 1980s, China remained a US ally, useful for checking Soviet activities in Afghanistan and South Asia. For example, after the USSR invaded Afghanistan in December 1979, Beijing assisted with American-backed arms sales to the Afghan *mujahadin* rebels seeking to defeat Soviet occupation.[18] Deng made his first visit to the United States in January 1979, despite the fact that, at least nominally, it was Hua Guofeng who had been designated Mao's official successor. In addition to meeting with President Jimmy Carter, he also toured a Coca-Cola factory in Atlanta, a space shuttle flight simulator in Houston, and a rodeo in a nearby town (the cowboy hat which he wore is now on display at the National Museum in Beijing). On a more serious note, Deng explained to Carter the need for China to send PLA forces over the border into Vietnam as punishment for Hanoi's decision to fully invade Cambodia in December 1978 and to oust the Khmer Rouge regime there, a move that China feared would solidify the hold of both Vietnam and the country's then-sponsor, the Soviet Union, on Indochina. The Carter administration did not support the brief invasion but did not condemn the action either.[19]

Nevertheless, during the early 1980s under the US presidency of Ronald Reagan the Sino-American relationship was largely held together by mutual antipathy towards Moscow. However, differences in foreign policy between the two sides frequently affected the relationship, especially the question of America's still-friendly policy toward Taiwan even though Washington had officially severed ties with the island after recognising Beijing in January 1979.[20] The Taiwan Relations Act, passed by the US Congress in April 1979, affirmed an ongoing commercial relationship between Washington and Taipei despite official recognition having been severed. By the end of the decade, China sought a more balanced position between the superpowers assisted greatly by the diplomatic overtures of the Soviet Union's last leader, Mikhail Gorbachev, after he assumed power in March 1985. By this time, China had experienced many years free of the diplomatic isolation of the Mao era and now began to develop more confidence in its diplomacy with both small and great powers.

The Tiananmen Incident of June 1989 resulted in China once more being isolated by the United States, ending any pretence of common diplomatic ground between the two sides. However, while economic ties between the two states were quick to recover, a ban on US weapons sales to Beijing remains in place. With the Soviet military withdrawal from Afghanistan in 1988–9, the fall of communism through much of Eastern Europe in 1989, and the breakup of the Soviet Union in 1991, China was no longer considered a partner

---

Box 6.1 "Just get on a plane and come"

"I welcome Nixon's winning the election. Why? There is a deceptive side of him as well, but there is less of it. Do you believe it? He is accustomed to use hard tactics, but sometimes also soft ones. If he wishes to come to Beijing, please tell him he should do it secretly, not openly – just get on a plane and come."

– Mao Zedong to journalist Edgar Snow, 18 December 1970.

and a buffer state by America, but rather as the largest remaining communist state and a looming revisionist power unhappy with the emerging post-Cold War unipolar order. At the same time, China's traditional views against global hegemony were sorely tested by the emergence of the United States as the lone global superpower. After the 1991 Gulf War, which demonstrated the superior weaponry of the US armed forces, there was talk by Bush of a "new world order", a phrase which Beijing rejected in favour of a "new international order" (*guoji xin zhixu* 国际新秩序) of a multipolar system rather than a unipolar one. However, as it became more obvious during the 1990s that the post-Cold War system was becoming more unipolar than multipolar, Chinese analysts began to speak of a "one superpower, many great powers" system (*yichao duoqiang* 超多强).[21] Concerns about US power and hegemonic behaviour would dominate Beijing's view of the United States in the years following the Cold War, while during the same period American attitudes toward China would go through several different phases.

The post-Cold War "containment versus engagement" question

The loss of China's status as a Cold War ally of the United States meant that several issues between the two states which could previously be successfully tabled, such as democratisation, the Taiwan question, human rights concerns, the status of the South China Sea and other matters suddenly resurfaced throughout much of the 1990s. It was during this time that the "China Threat" school rose to the fore in both academic and analytical areas, especially among realist scholars and commentators, as well as authors writing about the future of American power. For example, Samuel Huntington's controversial book *The Clash of Civilisations* (1996), which argued that future conflicts would be fought not over ideology but over "civilisational" fault lines, concluded with a hypothetical military scenario involving the United States versus China, and John Mearsheimer's *The Tragedy of Great Power Politics* (2001), examining the international relations theory of offensive realism, pointed to China's growing economic power which could readily be translated into military strength which might challenge the current international order.[22]

It was during the 1990s that the question of addressing China's rise assumed prominence among American policymakers. The issue of engagement versus containment was the core of this debate, which developed along with the "China Threat" School in the US. The containment option was viewed as a way of halting Chinese growth in power by adapting regional policies designed to deter China from developing a stronger regional and international power base. The idea resembles one proposed for the Soviet Union during the Cold War, and since the 1990s, Beijing has worried that the US is covertly attempting the same strategies. There have indeed been examples of American foreign policy behaviour since the early 1990s which have suggested a containment stance. For example, not only did the US not abandon its Cold War alliance with Japan, as a result of the USSR's fall, but instead strengthened it, affording Tokyo a more independent role in its security planning as a result of the 1996 agreement between then-leaders Bill Clinton and Ryutaro Hashimoto. As one scholar noted, the US–Japan relationship can act either as a "bottle cap", preventing Japanese re-armament, or an "eggshell", preparing Japan for an eventual fully independent military, one which could more effectively assist in countering China.[23] Beijing remains concerned that the United States is more accepting of the latter outcome. Since the 1990s the US also began to adapt warmer relations with India, Southeast Asia and states in the former Soviet Union, and deepened its strategic relationship with Australia, adding to concerns in Beijing about being ringed by pro-Western states.

> *Box 6.2* Power transitions
>
> "One of the reasons power transition theory continues to generate such interest is that it offers falsifiable expectations about the future of world politics. For example, if China continues to grow in power as it has for the past few decades, it will surpass the United States as the world's dominant power sometime before the middle of this century. Such overtakings among great powers have corresponded with the major wars of the past centuries. These two observations represent the most important strategic calculation of the twenty-first century."
>
> – Douglas Lemke and Ronald L. Tammen, "Power Transition Theory and the Rise of China", *International Relations* 29(4) (2003): 270.

The engagement option has been more complex, but has involved drawing China into existing regimes and international agreements in the hope of enmeshing Beijing in a complex network of international norms, making it much more difficult for China to challenge the status quo. This could be seen as a variation of so-called "sticky power" meaning the ability to bring states into complex regimes and organisations by promising benefits, and then once inside they cannot leave without incurring unacceptably high political or economic costs.[24] China would then become socialised within the international system and become a supporter of its processes. The engagement idea was seen by many analysts as a more pragmatic approach to China's rise, and today the idea of diplomatically or economically isolating China is believed to be unrealistic in light of the high levels of modern Chinese power.

Chinese nationalism and the United States

The United States has also been seen as a prime target for Chinese nationalism which on many occasions has had foreign policy dimensions. The 1990s and the first years of the 2000s saw many incidents and policy differences which added to Chinese nationalism, fed by concerns over US power. In July 1993, a Chinese cargo vessel, the *Milky Way* (*Yinhe* 银河), was halted by US warships in the Persian Gulf on the (mistaken) supposition that it was ferrying chemical weapons components to Iran, touching off diplomatic protests from Beijing.[25] Two years later, Washington and Beijing were at loggerheads over a US decision to permit Taiwanese president Lee Teng-hui to travel to America and make a speech at Cornell University, his *alma mater*. The relationship further deteriorated when in early 1996 Beijing initiated a series of missile exercises near Taiwan in the run-up to the island's first free elections, prompting two American aircraft carrier groups to approach the Taiwan Straits in a subtle balancing of power.[26] Sino-American tensions were increased in May 1999 when the Chinese Embassy in Belgrade, in the former Yugoslavia, was destroyed by an American bomber, killing three Chinese journalists, in the course of the NATO military campaign against the Yugoslavian government. The incident, blamed by the American government on faulty maps which mislabelled the building, touched off waves of anti-American protests in Chinese cities as well as widespread disbelief that the attack was accidental.[27] Even before the incident, China was unhappy at the NATO intervention because the United Nations Security Council, of which China is a permanent member with veto power, was bypassed in the decision to attack Yugoslavia.

Critical thinking about the United States and its political as well as socio-cultural roles in the post-Cold War world began to manifest itself within China during the 1990s. In 1996, a controversial and nationalist book appeared entitled *China Can Say No* (*Zhongguo keyi shuo bu* 中国可以说不) which was highly critical of American post-Cold War foreign policy, at one point accusing the US of acting like a "spoiled child" in the international arena.[28] The Chinese government did not directly comment on the work, although political writings in China are overseen by the government and this could have been interpreted by outside observers as further proof of worsening opinions of the United States. However, the book also came under heavy criticism within China, and there was a counter-argument published in 1998 entitled *China Should Not Be "Mr No"* (*Zhongguo bu dang 'Bu Xiansheng'* 中国不当'不先生') asserting that taking a rigid stance in international affairs and openly seeking to undermine international norms is exactly what hastened the end of the Soviet Union.[29] The fact that this book was also released without comment from the CCP suggested that the government was interested in getting a balance of opinions out into public discourse.

The status of the Sino-American relationship during the eight-year government of George W. Bush is difficult to summarise. He assumed office promising that Beijing would be treated as more of a strategic competitor than a partner and early events appeared to uphold that policy. Chief among these was the Hainan Incident of April 2001. On the first of that month, an American EP-3E *Aries* surveillance plane was challenged by two PLA Air Force J-8 fighter jets approximately 105 km from the southern Chinese island of Hainan. There was a collision between the US plane and one of the jets, causing the latter to fall into the Pacific Ocean and resulting in the loss of Wang Wei, the Chinese pilot. Heavily damaged, the American plane was forced to land at the PLA's Lingshui Airfield on the island, where the crew of 24 was taken into custody. This touched off a diplomatic incident lasting for 11 days as both sides blamed the other for the collision. Finally, Beijing was satisfied that the American government had adequately apologised for the incident after a letter was given to the Chinese Foreign Ministry from Washington which stated that the United States government expressed "great sympathy" (*feichang wanxi* 非常惋惜) for the loss of the Chinese pilot and was "extremely sorry" (*feichang baoqian* 非常報歉) that the American plane landed on Hainan without permission. However, the apology letter from the Bush government stopped short of using the word "*daoqian*" (道歉), which implied formal apologies and acceptance of blame. The return of the plane was a more complicated matter, as it was not released until July 2001 following extensive negotiations over costs and the participation of American personnel in recovering the plane.[30] This incident served to suggest that Sino-American relations at the turn of the century would continue to deteriorate, possibly to the level of a new type of Cold War.

11 September and after

Sino-American relations changed dramatically after the 11 September 2001 terrorist attacks in the United States by the *Al-Qaeda* terrorist group and the beginning of military operations in Afghanistan. President Bush visited Shanghai shortly after 9/11 to attend the annual Asia-Pacific Economic Cooperation (APEC) leadership conference, and soon afterwards the US and China signed agreements on sharing of information related to terrorist threats. Despite some reservations, China did not object to American military intervention in Afghanistan, begun by the end of the year, to topple the Taliban government there and destroy *Al-Qaeda* installations, even though this placed the American military very close to China's sensitive western borders.[31] As well, the Bush government agreed to grant China permanent favoured trade status in keeping with Beijing's membership in the WTO. In October 2002, Jiang Zemin was invited to meet the President at his ranch in Crawford, Texas, for talks which included mutual concerns about globalised terrorism as well as the deteriorating security situations in Iraq and North Korea. Not long after 9/11, Bush's original statements that China should be viewed as a "strategic competitor" were no longer heard. There were concerns in Beijing that the advent of the "Bush doctrine", which allowed for preventive conflict on the part of the United States, was a negative development for China's own security interests. However, despite these misgivings, the Jiang Zemin government opted to give its support to the US-led war on terror.[32]

The ongoing rise of China and the potential for political, economic and possibly even military rivalry between the two sides has led to arguments that both the Iraq conflict and the war on terror were distractions from the so-called "China challenge", namely China's growth and diplomatic inroads into many parts of the world, and that the best way to describe the current relationship is somewhere between an alliance and a rivalry. There is the general impression that although there are serious foreign policy differences between the US and China, including in the Asia-Pacific region, the United States would prefer to see a prosperous China capable of acting as a pivot in the international economy and a source for American trade, a stable China which does not seek to overturn the power distribution in the region, and an open China receptive to international organisations and confidence-building.

In addition to Chinese concerns about American attempts to contain Chinese power regionally or internationally, another longstanding worry that China has expressed towards the United States since the start of the reform era has been that of "peaceful evolution" (*heping yanbian* 和平演变).[33] A political euphemism in Chinese political circles, peaceful evolution refers to the undermining of the Chinese state through external support for organisations or ideals which stand against China's government. Both the "colour revolutions" (*yanse geming* 颜色革命) in the former Soviet Union in the mid-2000s and the 2011 "Arab Spring" protests across the Middle East and North Africa were commonly viewed by Chinese policymakers as by-products of external interference, including from the West and the United States.

China's American policy immediately after the Cold War was based upon the fact that despite the view in the 1990s that a multipolar world would appear, the United States would remain, at least for the near term, the largest power in the system. This view began to change in light of the post-2008 global recession and concerns about the loss of American economic power, events which suggested a shift in the power balance, at least economically, between China and the United States. After the recession took hold, estimates of the date when the Chinese economy would surpass that of the US were revised downward, with a report by the International Monetary Fund released in 2011 suggesting that the transition date may be as early as 2016, far earlier than predictions made a decade earlier. A subsequent IMF report released in October 2014 suggested that measured in terms of purchasing power parity (PPP) the Chinese economy had already surpassed that of the United States in terms of overall size, US$17.6 trillion versus US$17.4 trillion.[34] Of course, China's much larger population would mean that the country's financial gains would have to be balanced against the fact that many parts of the country are still addressing poverty and underdevelopment, but the IMF figures further underscored the dramatic shift in economic power between the two states in a very short time period.

Despite American difficulties in pacifying Iraq and Afghanistan, the US military is still viewed as superior to that of any other state's armed forces, and remains capable of addressing the challenge of high-technology modern warfare. Potential competitors to the United States, including China and also Europe, Japan and Russia, were seen by Beijing as having too many internal political and economic issues to concentrate on countering US power. In the current post-Cold War period, most international institutions remain Western and US-dominated, and therefore China must continue to acknowledge American preferences in foreign policy in order to obtain maximum benefit from joining these regimes. Conservative elements within the CCP, as well as policy actors within the PLA, have expressed dissatisfaction with American foreign policy and specifically its tendency towards hegemony. This explains China's modern foreign policy of strong support for the development of a multipolar world. Beijing remains sensitive to perceived attempts at containing Chinese power and about the possibility of American interference in Taiwan.

As noted in the previous chapter, Washington has been consistently wary of efforts by China to increase its power-projection capabilities, especially in terms of naval power which the US fears could be used to compromise American policy in the Pacific. Of concern is the security of the South China Sea, East China Sea, and the Malacca Straits, as well as increasingly the Indian Ocean, which is developing into an important conduit for energy and commodity trade between the Middle East, Africa and East Asia. Then-Secretary of Defence Donald Rumsfeld, for example, raised some ire in Beijing in 2005 when he asked why China was concentrating on building its military budget during a time of relative peace.[35] China has been careful to avoid any military actions which could touch off an arms race between itself and Washington, cognisant of the fact that such behaviour by the Soviet Union contributed to the acceleration of its demise because it could not keep up with American military technology.

However, there have been incidents involving both sides' militaries since the spy plane affair, including diplomatic damage done when the American aircraft carrier *USS Kitty Hawk* was refused entry into Hong Kong in November 2007 and subsequently angered Beijing by sailing through the Taiwan Straits.[36] Military demonstrations such as in January 2007 when China conducted a test of its anti-satellite system, and Chinese criticisms of a similar test conducted by the US in February 2008, when a faulty surveillance satellite was successfully shot down, further illustrate sensitivities over weapons development on both sides.[37] In 2009, Chinese military and civilian ships challenged the US surveillance vessel *USNS Impeccable* which was operating within China's 200-nautical mile exclusive economic zone (EEZ), further highlighting Chinese sensitivities over the country's surrounding waters, and a similar incident took place involving the *USNS Victorious* in May 2009. In December 2013, there was an encounter between a Chinese navy amphibious dock ship and the American Navy cruiser *USS Cowpens* as the latter vessel was traversing waters close to the Chinese carrier *Liaoning*, forcing the *Cowpens* to change course in order to avoid a collision. These incidents stemmed from ongoing differing interpretations between Washington and Beijing over the right of foreign vessels to traverse China's 200-nautical mile EEZ.[38] As noted previously, Beijing and Washington have differing views on the level of sovereignty granted by an EEZ, which has further complicated both countries' views of the security situation in the South China Sea.

The status of the South China Sea, which is almost wholly claimed by Beijing, also became an irritant to both sides after 2009 when China began to call for a fishing ban in the Sea, and the governments of two US allies, the Philippines and Vietnam, began to claim interference with both their passage and potential fossil fuel exploration in the disputed waters. Comments made by US Secretary of State Hillary Clinton at a July 2010 ASEAN Regional Forum (ARF) meeting in Hanoi that the United States retained interest in the security of the Sea and that multilateral diplomatic initiatives were the best means to settle the overlapping claims to the waterway were rebuffed by Beijing, whose spokespersons responded by saying that the status of the South China Sea was strictly a regional matter. Subsequent upgrading of US military ties with other governments surrounding the South China Sea, including Indonesia, the Philippines, Singapore and Vietnam, added to Chinese conviction that their claim to the Sea, and its potential resources, was being increasingly challenged by the United States.

After about 2010, there was a growing concern in American policy circles that although China and the US were unlikely to embark on an arms race, there was the possibility of strategic differences between the two countries diverging even more sharply. As well, there was the stronger possibility of what Joseph Nye termed an "arms walk",[39] namely a very low-intensity build-up of military power between the two militaries. As well, by this time, studies of the future of the Sino-American relationship began to deviate from the general consensus on how best Washington should engage China, an approach which could generally be termed "engagement plus hedging".[40] In other words, the United States should continue to encourage China's interactions with regional and international actors while at the same time making contingency plans in case strategic relations deteriorate. These views predominated throughout much of the 1990s and also exemplified American policy under the George W. Bush administration as the global war on terror was given priority in US strategic thinking. However, as the first term of the presidency of Barack Obama came to a close, a strong signal was given that American strategy towards China was moving towards more overt balance of power behaviour. This came in the form of American plans to increase its military presence in the Asia Pacific region, plans which were increasingly clarified in 2011–12.

The US pivot and China's responses

A United States Department of Defence paper, released in January 2012, was the first major official statement regarding a shifting of US defence priorities towards the Pacific. The introduction of the paper, entitled *Sustaining US Global Leadership: Priorities for 21st Century Defence*, contained the statement [italics in original]:

> U.S. economic and security interests are inextricably linked to developments in the arc extending from the Western Pacific and East Asia into the Indian Ocean region and South Asia, creating a mix of evolving challenges and opportunities. Accordingly, while the U.S. military will continue to contribute to security globally, *we will of necessity rebalance toward the Asia-Pacific region*.[41]

The report continued by noting that while China and the United States had a joint stake in promoting and protecting peace in East Asia as well as strengthening bilateral strategic ties, Beijing also had a responsibility to clarify its longer-term strategic goals in order to prevent "friction" in the region. Even before the paper was presented, however, there were signs from the Obama administration that a strategic shift to the Pacific Rim was in the works. For example, in an October 2011 article in the journal *Foreign Policy*, then-US Secretary of State Hillary Clinton argued that as the United States was beginning to draw down forces in Afghanistan and Iraq, the time had come for a stronger American security commitment to the Asia-Pacific given the region's expanded importance to the international system. She called for a strengthening of American alliances, including with Japan and South Korea, but also rejected the idea that such actions should be interpreted as overt balancing against China. "China," she noted instead, "represents one of the most challenging and consequential bilateral relationships the United States has ever had to manage."[42]

The process of building the "pivot to Asia" arguably began in November 2011, when US President Barack Obama, meeting with then-Australian Prime Minister Julia Gillard, announced a deployment of up to 2500 US Marines in the northern Australian port of

Darwin between 2012 and 2017. This announcement was the first concrete policy announced as part of the American regional "rebalancing", also referred to as the "pivot", a term less favoured in Washington out of concerns that it implied that the US was downgrading its security presence elsewhere in the world, including Europe. The Chinese government reacted negatively to the Darwin announcement, expressing concern that such a move would lead to the destabilisation of security in the region.[43] In April 2012, agreements were struck between Washington and Tokyo which updated their mutual strategies for the Pacific region, including a transfer of US forces stationed in Okinawa, Japan, whose presence had been a difficult Japanese domestic political issue since the 1990s, to other parts of the region. The northern Pacific US territory of Guam would receive between 4700 and 5000 US Marines under the transfer agreement while another approximately 4000 would be transferred to Hawaii, Australia or elsewhere in the region. Another product of talks between Washington and the government of Yoshihiko Noda in Japan was the possibility of joint operations and training both on Guam and in the Mariana Islands in the northern Pacific. During and after 2012, the United States also offered increased support and the promise of improved ties with the Philippines and Singapore, with Vietnam also proposing stronger strategic links with the US.[44] American relations with New Zealand and the Pacific Islands were also upgraded during this time, partially as a result of heightened Chinese economic diplomacy in Oceania.

Although the Obama government insisted these moves represented the growing importance of the Pacific to long-term American strategic interests and should not be interpreted as attempted "containment" of China, the proposed redistribution of American forces and interests created concerns in Beijing that the US was seeking just such an outcome. Policy specifics about the regional rebalancing were further articulated by US Secretary of Defence Leon Panetta, at the annual Shangri-La Dialogue in Singapore in June 2012. In addition to expressing concerns over the security situation in the South China Sea and promising to further enhance bilateral alliances and partnerships in the Asia-Pacific region, it was also announced that the US Navy would change its distribution of forces away from a 50/50 split between the Atlantic and Pacific so that 60 per cent of naval forces would be based in the Pacific Rim by 2020, including six US aircraft carrier groups. The statement also included the assertion that the rebalancing was not meant to be a challenge to China and that instead the increased American presence would be of benefit to China as well as the rest of the region.[45] It remained to be seen, however, whether this new balancing behaviour would increase or decrease regional tensions between the two great powers.

The reasons behind the American development of the pivot/rebalancing policy are many. First, there was the acknowledgement in Washington that the security situation in Asia had become more complex, and there was a demand among America's friends and allies in the region that the US take a greater role in ensuring stability and peace in the region. A second, related point was that although American policymakers routinely waved aside the "China factor" in the decision to engage in rebalancing, the pivot policies can be considered a response to Beijing's growing strategic influence in the Pacific Rim, especially in the area of maritime power, as well as in political and economic areas. Thus, the rebalancing has been widely viewed, including among Chinese policymakers, as a reminder to Beijing that the United States was not seeking to abrogate its traditional security roles in Asia. It is telling that in the Chinese press, neither the terms "pivot" nor "rebalancing" are used very often. Instead, the phrases "return to Asia" (*chongfan Yazhou* 重返亚洲), or "return to the Asia-Pacific" (*chongfan Yatai* 重返亚太) policy are favoured. One critique of the pivot policies suggested that making such a formal statement of a shift in American strategic priorities to the Pacific Rim all but validated fears in Beijing about containment.[46]

Third, as a result of the global economic downturn since 2008 and faltering economies in Europe, it has been acknowledged that East Asia, including China, had become the primary economic "tent-pole" of the international financial system, and therefore it made sound strategic sense for the United States to increase its strategic attention there. Any conflict in the region would have significant economic as well as political effects well beyond the Pacific Ocean. As well, since 2010 the United States signed on to the negotiation process designed to move forward the Trans-Pacific Partnership (TPP) free trade negotiations in the Asia-Pacific.[47] The TPP talks include twelve economies in the Asia-Pacific region, with others likely to follow, but the group excludes Beijing, and that omission has often been viewed in Chinese policy circles as both an attempt to blunt Chinese economic power in Asia and as a developing economic arm of the US pivot policy. One emerging question is whether China's role in the development of financial institutions such as the New Development Bank and the AIIB, as well as the "one belt and one road" trade routes proposed by Beijing, are attempts to curtail the effectiveness of the TPP.

Finally, as the Obama administration was ending its first term in office, it was seeking to draw a line under the previous phase in American military policy, which was dominated since the turn of the century by an unwavering focus on counter-terrorism, the Middle East and Central Asia. The rebalancing, therefore, was a strong signal that the United States was about to enter a new era in its security priorities, following a long period during which Washington's partners in Asia were feeling neglected and concerned that the United States was quietly pulling back from its security commitments in the region, an impression not helped by the recession in the United States and the possibility of defence cuts due to "sequestration" policies. Despite the rebalancing announcement, as well as the strengthening of American security commitments to Japan and other allies, the misgivings in the Asia-Pacific have not completely subsided, as since the pivot began to take shape there has been a series of crises outside of Asia, including Libya, Syria, Crimea/Ukraine, Iraq, Yemen, and the ISIL movement, all of which have repeatedly threatened to distract Washington from its strategic policies in the Pacific region.[48]

Tied to the military aspects of the pivot policies was the idea of "Air-Sea Battle" (ASB), meaning the use of networked military assets, including air and maritime defences, to counter attempts by an adversary to engage in anti-access / area denial (A2/AD) operations. An A2/AD strategy would involve military actions designed to halt or slow down an adversary's deployment into a given theatre of operations, as well as to impede activity within a given theatre. ASB was designed to swiftly and effectively disrupt such operations. Not surprisingly, although the ASB concept was also applied to potential conflicts in the Persian Gulf region, the South China Sea was frequently mentioned as the most likely region where such actions might be needed. Critics of the concept were concerned that applying ASB to waters near China would be seen as offensive in nature, coupled with questions as to whether the United States had the capabilities of following through on such a strategy.

These questions grew more pressing during 2014 as US security interests began to move back towards the Middle East as well as placing a stronger emphasis on East European defence in light of the Ukraine conflicts. In January 2015, the study of the ASB concept within the US Department of Defence was quietly discontinued, with some elements folded into a more nebulous model of "Joint Concept for Access and Manoeuvre in the Global Commons" or JAM-GC. Debate continues in American military circles, however, about the question of what has been called "archipelagic defence", meaning denying the Chinese navy access to waters around and beyond the Western Pacific's "first island chain", (comprised primarily of Japan, the Philippines and Taiwan).[49] However, the political, fiscal and strategic obstacles involved have kept this idea from advancing beyond the drafting stage.

Box 6.3 China and American "rebalancing"
"I know that many in the region and across the world are closely watching the United States–China relationship. Some view the increased emphasis by the United States on the Asia-Pacific region as some kind of challenge to China. I reject that view entirely. Our effort to renew and intensify our involvement in Asia is fully compatible – fully compatible – with the development and growth of China. Indeed, increased US involvement in this region will benefit China as it advances our shared security and prosperity for the future."
– US Secretary of Defence Leon Panetta, speech at the Shangri-La Dialogue in Singapore, 2 June 2012.

Great power accommodation and the shadow of 1914

This does not mean, however, that the US has remained unconcerned about China's rise. US policy has been seen as sensitive to potential balancing behaviour on China's behalf, creating a balance of power situation reminiscent of the Cold War. However, in practice China has largely avoided overt balancing behaviour, including within international regimes, and instead has often been seen as "bandwagoning" with the US on many key issues ranging from the international trade structure to the war on terror.[50] Although China has occasionally sided with Russia to create a coalition countering some US policies, such as over the civil conflict in Syria since 2011, China has shied away from building alliances meant specifically to balance US power. "China Threat" adherents argue this policy is temporary while China strengthens.

However, those arguing for engagement often assert that such direct balancing would do much more harm to China than good, given the demise of the Soviet Union which exhausted itself trying to maintain a farrago of allies against the West. It has been demonstrated historically that the mere act of seeking alliances can be viewed as a hostile act, and China has been highly critical of alliance systems which, it has argued, have outlived their usefulness in the twenty-first century. As well, China's "peaceful rise" developed under Hu Jintao stressed Beijing had no desire to develop as a great power by challenging the current American-led world order. Under Xi Jinping, while there have been policy differences with Washington over strategic issues, the disputes have largely remained on the diplomatic level.

Viewed through the lens of power transition theory, there is the issue of whether great power conflict becomes a stronger possibility as China approaches American levels of power. In 2012, American security scholar Graham Allison framed this question using the idea of a "Thucydides trap", which was sprung in the fifth century BCE when Sparta, fearing the rise in power of its northern neighbour, Athens, contributed to a breakdown in diplomacy and the start of the 30-year Peloponnesian War which eventually left both city-states in ruins. Allison asked whether a similar situation was developing between China and the United States given the former's power rise and calls for a greater voice in global affairs.[51] Historians have also traditionally pointed to the Anglo-Spanish War in the sixteenth century, and the rise of Imperial Germany challenging British power in the early twentieth century, as examples of violent power transitions.

Concerning the latter case, in 2014, as the hundredth anniversary of the start of the First World War was observed, there was much debate in scholarly and policy circles as to whether the conditions which resulted in the conflict could be replicated in East Asia given the dramatic shifts in power in that region and the number of strategic differences between China, the United States, and American allies such as Japan which have appeared in the region, such as the maritime sovereignty disputes. In the introduction of *The War that Ended Peace: The Road to 1914* by Margaret Macmillan, a 2013 history of the events which led up to the First World War, the author noted that the international system faces similar pressures a century later, including political and religious extremism, differing social movements, as well as the effects of rising and declining powers with the United States and China as examples. The author noted, however, that as the First World War was not inevitable, despite popular wisdom, nor should it be argued that conflict today should be considered inescapable.

While the major states in Asia have experienced major power shifts in the recent past, and the distribution of power between the United States and China has also changed abruptly during that time, it has been argued that the rigid alliance system in Europe, which led to "overbalancing" behaviour, (meaning the use of too many allies and assets to balance a perceived threat), as well as the specific isolation of some European powers, such as Wilhelmine Germany in the early twentieth century, is very much lacking in modern Asia. Nor is there in Asia today a focus on "offensive" strategies, i.e. the idea that an attack could bring about swift and substantial gains for those who strike first. That type of strategic situation, some political historians argued, contributed to what became a pan-European conflict in 1914 as opposed to an isolated Balkan one in the wake of the assassination of the Archduke Franz Ferdinand in June of that year, the primary catalyst for the conflict. Add considerable differences in geography, the nuclear weapons factor, and the fact that neither China nor the United States are fearful of direct attacks on their sovereignty, a fear very much in place amongst the belligerents in the First World War, and the analogy between Europe of the past and Asia today is further weakened.[52]

As well, not all such power transitions have been automatically marked by conflict, as evidenced by the US eclipsing British power after the Second World War. However, if the hegemonic state and the challenger have considerably different views on international relations, the possibility of these differences spilling over into war is considered elevated. Other alternative forms of balancing may appear should Chinese power continue to grow and policy differences between Beijing and Washington persist. For example, there is the potential for China to engage in "soft balancing" behaviour as a response to American power. While engaging in direct balance of power using military means (hard balancing), as occurred between the United States and the Soviet Union during most of the Cold War, is commonly seen as a provocative move, soft balancing theory suggests the use of tacit, low-level agreements and non-military policies (such as trade and diplomatic initiatives), which could be augmented when necessary.

Soft balancing strategies are less direct but still-viable approaches to preventing a hegemonic state from expanding its power unchecked.[53] China has engaged in such activity in international regimes such as the UN, for example expressing disagreements over past Western policies towards Iran, Myanmar and Syria. In each case, Beijing was concerned about the precedent which might be set should the West intervene, via the UN, in the internal affairs of a single state. Economic differences over Chinese trade, as well as new financial institutions such as the Chinese-led AIIB, could also be seen as soft balancing behaviour *vis-à-vis* American policies. It remains to be seen, however, whether soft balancing may actually "harden" as a result of growing Chinese power or developing opposition to American policies both in the Asia-Pacific and elsewhere in the world.

The economic relationship

The economic relationship between China and the United States, which has grown steadily since Beijing's economic reforms, is now one of the strongest trade ties in the world, greatly benefiting both sides. Total goods trade between the two countries exceeded US$590 billion in 2014 according to US Census Bureau figures, compared with approximately US$365 billion in 2009 and US$230 billion in 2004.[54] This trade relationship has created a situation of entrenched economic interdependence which has made it very difficult for one side to alter its format without affecting both sides. The American market has benefited from inexpensive Chinese goods, while China benefited from having a stable American consumer base, at least until the global financial crisis took root, for its exports. It is therefore understandable that the post-2008 downturn has been closely monitored in Beijing, even though its effects on the Chinese economy have been far less than on the United States, Europe and Japan. As well, in light of the perceived American origins of the recession, much frustration was expressed in Chinese government and media about US economics. Two widely-discussed books which were seen as following the same genre as *China Can Say No* appeared in China just as Western economies began to falter, namely *Currency Wars* (*huobi zhanzheng* 货币战争) in 2007 and *Unhappy China* (*Zhongguo bu gaoxing* 中国不高兴) in 2009 which were critical of American economic power, and called for Beijing to take a more active and independent stance regarding its own finances.

There have been some negative effects for the Sino-American relationship as a result of growing Chinese economic power. As China continues to grow as a trade giant and accumulates more foreign currency and economic "persuasive" power, concerns have been raised in the US over Beijing's respect for trade rules and the perceived advantages to China from its allegedly undervalued currency, inexpensive labour, and comparatively low level of regulation in areas such as environmental and labour laws. Beijing's foreign exchange policies became an especially difficult issue at the turn of the century as increasingly strident protests emanated from the American government about the tying of China's currency, the *yuan*, to the American dollar.[55]

In 2005, Beijing agreed to reform its currency policy, and since that year the value of the *yuan* (or *renminbi*) has been slowly rising in comparison to the dollar despite a tightening of Chinese currency regulations after 2008 in order to protect the economy from the growing financial chaos. Nevertheless, concerns remain from some US policymakers that China's currency is still undervalued, providing Chinese goods with an unfair advantage in international markets and exacerbating an imbalance of trade (imports versus exports) between America and China. By 2015 differences began to appear between major financial actors over the correct value of the *yuan*. In May of that year, the IMF began to shift from its earlier position and instead suggested that the Chinese currency was reaching a fair value versus the US dollar, a move that demonstrated disagreement with the ongoing stance of the Obama government that the *yuan* was still unacceptably undervalued.[56] Sino-American disagreements over monetary policies have become more acute given recent policies by Beijing to "internationalise" the *yuan* by making it more freely available as a trading currency, including establishing trading hubs in Doha, Frankfurt, London, Singapore, Taipei, Toronto and Zürich, among other cities,[57] as well as the issuing of bonds outside of China but denominated in *yuan*, colloquially known as "dim sum bonds" on global markets, a practice begun in 2007 in Hong Kong.

Although Beijing was prompted to drastically reform its trading policies, including its tariff programmes, before gaining entry to the World Trade Organisation in 2001, the United

Box 6.4 The Sino-American "dance"

"Although I am more familiar with Chinese *yangko* (a popular rural folk dance), while Secretary Lew may know American hip-hop dancing better, different types of dance enrich the stage performance. And the languages of dance also share something in common. Dialogues bridge communication. No matter it is a solo dance, a duet, or a group dance with both sides involved, China and the US will benefit from it."

– Chinese Vice Premier Wang Yang, at the 7th China–US Strategic & Economic Dialogue in Washington DC on 23 June 2015, with US Treasury Secretary Jack Lew.

States and China have continued to clash over Beijing's trade policies, with disagreements over products such as electronics, textiles and solar panels.[58] As Chinese corporations have increasingly been seeking joint ventures with international firms, a process known in China as the "going out" strategy (*zouchuqu* 走出去), there have been incidents of perceived American protectionism which caused concern in China. For example, when in 2005 a Chinese oil firm, CNOOC, attempted to purchase the American energy company, Unocal, the deal was abandoned due to strong protests from American policymakers. While there have been some successful Chinese deals with American firms, including the 2004 purchase by the Chinese firm Lenovo of the personal computer division of American technology giant IBM, questions remain as to whether future deals between American and Chinese companies might be affected by political concerns.[59]

The prospect of potential competition between Beijing and Washington for energy is another economic concern to both sides. China's growing demand for energy, especially in the form of oil and gas from international sources, has prompted Beijing to seek out supplies in the Middle East, Central Asia and Africa, and in some cases Chinese and American energy diplomacy has collided. For example, Beijing has sought energy deals with Iran and Sudan, both considered "rogue" states by Washington for their history of human rights abuses. As well, sub-Saharan Africa, with many regions containing potentially rich oil and gas fields, is being increasingly courted by Beijing, much to the concern of the United States.[60] Yet despite previous speculation that the United States and China would fall into overt competition for global supplies in energy-rich regions in the Middle East, Africa and elsewhere, the shale oil revolution in the US has greatly increased American fossil fuel supplies, contributed to a dramatic drop in oil prices at the end of 2014, and even presented the possibility of the United States exporting oil for the first time in three decades.[61]

In an acknowledgement of the growing importance of maintaining stable Sino-American economic relations, the bilateral Strategic Economic Dialogue (SED) was founded in 2006 between Presidents George W. Bush and Hu Jintao and designed to create a dialogue between high-level American and Chinese officials over potential areas of economic cooperation. In April 2009, the parameters of the dialogue were expanded by Presidents Obama and Hu to include more strategic issues, and as a result the meetings were renamed the "Strategic and Economic Dialogue". The S&ED is now held annually, with separate strategic and economic discussions taking place. These talks, along with the acknowledgement of the great combined economic power held by the two states, begged the question of whether a "Group of Two", or G-2, framework was slowly being created, if only in an informal fashion.

Sino-American cooperation and competition in Asia

As noted above, in the wake of developing Chinese power, there are many areas within Asia which are seen as platforms for either Sino-American competition or cooperation. Since the end of the Cold War there have been examples of both scenarios at work. Regional Asian security is another area in which China is concerned about American motives. At the onset of the Cold War, the United States attempted to establish a NATO-like alliance in the form of the Southeast Asian Treaty Organisation (SEATO) with Western allies in Asia, but by the 1960s the grouping had become largely defunct. Washington instead moved towards a "hub-and-spoke" approach to developing Asian regional ties, adapting the US–Japan agreement to other area allies such as South Korea, Thailand and Singapore. There, arrangements were collectively known as the "San Francisco System", named for the city where America and its Pacific allies met in 1951 to conclude an American peace treaty with Japan and to examine the post-war order in the Pacific Rim. Various agreements, including the US–Japan Pact, the Australia–New Zealand–United States pact (ANZUS), and the Philippines Treaty were all part of this rubric.[62]

With the Cold War's end, China began to advocate an informal cooperation model through the development of security communities rather than alliances, especially the ARF, East Asian Summit and ASEAN-Plus-Three as a preferable alternative in order to maintain regional security and stability. China has remained concerned about the possibility of an eventual alliance developing which could involve Asian states close to the US, including Australia, Japan, the Philippines, Singapore and South Korea, possibly under the guise of the rebalancing strategy developed by President Obama. The question of US ties *vis-à-vis* China has been especially complex for Australian foreign policy. While Australia remains a strong American ally, it does not want to alienate itself politically or economically from a rising China. Concerns about a Pacific alliance in China abated in response to the heavy American regional concentration on the Middle East by the George W. Bush administration, but during the first term of the Obama presidency, the prospect of tacit containment of China by the US returned as a long-term concern and a strong motivation for Beijing's ongoing "charm offensive" in Asia, and increasingly in other parts of the world. The "one belt and one road" trade routes in Asia and the Indian Ocean announced by the Xi Jinping government in 2013–14 can be seen not only as an endeavour by Beijing to offer an alternative to traditional, Western-centric forms of regional cooperation but also as a potential bulwark against any hardening of the US pivot/rebalancing policy in the region.

Taiwan also continues to be an important issue in Sino-American relations despite warmer cross-Strait relations since 2008. Beijing remains sensitive to any US attempts to prop up Taipei, and had routinely criticised past decisions of the United States to allow the sale of weapons to the island. Since 1979, the US has maintained a policy of ambiguity on the subject of whether Washington would intervene in a cross-Strait military conflict. With rare exceptions, such as in early 2001 when George W. Bush remarked that the US would do "whatever it takes" to defend Taiwan,[63] Washington has stuck to this policy. The 2008 election of Ma Ying-jeou of the Kuomintang (Nationalist) Party and the subsequent warming of cross-Strait relations allowed America's East Asian policies to focus elsewhere, including North Korea and regional maritime security. Nevertheless, it remains an open question in American policy in the Asia-Pacific as to whether Washington would defend the island if its relations with Beijing deteriorated to the point where force might be used. There has been some low-level debate as to whether, in light of growing Chinese power, the United States should scale back its security commitment to Taiwan (a controversial editorial in the *New York Times* in November 2011 argued for just that, in exchange for Chinese economic assistance to the US),[64] but at present there is general satisfaction with the status quo between Beijing and Taipei. Much may depend, however, on the results of the general elections in Taiwan in early 2016, and whether the opposition Democratic Progressive Party (DPP), which has traditionally favoured greater sovereignty, takes office again.

As well, the role of the US–Japan alliance in a potential Taiwan crisis has been enough to give both the CCP and the PLA pause, particularly after it was announced in 2005 that security in the Taiwan Strait would be a "common strategic objective" of the US–Japan defence agreement.[65] While Beijing is concerned about America's long-term Pacific presence, Beijing recognises the US as a force for strategic stability as well, preventing a potentially damaging arms race in Northeast Asia. China and the United States also serve as a useful pairing in the ongoing nuclear dialogue with North Korea, with the US providing pressure and China providing the quiet diplomacy. Both have recognised that the role of the other is essential in advocating that Pyongyang step back from developing as a nuclear power, a goal which the United States and China both desire, especially in the wake of Pyongyang's three nuclear tests and the uncertain future of the government of Kim Jong-un, which was hastily assembled in December 2011 after the sudden death of Kim's father, Kim Jong-il. Any solution to the North Korean nuclear standoff, and an overall negotiated peace settlement on the peninsula, would require the support of both Beijing and Washington.

Other forms of Asian multilateralism which China supports were more problematic for Washington, including the development of the East Asia Summit (EAS), which has met annually since 2005 and brings together China along with all of the major East and Southeast Asian states. When the EAS was founded, the United States was not permitted to join, while US partners Australia, India, New Zealand and Japan were able to secure seats in the organisation upon its founding, which mitigated to a degree China's status in the group. In November 2011, the United States, along with Russia, formally joined the EAS which now provides another forum for American and Chinese interests to be discussed. In the case of the Shanghai Cooperation Organisation (SCO), however, the United States remained outside of that agreement, which brought together China, Russia and most Central Asian states in a security community primarily created to fight terrorism and extremism. The fact that two large military powers are within the SCO, and that American rival Iran is an observer in the organisation, has meant that this group remains closely watched by American interests.

China under Xi Jinping has also been giving its increased support to the Conference on Interaction and Confidence Building in Asia (CICA), established in 1999 and bringing together 26 Asian states, including China, Russia, India, Iran, Pakistan, South Korea and Vietnam (Indonesia, Japan and the United States are among the observers). Beijing was granted the chair of the CICA for the period 2014–16, and when President Xi gave the keynote speech at the organisation's summit in Shanghai in May 2014, he suggested that "Asia's problems ultimately must be resolved by Asians and Asia's security ultimately must be protected by Asians." The Chinese president made similar remarks when Beijing hosted the Asia Pacific Economic Cooperation (APEC) Summit in Beijing in November 2014, suggesting that the region should work towards realising an "Asia-Pacific Dream" (*Yatai meng* 亚太梦) which would be "based on a shared destiny of all of the Asia-Pacific", and adding that Beijing would be in a position to provide "new initiatives and visions for enhancing regional cooperation".[66]

Conclusions

As noted at the beginning of the chapter, American scholarship on the direction of the Sino-American relationship has begun to both move away from the longstanding views supporting an "engagement and hedging" approach and to represent a more multifaceted set of views and policy recommendations. In addition to the literature described above on potential accommodation between Beijing and Washington on issues such as Asian security and the Taiwan question, another set of publications has also appeared which moves closer to the "China Threat" school and advocates not necessarily a containment strategy, but certainly policies more in keeping with traditional hard balance of power actions. For example, a 2015 book by Michael Pillsbury, *The Hundred Year Marathon*, argued that Beijing was tacitly seeking to undermine American power in a variety of areas, including politically and economically, in the coming years.

A Council on Foreign Relations paper released the same year by Robert Blackwill and Ashley Tellis asserted that the current American policy of engagement was no longer viable, and that Beijing was seeking to leverage the United States out of Asia while avoiding a direct military clash with America. The authors advocated a strengthening of American alliances in Asia, a development of a more formidable set of cybersecurity safeguards, and more effective preparation in order to counter Chinese A2/AD policies in the Western Pacific.[67] In the 2014 second edition of his classic work, *The Tragedy of Great Power Politics*, John Mearsheimer also suggested that in the tradition of offensive realism theory of international relations, as China continues to rise it will seek to maximise its power in Asia, at the expense of the United States if necessary, in keeping with historical great power behaviour. David Shambaugh, writing in the *Wall Street Journal* in June 2015, bemoaned the negative trajectory of the Sino-American relationship and noted that the long string of issues, including East and South China Sea security, cybersecurity, human rights and legal differences, and economic concerns were contributing to the difficult diplomatic atmosphere. "Hardly a day passes when one does not open the newspaper to read of more – and serious – friction. This is the 'new normal' and both sides had better get used to it – rather than naively professing a harmonious relationship that is not achievable," he concluded.[68]

In 2014–15, the major area of contestation between the two powers was the South China Sea and especially Chinese land reclamation and infrastructure projects on disputed reefs in the region. In May 2015, the United States dispatched a surveillance plane into the disputed waters, prompting an angry reaction from Beijing, with a Chinese Foreign Ministry spokesman calling the over-flight "very irresponsible and dangerous and detrimental to regional peace and stability". A US Congressional Research Service paper which was released shortly after that incident, posed the question of whether the United States had developed a strategy to counter Chinese activities in the South China Sea, especially if the decision was made in Beijing to implement an Air Defence Identification Zone in the region, similar to the one placed on the East China Sea in 2013.[69] The verbal sparring on this delicate issue spilled over into the Shangri-La Dialogue speeches in June 2015. Ashton Carter, US Secretary of State, was highly critical of the land reclamation efforts in the South China Sea and affirmed that the United States would "fly, sail and operate wherever internal law allows, as US forces do all over the world". The highest-level delegate from China at the Dialogue, Admiral Sun Jianguo from the PLA Navy, reiterated that China's construction activities within the South China Sea were well within Chinese sovereignty and internal laws, and called upon "relevant countries to work together" to ensure peace in the region.[70]

The question of American power versus Chinese in the coming years also continues to factor into research into the future bilateral relationship. For example, a March 2012 paper compiled by Wang Jisi and Kenneth Lieberthal, two veteran China scholars with the Brookings Institution, examined current perceptions of American and Chinese policymakers towards each other. Among their findings was the idea that in Beijing's view, much of the developing distrust between the two states stemmed from an American preoccupation with four specific changes in the international system. These were the post-2008 rise of China as a "first-class global power", the relative decline of American power during the same period, the appearance of emerging economies, including India and Brazil, which were less prone to accepting Western influence, and the development of a Chinese economic system which challenges the Western model of democratisation and market economies.

On the American side, the authors suggested that sources of unease regarding China stem from Beijing's military expansion, increasing zero-sum thinking on regional security issues, as well as Chinese foreign economic policies which Washington fears may impede a US recovery. The report concluded that both sides bore responsibility for creating new initiatives designed to improve bilateral relations not only strategically and economically, but also in the areas of cybersecurity and engagement with third parties, including regional organisations and key regional players like India and Japan.[71] However, with the American economy experiencing a slow but steady recovery and China experiencing an economic slowdown in 2014–15, as well as a change in leadership in the US following the November 2016 elections, it may be too early to determine the degree to which the power of the two states in relation to each other has really shifted.

Not all of the current writing on the relationship, however, is as pessimistic or as revisionist in interpreting the future shape of the Sino-American relationship. For example, the 2015 book by Thomas Christensen, *The China Challenge*, views the relationship as increasingly complicated but adds that there is plenty of room for further bilateral engagement and political cooperation and that American power is unlikely to be surpassed by China's rise in the near term. A similar view was upheld by Joseph Nye in his book *Is the American Century Over?* American power, he argued, was still very healthy and unlikely to be eclipsed by any challenger even though the US would no longer be the hegemon it was in the period immediately after the fall of the USSR. As well, in a paper written in April 2015 for the Belfer Centre, former Australian Prime Minister Kevin Rudd explained that

---

Box 6.5 How China and the US view each other

"Given China's modern history and its still-evolving domestic system, Beijing has deep concerns not only about America's strategic posture toward the PRC but also about Washington's ultimate intentions toward China's domestic political stability and economic growth. By contrast Washington, despite its current domestic difficulties, harbours no concerns about the continued viability of the American political system, and it tends to view its future prospects primarily as a function of how effectively America deals with its own domestic problems. It is more concerned about China's impact on the international system and how that might affect America's ability to promote its longstanding principles and interests."

– Kenneth Lieberthal and Wang Jisi, "Addressing US–China Strategic Mistrust", *John L. Thornton China Centre Monograph Series, Brookings* (4) (March 2012): 34–5.

the best way forward for both states was to develop a framework of engagement which he termed "constructive realism – common purpose".[72] This would involve recognising that there were significant areas of disagreement between the two powers and that protocols were required to contain their potential negative effects, acknowledging that there exist problems which both parties could agree to address as partners, and that it was possible over time to build trust as well as new regimes to better formalise regional cooperation and to work to remove the possibility of present and future discord from threatening the Asia-Pacific as a whole.

In all of these scenarios, the underlying question of modern Sino-American relations remains whether and how the United States will be willing and able to accommodate a rising China and whether Beijing will view the US in the future as a partner or as a barrier to its development as a great power. Thus, it can be argued that both sides will need to adapt an equal sense of responsibility *vis-à-vis* the other, knowing that this particular relationship can have dramatic effects on much of modern post-Cold War international relations. Since the formal opening of relations more than three decades ago, Sino-American engagement has become significantly more complex, incorporating issues well beyond security matters, including trade and finance as well as international organisations and norms. As a result, the relationship between China and the United States has developed into the most pivotal in the international system, and the question of whether this relationship will fall more on the side of cooperation or of competition remains open.

Discussion questions

- How has the relationship between China and the United States changed since the fall of the Soviet Union?
- What are the ways in which the US might continue to "engage" and is containment of Chinese power even possible for Washington today?
- Will the rising level of economic interdependence between the two states increase or decrease political tensions?
- Is a "power transition" taking place between the two states and will it be peaceful?
- Did the advent of the international war on terror after 9/11 result in the improvement of Sino-American security relations?
- What are the risks of a Sino-American military rivalry or an arms race given the announcement in the United States of a "rebalancing" strategy in the Pacific?
- What was meant by Xi Jinping's call for a "new type of great power relationship" with the United States?
- What accounts for the differing opinions and views in American policy analysis about the future of the Sino-American relationship?

Recommended reading

Bader, Jeffrey A. *Obama and China's Rise: An Insider Account of America's Asia Strategy* (Washington DC: Brookings, 2012).
Christensen, Thomas J. *The China Challenge: Shaping the Choices of a Rising Power* (New York and London: W.W. Norton, 2015).
Coker, Christopher. *The Improbable War: China, the United States and the Logic of Great Power Conflict* (London: Hurst, 2015).

Dyer, Geoff. *The Contest of the Century: The New Era of Competition with China* (New York and London: Allen Lane, 2014).

Feldman, Noah. *Cool War: The Future of Global Competition* (New York: Random House, 2013).

Foot, Rosemary and Andrew Walter. *China, the United States and Global Order* (Cambridge and New York: Cambridge University Press, 2011).

Friedberg, Aaron L. *A Contest for Supremacy: China, America, and the Struggle for Mastery in Asia* (New York and London: W.W. Norton, 2011).

Goldstein, Lyle J. *Meeting China Halfway: How to Defuse the Emerging US–China Rivalry* (Washington DC: Georgetown University Press, 2015).

Kissinger, Henry. *On China* (New York: Penguin Press, 2011).

Macmillan, Margaret. *Seize the Hour: When Nixon Met Mao* (London: John Murray, 2006).

Mearsheimer, John J. *The Tragedy of Great Power Politics* (2nd edn) (New York and London: W.W. Norton, 2014).

Nye, Joseph S., Jr. *Is the American Century Over?* (Malden, MA and Cambridge, UK: Polity Press, 2015).

Paulson, Henry M., Jr. *Dealing with China: An Insider Unmasks the New Economic Superpower* (New York and Boston: Twelve / Hachette Book Group, 2015).

Rosecrance, Richard N. and Steven E. Millar (eds). *The New Great War? The Roots of World War I and the Risk of US–China Conflict* (Cambridge, MA: MIT Press, 2015).

Steinberg, James and Michael O'Hanlon. *Strategic Reassurance and Resolve: US–China Relations in the Twenty-First Century* (Princeton: Princeton University Press, 2014).

Sutter, Robert G. *US–Chinese Relations: Perilous Past, Pragmatic Present* (Lanham, MD and Boulder, CO: Rowman and Littlefield, 2010).

Swaine, Michael D. *America's Challenge: Engaging a Rising China in the Twenty-First Century* (Washington DC, Carnegie, 2011).

White, Hugh. *The China Choice: Why America Should Share Power* (Collingwood, Australia: Black Inc., 2013).

Notes

1 "中美关系有足够韧性," ("China–US Relations Have Sufficient Toughness") *People's Daily*, 17 June 2015, < http://world.people.com.cn/n/2015/0617/c1002-27168868.html>.

2 Emma V. Broomfield, "Perceptions of Danger: The China Threat Theory," *Journal of Contemporary China* 12(35) (May 2003): 265–84.

3 Susan Shirk, *China: Fragile Superpower* (Oxford: Oxford University Press, 2007).

4 Remarks by President Obama and President Xi Jinping of the People's Republic of China Before Bilateral Meeting, Sunnylands Retreat, Palm Springs, California," 7 June 2013, *The White House, Office of the Press Secretary*, < https://www.whitehouse.gov/the-press-office/2013/06/07/remarks-president-obama-and-president-xi-jinping-peoples-republic-china->.

5 Machabe Keliher, "Anglo-American Rivalry and the Origins of US China Policy," *Diplomatic History* 31(2) (April 2007): 235–40.

6 "*Memorial*: Ch'i-ying Analyses the Treaty of Wang-hsia and Compares it with the British Supplementary Treaty, July 28, 1844," *China's Management of American Barbarians: A Study of Sino-American Relations, 1841–1861, with Documents*, ed. Earl Swisher (New York: Octagon Books, 1972), 160–4; Edward P. Crapol, "John Tyler and the Pursuit of National Destiny," *Journal of the Early Republic* 17(3) (Autumn 1997): 482–3.

7 Jonathan Fenby, *The Siege of Tsingtao* (Melbourne: Penguin Books, 2014).

8 Rana Mitter, *China's War With Japan, 1937–1945: The Struggle for Survival* (London: Allen Lane, 2013).

9 Ross Y. Koen, *The China Lobby in American Politics* (New York: Octagon Books, 1974), 29.

10 Odd Arne Westad, "Losses, Chances and Myths: The United States and the Creation of the Sino-Soviet Alliance, 1945–1950," *Diplomatic History* 21(1) (Winter 1997): 107–8.

11 Chen Jian, *Mao's China and the Cold War* (Chapel Hill and London: University of North Carolina Press, 2001), 38–48.

12 Qiang Zhai, *The Dragon, the Lion and the Eagle: Chinese–British–American Relations, 1949–58* (Kent, OH and London: Kent State University Press, 1994), 38–45.

13 Richard M. Nixon, "Asia after Viet Nam," *Foreign Affairs* 46(1) (October 1967): 111–25.

14 Henry Kissinger, *On China* (New York, Penguin Press, 2011), 203–13; Linda D. Dillon, Bruce Burton and Walter C. Soderlund, "Who was the Principal Enemy?: Shifts in Official Chinese Perceptions of the Two Superpowers, 1968–1969," *Asian Survey* 17(5) (May 1977): 456–73.

15 James Mann, *About Face: A History of America's Curious Relationship with China, From Nixon to Clinton* (New York, Vintage Books, 1998), 59–60.

16 "Hilsman Speech 1963," *China Confidential: American Diplomats and Sino-American Relations, 1945–1996* (New York: Columbia University Press, 2001), 193–6; James Peck, *Washington's China: The National Security World, the Cold War and the Origins of Globalism* (Amherst and Boston, University of Massachusetts Press, 2006), 219–20.

17 O. Edmond Clubb, "China and the United States: Beyond Ping-Pong," *Current History* 61(361) (September 1971): 129–34, 180.

18 Steve Coll, *Ghost Wars: The Secret History of the CIA, Afghanistan, and Bin Laden, from the Soviet Invasion to September 10th, 2001* (New York: Penguin Press, 2004), 66.

19 Christian Caryl, *Strange Rebels: 1979 and the Birth of the 21st Century* (New York: Basic Books 2013), 169–73.

20 Steven I. Levine, "China and the United States: The Limits of Interaction," *China and the World: Chinese Foreign Policy in the Post-Mao Era* (Boulder and London: Westview Press, 1984), 118–21.

21 Mel Gurtov and Byong-Moo Hwang, *China's Security: The New Roles of the Military* (Boulder and London: Lynne Renner, 1998), 66–7; Rosalie Chen, "China Perceives America: Perspectives of International Relations Experts," *Journal of Contemporary China* 12(35) (May 2003): 287.

22 Samuel P. Huntington, *The Clash of Civilizations: the Remaking of World Order* (New York: Simon and Schuster, 1996), 312–16; John Mearsheimer, *The Tragedy of Great Power Politics* (New York and London: W.W. Norton, 2001), 396–400.

23 Liu Jiangyong, "New Trends in Sino-US–Japan Relations," *Contemporary International Relations* 8(7) (July 1998): 1–13; Thomas J. Christensen, "China, The US–Japan Alliance, and the Security Dilemma in East Asia," International Security 23(4) (Spring 1999): 62.

24 Walter Russell Mead, "America's Sticky Power," *Foreign Policy* 83(2): 46–53.

25 Allen S. Whiting, "Chinese Nationalism and Foreign Policy after Deng," *The China Quarterly* 142 (June 1995): 312.

26 Michael D. Swaine, "Chinese Decision-Making Regarding Taiwan," *The Making of Chinese Foreign and Security Policy in the Era of Reform*, ed. David M. Lampton (Stanford: Stanford University Press, 2001), 319–27.

27 Peter Hayes Gries, *China's New Nationalism: Pride Politics and Diplomacy* (Berkeley and London: University of California Press, 2004), 13–18; Dingxin Zhao, "An Angle on Nationalism in China Today: Attitudes among Chinese Students after Belgrade 1999," *The China Quarterly* 172 (December 2002): 885–905.

28 Gries, *China's New Nationalism*, 34–5.

29 James Miles, "Chinese Nationalism, US Policy and Asian Security," *Survival* 42(4) (Winter 2000–01): 53–4.

30 Maria Cheng, "The Standoff: What Was Unsaid? A Pragmatic Analysis of the Conditional Marker 'If'," *Discourse and Society* 13(3) (2002): 309–17; Dennis C. Blair and David B. Bonfili, "The April 2001 EP-3 Incident: The US Point of View," *Managing Sino-American Crises: Case Studies and Analyses*, ed. Michael D. Swaine and Zhang Tuosheng with Danielle F.S. Cohen (Washington DC: Carnegie, 2006), 277–90; "China, US Agree on Freeing Plane Crew," *Reuters and Associated Press*, Beijing, 12 April 2001.

31 Aaron L. Friedberg "11 September and the Future of Sino-American Relations," *Survival* 44(1) (January 2002): 34–5.

32 Jing-dong Yuan, "The Bush Doctrine: Chinese Perspective and Responses," *Asian Perspective* 27(4): 111–45.

33 Russell Ong, "'Peaceful Evolution', 'Regime Change' and China's Political Security," *Journal of Contemporary China* 16(3) (2007): 717–27.

34 *International Monetary Fund*, April 2011, <http://www.imf.org/external/pubs/ft/weo/2011/01/weodata/weorept.aspx?sy=2009&ey=2016&scsm=1&ssd=1&sort=country&ds=.&br=1&pr1.x=47&pr1.y=12&c=924%2C111&s=PPPGDP&grp=0&a=#download>;   "World   Economic

Outlook, October 2014: Legacies, Clouds, Uncertainties," *International Monetary Fund*, October 2014, <http://www.imf.org/external/pubs/ft/weo/2014/02/pdf/text.pdf>.

35 Richard D. Fisher Jr., "'Power Projection' Chinese Style," *The Wall Street Journal* (Europe), 13 April 2006, 13.

36 "China Upset at *Kitty Hawk*'s Taiwan Strait Transit," *Reuters*, 4 December 2007.

37 Jonathan D. Pollack, "Chinese Military Power: What Vexes the United States and Why," *Orbis* 51(4) (Fall 2007): 636; "China Calls on US to Provide Data on Satellite Shootdown," *Agence France-Presse*, 21 February 2008.

38 Eric A. McVadon, "The Reckless and the Resolute: Confrontation in the South China Sea," *China Security* 5(2)(Spring 2009): 1–15; Ronald O'Rourke, "Maritime Territorial and Exclusive Economic Zone (EEZ) Disputes Involving China: Issues for Congress," *US Congressional Research Service* 7-5700 (24 December 2014): 3–7.

39 Joseph Nye, "China and the Future of the Asia-Pacific," International Institute for Strategic Studies (IISS) 39th Annual Conference, Singapore, September 1997.

40 Rosemary Foot, "Chinese Strategies in a US-Hegemonic Global Order: Accommodating and Hedging," *International Affairs* 82(1)(January 2006): 77–94.

41 United States Department of Defence, "Sustaining US Global Leadership: Priorities for 21st Century Defence," January 2012, 2.

42 Hillary Clinton, "America's Pacific Century," *Foreign Policy*, 11 October 2011, < http://foreignpolicy.com/2011/10/11/americas-pacific-century/>.

43 Jackie Calmes, "A US Marine Base for Australia Irritates China," *The New York Times*, 16 November 2011.

44 Yuka Hayashi, "Japan Leader in US to Pledge Security Efforts," *Wall Street Journal*, 29 April 2012; Robert Burns, "New Deal Calls for 9000 Marines to Leave Okinawa, Many Will Shift to Guam or Hawaii," *Associated Press*, 27 April 2012.

45 "The 11th Annual IISS Asian Security Summit: The Shangri-La Dialogue. First Plenary Session: The US Rebalance Towards the Asia-Pacific, 2 June 2012," *International Institute of Strategic Studies*, <http://www.iiss.org/EasySiteWeb/getresource.axd?AssetID=66624&type=full&service type=Attachment>.

46 Robert S. Ross, "The Problem With the Pivot: Obama's New Asia Policy Is Unnecessary and Counterproductive," *Foreign Affairs* 91(November–December 2012): 70–81.

47 Ann Capling and John Ravenhill, "Multilateralising Regionalism: What Role for the Trans-Pacific Partnership Agreement?" *Pacific Review* 24(5) (December 2011): 553–75.

48 "Obama Reassures Allies, but Doubts Over 'Pivot' to Asia Persist," *Reuters*, 29 April 2014.

49 Sam LaGrone, "Pentagon Drops Air Sea Battle Name, Concept Lives On," *US Naval Institute News*, 20 January 2015, <http://news.usni.org/2015/01/20/pentagon-drops-air-sea-battle-name-concept-lives>; Andrew F. Krepinevich, Jr., "How to Deter China: The Case for Archepelagic Defence," *Foreign Affairs* 94(2) (March/April 2015): 78–86.

50 See Avery Goldstein, *Rising to the Challenge: China's Grand Strategy and International Security* (Stanford: Stanford University Press, 2005), 32–5.

51 Graham Allison, "Thucydides's Trap Has Been Sprung in the Pacific," *Financial Times*, 21 August 2012.

52 Joachim Krause, "Assessing the Danger of War: Parallels and Differences between Europe in 1914 and East Asia in 2014," *International Affairs* 90(6) (2004): 1421–51; Ja Ian Chong and Todd H. Hall, "The Lessons of 1914 and for East Asia Today: Missing the Trees for the Forest," *International Security* 39(1) (September 2014): 7–43; Richard N. Rosecrance, "Allies, Overbalance and War," *The Next Great War: The Roots of World War I and the Risk of US–China Conflict*, ed. Richard N. Rosecrance and Steven E. Miller (Cambridge, MA and London: MIT Press, 2015), 45–69.

53 Robert A. Pape, "Soft Balancing Against the United States," *International Security* 30(1) (September 2005) 7–45; Judith Kelley, "Strategic Non-Cooperation as Soft Balancing: Why Iraq Was Not Just About Iraq," *International Politics* 42(2005): 41–2.

54 "Trade in Goods with China," *United States Census Bureau*, April 2015, < https://www.census.gov/foreign-trade/balance/c5700.html>.

55 Ronald McKinnon, "Why China Should Keep Its Dollar Peg," *International Finance* 10(1) (2007): 43–70.

56 Ian Talley, "IMF to Brighten View of China's Yuan," *The Wall Street Journal*, 3 May 2015.

57 Yu Yongding, "How Far Can Renminbi Internationalisation Go?" *Renminbi Internationalisation: Acheivements, Prospects and Challenges*, ed. Barry Eichengreen and Masahiro Kawai (Tokyo and Washington: Asia Development Bank / Brookings, 2015), 53–81.

58 Neil C. Hughes, "A Trade War with China?" *Foreign Affairs* 84(4) (July / August 2005): 94–106.

59 Joe McDonald, "China's Acquisitions Provoke Unease," *Associated Press*, 22 February 2008.

60 Zha Daojiong, "China's Energy Security, International and Domestic Issues," *Survival* 48(1) (Spring 2006): 179–90.

61 Timothy Gardner, "US Opens Door to Oil Exports after Year of Pressure," *Reuters*, 30 December 2014.

62 Kent E. Calder, "Securing Security through Prosperity: The San Francisco System in Comparative Perspective," *The Pacific Review* 17(1) (March 2004): 135–57.

63 Lanxin Xiang, "Washington's Misguided China Policy," *Survival* 43(3) (Autumn 2001): 9–10; Dennis van Vranken Hickey, "America, China and Taiwan: Three Challenges for Chen Shui-bian," *Journal of Contemporary China* 15(48) (August 2006): 459–77.

64 The editorial in question was by Paul V. Kane, "To Save Our Economy, Ditch Taiwan," *The New York Times*, 11 November 2011. On the debate, see also Charles S. Glaser, "A US–China Grand Bargain? A Hard Choice between Military Competition and Accommodation," *International Security* 39(4) (Spring 2015): 49–90, and Richard C. Bush, *Uncharted Strait: The Future of China–Taiwan Relations* (Washington DC: Brookings, 2013), 213–43.

65 Wu Xinbo, "The End of the Silver Lining: A Chinese View of the US–Japanese Alliance," *Washington Quarterly* 29(1) (Winter 2005 / 2006): 125–6.

66 "After 'Chinese Dream', Xi Jinping Outlines Vision for 'Asia-Pacific Dream' at Apec Meet," *South China Morning Post*, 10 November 2014.

67 Robert D. Blackwill and Ashley J. Tellis, "Revising US Grand Strategy toward China," *Council on Foreign Relations, Council Special Report* 72 (March 2015).

68 David Shambaugh, "In a Fundamental Shift, China and the US are Now Engaged in All-out Competition," *Wall Street Journal*, 11 June 2015.

69 Ben Dolven, Jennifer K. Elsea, Susan V. Lawrence, Ronald O'Rourke and Ian E. Rinehart, "Chinese Land Reclamation in the South China Sea: Implications and Policy Options," *Congressional Research Service, CRS Report* 7-5700 (16 June 2015).

70 "The United States and Challenges of Asia-Pacific Security: Ashton Carter," *Shangri-La Dialogue 2015*, 30 May 2015, <http://www.iiss.org/en/events/shangri%20la%20dialogue/archive/shangri-la-dialogue-2015-862b/plenary1-976e/carter-7fa0>; "Strengthening Regional Order in the Asia-Pacific: Admiral Sun Jianguo," *Shangri-La Dialogue 2015*, 30 May 2015, <http://www.iiss.org/en/events/shangri%20la%20dialogue/archive/shangri-la-dialogue-2015-862b/plenary4-b8e3/sun-0dfc>.

71 Kenneth Lieberthal and Wang Jisi, "Addressing US–China Strategic Mistrust," *John L. Thornton China Centre Monograph Series* (4) (March 2012).

72 Kevin Rudd, "US–China 21: The Future of US–China Relations under Xi Jinping, Toward a New Framework of Constructive Realism for a Common Purpose," *Harvard University Kennedy School, Belfer Centre for Science and International Affairs*, April 2015.

7 China's peripheral diplomacy

China in Asia: Emerging identities

In addition to Sino-American relations, the most visible means of measuring the dramatic changes which have taken place in China's foreign policy development over the past two decades has been the relationship between Beijing and its immediate neighbours in East and Southeast Asia as well as in the greater Pacific. China's rise in Asia has created a significant power shift in all major areas of international relations, and many of Beijing's neighbours are in the process of re-evaluating their policies towards the great power. There is shared understanding among many of China's neighbours that China represents a significant economic opportunity, especially in light of Beijing's regional diplomatic initiatives including the "one belt and one road" planning and the Asia Infrastructure Investment Bank, as well as China's push for free trade agreements on bilateral and regional scales.

However, from a diplomatic and strategic viewpoint, there is less agreement among other parts of the Asia-Pacific over what China represents. Relations between Beijing and Tokyo, especially since the return to power of Japanese Prime Minister Shinzō Abe in December 2012, and sharper differences over the political status of the East China Sea, continue to be problematic despite the still-healthy trading relationship. Economics also plays a significant role in the relationships China has with South Korea as well as among the states of Oceania. In the case of North Korea, Beijing still faces the dilemma of engaging a country with strong historical and strategic ties with China, but one which retains a Stalinist government which is politically and economically unreformed and a young leader, Kim Jong-un, who since assuming power after the death of his father, Kim Jong-il, in December 2011, has been prone to bellicose actions in the region. China remains hopeful for a multilateral solution to the North Korean nuclear question, but in the wake of still-frozen communications between Washington and Pyongyang and the DPRK's nuclear test in February 2013, the third such event, the security conditions for any resolution remain elusive.

In Southeast Asia, there are also differences among governments about the significance to the region of China's rise. While Beijing has cultivated closer relations with Cambodia and Laos, and is still a major player in the foreign policy of Myanmar despite the post-2010 reforms in that country which opened the door to greater Western engagement, relations between China and the governments of the Philippines and Vietnam became more toxic after Beijing introduced a series of policies designed to emphasise its sovereignty over the bulk of the South China Sea and island groups disputed by Hanoi and Manila. Other members of the Association of Southeast Asian Nations (ASEAN), including Indonesia, Malaysia and Singapore, have sought a balanced relationship between the United States and China. The beginning of the American pivot/rebalancing policies since 2011 have also drawn in several of China's neighbours, including in Oceania and Southeast Asia, who want to maintain cordial relations with Beijing while still keeping an American security presence nearby.

Despite a number of strategic differences between China and some of its neighbours regarding maritime sovereignty and nuclear issues, Beijing has, since the 1990s, largely attempted to keep these disputes relegated to the diplomatic level in order to develop a stable periphery and therefore concentrate both on domestic reforms and the expansion of Chinese foreign policy interests beyond Asia. However, despite the greater internationalisation of China's foreign policy interests, events closer to home will still form much of Beijing's political and strategic calculations in the near future.

The beginnings of China's "good neighbour" policies

In the wake of the damages to Chinese foreign policy incurred following the Tiananmen Incident of June 1989, the government of Jiang Zemin placed a priority on relations with Asian neighbours via a series of foreign policy initiatives which came to be known as "peripheral" (*zhoubian* 周边) diplomacy. This involved attempts to improve international ties with bordering states in the Asia-Pacific region, including those with which China had limited or even non-existent relations.[1] As a result, during much of the 1990s Beijing was engaged in improving its Asian relations, settling border and other disputes, and seeking to establish itself as a rising Pacific Rim power interested more in regional cooperation rather than competition.

Beijing's reasons for launching its peripheral diplomacy policies during that decade were manifold. Primarily, the Chinese government wished to assure its neighbours that in the wake of Tiananmen, the country would neither regress into the isolationism of the late Maoist era nor was it interested in radically challenging the political order in East and Southeast Asia. As well, Beijing wanted to forestall a collective attempt by its neighbours, especially those more directly aligned with the West, to restrain or contain China's growing power in Asia by means of encircling it with states hostile to Beijing's regional interests. Third, as China's economic and diplomatic power began to grow, Beijing sought to convince its smaller neighbours that it was not seeking a hegemonic role in Asia but rather aspired to become an indispensable partner and potential alternative to American-led Western power in the Pacific Rim. The impact of the Asian Financial Crisis (AFC) of 1997–8 further enabled Beijing to portray itself as a regional economic protector by offering aid and support to stricken Asian economies. Finally, during the 1990s the priorities of the Chinese government included reforms of China's economic system, which generally involved accelerating market reforms, and to a lesser degree reforming aspects of the party-state in order to modernise it and improve its accountability. Therefore, Beijing sought to create a stable, peaceful periphery in which to concentrate on these internal reforms since the country could ill-afford being drawn into regional conflicts as it had been in previous decades.

China's peripheral diplomacy, it can be concluded, has been very successful in achieving its primary goals despite some setbacks. Beijing resolved many border disputes with its neighbours during and after the 1990s and adopted a more conservative, diplomatic approach to addressing inter-state differences. This was especially the case in Central Asia, where there were many border disputes left over from the former Soviet Union. One interesting case of China's willingness to settle these disputes, fairly, was the final border demarcation agreement between China and Kyrgyzstan which concluded in 2004, from which Beijing only received 32 per cent of the territory under dispute. Beijing was also willing to concede much disputed land during similar negotiations with Tajikistan, as the final agreement in 2002 only gave China 1000 km² of land from the 28,000 km² which was originally under negotiation.[2]

With the exception of Taiwan, which did not factor directly into China's peripheral diplomacy, the chances of a conflict between Beijing and a neighbouring political actor became much lower than in previous decades. Moreover, China's growing economic power attracted considerable positive attention throughout the Pacific Rim, especially after the AFC which resulted in Beijing being perceived as both an island of stability and a helpful partner.[3] As American focus on the Pacific Rim from the start of the George W. Bush administration of 2001–9 was seen as waning in relation to other regions such as the Middle East, China sensed a strategic window opening, and began to increase both its soft power and its diplomatic presence in many parts of Asia.

This does not mean, however, that China was totally successful in solving all outstanding problems and issues between itself and its neighbours. Indeed, the successes of Chinese peripheral diplomacy were somewhat unevenly distributed. While Beijing, since the turn of the century, has begun to engage in more "cross-regional" diplomacy with states well beyond its immediate milieu (as examined in the next chapter), many issues remain to be addressed. China's relations with its neighbours during the Hu Jintao and Xi Jinping administrations have become more fluid, prompted by Beijing's developing military and economic power along with regional concerns that China's peripheral diplomacy may give way to greater pragmatism as China settles further into great power status.

Japan

The post-Cold War foreign policy climate between China and Japan is marked by many contradictions. Both countries have enjoyed peaceful relations since the Second World War and have expressed interest in developing an Asia-Pacific economy and more formal institutions. Historically, numerous political issues, both regional and international, have divided the two states. Specifically the Chinese government frequently expressed criticisms that Tokyo had not fully accounted for its historical war record. Today, both states are seen as regionally powerful, as although China has surpassed Japan as the second-largest economy in the world, Japan has been seeking to finally emerge from a long period of economic stagnation while re-evaluating its diplomatic and strategic posture to better reflect independent strategic thinking.

As a result, questions are being raised as to whether a low-level hard power competition is developing between them. In the years leading to the Second World War, Imperial Japan's goal was to enhance its security through the development of its own empire in order to ensure greater economic self-sufficiency. This led to the colonisation of Northern China, Korea and much of Southeast Asia before the decision was made in December 1941 to directly challenge American power in the Pacific Ocean via an attack on Pearl Harbour, Hawaii. The "Greater East Asian Co-Prosperity Sphere" was designed to protect Japan from blockades and trade disruptions, as well as to provide a ready source of economic goods. A major component of this drive towards colonisation was the puppet state of Manchukuo (*Manzhouguo* 满洲国), forcibly carved out of north-eastern China by Japanese forces since the Mukden Incident in 1931 and occupied until Japan's surrender at the end of the Pacific War in 1945.

A major focus on economic and financial modernisation dominated Japanese domestic and foreign policies throughout much of the 1950s and 60s, and the state's recovery from the war was extremely rapid, greatly assisted by American hegemony and protection against communist incursion. After the war, Japan adapted the Yoshida Doctrine, named after Shigiru Yoshida, prime minister during and for a few years after the American occupation. It called for a strong stand against communism, a resistance to Japanese rearmament, and a continued alliance with the United States in order to defend Japanese interests. Both Article IX of the Japanese Constitution, which states that "the Japanese people forever renounce war as a sovereign right of the nation and the threat or use of force as means of settling international disputes", and the 1960 US–Japan Mutual Security Treaty were seen as important elements of the Yoshida Doctrine and also influenced much current strategic thinking between China and Japan.

However, two important events occurred in the early 1990s, namely the first, albeit short-lived, fall from power of the Liberal Democratic Party (LDP) which had governed Japan throughout the post-war period, and second, the end of the Cold War, which caused a rethinking of some aspects of Tokyo's international and regional relations.[4] Political scientists argued that the military protection given to Japan during the Cold War allowed Tokyo to develop a strategy known as "mercantile realism", a security policy based on the development of economic power and high-technology-led growth in order to protect Japanese economic sovereignty. In addition to maintaining a strong Japanese pro-Western stance, Prime Minister Yoshida was pragmatic about eventually improving relations with China. He noted in 1948 that he didn't care if China was "red or green", but that the People's Republic was a natural market which Tokyo could ill-afford to ignore as it sought to develop its post-war economic relations.[5]

Post-war Sino-Japanese relations while initially frosty were not overtly hostile. Both Mao Zedong and Deng Xiaoping were unhappy with an extended American military presence nearby, but they viewed it as the best alternative to a re-militarised Tokyo. There was also considerable anger at Japan being used as a staging ground for UN forces during the Korean War. However, trade between China and Japan slowly increased during the 1960s, and relations were officially restored in 1972. The period from normalisation until recently was commonly referred to as the "1972 system", commonly used to describe bilateral ties marked by pragmatism and the tacit avoidance of discussion of difficult bilateral issues in favour of declarations of amity.[6] When Deng began to accept overseas development assistance, Tokyo became the largest single aid donor to China. Beijing, however, remained unhappy that Japan had not sufficiently acknowledged and apologised for atrocities committed in China during World War II, including the Nanjing (Nanking) Massacre in 1937, and routinely pressed Japan to make more open admissions of war crimes committed during that era.[7] However, there remains the question of whether Imperial Japan's wartime conduct is being used to increase levels of nationalism in China.

Interpretations of Japan's wartime conduct continue to affect Sino-Japanese relations for a variety of reasons. First is the controversy over Japan's Yasukuni Shrine, founded in 1869, which became a magnet for local and regional criticism when in 1978 fourteen Class-A war criminals, including wartime Prime Minister Hideki Tojo, were interred there. Visits by Japanese leaders to Yasukuni to honour Japanese war dead frequently aroused protests in China and South Korea, which saw such activity as condoning Japanese aggressiveness during the Second World War. The subject remains politically delicate in Tokyo while often being a focus of nationalist protests in China. This became a sore point in bilateral relations during the time in office (2001–6) of Prime Minister Junichiro Koizumi, who visited the shrine six times while in office. Another issue which flared up during Koizumi's tenure involved the teaching of Second World War history in Japanese schools. From that period, subsequent Japanese leaders declined to visit the site, a pattern which was only broken in December 2013 when Prime Minister Abe visited the shrine, causing a further chill in Sino-Japanese relations. In April 2015, he sent a ritual offering, a *masakaki* tree, to Yasukuni, which was viewed as a compromise position between visiting the shrine a second time and forgoing any further association with the site.

Both Beijing and Seoul expressed concerns that some Japanese history texts glossed over the country's wartime behaviour. Chinese frustration with the situation spiked in April 2005 with the limited release in Japan of a history textbook viewed as downplaying many examples of Japanese war crimes. News of the book was enough to spark anti-Japan riots in Beijing and other major Chinese cities. These demonstrations, which caused significant damage to many Japanese businesses and consulates, were allowed to proceed for a few days by Chinese authorities before being halted.[8] Other factors have also contributed to negative views in China about Japan, including Tokyo's unsuccessful campaign to join the UN Security Council as a permanent member, which Beijing opposes partially due to concerns about Japanese accounting for its record in the Second World War. As well, China was unhappy with Japan's 2005 decision to cease overseas development assistance to China, a move which Beijing saw as punitive despite China's rapid economic growth.[9] Chinese policymakers had often equated Japanese aid with *de facto* war reparations.

At the turn of the century, Beijing became concerned that with the Cold War over, Japan would trade in mercantile realism[10] for more traditional hard power realism and the ability to maintain a strong security relationship with the United States. The US–Japan security treaty has been strengthened since the 1990s, and after 2011 the relationship between the countries became even closer in light of Washington's announced plans to "rebalance" its naval forces with a greater focus on the Pacific and to cooperate with Japan militarily not only in Asia but also in the North Pacific, through proposed joint facilities in Guam and the Marshall Islands. Japan is a central player in emerging US strategic rebalancing policies in the Pacific, as evidenced by the announcement in April 2015 that US–Japan defence cooperation guidelines would be further enhanced to allow Tokyo to exercise its right to "collective self-defence" under specific circumstances. For example, Japan could intervene in an attack on the United States, and aid third party countries under attack. Moreover, since the 1990s, Washington and Tokyo have pledged support for the development of an anti-missile system which Beijing fears could be used to negate their missile arsenal. The participation of Japanese forces in supporting roles, both in the allied operations in Afghanistan and during the Iraq War, increased Chinese concerns about a more independent Japanese military. Japan, in turn, worries about the ongoing development of Chinese military power and the possibility of Chinese hegemony in East Asia.[11]

In addition to the question of historical interpretation of the Second World War and problems of nationalism, the status of the disputed Senkaku / Diaoyu Islands (*Diaoyu dao* 钓鱼岛) in the southern part of the East China Sea (*Dong Hai* 东海), and the maritime boundaries of the East China Sea itself, have also been serious areas of bilateral dispute. The small (less than 7 km^2 in total area) and uninhabited islands, known in Japan as the Senkakus, are formally administered as part of Okinawa on the Japanese side. However, according to Beijing, the Diaoyu Islands (also claimed by Taiwan as the *Diaoyutai* 釣魚台) were listed in Chinese historical records as part of Imperial Chinese holdings at least as far back as the fourteenth century. According to one Chinese publication on the matter, Japan only sought to annex the islands, claiming them to be *terra nullius* (land claimed by no one) in the late nineteenth century. Qing-Dynasty China, according to current Chinese government discourse, was forced to relinquish the islands, along with Taiwan, as part of an unequal treaty, the 1895 Treaty of Shimonoseki (known in Chinese as *Maguan Tiaoyue* 马关条约).[12] Japan has maintained that because the disputed islands were not part of the Treaty the country is under no obligation to cede them.

In addition, studies suggested the islets may be sitting on substantial fossil fuel supplies, further attracting the interest of both states. The disputed zone that both countries claim in the East China Sea includes the Xihu Trough (*Xihu Aoxian* 西湖凹陷), an area believed to hold considerable natural gas reserves. As both countries are now net energy importers, the possibility of having local access to such supplies has exacerbated the dispute. Tensions began in May 2004 when Japan noticed that China had begun drilling operations in the Chunxiao gas field (*Chunxiao youqitian* 春晓油气田 or *Shirakaba* in Japanese) very close to the disputed zone. Chinese drillers have expanded operations since then and Japan is growing increasingly worried that gas supplies, which Tokyo claims, are being confiscated.[13]

In 1996, a makeshift lighthouse was assembled on the islands by a Japanese youth group, and also that year Tokyo claimed the islands as part of their exclusive economic zone (EEZ). Then in 2004, Chinese fishing vessels near the islands were driven off by Japanese patrol vessels and later that year Chinese activists landing on the islands were detained by Japanese authorities.[14] Although both Beijing and Tokyo have stated a preference for a diplomatic solution to the dispute, neither side has retreated from their claims. Moreover, adding to the complexity of the issue is the fact that Japan has not formally recognised that there is a dispute over the islands. The closest that the Japanese government came to acknowledging a difference of policy stance only came in November 2014, after talks between Chinese State Councillor Yang Jiechi and Japanese National Security chief Shotaro Yachi resulted in a four-point document which included the statement, according to the Japanese Foreign Ministry, "both sides recognised that they had different views" on the source of troubles in the East China Sea.[15]

The sensitivities surrounding the region were further illustrated in September 2010 when a Chinese fishing vessel, the *Minjinyu 5179*, was challenged by Japanese Coast Guard vessels in the disputed waters, resulting in the fishing boat colliding with two of the Japanese ships and the Chinese crew being taken into custody. However, diplomatic pressure from China along with a temporary suspension of rare earth mineral shipments, necessary for high-technology manufacturing, from China to Japan during the diplomatic standoff prompted a policy reversal, and the trawler captain was released without trial.[16] The dispute intensified after March 2012 when it was revealed that the Japanese government was seeking to purchase three of the disputed islands from a private owner, a move harshly condemned by Beijing, which argued that the islands were Chinese historical property.[17]

In January 2013, Japan accused a Chinese PLAN frigate, the *Lianyungang* (连云港), of deliberately locking its targeting radar on a Japanese Maritime Self-Defence Force (MSDF) vessel in a disputed zone of the East China Sea, a charge Beijing initially denied then admitted in March of that year, saying that the locking had been a judgement error. The increase of naval and air force activity by both parties in the East China Sea, coupled with the increased use of unmanned aerial vehicles (UAVs) over the waters (the Japanese Defence Ministry announced in October 2013 that any foreign drones operating in Japanese airspace would be shot down), substantially increased the risk of a miscalculation leading to a direct conflict. The November 2013 announcement by Beijing of an Air Defence Identification Zone (ADIZ) in the East China Sea, which overlapped that of Japan's, caused a further intensification of the dispute, as did the announcement in April 2014 by US President Obama confirming that the Senkaku/Diaoyu Islands were safeguarded under Article V of the US–Japan Security Treaty.[18]

Sino-Japanese relations since the end of the Koizumi government in Tokyo have seen a great deal of waxing and waning due to the very short terms in office held by Koizumi's immediate successors. The 2006–7 tenure of Shinzō Abe and his successor, Yasuo Fukuda, as Japanese prime minister created some opportunities for improvements to the Sino-Japanese relationship as both leaders called for "ice breaking" and "ice-melting" relations with Beijing. The ice made a swift return however with the coming to office of Taro Aso in 2008. As a former foreign minister, Aso had made inflammatory statements about China, Taiwan, and Japanese nationalism which threatened further diplomatic setbacks. However, he was ousted after a little less than a year in office and the opposition Democratic Party of Japan (DPJ) formed the next government under Yukio Hatoyama, who promptly made promises to move Japanese foreign policy further away from the US and closer to Asia. His promise, however, to close the American military facilities in Okinawa proved to be his political undoing when he reversed that decision and then resigned in 2010 under a cloud of criticism.

Hatoyama was succeeded by Naoto Kan, and it was during Kan's tenure that Japan experienced its worst disaster since the Second World War. On 11 March 2011, a magnitude 9.0 earthquake struck the Tōhoku region of eastern Japan, setting off a tsunami which devastated coastal cities and caused critical damage to the Fukushima Daiichi nuclear power facilities in the north-eastern part of the country, leading to a meltdown of three of the plant's six reactors. At least 15,800 casualties were reported, and massive efforts were required to contain a radiation leak from the Fukushima reactors. Beijing responded with aid and a rescue team and bilateral relations improved once again. However, with the announcement of closer US–Japanese military cooperation by American President Barack Obama and Japanese Prime Minister Yoshihiko Noda shortly after the latter's assuming office in September 2011, Chinese concerns about Tokyo's role in "containing" Chinese power resurfaced.

The tenure of Prime Minister Noda lasted only a little more than a year when his party was defeated in the December 2012 elections, paving the way for the return of Shinzō Abe as leader and for the Liberal Democratic Party to once again assume a governmental role. The election brought to an end the Democratic Party of Japan's brief period in government (2006–12), as well as the DPJ's attempts to realign Japanese foreign policy to reflect a more centrist stance between China and the United States. These moves reflected an acknowledgement of Beijing's growing economic and political power as well as concerns that the Asia-Pacific was being downgraded as a priority in Washington in favour of the Middle East and other regions. However, the start of the US pivot policy in Asia, as well as growing concerns about Chinese intentions in the East China Sea, eroded enthusiasm for a more Beijing-centric foreign policy.[19] Upon resuming office, it was clear that Prime Minister Abe strongly preferred a more independent Japanese defence stance along with increased strategic ties with the United States. Unlike during his first term, Abe began to demonstrate a greater emphasis on balancing China and building up Japanese defensive capabilities despite Article IX. For example, shortly after Abe resumed office, concerns were raised that he was seeking to revise, or at least downplay, the 1993 Kono Statement, which included a formal apology for forced prostitution policies during the Second World War.

By early 2015, Abe was also publically calling for changes to the Japanese constitution, including a potential alteration of Article IX, to allow for a more independent defence policy. These announcements created further concerns in China that Japan was seeking a rightward shift in its foreign policy and was attempting to develop a more activist military. Events such as the launch of a new helicopter carrier (or destroyer, according to the Japanese government), the *JS Izumo*, in August 2013 was one source of concern in China, due to both the vessel's potential offensive capabilities and the fact that it shares its name with an Imperial Japanese Naval cruiser which was active in the Pacific War before being sunk in July 1945.

As Chinese power grows and Japanese power begins to re-define itself after two decades of economic stagnation and frequent political instability, the relationship between the two countries continues to be marked by a considerable disconnect between political and economic relations. The post-2008 recession dealt a considerable blow to already sluggish Japanese finances, and the reconstruction required after the 2011 Tohōku earthquake further affected Japan's economy as well as its foreign policy. The Abe government has sought to revive the Japanese economy via a "three arrows policy" involving fiscal stimulus, monetary easing to lower the value of the *yen*, and domestic structural reforms. While various political issues continue to aggravate the relationship, from a trade viewpoint, both sides are eager to deepen their economic engagement and help build greater regional trade though such organisations as the ASEAN-Plus-Three, the East Asian Summit and the Regional Comprehensive Economic Partnership (RCEP). However, the political differences between the two states have also spilled over into the institutional realm. China is not a member of the Trans-Pacific Partnership, which Japan agreed to join in early 2013, while Tokyo opted not to become a founding member of the Beijing-backed AIIB in March 2015, out of deference to American concerns about the new bank.

By the end of 2014, tensions between China and Japan eased somewhat, as Chinese President Xi Jinping and Prime Minister Abe met briefly on the side-lines of the Asia-Pacific Economic Cooperation summit in Beijing in November of that year, where they were photographed shaking hands, albeit with somewhat pained expressions. However, a follow-up meeting in Jakarta in April 2015 between the two leaders was more cordial in tone. From a power-politics viewpoint, there is the question of what will happen should both China and Japan claim to be the fulcrum state in East Asia. The wildcard in this debate remains the United States, and much will depend on whether Washington continues to maintain its military commitments in the region. Although Japan seeks to deepen political and economic ties with China, its relationship with the United States has also remained a high priority for Tokyo. As Chinese scholars have noted, the relationship with Japan can best be described as "cold politics, hot economics" (*zhengleng jingre* 政冷经热),[20] a situation which appears likely to persist.

South Korea

Relations between the Republic of Korea (ROK) and China were seriously strained in the wake of the Korean War (1950–3) which resulted not only in the Communist North failing to annex the pro-Western south but also in thousands of American forces being stationed in the Demilitarised Zone (DMZ) between the two Koreas, uncomfortably close to China's north-eastern frontier. However, as China began to open up to the West and to its economic regimes in the 1980s, a policy not copied by North Korea, South Korea began to be looked upon by Beijing under Deng Xiaoping and Jiang Zemin as an attractive economic model for Beijing to emulate. As the Cold War began to fade, China reconsidered its traditional stance that there was only one Korean government, namely in Pyongyang, and began to support a "two Korea" regional policy, much to the dismay of North Korea.

This stance was codified in 1991 when China gave its support for both Koreas obtaining seats in the United Nations General Assembly, and then the following year when diplomatic relations between Seoul and Beijing commenced. Even before formal talks began, relations between the two countries on the sub-state level began to warm when Beijing agreed to send teams to Seoul for both the Asian Games in 1986 and the Olympics in 1988. The talks on opening diplomatic relations, referred to as "Operation East Sea" in Seoul, ultimately led to the establishment of relations in August 1992.[21] The decision to open negotiations was largely trade-driven, and shortly after relations were established, bilateral trade between the two states began to be much more valuable to Beijing than Sino-North Korean economic links.[22] South Korea was also adept at making use of its middle-power diplomacy in breaking the diplomatic stalemate which allowed China, along with Taiwan and Hong Kong, to join the APEC forum in 1991,[23] and the growing number of regional organisations in Asia has provided many more occasions for the two governments to confer on mutual international interests.

Sino-South Korean bilateral relations have often varied depending on specific South Korean administrations. The governments of Kim Dae-jung (1998–2003) and Roh Moo-hyun (2003–8) were comparatively more pro-Beijing than that of Lee Myung-bak (2008–13), which took on a more balanced position between China and the United States.[24] The post-2013 government of Park Geun-hye also attempted to balance between the two great powers. In April 2015, South Korea made a formal request to join the TPP trade talks, but during the previous month, the Park government also agreed to South Korea becoming a founding member of the AIIB despite American and Japanese concerns. In mid-2015, China–South Korea relations were also affected by an outbreak of Middle East Respiratory Syndrome (MERS) in the ROK, which prompted Beijing to issue a health warning in May of that year for Chinese nationals travelling to South Korea.

With China's rise and the American role in East Asia in transition, Seoul has been seeking a more equalised policy between the two powers and has been careful not to directly antagonise Beijing in strategic matters. For example, when the United States began to develop plans for a Theatre Missile Defence (TMD) system which would in theory protect American allies in Asia against rogue missiles, South Korea, unlike Japan, stated in 1999 that it would not participate in its development, believed due to both concerns over China's reaction and its stance against proliferation.[25] However, South Korea continued to be courted by the United States as missile interception technology improved, and in 2014–15 Seoul faced the difficult decision over whether to sign on to American plans to deploy its Terminal High Altitude Area Defence (THAAD) missile defence system on the peninsula. Although the mechanism could be used to defend against North Korean missile attacks, China has been critical of the system which it sees as an attempt by the United States to curtail Chinese military power in northeast Asia via its ally. As well, the successful deployment of a THAAD system in South Korea would disrupt Beijing's development of its anti-access / area denial (A2/AD) strategies designed to leverage American forces from waters bordered by the "first island chain" in the Western Pacific.

On a multilateral level, representatives from Beijing and Seoul met regularly during rounds of the Six-Party Talks (SPT) designed to promote security on the Korean Peninsula and to convince North Korea to cease its development of nuclear weapons. When the SPT was suspended after 2009 however, there appeared to be a widening of divisions regarding North Korean policy. This was illustrated when the South Korean corvette *ROKS Cheonan* was sunk in March 2010, reportedly after being hit by a North Korean torpedo. Pyongyang denied responsibility for the incident, later evidenced to the contrary, and China refrained from condemning Pyongyang, much to Seoul's dismay. The Chinese government also did not criticise North Korea for its shelling of South Korea's Yeonpyeong Island in November 2010, instead calling upon both sides to work towards peaceful relations. Since North Korea's second nuclear test in 2009, China began to demonstrate a softer approach towards Pyongyang and became more hesitant to criticise the policies of the Kim Jong-il government and its successor regime under Kim Jong-un. Strategically, China and South Korea share a concern that the Peninsula should be made into a nuclear weapons-free zone, and both states are committed to finding a multilateral solution to the North Korean crisis.

More than a decade after recognition, trade continues to dominate the Sino-South Korean relationship, and Beijing is now the centrepiece of what was called South Korea's "three number ones", namely that China is Seoul's biggest trading partner, largest export market and trade surplus source.[26] The bilateral economic relationship was further strengthened after the Xi government completed free trade negotiations with the Korean government of President Park in November 2014, with the agreement signed in June 2015, the largest such agreement in terms of trade volume which Beijing had signed to date. The China–South Korea free trade agreement (FTA) was also viewed in Beijing as a strong sign that China was prepared to negotiate more effectively with developed economies, as well as a potential building block for a trilateral FTA, possibly involving Japan.

Although political and economic relations are warm, there have been some concerns about the effect on South Korea of China's continued growth as a regional and international power. Beijing and South Korea are also involved in a maritime sovereignty dispute over a submerged rock in the Yellow Sea, historically named Socotra by British explorers but called Ieodo in Korean and Suyan Rock (*suyan jiao* 苏岩礁) in Chinese. Despite international law, which specifies that underwater features outside of a country's 12 nautical mile territorial sea limit cannot be claimed and cannot generate an exclusive economic zone, both China and South Korea nonetheless view the rock as part of their territory. Although the issue has not generated the same degree of political rancour as the Senkaku/Diaoyu dispute, there has been no resolution to the dispute. In the wake of Beijing's announcement that it was placing an ADIZ in the East China Sea, which included the Socotra Rock, Seoul responded the following month by expanding its own ADIZ, which was originally put into place in 1951 by the American military, during the height of the Korean War, to include the rock.[27] China's response was muted, and Beijing has since downplayed any talk of bilateral differences over the status of the region.

Another incident which highlighted sensitivities in this area took place in 2002–7 when Chinese historians, undertaking what was titled the "Northeast Project" (*dongbei gongcheng* 东北工程), suggested that the kingdom of Koguryo (Goguryeo) which existed on the Korean Peninsula from the first century BCE to the seventh century CE was actually a tributary government of Imperial China. The project upset many Koreans and created concerns about Chinese nationalism and attempts by Beijing to revise sensitive aspects of Korean history, more troublesome in light of China's growing regional power.[28] In June 2012, China's State Administration of Cultural Heritage agency added more fuel to bilateral historical debates when it presented evidence suggesting that China's iconic Great Wall extended far further eastwards than previous historical accounts indicated, as far as the ancient northern Korean kingdoms, including Koguryo.[29]

Despite these diplomatic differences, Beijing has been successful in engaging South Korea and strengthening ties with a country which had been shut out of Chinese foreign policy until less than 20 years ago, and the relationship is one of the strongest Beijing maintains in Asia. Moreover, China has been able to promote the greater balance in South Korean foreign policy between itself and the United States while benefiting from the many economic opportunities Seoul can provide. Although there are some diplomatic differences affecting bilateral relations, the China–South Korea relationship is one of the most visible examples of China's post-1990s peripheral diplomacy.

North Korea

In the 1940s and 50s, Mao Zedong's successful campaign of re-unifying China under the socialist banner greatly motivated then-North Korean leader Kim Il-sung to do the same for the Korean Peninsula, by force if need be.[30] Since he was unsuccessful, and after failing in the Korean War (1950–3) to conquer the Western-backed Republic of Korea, North Korea adopted a policy of ostensible diplomatic and economic "self-reliance" (*juche*), and today the country remains one of the most closed in the world. This barrier against excessive foreign influence moulded political, economic and military policies around the core ideological objective of eventual unification of Korea under Pyongyang's control. In reality, however, the country was heavily dependent upon Soviet and Chinese assistance, and with the fall of the USSR, North Korea was left with few allies save for China, which protected the DPRK during much of the Cold War and traditionally referred to the relationship as "close as lips and teeth" (*chunchi* 唇齿).

A formal alliance between Beijing and Pyongyang was codified in 1961.[31] However, the ties which brought the two together, including suspicion of the West and strong adherence to traditional Marxism-Leninism, quickly eroded as Beijing launched its economic and foreign policy reforms in the 1980s.[32] The state is run as a totalitarian regime with a corresponding cult of personality. Kim's son, Kim Jong-il, was officially designated as Kim's successor in 1980 and assumed a growing political and managerial role until his father's death in 1994, when he assumed full power without opposition. Kim Il-sung remains "eternal" head of state while the younger Kim was head of government and of the sole legal governing body, the Korean Workers' Party (KWP), until his death in December 2011. Both leaders built a near-unshakeable isolated regime which endures today, long after the end of the Cold War and despite many outside pressures and internal crises. Kim Jong-il's successor, his son Kim Jong-un, showed little sign during his first few months in power of moving towards any significant reforms of the hermit state.

While reliable information about the state's domestic and international politics is extremely scarce, the economy of the state is known to have all but collapsed due to faulty central planning, and industrial output has been in steady decline for decades. The state has experienced severe food shortages since the 1990s, including the Great Famine of 1996–9.[33] Part of the reason for the ongoing shortages was a massive flood in June 1995, from which the country is still trying to recover. The famine touched off much controversy in the United States and Asia over whether to provide assistance to a hostile regime. The country is also facing chronic shortages of energy and hard capital, with poverty rampant throughout. However, unlike in Eastern Europe in the 1980s, the isolation of the regime and the refusal of Kim to attempt political reform have prevented the rise of opposition forces or other pressures from globalisation. China remains North Korea's only major financial backer and trade between the two sides reached US$6.39 billion in 2014, a slight drop from the previous year.[34] Beijing still gives millions in aid and technical assistance to Pyongyang annually, and has sought to purchase larger supplies of North Korean coal, metals and minerals. However, political relations between the two sides have been less warm than during the Cold War, due to uncertainties regarding North Korea's future nuclear weapons policies as well as the DPRK's stubborn resistance to implement even the most basic of economic reforms.

Full societal control in the DPRK has been accomplished through two methods. First, there is complete control of information and state media, foreign contact and travel. Second, there is the constant psychological pressure of the *juche* programme and the personality cult. Anti-imperialism and capitalism are maintained. As well, North Korea's *seongoon chungchi* ("military-first" politics) emphasises that top policy priority should be given to the Korean People's Army and its military capabilities, adding to the psychological insulation. A 4-kilometre wide, 250 kilometre-long Demilitarized Zone (DMZ) has separated North from South Korea since 1953, with only 194 kilometres separating Pyongyang from Seoul. The region remains one of the most heavily armed in the world, with roughly 25,500 American forces augmenting a South Korean military of approximately 655,000 personnel as of 2014. North Korea is estimated to have armed forces of 1.02 million, most of which are thought to be deployed near the DMZ.

Since the 1990s North Korea, strongly encouraged by China, had been haltingly emerging from its diplomatic isolation, by participating in "Track II" dialogues as well as in the ASEAN Regional Forum (ARF) which was created in 1994 as an international discussion forum for Asian security. China also attempted to encourage the Kim Jong-il government in North Korea to develop its own Special Economic Zones to promote reform, and the most ambitious of these has been the Tumen River Development Project designed to develop a hydroelectricity sector between China, North Korea and Russia. However, progress has been very slow and it remains unclear when and if this project will ever be completed.

The political wariness between the two countries since the Cold War could be attributed to two factors. First, despite much prodding from Beijing, Pyongyang refused to accept anything but the most minute attempts at economic reform. For example, an attempt by Kim Jong-il to revalue the North Korean currency, the *won*, in late 2009 created major disruptions, reports of public protest, and the execution of a Planning and Finance director early the following year. Second, despite China's Cold War history of assisting North Korea with nuclear weapons development, Beijing was hopeful it could persuade Pyongyang not to test such a weapon, attempts which failed in October 2006. North Korea has a long history of seeking nuclear weapons, dating to the 1950s when the DPRK sought the bomb in order to respond to veiled American threats of nuclear weapons possibly being used during the Korean War.

In 1993, Pyongyang announced that it would withdraw from its membership in the Nuclear Non-Proliferation Treaty (NPT), touching off the first major Korea nuclear crisis. The American government under President Bill Clinton responded by entering into direct negotiations with Pyongyang in 1993–4, resulting in the Agreed Framework in October 1994. Under the agreement, North Korea would remain within the NPT and suspend further nuclear weapons development in exchange for an agreement by the US not to attack the DPRK. As well, the US, Japan and South Korea would provide two light water nuclear reactors which were to have been completed in 2003, as well as periodic oil shipments. A multilateral regime, the Korean Peninsula Energy Development Organisation (KEDO), would be created to oversee the energy-related aspects of the agreement.[35] However, North Korea later accused the US of being tardy with its commitments, and when George W. Bush came to power he was highly critical of the Framework, stating that it rewarded aggression and did not solve the problem of future conflicts with the North. North Korea, at the same time, was unhappy with the slow pace in both providing regular oil shipments and building the reactors. By the end of the 1990s, both the Agreed Framework and KEDO were being regarded more sceptically by both Pyongyang and Washington.

A subsequent North Korean nuclear crisis began in October 2002 when DPRK officials informed the American government that in defiance of the 1994 Framework Agreement they were again developing a uranium-enrichment programme in preparation for the development of nuclear weapons. North Korea was also furious at being cited as part of the "axis of evil" by Bush.[36] Unlike in the Iraq case, the United States responded to this potential WMD threat by urging a diplomatic solution and encouraging confidence-building in hopes of persuading the Kim regime to reverse its decision. Nevertheless, seals placed on North Korean nuclear reactors by the IAEA were removed that December, during the same month that the DPRK announced it was withdrawing from the Nuclear Non-Proliferation Treaty.[37] Washington ignored requests from Pyongyang for direct bilateral talks and instead China organised multilateral negotiations to solve the crisis.

As China was not directly involved in either the Agreed Framework or the creation of KEDO, Beijing wished to play a more direct role in subsequent Korean disarmament talks. As well, China was concerned that the United States might use force to deal with Pyongyang, an outcome no more appealing now than it had been in the early 1990s during the first crisis. In addressing this latest emergency, Beijing insisted upon a negotiated settlement, which included a complete de-nuclearisation of the peninsula and the maintenance of regional peace and stability. Using shuttle diplomacy, then-Deputy Foreign Minister Dai Bingguo was directed in early 2003 by President Hu Jintao to lay the groundwork for negotiations. The United States agreed to the diplomatic initiative, in no small part because it was currently engaged in Afghanistan and was commencing the first stages of an invasion of Iraq.[38]

North Korea followed through on its threat to leave the NPT in April 2003. However, in 2003–4, three rounds of Six-Party Talks between the Koreas, China, Japan, Russia and the United States were held in Beijing, opening communications but producing limited results.[39] During that time, North Korea was accused of continuing to prepare materials for nuclear weapons, which the government claimed was necessary for their defence. China's patience with Pyongyang had been tested in 2003 by two incidents. First, in February there was a shutdown of an oil pipeline between China and North Korea, which the former blamed on a technical fault but was widely seen as a pressure tactic. Second, in September Beijing announced the replacement of civilian police guarding the North Korean border by People's Liberation Army soldiers.[40]

The country has one known functioning nuclear reactor, in the city of Yongbyon, which can supposedly produce enough plutonium for approximately one nuclear weapon per year. However, it is unknown whether other forms of nuclear weapons development are being pursued elsewhere in the country. As well, North Korea has stockpiles of short-range *Nodong* missiles capable of striking South Korea and Japan, and has tested a longer-range *Taepodong* missile which if fully operational, some analysts fear, could strike the North American west coast. The August 1998 test of a *Taepodong I* missile, which flew over Japanese airspace before crashing into the Pacific, was seen as proof that North Korea was close to developing heavy-lift and ICBM technology. Pyongyang stated it had been attempting to launch a satellite, a claim neither Washington nor Tokyo believed. This test was also seen as the impetus for American attempts at developing theatre missile defence, with increased Japanese assistance. In February 2005, North Korea announced the suspension of its participation in talks concerning its nuclear programme for an "indefinite period", blaming the Bush administration's lack of respect for Pyongyang's security, and KEDO lapsed into inactivity in May 2006. Since the crisis began the US had repeatedly refused DPRK demands for direct one-to-one talks, and the US remains unwilling to offer another version of the oil and assistance deal of 1994, out of concern that such actions would reward bad behaviour. Pyongyang inched closer to a regional confrontation when in July 2006 it conducted tests of seven missiles, six of which were short-range vehicles (*Nodong* and *Scud* missiles) and the last was a suspected *Taepodong II* missile. Although the *Taepodong* crashed well short of target and was regarded as a failure, China joined other regional powers in expressing their concerns about this seemingly provocative act.[41]

Finally, on 9 October 2006 North Korea detonated an approximately 1 kilotonne nuclear device near the city of Gilju near the border with China, thus making the DPRK the *de facto* ninth nuclear power, although it has not been formally recognised as such. Beijing received warning only minutes before the test via a phone call from Pyongyang, and the Chinese government launched an unusually strong public criticism of the blast, calling it "flagrant" (*hanran* 悍然), wording normally used by Beijing when an adversary commits an objectionable act.[42] Shortly afterwards, China sided with the rest of the UNSC in passing Resolution 1718, imposing economic and military sanctions on the DPRK. However, Beijing favoured a return to the Six-Party Talks rather than threats of force to solve the crisis. The talks restarted at the end of 2006 and produced a tentative, and temporary, stopgap agreement in March 2007.[43]

The 2006 nuclear crisis and its after-effects placed Beijing in a difficult position for several reasons. First, the test proceeded despite Chinese pressure, illustrating the degree of erosion of Beijing's diplomatic power over the DPRK since the Cold War. As well, Beijing had placed much political capital on the Six-Party Talks, but this process will be greatly complicated now that North Korea has crossed the nuclear threshold. Many Chinese government officials still view North Korea as an essential ally, and fear an implosion of the country would bring American forces back to the Chinese border as well as a massive influx of North Korean refugees (*taobeizhe* 逃北者) into China's northern provinces.[44] However, China does not want another nuclear power on its doorstep. Despite China and North Korea remaining nominal allies, Beijing remembers the example of Vietnam demonstrating that even ideological partners can turn on each other in the name of *realpolitik*. There is also the possibility of a "fire-chain" scenario, where Japan, South Korea and possibly Taiwan also develop the bomb in order to counter North Korea. Pyongyang has remained wary of Japan, and at times is overtly hostile as for example the former threatened in September 2004 to turn the latter into a "nuclear sea of fire",[45] and Beijing fears that Tokyo, if provoked to extremes, may also respond by developing a nuclear weapon.

China, Japan and the United States are all wary of the possibility the DPRK may export nuclear technology to hostile states and perhaps even to terrorist organisations in exchange for hard capital. These concerns appeared justified when it was reported that a suspected Syrian nuclear facility, destroyed by Israel in September 2007 in what was called Operation Orchard, was partially supported by North Korea. Beijing has been insistent that North Korea should not be allowed to help other nuclear threshold states develop a nuclear capability.[46] A promising breakthrough was made in June 2008 when Pyongyang destroyed a cooling tower at its Yongbyon site and expressed willingness to negotiate a possible disarmament blueprint in exchange for a resumption of fuel shipments.[47] However, that victory proved short-lived,

---

Box 7.1 North Korea's "brazen" nuclear test

"China's punctilious Foreign Ministry reserves the word *hanran*, which translates as brazen or flagrant, for serious affronts to the nation's dignity by countries that have historically been rivals or enemies.

North Korea, a longstanding ideological ally, has had increasingly testy relations with China in recent years. But it was not until Monday, moments after North Korea apparently exploded a nuclear device, that China accused it of a 'brazen' violation of its international commitments."

– Joseph Kahn, *The New York Times*, 10 October 2006.

as Pyongyang began to make preparations towards a second nuclear test which it conducted in May 2009 along with a renewed series of missile launchings. Beijing's response was more muted than after the previous test, but an official statement stressed that the Chinese government was "resolutely opposed" to the test. As noted above, Beijing's responses to the 2010 sinking of the South Korean naval vessel *Cheonan* warship and DPRK shelling of Yeonpyeong Island later that year were also restrained.

Although the Sino-DPRK relationship has cooled, China is still viewed as the only state with enough diplomatic leverage against Pyongyang to convince it to abandon its nuclear programme. However, there is the question of whether any progress on rolling back a North Korean bomb will require pressure from both China and United States. Pyongyang has long called for direct, strictly bilateral talks with the United States, but Washington has been unwilling to participate and Beijing insisted that China needed a chair at the negotiating table. In the last round of Six-Party Talks in September 2007, Pyongyang agreed to disable its nuclear programme indefinitely and to allow for inspection in exchange for increased diplomatic and economic contacts with the US and Japan. Attempts to continue the SPT again since 2009 produced few results despite frequent prodding from Beijing. While the United States would not remove the option of using force to deal with North Korea's potential regional security threats, Beijing has denounced any talk of a military solution or invasive sanctions in favour of ongoing diplomacy.

By 2012 there appeared to be a waiting game being played in light of the power transition in China, the elections in South Korea scheduled for December of that year, and the still uncertain political leanings of Kim Jong-un, who was viewed as requiring the support of the North Korean army and his own family in order to retain power. Kim's political status was placed further in doubt in April 2012 when an attempt to launch a rocket to commemorate the hundredth anniversary of Kim Il-sung's birth failed when the missile broke up minutes after lift-off amid US criticism and China's calls for "calm and restraint".[48] In January 2013, the Kim Jong-un government conducted North Korea's third nuclear test, with a yield of approximately 7 kilotonnes. This latest test resulted in international outcry and protests from Beijing, with the Chinese Foreign Ministry announcing that it "resolutely" opposed the test. These events not only demonstrated the limits of Chinese nuclear diplomacy, but also the steadfastness of the Kim Jong-un regime to retain a nuclear capability in order to prevent US-led attempts at forced regime change along the same lines as in Iraq as well as Western support for the Arab Spring and Ukraine protests. North Korean officials were candid about the idea that the Gaddafi regime in Libya would not have fallen in 2011 had Tripoli not abandoned its previous nuclear weapons programmes.[49]

In December 2014, China found itself in the middle of diplomatic crossfire between North Korea and the United States over the release of an American satirical film, *The Interview*, which parodied the Kim Jong-un regime. During the diplomatic melee both the studio releasing the film, Sony, and North Korea's internet experienced what were likely hacking attacks. Although the Chinese media was critical of the movie's release, the film did circulate extensively in China. Despite cooling relations between Beijing and the Kim Jong-un government, there was little sign that Beijing was willing to place added economic pressure on Pyongyang to encourage nuclear disarmament, and as North Korea began to face a severe drought in mid-2015,[50] Beijing expressed its willingness to send support. Despite cordial political and improving economic relations between China and North Korea, Beijing's future policies towards the DPRK will greatly depend upon whether Pyongyang can be convinced to forgo its nuclear programme.

Southeast Asia

China's southern neighbours have undergone a variety of changes since the end of the Cold War, with the removal of the ideological splits in Southeast Asia permitting the region to build stronger ties and slowly develop the main regional organisation in the area. The Association of Southeast Asian Nations (ASEAN) was created in 1967 in part due to concerns about socialist expansion, including from China. The China challenge in Southeast Asia had assumed a more benign visage due to Beijing's good-neighbor policies towards the south in the 1990s. Until outstanding regional issues, including the status of the South China Sea, between China and parts of Southeast Asia began to intensify, the ASEAN region had been another example of China's peripheral diplomacy producing positive tangible results in both the diplomatic and the economic fields. In some cases Beijing was successful in developing a more congenial identity in Southeast Asia, but at present there are significant differences among ASEAN members about the significance to them of China's rise in the region.

Before the thawing of Sino-Southeast Asian relations in the 1980s, Beijing often viewed its southern neighbours primarily as metaphorical chess pieces, first in competition with the United States and then later with the Soviet Union. Southeast Asian policy under Mao was marked by strong support of communist movements in the region, most notably in Indonesia, where China was blamed for backing an attempted communist coup against the Sukarno regime in Jakarta in 1965.[51] After Sino-Soviet relations deteriorated in the early 1960s, Beijing began to view Vietnam as a Soviet proxy when Hanoi refused to support China against the USSR. As a result of border disputes followed by Hanoi's overthrow of the Khmer Rouge government in Cambodia in 1978, which was nominally allied with China, Beijing attempted, unsuccessfully, to fight what it termed a "self-defence counterattack" (*ziwei fanji zhan* 自卫反击战) via a limited war in northern Vietnam.

Border conflicts erupted during February–March 1979 before China declared that its aims had been realised and withdrew, with both sides suffering heavy casualties and economic damage. Not only were Vietnamese forces not dislodged from Cambodia, but the weaknesses of the People's Liberation Army in fighting out-of-area were exposed despite China's determination to "teach Vietnam a lesson".[52] However, as a result of the Dengist reforms and a desire to disengage from supporting communist elements in Southeast Asia, Beijing undertook a more conciliatory approach to peacebuilding in the area. China sat with the other permanent members of the UN Security Council to draft the 1989 Paris peace agreement designed to end fighting in Cambodia, and assented to a UN peacekeeping force being deployed there in order to facilitate elections in Phnom Penh in 1993,[53] a move away from Beijing's previous misgivings about the use of UN peacekeepers in Asia.

Southeast Asia assumed a very important role in Jiang Zemin's peripheral diplomacy, as two states which were isolated from China, Brunei and Singapore, successfully negotiated full diplomatic relations in 1991. As well, China agreed to join the ASEAN Regional Forum (ARF) in 1994 despite its traditional mistrust of security regimes, and shortly afterwards China became a formal dialogue partner with ASEAN.[54] The onset of the 1997–8 Asian Financial Crisis did much to underscore the changed economic relationship between China and ASEAN, as many of the worst-hit economies as a result of the currency value meltdown were in that region, including Thailand, Indonesia, Malaysia and the Philippines. During that tumultuous time, Beijing assumed the unlikely role of the region's "white knight" through a variety of actions. First, it refused, unlike Taiwan, to devalue its own currency as a defensive measure against the rising prices of its exports in comparison with Southeast Asia. Second,

Beijing arranged for emergency financial assistance to crisis-hit states, including authorising a US$1 billion transfer to the International Monetary Fund (IMF) to assist the flagging Thai economy. Third, it was able to accomplish this while also protecting Hong Kong's currency, which also risked a meltdown in the wake of the former colony's stock market crash in October 1997. Finally, Beijing was widely viewed in Southeast Asia as an island of stability and increasingly as an economic pivot for its conservative and helpful approaches to dealing with the economic chaos.[55] In the aftermath of the AFC, China became a major contributor to the development of the ASEAN-Plus-Three (APT), which brought together ASEAN, China, Japan and South Korea to discuss mutual economic interests.[56]

From a strategic viewpoint, however, there were still serious issues between China and ASEAN which affected the relationship in the 1990s. The largest of these was the status of the South China Sea and the administration of the small island chains within it, as noted in previous chapters. Beijing has maintained that it has full sovereignty over the whole of the Sea, and official Chinese maps feature a loosely-defined nine-dashed line (*jiu duanxian* 九段线) boundary which cordons roughly 80 per cent of the waterway. The two main island groups in the Sea, namely the Spratly (*Nansha* 南沙) and Paracel (*Xisha* 西沙) groups, are claimed by China in full. However, Vietnam also claims the Paracels, which were seized by China from Hanoi in 1974, and the Spratlys are in the middle of an even thornier legal dispute, as they are claimed by China, the Philippines, Taiwan and Vietnam and in part by Brunei and Malaysia.[57] Indonesia has no claims to the Spratlys, but the waters surrounding Indonesia's Natuna Island are also disputed by Beijing. Although the islands themselves are small and uninhabited, they are seen as valuable both due to potential oil and gas supplies which may lie under them, and because they are located along heavily-trafficked sea routes.

Concerns among the ASEAN nations over China's territorial designs for the Spratlys came to a head in 1995 when the PLA Navy seized one island, the aptly-named Mischief Reef (*Meiji jiao* 美济礁), and ejected Philippine fishermen while subsequently setting up permanent structures in order to assert Chinese claims. The ASEAN membership reacted with concern but restraint, and eventually presented Beijing with a joint expression of their dismay over China's actions.[58] In the wake of the loss of Mischief Reef, the Philippines in 1999 authorised the beaching of an elderly naval vessel, the *Sierra Madre*, at the nearby Ayungin Shoal (which China claims as *Ren'ai Jiao* 仁爱礁), establishing a makeshift military garrison. The prospect of a heightened level of tension over the final status of the Spratlys seemed a strong possibility. However, since then Beijing has sought to allay

---

Box 7.2 The South China Sea

"Sovereignty disputes in the South China Sea involve five countries plus Taiwan. China (and Taiwan) claim sovereignty over all its islands. Vietnam, the Philippines, Malaysia, and Brunei each claim some of the land features. Further complicating the labyrinth of claims is the 'nine-dash line' that appears in official Chinese maps. It loops down from the coast to take in most of the South China Sea – 60 to 90 per cent depending on the assumed geographic extent of the sea – significantly overlapping exclusive economic zones asserted by the other claimants and by Indonesia. Though the area has seen a pattern of confrontations followed by periods of relative calm for decades, volatility has increased in recent years and the lulls grown shorter."

– "Stirring Up the South China Sea (III)", *International Crisis Group Asia Report* 267 (7 May 2015).

fears about further aggressive moves towards Southeast Asia in the Spratleys while at the same time not relinquishing its claims. In November 2002 China struck an agreement with ASEAN in Phnom Penh to commit to a peaceful solution to the dispute, and the following year Beijing signed the treaty of Amity and Cooperation (TAC) with ASEAN governments which included a promise not to threaten the security of other signatory states.[59] This led to a period of quiet in the region as all sides avoided any provocative actions.

However, after 2009 Chinese tensions rose again with the Philippines and Vietnam. The United States, traditionally unwilling to make official comments on the legal status of the South China Sea, now found itself being more fully drawn into the dispute. After Chinese policymakers allegedly referred to the South China Sea as a "core interest" (*hexin liyi* 核心利益) of Beijing in 2010, it appeared to signify that Beijing was now in a position to more fully press its claim to the waterway, even though the term was not subsequently used in official Chinese government statements.[60] The response by the US government that its own interest was to promote freedom of navigation in the South China Sea led to Chinese criticism. In May 2011 a Vietnamese fossil fuel survey vessel was allegedly harassed and damaged by three Chinese maritime patrol ships, and starting in April 2012 a standoff began between Chinese and Philippine fishing and patrol vessels near the Scarborough Shoal, an islet both countries claim and what China names Huangyan Island (*Huangyan dao* 黄岩岛). Chinese officials described its actions there as a "cabbage" strategy, meaning the surrounding of a disputed islet with fishing and civilian vessels in addition to naval ones to provide several layers of protection. The incident came to an end in June 2012 when the ships from both sides withdrew, but during the following month the Chinese navy took full control over the region and barred the entrance of other vessels into the shoal.

After 2012, Washington and Manila began negotiations involving potentially closer military cooperation, including improving ties to levels seen before the US closed its military bases in the Philippines in 1991. In the wake of the Scarborough fiasco and other previous encounters with China in the region, Manila began to consider a legal challenge to Chinese actions in the Spratlys, and in January 2013 the Philippines formally filed a case with the International Tribunal for the Law of Sea, a move which Beijing criticised as invalid.[61] The legal challenge had the full support of Philippine President Benigno Aquino III, who was highly critical of Chinese actions in the South China Sea. In September 2012, he issued an administrative order which renamed the waters the "West Philippine Sea", and twice the Philippine President compared Chinese actions in the region to the expansionist policies of Nazi Germany in the period before the Second World War, drawing criticism and concern from Beijing.[62] In June 2015, personnel with the Philippine military accompanied Japan's Self-Defence forces in a joint operation near Reed Bank, a region thought to be potentially rich in fossil fuels, and another area claimed by Beijing and Manila. China, which refers to Reed Bank as *Li Yuetan* (礼乐滩), protested to both the operations and the possibility that Tokyo might involve itself more directly in future South China Sea disputes.[63]

US–Vietnamese military relations also looked to improve that year as a result of joint concern about Chinese actions in the waterway. However unlike the Philippines, which has a security treaty with Washington, Vietnam has sought to develop stronger relations with several powers, including India and Russia as well as the United States, to balance against China. The decision by China to place an oil rig in disputed waters near the Paracel Islands in mid-2014 marked a low point in the bilateral relationship, and Hanoi has also been wary of efforts since that time by China to engage in land reclamation of reefs which Vietnam has claimed. By mid-2015, bilateral relations appeared ready to enter another difficult patch as the Chinese oil rig was returned to another disputed part of the South China Sea in an area where the EEZs of Vietnam and China overlap.[64] However, the trading relationship between the two countries remains strong, and the Vietnamese government has frequently debated to what degree it should align itself with US strategic interests in the Asia-Pacific given the country's longstanding "three no's" approach to military strategy, meaning no military alliances, no foreign bases on Vietnamese soil, no reliance on an external partner for assistance during times of warfare.[65] Given Vietnam's unhappy history of great power conflict in the twentieth century, including wars against France, the United States and briefly with China, Hanoi remains sensitive on the subject of great power alignment.

A related issue for China in Southeast Asia is the security of sea lanes of communication, or SLoCs, vital to Chinese trade. Chief among these is the Malacca Straits, a corridor for an increasing amount of Chinese imports, especially oil and gas. Security for the very narrow maritime passage is largely overseen by the surrounding states, namely Indonesia, Malaysia and Singapore, but Beijing is concerned that should passage through the Straits be blocked either by terrorists or by a state seeking to interdict Chinese trade, Beijing would be vulnerable as it currently lacks the means to effectively patrol the region. Hu Jintao remarked on this "Malacca Dilemma" (*Maliujia kunju* 马六甲困局) in a 2003 speech, noting that China's increasing energy imports would be at risk if another state attempted to blockade the Malacca region. Beijing responded by seeking to modernise its naval capability as well as seeking to work with Southeast Asian states to augment security in the region.[66] This case study further underlined the fact that Chinese and Southeast Asian security issues are becoming increasingly interlinked. The "one belt and one road" trade corridors proposed by President Xi Jinping in 2013 would also of necessity make use of the South China Sea, the Malacca region, and the Indian Ocean for increased Chinese commerce.

In recent years, economics have begun to dominate the relationship between China and Southeast Asia, as illustrated when Beijing in 2000 proposed an ASEAN–China Free Trade Agreement (ACFTA) which would liberalise trading links between Beijing and the ten ASEAN economies.[67] The first stages of the ACFTA agreement came into effect in January 2010, creating the world's largest free trade area in terms of population. The ten states of ASEAN are also all members of China's Asian Infrastructure Development Bank, but the Trans-Pacific Partnership (TPP) trade agreement has been divisive, given that while China remains out of the collective, Brunei, Malaysia and Vietnam are members of the negotiations while the Philippines announced its intention to join the talks in June 2015, and other ASEAN members might follow suit.

After the turn of the century, Beijing made great diplomatic strides in other parts of Southeast Asia, and this region had been one of the main beneficiaries not only of China's peripheral diplomacy but, it has been argued, Beijing's economic "charm offensive" under Hu Jintao.[68] Beijing has developed especially strong relations with Cambodia and Laos, and the government of Thailand also began to improve relations with China in the wake of a coup in May 2014 which led to the coming to power of a military junta, the National Council for Peace and Order, led by Prayut Chan-ocha. In February 2015, Bangkok and Beijing agreed to upgrade military relations and lay the groundwork for future defence cooperation in the wake of cooling relations between Thailand and the United States since the coup.[69] Bilateral relations between China and Malaysia were strained in March 2014 in the aftermath of the disappearance of Malaysia Airlines Flight 370 (MH370), which vanished while en route from Kuala Lumpur to Beijing; of the 227 passengers on board, 152 were Chinese citizens.

Events in Myanmar (Burma) since 2007 further highlighted challenges for China's regional diplomacy with ASEAN. The two countries had traditionally been close, with Burma being the first non-communist government to recognise the Maoist government in China, and the two states signed a friendship treaty in 1954. China slowly became Myanmar's closest regional partner when the latter became increasingly isolated after a 1962 military coup, and a crackdown on protests in August 1988 which resulted in another coup and the formation of the State Law and Order Restoration Council (SLORC), renamed the State Peace and Development Council in 1997. The United States encouraged the diplomatic and economic isolation of Myanmar, and although the country was admitted to ASEAN in 1997, its relations with much of Asia were limited, and therefore China–Myanmar relations became closer during much of this period. However, when anti-government demonstrations ignited in September 2007, protests which were given the misleading name "Saffron Revolution", the subsequent government crackdown prompted an international outcry and placed Beijing in a difficult position. The Hu Jintao government first maintained a non-interventionist stance but later called upon the government to settle the dispute in a more peaceful manner.[70]

In 2010, however, Sino-Burmese relations would be affected by a series of sweeping political reforms implemented by the military junta. A flawed election was held in November 2010 with the military officially abdicating power in favour of a civilian government, and during the same month jailed opposition leader Aung San Suu Kyi was released after long periods of detention since 1989, and she and her political party, the National League for Democracy (NLD) were allowed to participate in a subsequent vote in April 2012. Since taking office in March 2011, former military leader turned civilian president Thein Sein promised further reforms and the long-chilled relations with the United States and Europe began to thaw. A new election was promised for the end of 2015, with the Myanmar military retaining a degree of government oversight regardless of the results of the vote.

The post-2010 Myanmar reforms opened the door to renewed political and economic relations with the United States and Western Europe, as well as India, Japan and other parts of Southeast Asia. This opening took place at a time when relations between China and Myanmar cooled. In August 2009, fighting between Myanmar armed forces and rebel militias in the country's Kokang region bordering southern China precipitated a massive exodus of refugees, involving possibly as many as 30,000 persons, across the frontier into China's Yunnan province, prompting rare criticism from Beijing towards the Myanmar government. In October 2011, the Myanmar government called a halt to construction of a controversial dam project at Myitsone, in the northern part of the country, which was designed to provide needed electricity to southern China. The multimillion-dollar project, which was heavily supported by Chinese investment, had been criticised by both environmentalists and local leaders due to the potential damage to the region.

In April 2015, four Chinese nationals were killed in Linceng, Yunnan, during a bombing incident by the Myanmar armed forces in pursuit of rebel militants. Afterwards, both governments pledged to bolster border security, but the ongoing ethnic violence in northern Myanmar remains a strong challenge to the stability of that border region. In June 2015, China's PLA held military drills in Yunnan close to the Myanmar border, a move which further illustrated Beijing's concerns about the stability of that region. However, later that month, Aung San Suu Kyi was invited to Beijing for a dialogue with President Xi Jinping, a sign that China was still placing a great deal of importance on its Myanmar relations. Despite the possibility of several new economic partners for the country, China remains as the key player in Myanmar trade. One often-repeated local saying in Myanmar is that the United States and Japan are boulders which can be moved, but that China is a boulder which cannot be moved.

Oceania

In Australia, China's growing presence in the Asia-Pacific has become a major foreign policy issue since the turn of the century, with Beijing representing a growing interest in Australian trade. Bilateral trade has especially been dominated by raw material exports to China, especially iron ore, coal and liquefied natural gas.[71] China and Australia first formally agreed to commence negotiations on a free-trade agreement in 2005 under the then-government of John Howard in Australia. However, despite numerous negotiation rounds, divisions between the two sides persisted and the outcome of the talks was placed in doubt.

For example, in early 2012, there were differences between the two sides over what degree of access Chinese state-owned enterprises should have to Australian assets. There were hopes that after the very pro-American stance of the Howard government, the election of Kevin Rudd in 2007 would mark a warming of relations with Beijing, especially given that Rudd was a fluent Mandarin speaker and a scholar of Chinese history. However, despite the initial enthusiasm for the Rudd government towards widening Chinese ties, including supporting the opening of the Centre for China and the World research institute at the Australia National University (ANU) in Canberra in 2010, bilateral diplomatic complications would appear at the same time. The most visible of these was the July 2009 arrest of an Australian national and three Chinese colleagues, all employees of the UK–Australian metals firm Rio Tinto, by Chinese authorities for espionage, which resulted in a diplomatic cooling.

As well, Australia's strategic stance appeared to suggest that it was concerned about China's military advancements. This was demonstrated by the country's 2009 Defence White Paper which called upon Beijing to better clarify its longer-term strategic goals.[72] Beijing's concerns about Australia's defence posture and strategic alignment with the United States grew under Rudd's successor, Julia Gillard, after it was announced in late 2011 that the northern Australian city of Darwin would begin to house US Marines as part of an increased United States military presence in the region. This prompted criticism of Australia during the first half of 2012 in some parts of the Chinese press for growing partisanship in Canberra's regional policies. When Tony Abbott became Prime Minister in September 2013, the stage appeared to be set for further diplomatic turbulence. The Abbott government was especially critical of the Xi government's decision to establish an ADIZ in the East China Sea in late 2013, and invited Japanese Prime Minister Abe to Canberra after referring to Japan as Australia's "best friend" in Asia.

However, Sino-Australian diplomatic relations bounced back when the free trade talks were finally completed at the end of 2014, with the deal officially signed in June the following year. The Abbott government celebrated what it called the completion of a "historic trifecta", given Canberra's signing of free trade agreements with Japan and South Korea in 2014.[73] Australia was also an early supporter of the AIIB project and agreed to become a founding member of the new bank. As the Bank's constitution was being prepared for signing by the 57 member states of the institution, the Australian government announced that it was in place to be the AIIB's sixth-largest stakeholder after China, India, the Russian Federation, Germany and South Korea.[74] With these developments, Australia appeared to be preparing for more overt balancing policies between China and the United States.

Relations between China and New Zealand became increasingly warm and trade-dominated in the wake of the two nations signing their free trade agreement in April 2008, with NZ being the first Organisation for Economic Cooperation and Development (OECD) member to sign such a bilateral agreement with China. The strong economic relations with China were partially a result of the cooler relationship between NZ and the United States after the alliance between the two governments was severed in the mid-1980s over New Zealand's nuclear weapons

Box 7.3 China and the United States in the Pacific

"What the Asia-Pacific countries care about most is to maintain economic prosperity and build on the momentum of economic growth and regional cooperation. At a time when people long for peace, stability and development, to deliberately give prominence to the military security agenda, scale up military deployment and strengthen military alliances is not really what most countries in the region hope to see.

The vast Pacific Ocean has ample space for China and the United States. We welcome a constructive role by the United States in promoting peace, stability and prosperity in the region. We also hope that the United States will fully respect and accommodate the major interests and legitimate concerns of Asia-Pacific countries."

– Xi Jinping, interview with the *Washington Post*, 13 February 2012.

ban, which prevented US naval vessels from entering NZ waters. Relations between the two states improved greatly after November 2010 when then-US Secretary of State Hillary Clinton visited New Zealand and co-signed the Wellington Declaration which significantly restored ties,[75] but NZ remains wary of aligning with the United States to the same degree that Australia had under the Gillard and Abbott administrations.

Shortly after the free trade agreement went into effect, China displaced the United States as New Zealand's second-largest trading partner after Australia. Dairy products, wood, wool and seafood grew to dominate NZ exports to China. New Zealand, like Australia, had managed to bypass the worst of the post-2008 economic downturn largely due to its economic links with China and Asia, but both states also remain wary of the potential side-effects of a slowdown in the Chinese economy. Chinese President Xi visited New Zealand in November 2014, with the Chinese leader and Prime Minister Key promising to further widen and deepen their trade relationship. New Zealand was also a strong early supporter of the AIIB.

In the South Pacific, China's strategic, diplomatic and economic presence increased considerably after the turn of the century, especially in Melanesia and Polynesia. After 2004, China's naval modernisation under Hu Jintao included planning an expansion of "far seas operations" (*yuanhai zuozhan* 远海作战) as an essential means to better project Chinese military capabilities further away from its coastline. Strategic distinctions were made between the "second island chain" (*di'er daolian* 第二岛链) in China's developing maritime security thinking, which included Japan's Kurile Islands, the US territory of Guam, the Marianas, Micronesia and Papua New Guinea. The waters between this chain and the "first island chain" (*diyi daolian* 第一岛链) of Japan, Taiwan and the Philippines, were referred to as the "middle seas", and the Pacific Ocean to the west of the second island chain was thus the "far seas". The potential role of Guam and the Mariana Islands in the proposed re-deployment of American naval assets in the Pacific would in theory suggest that the region might be seen as a potential location for strategic manoeuvres between China and the US.

However, Beijing sought to downplay the idea that the mid-Pacific would be a Chinese military interest. For example, in August and September 2010, two PLAN ships, the frigate *Mianyang* (绵阳) and the training vessel *Zhenghe* (郑和) made well-received visits to PNG, Vanuatu and Tonga as well as Australia and New Zealand as part of a naval goodwill tour. In 2014, the PLA's medical vessel, the *Peace Ark* (*Heping fangzhou* 和平方舟), also made tours to Fiji, Papua New Guinea, Tonga and Vanuatu.[76] Beijing has also been seeking to improve its diplomatic reputation in the region after riots erupted in 2006 in the Solomon Islands and Tonga, which targeted Chinese businesses.

Until the diplomatic truce of 2008, the South Pacific had been a key diplomatic battleground between Beijing and Taipei and was frequently an arena for "chequebook diplomacy" (*zhipiaobu waijiao* 支票簿外交) between both sides, as financial incentives were often part of the negotiations for a given South Pacific state to recognise either China or Taiwan. This situation frequently saw many South Pacific nations switch recognition from one side to another, in some cases more than once, largely prompted by competing promises of aid. For example, in November 2004 then-Vanuatu Prime Minister Serge Vohor sought to switch recognition from Beijing to Taipei while seeking to maintain economic links with both sides. However, Vohor's government collapsed over that policy, and relations resumed with Beijing less than a month after the agreement with Taiwan was signed.[77] Since the truce, six South Pacific nations were among the governments which recognised Taiwan, namely Kiribati, the Marshall Islands, Nauru, Palau, the Solomon Islands and Tuvalu.

Even with the diplomatic truce with Taipei in place, Beijing continued to offer loans, aid and assistance with infrastructure projects to its Pacific allies. Premier Wen Jiabao attended the 2006 Pacific Islands Forum (PIF) summit in Nadi, Fiji and announced a regional loan package totalling US$375 million. During the same year, the China–Pacific Island Countries Economic Development and Cooperation Forum was founded. At a November 2013 meeting of that group in Guangzhou, it was announced by the Chinese government that the Pacific Islands would be the recipient of a concessional loan package worth US$1 billion.

China also provided economic support for the regional Melanesian Spearhead Group (MSG), providing the funding for the organisation's secretariat building in Port Vila, Vanuatu, which opened in 2007. A majority of Chinese regional aid, both multilaterally and bilaterally, was in the form of "soft loans" with below-market-level interest rates and featuring flexible repayment rates. However, in some cases Chinese soft loans were beginning to represent a sizeable portion of individual Pacific nations' GDP. For example, figures for 2005–9 suggested that Chinese loans to the Cook Islands and Samoa each represented 16 per cent of their economy's GDP, and in the case of Tonga, 32 per cent.[78] The high numbers in some cases led to concerns about repayment of these loans and the long-term political and economic effects on some aid recipients.

According to a March 2015 study released by the Lowy Institute in Sydney, Chinese aid to the Pacific Islands from 2006 to 2013 totalled approximately US$1.06 billion, and was on the same level as that of New Zealand, with China in a position to overtake Japan as the third-largest aid donor in the Pacific. Although China was not in a position to usurp Australia as the largest Pacific aid donor (Australian aid during the 2006–13 period stood at US$6.8 billion), Beijing was increasingly being seen in the region as the main alternative supplier of aid and investment, especially for infrastructure projects.[79] Examples include a joint project between China, New Zealand and the Cook Islands to refurbish waterworks infrastructure in the Cooks' capital of Rarotonga, upgraded tourism facilities in Fiji, and aid to Vanuatu after the Pacific nation suffered heavy damage from a tropical cyclone in March 2015. As well, a nickel mine in Papua New Guinea is majority-owned by a Chinese firm.

China, along with other donors in Asia, maintained economic links with Fiji despite Australian and New Zealand sanctions placed on the country after a military coup by Commodore Voreqe "Frank" Bainimarama in 2006, much to the dismay of Canberra and Wellington, which had been hoping to use economic pressure to ensure that the island state returned to democracy after the elections Bainimarama promised for 2014. In the months before the Fiji elections, both Australia and NZ eased sanctions on Fiji, and Bainimarama was formally elected to office after the vote in September 2014, promising to further improve relations with Beijing.

Another dimension of China's engagement with the South Pacific has been a development in trade for raw materials and resources which Beijing increasingly requires to maintain its economic reforms and burgeoning growth rates. However, unlike in Africa and Latin America, natural resources are fewer in number and more expensive given the region's remoteness. Fishing is one area in which Beijing has increased its presence in the South Pacific, and in the case of Papua New Guinea, metals and minerals as well as the possibility of joint fossil fuel development. Although it is unlikely that there will be as great a competition for resources in the South Pacific as is perceived in other parts of the world, China's growing interests there may lead to more overt diplomatic competition between Beijing and the traditional powers in the region, namely the United States, Australia and New Zealand.

Conclusions

These case examples illustrate the progress which Beijing attempted to make in developing stronger and more peaceful relations with its immediate neighbours in the Asia-Pacific region, and how the results have been successful in some cases but less so in others. Since the 1990s, many outstanding political issues have either been directly addressed or placed into a better position to be solved in the future. At present, unlike in previous decades, the possibility of a border war or regional conflict involving China, despite the shaky security situation in the South China Sea after 2009, remains remote. Beijing had linked regional stability with its own domestic reforms in the hopes of concentrating more on internal development issues. Many of its evolving strategic views on creating security communities and partnerships have been tested, often with great success, in East and Southeast Asia. Moreover, China's diplomatic approach combining improved governmental relations with economic incentives has attracted the attention of many actors in China's periphery and sought to dispel assumptions being held during the Cold War of a China seeking to overturn the regional order. Warmer relations with South Korea and parts of ASEAN, despite some political and territorial issues affecting the latter relationship, have suggested that this mixed diplomacy on China's part has produced some positive political change. However, in the cases of Japan, the Philippines and Vietnam, China's periphery diplomacy has been seen as giving way to greater assertiveness.

China's growth as a regional and international power will have many effects on the country's neighbours, but Beijing is seeking to mitigate its rise by demonstrating a policy of cooperation and joint problem-solving. However, as the cases of Japan and North Korea demonstrate, there are still outstanding regional issues which require Beijing's attention, both bilaterally and multilaterally. In the case of Japan, there is the concern that a rising Beijing and a recovering Tokyo, despite their strong economic ties, may run into other areas of political and strategic conflict which could be further affected by nationalism on both sides. As for North Korea, despite some positive movement it retains a nuclear weapons capability which Beijing does not want to see develop. At the same time, China is concerned a collapsed state would have a negative security impact on the entire Northeast Asian region. Thus, Beijing faces the problem of applying just enough pressure on Pyongyang to improve its regional relations but not enough to impact the Kim regime as it begins its third iteration.

Changed diplomacy with China's neighbours in East and Southeast Asia and the greater Pacific has not only provided Beijing with greater security and improved regional relations but has also increased China's confidence in expanding its relations with actors well beyond its periphery. As will be argued in the next chapter, while the 1990s were the heyday of China's peripheral diplomacy, the following decade saw an advancement of China's international interests into cross-regional diplomacy.

Discussion questions

- What were the reasons behind Beijing's decision to undertake "peripheral diplomacy"?
- What role does nationalism play in affecting current Sino-Japanese relations? Will the growing economic ties between the two states improve their political relationship?
- How does history continue to affect the Sino-Japanese relationship, and how does the US continue to play a role?
- What were the incentives for China and South Korea to set aside their Cold War mistrust and open relations in the 1990s?
- Why is China limited in its options for dealing with North Korea's nuclear weapons programme? What, in Beijing's view, are the best solutions for peace in Korea?
- What are Beijing's views on developing greater regional cooperation between itself and Southeast Asia?
- Will China and ASEAN states be able to reach an agreement on the status of the South China Sea?
- What have been China's economic and political interests in Oceania, including the South Pacific?

Recommended reading

Chachavalpongpun, Pavin. *Entering Uncharted Waters? ASEAN and the South China Sea* (Singapore: ISEAS Publishing, 2014).

Chung, Jae Ho. *Between Ally and Partner: Korea–China Relations and the United States* (New York: Columbia University Press, 2007).

Freeman, Carla. *China and North Korea* (New York: Palgrave, 2015).

Funabashi, Yoichi. *The Peninsula Question: A Chronicle of the Second Korean Nuclear Crisis* (Washington DC: Brookings, 2007).

Hayton, Bill. *The South China Sea: The Struggle for Power in Asia* (New Haven and London: Yale University Press, 2014).

Kang, David C. *China Rising: Peace, Power and Order in East Asia* (New York: Columbia University Press, 2007).

Katzenstein, Peter J. (ed.). *Sinicization and the Rise of China: Civilizational Processes between East and West* (New York and London: Routledge, 2012).

Li, Rex. *A Rising China and Security in East Asia: Identity Construction and Security Discourse* (New York and London: Routledge, 2009).

Liao, Tim F., Kimie Hara and Krista Wiegand (eds). *The China–Japan Border Dispute: Islands of Contention in a Multidisciplinary Perspective* (Farnham, UK and Burlington, VT: Ashgate, 2015).

Manicom, James. *Bridging Troubled Waters: China, Japan, and Maritime Order in the East China Sea* (Washington DC: George Washington Press, 2014).

Nicolas, Françoise (ed.). *Korea in the New Asia: East Asian Integration and the China Factor* (New York and London: Routledge, 2007).

Percival, Bronson. *The Dragon Looks South: China and Southeast Asia in the New Century* (Westport, CT: Praeger, 2007).

Reilly, James. *Strong Society, Smart State: The Rise of Public Opinion in China's Japan Policy* (New York: Columbia University Press, 2011).

Shambaugh, David and Michael Yahuda (eds). *International Relations of Asia* (2nd edn) (Lanham, MD and Plymouth, UK: Rowman & Littlefield, 2014).

Smith, Sheila A. *Intimate Rivals: Japanese Domestic Politics and a Rising China* (New York: Columbia University Press, 2015).

Storey, Ian. *Southeast Asia and the Rise of China: The Search for Security* (London and New York: Routledge, 2011).

Teo, Victor and Lee Guen (eds). *The Koreas between China and Japan* (Newcastle: Cambridge Scholars Publishing, 2014).

Thant, Min-U. *Where China meets India: Burma and the New Crossroads of Asia* (London: Faber and Faber, 2011).

Wu, Shicun and Keyuan Zou (eds). *Maritime Security in the South China Sea: Regional Implications and International Cooperation* (Farnham, England and Burlington, VT: Ashgate, 2009).

Yahuda, Michael. *Sino-Japanese Relations after the Cold War: Two Tigers Sharing a Mountain* (New York and London: Routledge, 2014).

Yang, Jian. *The Pacific Islands in China's Grand Strategy: Small States, Big Games* (New York: Palgrave, 2011).

Notes

1   James C. Hsiung, "China's Omni-Directional Diplomacy: Realignment to Cope with Monopolar US Power," *Asian Survey* 35(6) (June 1995): 573–86.
2   M. Taylor Fravel, *Strong Borders, Secure Nation: Cooperation and Conflict in China's Territorial Disputes* (Princeton, NJ: Princeton University Press, 2008), 163–6.
3   Thomas G. Moore and Dixia Yang, "Empowered and Restrained: Chinese Foreign Policy in the Age of Economic Interdependence," *The Making of China's Foreign and Security Policy in the Era of Reform*, ed. David M. Lampton (Stanford: Stanford University Press, 2001), 202–24.
4   Bert Edström, "The Yoshida Doctrine and the Unipolar World," *Japan Forum* 16(1) (2004): 63–85.
5   Lowell Dittmer, "The Sino-Japanese–Russian Triangle," *Journal of Chinese Political Science* 10(1) (April 2005): 6–7.
6   Ming Wan, *Sino-Japanese Relations: Interaction, Logic and Transformation* (Washington: Woodrow Wilson Centre Press, 2006), 83–108.
7   Nicholas D. Kristof, "The Problem of Memory," *Foreign Affairs* 37(1) (November / December 1998): 37–49; Daiki Shibuchi, "The Yasukuni Shrine Dispute and the Politics of Identity in Japan," *Asian Survey* 45(2) (March / April 2005): 204–5.
8   Christopher R. Hughes, *Chinese Nationalism in the Global Era* (Milton Park, UK and New York: Routledge 2006), 151.
9   Lam Pang Er, "Japan's Deteriorating Ties with China: The Koizumi Factor," *China: An International Journal* 3(2) (September 2005): 275–91.
10   "Mercantile Realism and Japanese Foreign Policy," *Unipolar Politics: Realism and State Strategies After the Cold War*, ed. Ethan B. Kapstein and Michael Mastanduno (New York: Columbia University Press, 1999), 182–217.
11   Thomas J. Christensen, "Failing Instability or Creating a Monster? The Rise of China and Instability toward East Asia," *International Security* 31(1) (September 2006): 88–9.
12   Shu Zhenya and Zhang Haiwen, *The Diaoyu Islands* (Beijing: China International Press, 2014), 55–69.
13   "Chinese State Oil Chief Mum on Gas Field Exploitation in Disputed Water," *Kyodo News*, 24 March 2007; James C. Hsiung, "Sea Power, The Law of the Sea, and the Sino-Japanese East China Sea 'Resource War'," *American Foreign Policy Interests* 27(2005): 516–19.
14   Zhongqi Pan, "Sino-Japanese Dispute over the Diaoyu / Senkaku Islands: The Pending Controversy from the Chinese Perspective," *Journal of Chinese Political Science* 12(1) (April 2007): 71–92.
15   "Regarding Discussions toward Improving Japan–China Relations," *Ministry of Foreign Affairs of Japan*, 7 November 2014, <http://www.mofa.go.jp/a_o/c_m1/cn/page4e_000150.html>.
16   Chien-peng Chung, "China–Japan Relations in the Post-Koizumi Era: A Brightening Half-Decade?" *Asia-Pacific Review* 19(1) (2012): 88–107.
17   "Japan Confirms Disputed Islands Purchase Plan," *BBC News*, 10 September 2012.
18   Aoki Mizuho, "Obama assures Abe on Senkakus," *Japan Times*, 24 April 2014.
19   Daniel Sneider, "The New Asianism: Japanese Foreign Policy under the Democratic Party of Japan," *Japan under the DPJ: The Politics of Transition and Governance*, ed. Kenji E. Kushida and Phillip Y. Lipscy (Washington, DC: Walter Shorenstein Asia-Pacific Research Centre, 2013), 384–91.

20 Lowell Dittmer, "China's 'New Thinking' on Japan," *The China Quarterly* 184 (March 2006): 848.

21 Jae Ho Chung, *Between Ally and Partner: Korea–China Relations and the United States* (New York: Columbia University Press, 2007), 71–5.

22 George T. Yu, "China's Response to Changing Developments on the Korean Peninsula," *The US and the Two Koreas: A New Triangle* (Boulder and London: Lynne Renner, 1998), 260–1.

23 Jia Hao and Zhuang Qubing, "China's Policy toward the Korean Peninsula," *Asian Survey* 32(12) (December 1992): 1147.

24 Uk Heo and Terence Roehrig, *South Korea's Rise: Economic Development, Power and Foreign Relations* (Cambridge: Cambridge University Press, 2014), 77–8.

25 Jae Ho Chung, "South Korea between Eagle and Dragon: Perceptual Ambivalence and Strategic Dilemma," *Asian Survey* 41(5) (September / October 2001): 792–3.

26 Taeho Kim, "China's Ascendancy and the Future of the Korean Peninsula," *Korea in the New Asia: East Asian Integration and the China Factor*, ed. Françoise Nicolas (London and New York: Routledge, 2007), 117.

27 Akihiko Kaise, "Seoul to Expand Air Defense Zone over Reef also Claimed by China," *Asahi Shimbun*, 4 December 2013.

28 David Shambaugh, "China Engages Asia: Reshaping the Regional Order," *International Security* 29(3) (Winter 2004/05): 79–80; Taeho Kim, "Korea in the New Asia," 125–6.

29 Moon Gwang-lip and Kim Ki-hwan, "China Says Great Wall Extended to Ancient Korea," *Korea Joongang Daily*, 8 June 2012.

30 David Halberstam, *The Longest Winter: America and the Korean War* (New York: Hyperion, 2007), 47–52.

31 David Kerr, "The Sino-Russian Partnership and US Policy towards North Korea: From Hegemony to Concert in Northeast Asia," *International Studies Quarterly* 49(3) (September 2005): 425.

32 Gregory J. Moore, "How North Korea Threatens Chinese Interests: Understanding Chinese Duplicity on the North Korean Nuclear Issue," *International Relations of the Asia-Pacific* 8 (2008): 4.

33 Andrei Lankov, "Staying Alive: Why North Korea Will Not Change," *Foreign Affairs* 87(2) (March / April 2008): 9–16.

34 "N. Korea's 2014 Trade with China Marks 1st Drop in 5 Years," *Yonhap News Agency*, 26 January 2015, <http://english.yonhapnews.co.kr/northkorea/2015/01/26/37/0401000000AEN201501260 04900315F.html>.

35 Joel S. Wit, Daniel B. Poneman and Robert L. Gallucci, *Going Critical: The First North Korean Nuclear Crisis* (Washington DC: Brookings 2004), 295–330.

36 "North Korea Says 'Evil Axis' Remark Isn't Far From a Declaration of War," *Associated Press*, 31 January 2002.

37 Chaim Braun and Christopher F. Chyba, "Proliferation Rings," 9–10.

38 Yoichi Funabashi, *The Peninsula Question: A Chronicle of the Second Korean Nuclear Crisis* (Washington, DC: Brookings, 2007), 262–99.

39 John S. Park, "Inside Multilateralism: The Six-Party Talks," *Washington Quarterly* 28(4) (Autumn 2005): 75–91.

40 Marc Lanteigne, *China and International Institutions: Alternate Paths to Global Power* (Milton Park, UK and New York: Routledge, 2005), 112.

41 "North Korea's Missile Tests: Troubling Trajectories," *Strategic Comments* 12(6) (July 2006): 1–2.

42 "China Denounces 'Brazen' Nuclear Test," *Reuters* 9 October 2006; Zhu Feng, "Shifting Tides: China and North Korea," *China Security* 2(3) (Autumn 2006): 35–51.

43 "Macao Unfreezes N. Korea Funds with Immediate Effect," *Asia-Pacific News Agencies*, 10 April 2007.

44 Moore, "How North Korea Threatens China's Interests," 16.

45 Llewellyn Hughes, "Why Japan Will Not Go Nuclear (Yet): International and Domestic Constraints on the Nuclearization of Japan," *International Security* 31(4) (Spring 2007): 71.

46 Glenn Kessler, "North Korea, Syria May be at Work on Nuclear Facility," *Washington Post*, 13 September 2007, A12.

47 Jim Yardley and Jake Hooker, "Negotiators Move Closer to Disarming North Korea," *International Herald Tribune*, 14 July 2008, 1.

48   Christian Oliver, Geoff Dyer and Mure Dickie, "North Korea Admits Missile Failure," *Financial Times*, 13 April 2012.
49   Hazel Smith, *North Korea: Markets and Military Rule* (Cambridge: Cambridge University Press, 2015), 299–300.
50   Ben Blanchard, "China Says Willing to Help Drought-hit North Korea," *Reuters*, 18 June 2015.
51   Bronson Percival, *The Dragon Looks South: China and Southeast Asia in the New Century* (Westport, CT: Praeger, 2007), 6–7.
52   Daniel Tretiak, "China's Vietnam War and Its Consequences," *The China Quarterly* 80 (December 1979): 740–67.
53   See *The United Nations and Cambodia: 1991–1995* (New York: United Nations Department of Public Information, 1995): 7–48.
54   Ralf Emmers, *Cooperative Security and the Balance of Power in ASEAN and the ARF* (London and New York, 2004), 30–2; Percival, 7.
55   Thomas G. Moore and Dixia Yang, "Empowered and Restrained: Chinese Foreign Policy in the Age of Economic Interdependence," *The Making of Chinese Foreign and Security Policy in the Era of Reform*, ed. David M. Lampton (Stanford: Stanford University Press, 2001), 218–22.
56   Noel M. Morada, "ASEAN and the Rise of China: Engaging, While Fearing, an Emerging Regional Power," *The Rise of China and a Changing East Asian Order*, ed. Kokubun Ryosei and Wang Jisi (Tokyo and New York: Japan Centre for International Exchange, 2004), 229–30.
57   J. Peter Burgess, "The Politics of the South China Sea: Territoriality and International Law," *Security Dialogue* 34(1) (March 2003): 7–9; M. Taylor Fravel, "Power Shifts and Escalation: Explaining China's Use of Force in Territorial Disputes," *International Security* 32(3) (Winter 2006/07): 73–6.
58   Gerald Segal, "East Asia and the 'Constrainment' of China," *International Security* 20(4) (Spring 1996): 116–23; Daojiong Zha and Mark J. Valencia, "Mischief Reef: Geopolitics and Implications," *Journal of Contemporary Asia* 31(1) (January 2001): 86–8.
59   Sujit Dutta, "Securing the Sea Frontier: China's Pursuit of Sovereignty Claims in the South China Sea," *Strategic Analysis* 29(2) (April–June 2005): 270.
60   Alastair Iain Johnston, "How New and Assertive Is China's New Assertiveness?" *International Security* 37(4) (Spring 2013): 17–20.
61   "Stirring Up the South China Sea (III): A Fleeting Opportunity for Calm," *International Crisis Group: Asia Report* No. 267 (7 May 2015): 16–18.
62   "Whipping up Philippine Nationalism a Dangerous Game," *Xinhua*, 15 June 2015.
63   Michael Mogato, "Japanese Plane Circles over China-claimed Region in South China Sea," *Reuters*, 23 June 2015.
64   Ben Blanchard, "China Moves Controversial Oil Rig Back towards Vietnam Coast," *Reuters*, 26 June 2015.
65   "Vietnam Reiterates '3 Nos' Policy," *Vietnam News*, 26 August 2010, <http://vietnamnews.vn/Politics-Laws/202996/Vietnam-reiterates-3-nos-defence-policy.html>.
66   Marc Lanteigne, "China's Maritime Security and the 'Malacca Dilemma'," *Asian Security* 4(2) (May 2008): 1–19.
67   John Wong and Sarah Chan, "China–ASEAN Free Trade: Shaping Future Economic Relations," *Asian Survey* 43(3) (May–June 2003): 507–26; Cheng Siwei, "China–East Asia Cooperation – In the Context of Economic Globalisation and Regional Integration," *China International Studies* 4 (Fall 2006): 13.
68   Joshua Kurlantzick, *Charm Offensive: How China's Soft Power is Transforming the World* (New Haven and London: Yale University Press, 2007), 1–11.
69   Wassana Nanuam and Patsara Jikkham, "Thailand, China Bolster Military Ties as US Relations Splinter," *Bangkok Post*, 8 February 2015.
70   Charles Hutzler, "China Nudges Myanmar on Protests," *Associated Press*, 26 September 2007.
71   Baogang He, "Politics of Accommodation of the Rise of China: The Case of Australia," *Journal of Contemporary China* 21(73) (2012): 59–61.
72   Australian Government Department of Defence, "Defending Australia in the Asia Pacific Century: Force 2030," *Defence White Paper* 2009.
73   Anthony Fensom, "China Deals Up Pressure On TPP," *The Diplomat*, 22 June 2015, < http://thediplomat.com/2015/06/china-deals-up-pressure-on-tpp/>.
74   Shannon Tiezzi, "It's Official: AIIB Constitution to Be Signed on June 29," *The Diplomat*, 26 June 2015, <http://thediplomat.com/2015/06/its-official-aiib-constitution-to-be-signed-on-june-29/>.

75 Tracy Watkins, "It's all Good, Just Don't Mention the Nukes," *Dominion Post*, 23 May 2013.
76 "Chinese Training Ship, Frigate Visit Tonga," *Matangi Tonga / BBC Monitoring* 6 September 2010; "China's Peace Ark Starts Medical Assistance Mission in Fiji," *Xinhua*, 22 August 2014.
77 Joel Atkinson, "Vanuatu in Australia–China–Taiwan Relations," *Australian Journal of International Affairs* Vol. 61, No. 3 (September 2007): 351–66.
78 Hanson, "China in the Pacific," 16.
79 Philippa Brant, "The Geopolitics of Chinese Aid," *Lowy Institute for International Policy*, 4 March 2015, <http://www.lowyinstitute.org/publications/geopolitics-chinese-aid>. Statistics from the survey can be read at <http://www.lowyinstitute.org/chinese-aid-map/>.

8　Moving beyond the Asia-Pacific
China's cross-regional foreign policies

Beijing adapts cross-regional diplomacy

Even before the end of the Cold War, a great focus in the study of international relations was placed upon the development of *regions* rather than alliances, and the methods by which these regions established their own political, economic and strategic identity. This trend appeared to accelerate after the fall of the Soviet Union, as states which were closely tied to one superpower camp or another could now more directly engage their own neighbours and develop regional organisations more suited to local geopolitics. However, with the onset of globalisation and the ever-growing number of linkages via organisations, trade, laws and person-to-person connections ranging from government contacts to individuals, it has been argued that the world's regions are growing more "porous" and often more difficult to differentiate. This is due not only to increased economic ties but also shared diplomatic and strategic concerns.[1] As a result, much study in international relations is now being devoted to "cross-regional" diplomacy, which has been a common practice of superpowers and great powers but a facet of foreign policy which China has only recently embraced to any great degree.

As noted in previous chapters, during the first decade of China's foreign policy reforms under Deng Xiaoping and Jiang Zemin, a great deal of attention was placed on the superpowers and great powers, including the United States and the USSR / Russian Federation, as well as China's immediate neighbours in East, Southeast and Central Asia. China sought to establish a stable periphery by improving relations with surrounding Asia-Pacific states such as with Japan and the Koreas, through improving bilateral ties and multilateral cooperation with regional regimes such as APEC, the ARF and EAS, and the SCO. However, in the last few years of the Jiang government, and especially after the start of Hu Jintao's presidency, Beijing began seeking to build upon its earlier Asia-Pacific diplomatic initiatives and has sought to forge deeper ties with states and regions far beyond the Pacific Rim. Since the turn of the century, China has been active in improving diplomatic relations through summitry, economic cooperation and multi-faceted diplomatic initiatives. In the 1990s, Jiang sought improved ties with selected states via the seeking out of bilateral "partners" (*huoban* 伙伴) based on closer international cooperation and shared regional and/or global interests.[2] These agreements signalled China's first tentative steps into modern cross-regional diplomacy and provided Beijing with the first windows into regional political and economic affairs beyond China's periphery.

These policies, often referred to as essential elements of Beijing's overall global "charm offensive" have introduced a question once considered a non-issue by international relations scholars, namely does China have so-called "soft power" (*ruan shili* 软实力) capabilities to wield power via attraction rather than coercion? As previous chapters have noted, while China's current foreign policy has been influential on an increasing number of states, China's more activist foreign policy in further-flung regions has raised the issue of Beijing's potential competition with the United States for diplomatic influence, especially in regions such as Africa, Latin America and the Middle East, where the United States and Europe have traditionally enjoyed unchallenged levels of influence since the end of the Cold War. The onset of China's cross-regional diplomacy could be seen during much of the presidency of Hu Jintao, who along with then-Premier Wen Jiabao engaged in extensive summit diplomacy not only in East and Southeast Asia but frequently in many other regions. The trend continued during the first years of the Xi Jinping administration, as he and Premier Li Keqiang continued to travel extensively to meet with leaders and policymakers around the world, meetings which often culminated in economic deals and partnerships which reflected Beijing's growing financial capabilities.

As with China's peripheral diplomacy, Beijing has enjoyed different levels of success with its still-developing cross-regional foreign policy initiatives, but it can be argued that even under Xi Jinping, we have seen only the beginning stages of this process, and further progress will depend greatly on the politics of both China and those states with which it is seeking deeper relations. The evolution of China's cross-regional diplomacy in recent years will be studied in this chapter, using case examples of this process, specifically the regions of Europe, Africa, Latin America, the Middle East, South Asia and even the world's polar regions.

Europe

Since its creation in 1993, the European Union has continued to provide one of China's most visible multilateral challenges, as Beijing has had to adjust its European policies to take into account both Union and country-level decision-making procedures, further complicated by the lack of a single cohesive EU foreign, and often economic, policy. Nevertheless, since the 1970s, China has embraced a policy of cooperation with Europe and views the continent as an important alternative pole to the United States. By the 1980s, China was seeking a more independent foreign policy which did not lean too far towards either the West or the Eastern Bloc, and encouraging ties with Europe was seen as a means for Beijing to diversify its foreign policy interests. At this time, Europe had begun the first tentative steps towards creating a common market, and China was aware of the potential economic benefits of encouraging closer ties. In 1985, Deng Xiaoping remarked to former British Prime Minister Edward Heath that Europe was becoming increasingly important to Beijing's nascent reformist trade policy, both as a source of technology transfer and a developing trade conduit. Deng concluded by noting "For the past three years we have been considering how to increase economic ties with Europe. It is our policy to do so."[3]

China had normalised relations with the then-European Community in 1975, and during that decade many European states had opted to switch their diplomatic recognition from Taiwan to the People's Republic. For example, France, despite American pressures, recognised Beijing in early 1963, followed by Italy in 1970 and other Western European states in the early 1970s. The United Kingdom, concerned about the status of Hong Kong and cognisant of pro-Beijing opinions among many Commonwealth members, took the step of recognising the PRC much earlier, in January 1950, the same year as Denmark, Finland and Switzerland, with Norway recognising Beijing in 1954. When the Soviet Union dissolved in 1991, all 15 of its successor states opened relations with Beijing as well. Despite concerns expressed by many European governments about China's political system and its still-reforming economy, the region continues to recognise Beijing's growing political and economic importance. Today, the only European state which does not recognise Beijing is the Vatican (Holy See). China did not recognise the state of Kosovo after it declared independence from Serbia in February 2008, but the Chinese government does maintain a representative office in the Kosovo capital of Priština.

Since the European Union's creation and expansion after 1992, it has developed into Beijing's largest trade partner, with overall trade increasing by a factor of 60 between 1975 and 2005 to €210 billion (US$326 billion).[4] Beijing formally established relations with the European Economic Community in 1975, and since that time considered Europe to be a crucial economic partner. China published a White Paper on its European ties in 2003, which acknowledged differences over human rights issues but noted the growing number of shared geo-political interests,[5] and signed a partnership agreement with Brussels two years later. A short follow-up government paper on China–Europe relations was released by the Chinese government in April 2014 in the wake of European visits, including to Brussels, by President Xi. Within the document were calls for increased political and economic cooperation as well as greater communication in defence issues, urbanisation, education, energy and climate change.[6]

China has been enthusiastic about increasing political, educational and cultural ties with EU states. By the 1990s and following a brief break in the Sino-European Economic relationship after the Tiananmen Incident in 1989, the European Union began to further codify its political relations with Beijing, and in 1995, the European Commission (EC), the executive branch of the Union responsible for law-making and governance, outlined its goals for future Chinese engagement. These included improving political dialogue and encouraging the development of human rights and legal reform in China, further integrating China into the global economy, making better use of the EC's resources in engaging China and raising the Commission's profile in China.[7]

Currently, both China and the EU consider each other to be alternative trading partners to North America. However, Beijing faces the daunting task of developing an economic relationship with a European entity which is neither a single super-state nor a normal collection of states, but rather something in between. Despite attempts since the 1980s to develop a Common Foreign and Security Policy (CFSP) for Europe, a process which was finally standardised with the Treaty of Lisbon in December 2009, there remain many divisions within the EU over foreign policy directions. This made it difficult for China along with many other states, to develop a coherent policy of engaging "Europe".[8]

As a result of the 2008 credit crunch and subsequent recession, which also sparked a debt crisis within some EU members including Greece, Spain, Ireland, Portugal and Italy, China–European Union relations shifted considerably when Beijing was asked to contribute financial assistance to stricken eurozone countries. Relations between China and Germany, one of the few countries which was able to maintain economic stability during the worst of the crisis, also improved with much summit diplomacy taking place between German Chancellor Angela Merkel and President Xi. During Greece's debt crisis after 2009, and often rancorous negotiations with the EU over repayments, the Greek government sought stronger economic ties with both China and Russia as alternative economic partners under a cloud of uncertainty by 2015 over whether Greece would be forced to leave the euro area and even the Union itself (a "Grexit"). China Cosco Holding Co., a major Chinese shipping and port concern, acquired a 35-year concession to part of the container terminal at the main Greek port of Piraeus in 2009, and wished to increase its investments there.[9]

Even before the recession, there was some debate as to whether closer economic ties between China and Europe would also lead to stronger political links between the two

---

Box 8.1 China and the European chimera

"It is unlikely that the EU will overcome its ambiguous geopolitical identity and so it will continue to live a compromise between its several souls. This implies that it continue to be part of the transatlantic security alliance and therefore never as independent a pole in world politics as the Chinese would like."

– Frank Gaenssmantel, "China's Rise and the Geopolitical Identity of the European Union", *Interpreting China as a Regional and Global Power: Nationalism and Historical Consciousness in World Politics*, ed. Bart Dessin (Basingstoke, UK: Palgrave, 2014), 287.

---

great powers. This discussion attracted new focus in the wake of the American decision to intervene militarily in Iraq in 2003, a move which was greeted with suspicion by Beijing as well as many European states who were unhappy that the decision was made without direct consultation with the UN Security Council. Further European engagement was beneficial to Beijing as a means of tacitly balancing American power as well as encouraging "multipolarisation" (*duojihua* 多极化) in the international system. There have been differences of opinion between American and European views on China's rise, with the US focusing on the development of Chinese hard (military) power and European states tending to view the rise through the lens of China's ongoing domestic reforms and transition to a more liberalised economic system. At the same time, Europe has tended to define its principal security concerns as being non-traditional in nature as opposed to hard military threats. These "softer" threats involve transnational crime, environmental issues, health, energy and poor governance, and countries in Europe have tended to view China as a necessary partner in addressing these issues.[10] Since 2005, Chinese and EU representatives have met in the name of developing a "strategic dialogue" on mutual concerns, but so far the dialogue has been very broad-based with decisions yet to be made on which topics could and should be included in the process.[11] After the recession took hold in Europe, the question of economic affairs assumed a position of much higher importance in many bilateral dialogues.

High-ranking members of the Chinese government meet with European leaders every other year at the Asia–Europe Meeting (ASEM), which Beijing joined in 1996 when the forum was founded. ASEM seeks a strengthening of political, cultural and economic ties between the EU and Asia in recognition of the growing cross-regional ties between the two continents. Since its creation, ASEM's membership has grown to include 53 members, representing many European and Asian governments, along with two partner organisations, the European Commission and the ASEAN Secretariat. The ASEM process was designed to act as the third "leg" in the triangle of institutions connecting North America, Europe and Asia, with the other two being the Asia-Pacific Economic Cooperation (APEC) forum and the Organisation for Economic Cooperation and Development (OECD) which connects European and North American economic interests, among others. The ASEM process is composed of three major "pillars": political cooperation, economic linkages and social-cultural engagement between Europe and Asia.[12] However, as with APEC, the membership of ASEM is very large, and its role to date has been more in line with that of a policy discussion forum.

The China–EU relationship has not been without problems, both economic and political, even before 2008. Pre-recession, Brussels frequently expressed frustration with its growing trade deficit with Beijing and has periodically cited China for improper "dumping" (selling goods at below production costs) practices. In the latter half of 2007, the Union's trade deficit with China had grown to €132.2 billion (US$195.5 billion) which raised some concerns among European companies about access to the Chinese market, and despite the recession, by 2011 that figure had grown to almost €156 billion (US$197 billion), but retreated by 2013 to €131.8 billion (US$147.1 billion).[13] Like the United States, the EU has been critical of China's monetary policy, expressing concerns that the low value of the Chinese *yuan* gives Chinese products an unfair advantage in global markets. China and the European Union have also clashed within the World Trade Organisation over Chinese subsidies in sectors including steel and solar panels.

Concerns about the maturity of China's market and trade practices prompted the decision by the EU in 2004 to withhold from Beijing official "market economy status" (MES), which would have been the next higher classification from China's current designation of "transitional economy". In making the decision, EU officials pointed to incomplete Chinese reforms including paring down the number and output of inefficient state-owned enterprises, undertaking deeper legal reforms, and further separating the Chinese financial sector from control by the state. However, the MES decision was seen by Beijing as being primarily influenced by political motivations, noting that Russia was granted that status by the EU even before Moscow was accepted into the WTO.[14] Moreover, the decision was seen as flying in the face of the increasing amount of trade and economic links in Sino-European relations. Nonetheless, despite the growth of the Chinese economy since the EU decision was made, the question of MES continued to be unresolved during 2015, when the European Commission's legal service produced an opinion that MES should be granted to the Chinese economy by December 2016,[15] despite ongoing concerns from some Union member economies about alleged dumping practices by some Chinese firms.

At the China–EU bilateral conference in Helsinki in September 2006, Chinese and EU representatives agreed to launch talks to create a Partnership and Cooperation Agreement (PCA), and negotiations commenced the following January.[16] The negotiations have yet to address the more central issues related to tariffs and investment, nor has ASEM acted as a viable vehicle from which to jump-start preferential trade negotiations between Europe and China. Alternatively, China opted to seek out non-EU European states for free trade talks, and negotiations with Iceland began in late 2006. Two years later, the groundwork was laid for similar talks with Norway and Switzerland, as all three states had decided to grant China MES. As well, all three states, along with Liechtenstein which maintains a common economic area and currency with Switzerland, are members of the European Free Trade Association (EFTA), a looser economic organisation of states which had declined to join the EU. This "side-door" approach on China's part to liberalising trade with Europe has allowed Beijing to gain greater understanding of European economic policies without committing itself to direct negotiations with the EU.

China's free trade negotiations with the EFTA states produced mixed results however. Despite many successful negotiation rounds with Iceland since 2007, the talks were suspended after 2009 in the wake of the Icelandic banking crash followed by a deep recession late in the previous year. The weakness of the Icelandic currency, the *krona*, prompted talks with the EU for potential membership, despite tepid public support for joining.[17] Any potential free trade agreement with China would be nullified upon Iceland's admission to the Union under EU membership rules. However, public support in Iceland for EU membership quickly cooled again, especially in the wake of ongoing financial crises in the eurozone, and China continued to develop economic ties with Reykjavík, with then-Premier Wen Jiabao's visit to the island state in April 2012 resulting in lucrative economic deals. The free trade agreement, the first China signed with a European economy, was completed in April 2013.

Free trade talks between China and Norway were initiated in September 2008, but after eight rounds of negotiations the process was abruptly halted in the wake of the decision by the Oslo-based Nobel Committee to award its Peace Prize in 2010 to imprisoned Chinese political activist Liu Xiaobo.[18] The Chinese government viewed the award as unacceptable interference in its internal affairs and suspended all bilateral governmental contacts, although trade between the two states continued to grow, and governmental contacts remain in place in multilateral organisations such as the Arctic Council. FTA negotiations with Switzerland were far more successful. The talks, which formally began in February 2011, were concluded with an agreement in July 2013. The Sino-Swiss FTA became among the most prominent of China's free trade agreements, given the comparatively large size of the Swiss economy and its position in the heart of Europe. Among the many sectors in the Swiss economy which looked forward to increased access to the Chinese market were Switzerland's luxury watchmakers whose products were gaining popularity among China's growing new rich. However, sales to China did drop in the wake of Beijing's anti-corruption crackdown starting in 2012–13, before recovering somewhat.[19]

There have been some political differences between China and the EU and some of its members in recent years. In 2004–5, some European states began to quietly debate lifting the post-1989 arms embargo against China. Beijing had been arguing for a lifting of the ban, noting that the strategic relationship between China and Europe had grown to the point where maintaining the embargo was contradictory and outdated. As well, Beijing noted that its strategic dialogue with Brussels was becoming increasingly incompatible with the maintenance of an EU arms ban. However, the United States argued staunchly against moves by any European country to lift the ban, exacerbating Washington–Brussels divisions over the issue and prompting much debate within the EU membership. France under President Jacques Chirac, for example, had expressed support for removing the embargo late in his last term.

However, the elections of Nicolas Sarkozy in France (2007), Gordon Brown and then David Cameron in the United Kingdom (2007 and 2010) and Angela Merkel in Germany (2005), all of whom advocated a more cautious line on Chinese economic relations, slowed momentum on potentially reversing the ban. That debate in Europe was also affected by Beijing's ratification of the Anti-Secession Law in March 2005, which allowed for the use of force in the event of a Taiwanese push for independence.[20] China remains hopeful, however, that the issue may again be considered by future European governments as the country is interested in diversifying its markets for both military and "dual-use" technologies, markets which at present remain dominated by Russia. The case of the embargo underlined the still-sensitive path that Europe must walk between maintaining its traditional ties with the United States and engaging a country which it is believed will continue to grow as a strong player in future international relations. However, as a result of Europe's financial troubles since 2008 and the growth of China's economy in that time, there have been many debates in European governments as to how to best establish their own "pivot" policies towards China, only on an economic basis.

The February 2008 unilateral declaration of independence of the province of Kosovo from Serbia also highlighted Chinese and European political differences. Since 1999, the province had been in a state of quasi-independence largely under United Nations administration. Serbia, which had considered Kosovo (with an Albanian Muslim-majority population) part of its historical territory, had refused to agree to a negotiated secession, thus creating a political stalemate. Shortly after the declaration, a majority of European Union member states (some exceptions being Greece, Slovakia, Spain and Romania), along with the United States, Australia, Canada and Japan, announced that they would recognise the new Kosovo state, while China and Russia, both concerned about legal precedent and respect for state sovereignty, announced that they would decline to recognise Kosovo independence. Beijing explained its position by noting that the move by Kosovo constituted a "severe and negative impact on peace and stability of the Balkan region" and called upon representatives from Serbia and Kosovo to resolve the issue.[21]

To conclude, while there are a number of outstanding economic and political issues which divide China and European states, the trading relationship between both sides continues to flourish with an understanding that differences are best resolved via dialogue rather than confrontation. As one specialist notes, the integration and expansion of the European Union is itself an example of peaceful rise, since today's EU began with a much smaller membership and cooperation in much fewer areas, but over time grew and developed expanded methods of cooperation in political, economic and strategic fields to become one of the most peaceful regions of the world as well as an example of the effective use of soft power and the use of international institutions. Thus China could and should view the EU as a useful model.[22] However, the European financial crises, including the Greek debt imbroglio, as well as the mass refugee crisis from the Middle East on the continent in 2015, caused much concern in China both over the long-term health of the major European economies and the possibility that the EU's common currency might actually dissolve under severe financial pressures. Beijing had pledged support for assisting the EU in addressing its most crisis-hit members but preferred to do so in a multilateral fashion. In short, the number of linkages between the two sides continues to grow due to converging economic interests as well as changing geopolitics.

The power next door: Russia

China's relations with Russia, especially since the return to power of President Vladimir Putin in 2012, have been marked by a great deal of foreign policy cooperation, not only within organisations such as the Shanghai Cooperation Organisation and the BRICS but also on a bilateral basis. Warm relations between Jiang Zemin and Boris Yeltsin gave way to somewhat more pragmatic relations between Hu Jintao and Vladimir Putin, but upon taking office Moscow was the first overseas destination visited by President Xi in March 2013. The two leaders also had several opportunities to confer in multilateral meetings, including not only the BRICS and SCO gatherings but also APEC, the AIIB, and the security organisation Conference on Interaction and Confidence Building in Asia (CICA). Russia has also been a key component of the "Silk Road Economic Belt" (*sichouzhilu jingjidai* 丝绸之路经济带), the land-based component of President Xi's proposed "one belt and one road" trade corridors, which would stretch across Central Asia and the Caucasus and Bosporus regions, with one link to Moscow and another to ports in Northern Europe.

Bilateral border demarcation issues, which had contributed to the tense relations between China and USSR, began to be negotiated in the 1990s with the last of the disputes settled in 2008. From a strategic viewpoint, China and Russia began to develop similar policies toward concerns over possible Western intervention in civil conflicts such as in Syria in 2011–12, and both states have upgraded their military cooperation and coordination since President Xi took office. However, the two states retained some policy differences, including Russian concerns about Chinese migration in Siberia, Beijing's expanding influence in Central Asia, and unease in China over Russian military intervention against Georgia in South Ossetia in August 2008. Beijing declined to join Moscow in recognising South Ossetia as an independent state after that conflict.

Since the Russian government under President Vladimir Putin announced its watershed "Pivot to Asia" foreign policy initiative in 2013,[23] the economic and strategic relationships between China and Russia have come under much greater international scrutiny. The decision made by Moscow to deepen its diplomatic and economic relations with East Asia, especially China, came as an acknowledgement that the centre of financial power in the international system had greatly shifted to the Pacific Rim in the wake of the post-2008 global recession, as well as concerns in Russia that its relations with the West, including Europe, were beginning to sour. Despite optimism after a "reset" policy, announced by President Obama during a July 2009 visit to Moscow, was initially viewed as a way of warming the US–Russia relationship,[24] it was not long before the two powers were again finding themselves at odds over a variety of security issues.

Moscow's involvement in the 2014 Ukrainian conflict proved to be a crucible not only for Russia's relations with the West, which experienced a sharp decline, but also for the Sino-Russian relationship. These events included the annexation of the Crimea region by pro-Russia irregular militias and alleged Russian support for ongoing violent secessionist movements, and the carving out of a declared "Novorossiya" confederation, in the Donbas region of eastern Ukraine.[25] Russian culpability alleged by the United States and other Western governments in the fighting in Ukraine, as well as the shooting down of a Malaysian civilian jetliner over the disputed zone, allegedly by pro-Russian separatist forces, in July 2014, created an even more toxic diplomatic atmosphere between Russia on one side and Europe and the US on the other.

Although China viewed the events in Ukraine with great concern, given Beijing's traditional antipathy towards intervention on sovereign state affairs and the strong economic relationship between Beijing and Kiev, Beijing stopped well short of criticising Russian actions and did not support economic punishment in the form of sanctions undertaken by the United States and Europe. Regarding the security situation in Ukraine, a Chinese Foreign Ministry spokesperson stated that while Beijing recognised and respected the role of non-interference and international law, "we take into account the historical facts and realistic complexity of the Ukrainian issue".[26]

The Ukraine crises further bolstered international perceptions of Russia as the "loud dissenter" and China as its "cautious partner", especially in relation to opposition to Western strategic policies.[27] In March 2014 comments regarding the security situation in Ukraine, a Chinese Foreign Ministry spokesperson stated that while Beijing recognised and respected the role of non-interference and international law, "we take into account the historical facts and realistic complexity of the Ukrainian issue".[28] These remarks were made in the wake of Beijing's decision to abstain during a UN Security Council vote which would have condemned the referendum held that month on whether the Crimea region should become part of the Russian Federation; the resolution was defeated after an anticipated veto by Russia itself. Beijing, while being critical of Western economic pressures on Moscow, had since sought to define itself as more of a neutral arbiter in the dispute, proposing a three-point plan (an international coordinating mechanism for tension-reduction, greater restraint from all parties, and a focus on regional economic assistance) shortly after the vote.[29]

Concerns have been raised in the West about whether the warming Sino-Russian diplomatic relationship would evolve into a *de facto* alliance, especially since military relations between the two countries also became closer after Putin returned to office. The two countries cooperate via the SCO and CICA, and in May 2015 the Chinese and Russian navies held a joint exercise, the first of its kind, in the Mediterranean Sea.[30] Yet for the most part, the bilateral partnership has been much more dominated by mutual economic interests, especially after Moscow began to struggle with Western sanctions after 2014. During the Hu Jintao presidency, China expressed much interest in developing pipelines for oil and gas via the Russian hinterland. Under Xi, these ideas began to assume a more definite form. During the Putin–Xi summit in March 2003, deals were struck which would allow China to purchase substantial quantities of petroleum from Russian state-owned company OAO Rosneft, as well as agreeing to the joint development of a gas pipeline to China.

In addition, Rosneft agreed to partner with the China National Petroleum Corporation (CNPC) to jointly explore the waters north of the Russian coast for fossil fuels.[31] In May 2014, an even more ambitious 30-year Sino-Russian natural gas deal worth US$400 billion was completed assuring cooperation between CNPC and the Russian energy firm Gazprom. China also agreed to underwrite the development of a liquefied natural gas project in the Siberian region of Yamal in November 2014, proposing up to US$10 billion in initial investment.[32] Despite the rapid fall of international fossil fuel prices since the end of 2014 potentially slowing down new bilateral oil and gas projects, China and Russia expressed their interest in developing longer-term energy projects, given the ongoing uncertainty of the market. As well, in late 2010, both countries agreed to conduct bilateral trade using their own respective currencies rather than the American dollar in a show of support for each other's economic strengths.

Strategically, Moscow has sought to maintain its dominant position in many parts of the former Soviet Union, including in Central Asia, despite Chinese economic and diplomatic inroads. China is the largest trading partner of many Central Asian states including Tajikistan, Kazakhstan, Kyrgyzstan and Turkmenistan. The former Soviet republics in Central Asia are seen as crucial components of Beijing's developing "one belt and one road" strategies, and especially the Eurasian overland trade corridors between Asia and Europe. As well, energy-rich states including Kazakhstan and Turkmenistan had been courted by China since the 1990s, and pipelines transporting oil and gas from these countries to China have been essential for Beijing's policies of diversifying its energy sources and partners. Among the pipelines which China has supported has been the China–Central Asia pipeline, which comprises three links which originate in Turkmenistan and transport natural gas via Uzbekistan and Kazakhstan before reaching China's own pipeline network.[33] This line, which formally began operations in late 2009, ended Russia's monopoly on gas transport and further confirmed China's status as a major energy partner in Eurasia.

Africa

China's post-1949 history with sub-Saharan Africa has been long and complex, with the focus of the relationship evolving from that of ideology, especially opposition to colonialism and neo-imperialism, both the Western and Soviet varieties, to one which has stressed mutual benefits, partnerships and trade, especially in energy and commodities. The Sino-African relationship has become, since the turn of the century, one of the most visible examples of China's growing confidence in cross-regional diplomacy, while further underscoring Beijing's commitment to expanding trade with developing regions.

During the Maoist era the African continent grew in importance to China as Beijing sought to begin distancing itself from its previously staunch pro-Soviet policy and instead moving towards a more "three worlds" (*sange shijie* 三个世界) approach by the 1960s, recognising the growing importance of the developing world in international affairs. Mao would later articulate his "three worlds" thinking in a dialogue with President Kenneth Kaunda, the first leader of Zambia, in 1974. His statements referred to the United States and the Soviet Union as being part of the "first world" and smaller developed states such as Japan, Europe and Canada were members of the second. Mao saw China is being part of the "third world" with the majority of developing nations.[34] It was this shift in emphasis on Beijing's part which opened up many new diplomatic channels with Africa. In the wake of decolonisation in Africa along with Asia in the 1950s, Beijing sought to position China as a friend of the developing world and a potential leader and guide.

In one speech in 1959, Mao described Africa as an important player in the "struggle against imperialism", stating that China stood ready to assist the continent in what the Chinese leader saw as a long and protracted conflict.[35] This viewpoint had been introduced at the now-famous 1955 conference in Bandung, Indonesia, which saw the gathering of many developing world heads-of-state. Premier Zhou Enlai took this opportunity to further articulate the "Five Principles of Peaceful Co-existence" (*heping gongchu wuxiang yuanze* 和平共处五项原则) theory, which had first been drawn up as a guideline for cordial Sino-Indian relations, a year earlier. As a result of the momentum from the contacts made at Bandung, China established its first diplomatic relations with an African country, namely Egypt, in 1956.

As relations between China and the Soviet Union continued to falter towards the end of the decade, Beijing attempted to align itself closer to the developing world, and references to the "Bandung Spirit" became common in Chinese foreign policy speeches by the early 1960s. In 1963, Zhou made a well-publicised tour of several African states in the hopes of gathering support for greater cooperation among non-aligned states. However, his attempt to play both the diplomat and the revolutionary simultaneously during his tour was not well received.[36] Much of the talk about cooperation and leadership was rhetorical and very much influenced by ideology, as well as the hopes that Beijing could establish a diplomatic beachhead on the continent in competition with both the United States and the USSR.

However, in Africa there were some concrete policies which brought China politically and economically closer to the continent. One of these was the TanZam (Tanzania–Zambia) Railway, constructed in 1970–6 and representing one of Beijing's most ambitious aid and development projects, more so given China's limited financial resources during the latter years of its Cultural Revolution. China also offered medical aid and loan assistance to sub-Saharan Africa, but at the same time supported various liberation movements in the region. Some of these liberation movements found themselves undecided over whether to accept Soviet or Chinese patronage. During the Cold War, China provided military support to several guerrilla and liberation movements in Africa, including leftist armed groups in Algeria, Angola, DR Congo, Mozambique and Rhodesia / Zimbabwe.[37] However, in comparison with the two superpowers, China was unable at that time to maintain a very high visibility in the region, except arguably in Tanzania under Julius Nyerere. China unseated the United Kingdom as Dar es Salaam's primary aid-giver in 1971.[38]

After the death of Mao and the coming to power of Deng Xiaoping, the ideological justifications for African engagement faded and China began to concentrate on domestic rebuilding following the Cultural Revolution. It was not until the 1990s that Africa again became a foreign policy priority for Beijing for three major reasons. These included the desire of Beijing to repair international relations after Tiananmen, growing interests in joint development of African commodities and energy resources, and China's growing comfort and confidence with cross-regional diplomacy. Beijing's lack of a colonial legacy in Africa has allowed it to symbolically separate itself from the continent's other great power trading partners. As a result of both diplomacy and the large volume of China's trade capabilities, China's political and economic presence in many African states has grown in a few short years from negligible to highly visible.

Africa had also been the subject of much diplomatic competition between Beijing and Taipei over the issue of recognition. As the economy of the PRC began to expand in the

1990s, it was in a much better position to practise *"yuan* diplomacy" (i.e. the offering of trade deals and other economic incentives to African states in exchange for recognition), and as a result Taiwan's diplomatic influence began to diminish as governments on the continent switched their allegiances to Beijing. The decision by South Africa, after long negotiations with Beijing, to break with Taiwan and recognise the PRC in January 1998, was an especially pivotal event which underscored China's growing presence in the region.[39] Since that time, Taipei has continued to lose ground in the region's diplomatic chess game, a far cry from the situation in the 1970s when Taiwan was able to make use of its superior economic resources to link recognition with economic assistance. In January 2008, Malawi became the most recent African state to cut ties with Taiwan and recognise Beijing, leaving only Burkina Faso, São Tomé e Principe and Swaziland which continue to maintain diplomatic relations with Taipei. In November 2013, President Yahya Jammeh of Gambia announced that his government would sever ties with Taipei, likely in the hopes of gaining greater access to aid and investment from Beijing. However, the Xi government declined to open relations with Banjul, preferring to keep the post-2008 diplomatic truce with Taiwan intact.[40] From 2013, Gambia had the dubious distinction of having a "no China" policy.

The ideological dimension of Sino-African relations has largely been replaced today by expanded economic considerations. The continent has been a major recipient of Chinese investment in the wake of Beijing's "going out" business strategies of the late 1990s and many Chinese businesses of varying sizes have sought to develop a presence in Africa. Jiang Zemin, during his 1996 tour of the continent, outlined China's "Five Points Proposal" for Africa which was based on reliable friendship, sovereign equality, non-intervention, mutually beneficial development and international cooperation,[41] an echo of Zhou Enlai's proposals from the 1950s but reflecting modern political pragmatism rather than socialist ideology. Although China has sought increased African trade in agricultural products, timber, precious and base metals, and foodstuffs, energy trade has been the most illustrative example of the growing economic linkages between the two sides. As China has been seeking to diversify its energy trade away from the Middle East, African oil and gas resources, which have been comparatively underdeveloped, are of great interest to Beijing. China has been able to compete with other international firms and secure petroleum deals with several African states, with Beijing's largest suppliers on the continent being Angola, Equatorial Guinea,

---

Box 8.2 China in Africa

"China is now a powerful force in Africa, and the Chinese are not going away. Their embrace of the continent is strategic, planned, long term, and still unfolding."
  – Deborah Brautigam, *The Dragon's Gift: The Real Story of China in Africa*
      (Oxford and New York: Oxford University Press, 2009), 311.

"The general patterns and key features of how China is perceived in Africa seem to suggest that China is poised to further extend its presence in Africa and Beijing has acquired substantial goodwill among Africans yet is developing deep issues and facing uncertain challenges and growing obstacles. China has encountered uphill battles that are often quite cost-ineffective in its much-speculated competition with the West in Africa, if Beijing indeed had a coherent grand strategy for such a rivalry."
  – Fei-ling Wang and Esi A. Eliot, "China in Africa: Presence, Perceptions and
      Prospects", *Journal of Contemporary China* 23(90) (2014): 1013.

Nigeria, DR Congo and Sudan. In the case of Nigeria, China was for a long time unable to enter its fossil fuels market due to the domination of Western energy interests there, but a series of development deals between Beijing and Abuja opened the door in the 2000s to energy investment by Chinese firms.[42]

Spurred on by energy and commodity development, Sino-African trade grew to approximately US$222 billion by 2014, and in 2009 China had overtaken the United States to become Africa's largest trade partner. Angola, South Africa, Sudan, Nigeria and Egypt represented Beijing's top five trading partners in Africa in terms of volume. Beijing has sought to position itself as an alternative trade and assistance partner for Africa, and one less interested in interfering in local governance or attaching conditions to its economic deals. As part of its economic expansion into sub-Saharan Africa, Beijing has engaged in sector-specific investments in countries including Angola (agriculture, waterworks), Namibia (agriculture, processing) and Zambia (cotton). China has also provided low-interest loans to nations which are more reliant on commodities, such as fossil fuels or mineral resources, as collateral, a process which has been called the "Angola model".[43] As recent surveys of the China–Africa relationship have also noted, the deepening bilateral economic relationship cannot be measured only in terms of aid and investment in addition to trade, but also in terms of the volume of Chinese workers who have entered Africa in recent years to work in primary and secondary sectors in addition to services.[44]

The Forum on China–Africa Cooperation (FOCAC) has brought together Chinese policymakers and 45 African leaders to discuss cross-regional political and economic cooperation. This gathering was the culmination of years of Chinese diplomacy in Africa, and cemented Beijing's status as a great power supporter of the continent. The first Forum met in October 2000, also in Beijing, and was attended by nearly 80 ministers from African countries, with a second ministerial conference held in Addis Ababa, Ethiopia, in December 2003. The sixth FOCAC summit, the first meeting held since Xi Jinping assumed the Chinese presidency, will be held in South Africa in late 2015. Africa has been referred to during these summits as a "strategic partner" for China, and Beijing has been prepared to back its commitment to the FOCAC process financially with new loans, buyers' credits and an investment fund. China's commitment to Africa was further illustrated in January 2012 when the new headquarters of the African Union (AU), funded by a US$200 million donation by Beijing, was formally opened in Addis Ababa.

At the same time, China has matched its stated concern for improving security and stability in Africa by contributing to United Nations peacekeeping missions there. By 2007, Chinese personnel were serving as blue helmets in UN missions in Africa including the Democratic Republic of the Congo, Liberia, Mali, South Sudan, Sudan and Western Sahara, and China's peacekeeping interests in Africa make up the vast majority of Chinese forces stationed abroad for the United Nations.[45] However, China's growing strategic presence in Africa has caused some concern in the United States and Western Europe. The "United States Africa Command" (AFRICOM) formally began operations in 2008, and was viewed as a response to the growing strategic presence of non-Western actors, including China, on the continent. During the first half of 2015, reports surfaced that Beijing was negotiating for the possible construction of a military base in the small but strategically located eastern African country of Djibouti, where American and French military bases had already been placed.[46] Djibouti is located near several regional hotspots and conflicts, including the Central African Republic, Libya, Somalia and Yemen. In all, Africa is fast developing as a model for China's changing views on security and diplomacy as well as development. African diplomacy is another showcase for China's "peaceful rise/development" policy, along with problem-solving through joint cooperation and the development of a more equitable multi-polar world.

China's evolving African diplomacy has also created some international controversy in the West, mainly due to Beijing's policies of seeking to maintain a clear division between economic partnerships and issues of governance with some of its trading partners in the region. The case of Sudan, which was the second African state to recognise Beijing (in 1958), has been the source of much international debate. China increased economic ties with Khartoum at a time when Western firms were being strongly encouraged to leave Sudan due to the civil war between the northern and southern regions of the country in the late 1990s. Beijing was especially interested in developing Sudanese petroleum trade, and has invested heavily in fossil fuel industries in the state despite international pressures. Since the 1990s, China's overall economic presence in Sudan strengthened to the point that by 2007 Beijing's trade represented about 64 per cent of Sudan's overall trade volume. Despite international pressures, China's extensive economic interests in Sudan have continued, as Beijing has been a longstanding investor in Sudanese energy, illustrated by the 1996 purchase by the CNPC of a 40 per cent share of the Greater Nile Petroleum Operating Company in Khartoum. By 2005, Sudan's share of China's oil imports had surpassed five per cent and by 2006 China was importing 47 per cent of Sudan's total petroleum production.[47]

Beijing's economic presence in Sudan became considerably more complicated after 2011 when that country formally broke in two after a long north–south civil war. The Republic of South Sudan was quickly recognised by Beijing, which wasted little time in developing economic and energy partnerships with the new government. However, when relations between Khartoum and South Sudan began to deteriorate over border and energy disputes, China found itself in the awkward position of being approached by both sides for support.[48] In the months following its independence, South Sudan's economy became heavily dependent upon oil exports and its government wished to retain China as a primary market, forcing Beijing to walk a delicate diplomatic tightrope as relations between the two "Sudans" eroded further after 2012, and the security situation in South Sudan itself which fell into civil war by December 2013.

Zimbabwe was another regional foreign policy headache for Beijing in light of the longstanding relationship between the two states dating from early Chinese support of then-opposition leader and now President Robert Mugabe. Since the turn of the century the Mugabe government came under increasing international criticism both for an increasingly authoritarian stance, suppression of personal freedoms and for widespread economic mismanagement and draconian land reform which exacerbated poverty levels in the southern African country. As Western concerns over Zimbabwe grew, the Mugabe government launched a "Look East" foreign policy in 2003 to reduce dependency upon the West in favour of China.[49] Widespread violence and accusations of intimidation of opposition figures during summer 2008 elections in the country galvanised Western-led efforts to sanction the Mugabe government at the United Nations. However, when the matter was brought to the UN Security Council in July 2008, China along with Russia vetoed an American-proposed arms embargo and travel restrictions on the Zimbabwean government. Both governments had argued that the issue was an internal matter outside of the UNSC's jurisdiction and best solved by talks between the government and opposition leaders.[50] Both the Sudan and Zimbabwe cases have showcased the problems of China's policy of drawing a solid line between economics and politics in its dealings with some African regimes.

China's African diplomacy has started to factor more prominently in local politics in the region. The subject of Chinese investment and its potential damage to the indigenous economy was a hotly debated topic during the September 2006 Zambian elections, when opposition leader Michael Sata ran on a platform of reducing economic ties with China and instead recognising Taipei. Popular resentment against Chinese companies was spurred by an explosion in April of that year in a Chinese-owned Zambian copper mine.[51] Although the government of incumbent president Levy Mwanawasa was able to hold power after the vote, the event underscored some limitations to China's economic relationship with Africa, and after the elections China sought to portray itself as a more responsible economic actor in the region. Sata would go on to win the subsequent presidential election in September 2011 on a platform of developing a more independent economic relationship with Beijing, but bilateral relations remained strong up to Sata's death in 2014.

The rise of China as an economic power, along with the growing trade presence of other large emerging markets such as Brazil, India and Indonesia, has revived long-dormant research into the question of "south–south trade", meaning trading patterns among developing states. Africa has factored much more often into these new debates as has the discussion about whether China is presenting a new model of economic growth for developing states. Much attention has been paid to the economic dimensions of Sino-African trade, especially in the area of energy, and certainly resource diplomacy is driving many aspects of Beijing's engagement with many African states. Nevertheless, there are also important political and cross-regional diplomacy elements to this relationship. In January 2006, Beijing released a foreign policy white paper, "China's African Policy",[52] which promoted not only economic linkages but also the requirement for stronger political ties via exchanges between leaders and governments, coordination of international affairs and actions against traditional and non-traditional security threats, and cooperation between China and the African Union.

Among various follow-up papers on the subject of Sino-African economic relations was a 2013 report which outlines more specific areas of bilateral cooperation in the areas of deepening overall trade, promoting investment and infrastructure development, cooperating in areas of agriculture and food security, encouraging greater dialogue on human security in Africa, and promoting stronger bilateral and multilateral relations.[53] As the Xi government continued to develop its "one belt and one road" policy, it was apparent that Africa, and especially its east coast, was shaping up to be a key trading area for China as Beijing's resource diplomacy on the continent continued. As economist Justin Yifu Lin noted in a January 2015 editorial, given the growing importance of Africa for China's diplomatic and economic interests, the Chinese government should also pursue what he termed a "one belt, one road and one continent" approach.[54] While there remain many issues to be resolved in this bilateral relationship, China has maintained its commitment to developing Africa relations as a key part of its expanded diplomacy beyond the Pacific Rim.

Latin America

For many decades, Latin America had been considered, both politically and economically, as being within the United States' sphere of influence. During the Cold War, the US was active in combating communism and soviet influence in the region. As with Africa, China's engagement of Latin America under Mao was greatly ideologically-driven, and with the exception of Cuba, which established ties with China early in the Cold War, China's engagement process with the rest of the region was slower to develop. Under Deng Xiaoping and Jiang Zemin, the focus shifted to economic considerations but there were some political issues which affected Beijing's ties with the region. In the 1990s, Beijing threatened to veto a United Nations mission to Haiti and did veto a proposed UN mission to Guatemala in consideration of both states' ties with Taiwan at that time. Nevertheless, these political differences did not stop growth in regional trade with China starting in the 1980s.[55] With the fall of the Soviet Union, the stage appeared to have been set for further cooperation in the Americas with the signing of the North American Free Trade Agreement (NAFTA) and the promise of increased trade between the US and South America. However, due to increased Chinese engagement, Beijing's presence in Central and South America has grown considerably in the space of a few short years.

Chinese President Hu Jintao made a celebrated regional tour in 2004, visiting Argentina, Brazil, Chile and Cuba, and many regional leaders have also attended summits in Beijing. President Xi continued that tradition in 2013–14 with visits to several countries in the region including Argentina, Brazil, Costa Rica, Mexico, Trinidad and Tobago, and Venezuela. During President Xi's visit to Fortaleza, Brazil, for the BRICS Summit in July 2014, the New Development Bank (NDB) and the BRICS Contingent Reserve Arrangement (CRA) were formally founded between China and fellow members Brazil, India, Russia and South Africa.[56] Also in attendance were representatives of the 12 members of the Union of South American Nations (UNASUR). In the wake of the meeting, the government of Argentina expressed interest in becoming the next member of the BRICS grouping, but it was decided by the membership to table discussion on the expansion of the organisation until the new institutions, including the NDB, were in operation.

China's interest in engaging the Latin American economies has been prompted by the PRC's requirement for raw materials, foodstuffs and agricultural products, and Chinese demand as well as its interest in regional investment has greatly benefited commodity industries in Latin America. To cite just one example, rapidly-growing Chinese requirements for copper imports have been a boon to production in Chile and greatly influenced that country's economy,[57] and overall Chinese demand for other raw materials such as tin, aluminium, zinc and iron ore were also of benefit to Latin American economies. However, those regional economies, including Mexico and some Central American states, which are more dependent upon manufactured goods such as textiles, have been more wary of China's economic expansion in the region. Even larger economies such as Argentina and Brazil are worried about their increasingly lopsided trade balance with China and actual and potential job losses and lower-skilled sectors in the wake of Chinese competition.[58] When the Chinese economy began to slow down after 2014, many Latin American states which were greatly dependent on resources trade with China began to experience economic troubles.

Overall trade between China and the Latin American–Caribbean states rose from US$8.2 billion to almost US$70 billion between 1999 and 2006 (by 2011, the figure had jumped again, to approximately US$240 billion for the year). China was also successful in improving political ties with left-wing governments in Latin America, including those of Luiz Inácio Lula da Silva and his post-2011 successor Dilma Rousseff in Brazil (a fellow member of the BRICS group), and Raúl Castro in Cuba.

Sino-Venezuelan political ties have been augmented by the growing energy relationship between the two states as Caracas has sought to distance itself from over-reliance upon Western markets and Beijing seeks a greater presence in Latin American oil and gas trade. In May 2008, the two sides agreed to jointly construct a refinery in China's Guangdong province for the specific purpose of refining Venezuelan oil. Despite the great distance between the two states and the costs of maritime oil shipping, the Hugo Chávez government had vowed to increase petroleum shipments to China to a million barrels per day by 2011.[59] China was also seeking energy and commodity deals with Bolivia, Brazil, Colombia and Ecuador. Brazil has been of special interest to China due to both its robust economy and its potentially large oil reserves off the country's coast. In mid-2008, increased links were discussed between the Chinese National Offshore Oil Corporation (CNOOC) and Brazilian energy giant Petrobras to jointly develop both Chinese and Brazilian offshore energy reserves,[60] and Brazil had been looking at China as a primary destination for its energy exports until prices began to slide in late 2014. The increasing closeness of Beijing to select Latin American states, including Brazil, has become of growing concern to the United States.

As a result of these political and economic shifts, China is being considered more seriously in the region as an alternative diplomatic and economic partner to Washington.[61] Since the 1990s, China has sought to engage various Latin American regional institutions, becoming a member of the Caribbean Development Bank in 1994, meeting with the South American Common Market (MERCOSUR) and the Inter-American Development Bank, and developing links with Chile, Mexico and Peru via annual meetings of the Asia-Pacific Economic Cooperation forum.[62] China also offered aid and assistance to its Caribbean trade partners, including infrastructure projects such as a stadium in the Bahamas, a presidential residence in Trinidad and Tobago and educational facilities in Dominica, and in 2011 Beijing promised a US$6.3 million loan to its partners in the Caribbean.[63]

Beijing signed a free trade agreement with Chile in November 2005, the first such deal for a Latin American economy, to be followed by like agreements with Peru in April 2009 and Costa Rica in April 2010. During 2015, China and Colombia began to move closer to initiating free trade talks as well, and in May 2004, China was granted permanent observer status by the Organisation of American States (OAS). Beijing also sent military personnel to Haiti as part of the UN's peacekeeping mission there despite the lack of formal relations between Beijing and Port-au-Prince, marking the first time Chinese forces were engaged in such a mission in the Western Hemisphere. When Haiti was devastated by an earthquake in January 2010, eight Chinese UN personnel, including four peacekeepers, lost their lives, and Beijing pledged aid to the country despite the lack of formal diplomatic ties.[64]

Like in Africa, before the 2008 cross-Strait truce, Latin America had been a diplomatic battleground between Beijing and Taipei, as Taiwan had made considerable economic inroads in the region and was able to secure much diplomatic support. Since the truce went into place, 12 Latin American and Caribbean states recognised Taiwan and had no official diplomatic ties with China, including El Salvador, Haiti, Honduras, Nicaragua, Panama and Paraguay. In more recent years, Dominica (2004), Grenada (2005) and Costa Rica (2007) switched recognition from Taipei to Beijing, and in the case of Grenada the transition was complicated by a financial dispute over outstanding loans which Taiwan had provided for the construction of the island nation's airport. As well, the tiny Caribbean island of St. Lucia, after recognising Beijing since 1997, decided ten years later to reverse that decision and reinstate relations with Taipei. Despite these events, Beijing's economic and diplomatic presence in the Caribbean and Latin America were seen to be growing, partially as a result of perceived American disengagement from the region.

The Middle East

The Middle East / Southwest Asian region had also seen an increase in Chinese diplomatic attention since the end of the Cold War for both political and economic reasons. The region was the recipient of Hu Jintao's shuttle diplomacy soon after the Chinese president took office. An early 2004 tour by Hu, of Algeria, Egypt and the League of Arab States (LAS, also known as the Arab League) brought forward two sweeping policy proposals. The first was the creation of the China–Arab Cooperation Forum (CACF) which would act as a conduit for China and the LAS, and the second was a proposed set of guiding principles for future relations which included improved political relations on the basis of mutual respect, as well as strengthened economic, social and cultural links and greater cooperation in the name of improving peace and development. Several high-level leadership meetings between Beijing and Middle East policymakers took place afterwards, and the CACF continues to hold biannual governmental conferences, with the most recent held in Beijing in June 2014, with the "one belt and one road" plans high on the meeting's agenda. As well, China has been seeking since 2004 to develop a free trade agreement with the Gulf Cooperation Council (GCC), an economic grouping which includes the energy-rich states of Saudi Arabia, Kuwait and the United Arab Emirates.

Like many other outside actors, China had to make rapid adjustments to its regional diplomacy as a result of the 2011–12 "Arab Spring" uprisings which unseated many longstanding regional governments, including those of Egypt, Libya, Tunisia and Yemen, and resulted in widespread violence in Syria between the government of Bashar Assad and various rebel groups seeking Assad's ousting and an end to over 50 years of Ba'athist rule in the country. Beijing attempted to retain a neutral stance on the uprisings while continuing to seek improved relations in the region. However, China's habitual nonpartisan stance was sorely tested first in March 2011 when it abstained in a UN Security Council vote which authorised the use of force against the Libyan regime of Muammar Gaddafi, which would be toppled in August of that year. The governments of both China and Russia felt that they had been deceived by the West into supporting a vote which directly led to forced regime change in Libya. With these concerns in mind, in February 2012 China along with Russia vetoed a UNSC resolution calling for Syrian President Assad to resign in the wake of worsening civil conflict. Beijing justified the decision by noting that overt support for one side of the dispute would only lead to a further deterioration of conditions in Syria.

However, China's veto and its unwillingness to support deeper sanctions was sharply criticised in the United States and Europe and was greeted with unease among other Arab governments. By April of that year, Beijing had shifted its stance on the conflict and agreed to include Chinese personnel in the multilateral UN Supervision Mission in Syria (UNSMIS) charged with overseeing a ragged cease-fire in the country. In May 2012, the Assad government was accused of supporting attacks on civilians in the western Syrian town of Houla. The Chinese government condemned the violence and maintained that the UNSMIS mission and UN mediation were the best methods of resolving the conflict. However, the UNSMIS operations folded by the end of 2012, with the civil conflict in Syria continuing, and made more complicated by the rise of the Islamic State in Iraq and the Levant (ISIL) which began to carve out territory in the country as well as in next-door Iraq. Although Beijing did not join the US-led coalition to combat ISIL in a formal capacity, China has joined the international community in condemning the movement and has raised concerns about a possible extremist spillover into China's Far West, including potentially Xinjiang.

During the first two years of his presidency, Xi Jinping was less directly active in the Middle East in comparison with his predecessor. Xi's planned visit to Egypt and Saudi Arabia in April 2015, which would have been his first to the Middle East, was delayed due to the intensifying fighting between the Saudi-backed government of Yemen and Shi'ite Houthi rebels and other splinter groups loyal to ISIL. Despite the lack of summit diplomacy in the region, the Xi government continues to view the region not only as an important source of energy and resources but also as an important component of the "one belt and one road" strategy. In addition, several Middle East and North African countries agreed to join the

Asian Infrastructure Investment Bank (AIIB) in early 2015, including Iran, Israel, Jordan, Kuwait, Qatar, Saudi Arabia and the United Arab Emirates.

While Chinese relations with many Arab states have been longstanding, Sino-Israeli diplomatic relations were only formally established in 1992, despite Israel having recognised Beijing in 1950, and China traditionally preferred to remain aloof from the complex Israeli–Palestinian issue. However, trade and economic contacts between the two states existed at least as far back as the mid-1980s. Beijing, since that time, sought to maintain an even-handed diplomatic approach to Israel and its Arab neighbours, while maintaining its support for the eventual creation of a Palestinian state. However, under Xi Jinping, China began to move towards a somewhat more active role in the Middle East peace process, including a four-point peace proposal released in May 2013. These points included an independent State of Palestine in peaceful co-existence with Israel, negotiations on issues including Israeli settlement activities, violence against civilians, the blockade of the Gaza Strip, upholding the "land for peace" concept, and ongoing participation by the international community to encourage a peaceful resolution to regional disputes.[65] It was during the same month that President Xi met separately with Israeli President Binyamin Netanyahu and Palestinian President Mahmoud Abbas.

Trade in commodities has also dominated the Sino-Middle Eastern relationship, as Beijing now views the region as an important source of raw materials including phosphate, manganese, cobalt and fibres for China's burgeoning textile sector.[66] As with the United States and Europe, China has paid very close attention to the Middle East as a source of fossil fuels, and much of Beijing's diplomacy in the region has focused on energy trade. Despite being a latecomer to Middle East energy politics as compared with America, Europe and Japan, Beijing has nevertheless been successful in establishing itself as a crucial consumer base for regional oil and gas. Despite attempts to diversify its energy partners as described previously, the Gulf Region remains China's primary source of imported oil and gas, and by 2013 Beijing's major regional oil suppliers were from the Gulf Region, especially Saudi Arabia, Iran, Qatar but also increasingly Iraq and Yemen.

Iraq had also been viewed as a primary energy partner for China, but because of the uncertainty of the conflict there since 2003 and the post-war American role in Baghdad, China's future trading role remained unclear.[67] Beijing was unhappy with the decision made by the United States to lead a "coalition of the willing" to invade Iraq without a United Nations mandate, as well as the fact that the UN-backed inspections for potential Iraqi weapons of mass destruction were unable to continue. Concerns remain in Beijing that American goals for Baghdad will involve a long-term US presence in the country even after formal military operations have ceased. The Anglo-American build-up to the conflict in Iraq was one of the motivating factors behind Beijing's decision to begin developing energy stockpiles and improving infrastructure,[68] and as Western forces withdrew from Iraq in 2011–12, the future of the country's foreign and economic relations became less predictable, especially with the rise of the Islamic State in the centre of the country and the possibility of renewed American and Western military involvement in the country in 2015.

China, like the other large energy-consuming powers, has a vested interest in ensuring that energy exports from the region are maintained even as prices began to drop. While throughout much of the Cold War China's interests in the Middle East were ideological and strategic, more economic issues began to take precedence as China recognised the need to import fossil fuels, and Beijing has sought a balance in its policies on the Arab–Israeli conflict, acknowledging the economic consequences of favouring either side. As one author noted, the size of the Chinese market and the country's increasing global trading presence make it unlikely that Beijing would be subject to a fuel embargo.[69] However, the strong American presence in the region, not only in terms of Iraq but also considering Washington's established political ties with Riyadh, does present a challenge for long-term Chinese energy diplomacy.[70] There is the possibility that Saudi Arabia may increasingly view China as a counterweight to the West, while ensuring that ties to American and European markets are not seriously damaged.

China has also sought to maintain energy relations with Iran despite a concentrated international campaign led by the United States to isolate and sanction Tehran, especially in light of concerns about possible Iranian nuclear weapons development. Sino-Iranian ties were strong throughout much of the late Cold War period, with the two countries establishing diplomatic ties in August 1971, despite considerable ideological differences between Beijing and first the Iranian regime of Shah Reza Pahlavi and then the post-1979 theocratic rule of the Ayatollah Khomeini and his successors. China's insistence upon maintaining strong economic ties with Tehran, despite differences in political outlook, has run up against American efforts to curtail international investment in Iran and isolate its leadership. As with Sudan, Beijing has attempted to maintain a strict division between bilateral growing economic ties and non-interference in local governance. Total Sino-Iranian trade, despite US-led pressures for economically isolating Tehran, rose to US$45 billion in 2011, a 50 per cent rise from the previous year,[71] with China importing increasing amounts of Iranian oil, gas and petrochemical products, and Tehran receiving more Chinese manufactured goods. By early 2012, Iran represented 11 per cent of Beijing's oil imports. China has also been involved in non-energy-related projects in Iran including the development of the Tehran metro system as well as other transportation projects.[72] In short, Beijing had disagreed with the American-led policy of economic isolation of Iran.

As with Central Asia, China has also been investing in Iranian energy infrastructure, much of which had been deteriorating in the wake of US-led sanctions after 1980, including investment in Iran's Yadavaran oilfield in 2004 and a 2007 deal to jointly develop Iranian natural gas in the North Pars region.[73] Iran's status as the fourth largest oil producer in the world after Saudi Arabia, Russia and the US, and as the second largest global gas producer after Moscow, meant that China as a growing energy consumer felt it could ill-afford to ignore the benefits of maintaining economic ties with Tehran. The identification of Iran as part of the "axis of evil" by the American government under George W. Bush after 2002 provided further diplomatic openings for both China and Russia. Geography has also played a role in Iranian energy trade, as the country is close enough to Russia, as a fellow oil and gas producer, and to China as an energy consumer, to form what some analysts feared could be an Asian energy bloc which might be considerably more resistant to Western diplomatic pressures.[74] Iran is an observer state in the Shanghai Cooperation Organisation, and the government of Mahmoud Ahmedinejad made little secret of its desire for Iran to become a full SCO member.[75] The SCO continues to debate the option of granting Iran full membership and whether it would be beneficial to the organisation or too risky in terms of straining relations with the West.

However, in more recent years both the Iranian nuclear weapons question and the possibility of a US–Iran *rapprochement* during 2014–15 seriously complicated Beijing's diplomacy with Tehran. In April 2015, an initial breakthrough was reached with the Iranian government of Hassan Rouhani and the "P5 plus one" group, made up of China, France, Russia, the United Kingdom and the United States as well as Germany, which would allow for restrictions on the Iranian nuclear programme under international supervision. Beijing has been supportive of the process and has expressed hopes that a deal could see Tehran finally

---

Box 8.3 China's approaches to modern conflicts

"China's policies on diplomacy in the UNSC cases of Iran, Sudan and Myanmar indicate that it has succeeded in presenting a coexistance-based alternative to Western calls for using Chapter VII of the UN Charter to counter grave violations of civil and political rights. China's alternative is a revised version of existing UN Charter provisions founded in the coexistance principles of mutual rspect for sovereignty and territorial integrity, nonaggression, equality and mutual benefit, and noninterference with the internal affairs of other states."

– Lisette Osgaard, *China and Coexistance: Beijing's National Security Strategy for the Twenty-First Century* (Washington, DC: Woodrow Wilson Centre Press, 2012), 149.

---

emerge from international isolation. Since the turn of the century, concerns expressed by the United States and Europe that Iran was seeking to develop a nuclear weapon intensified political pressures on Iran and raised the possibility of military action against suspected Iranian nuclear sites. This had placed China in the difficult position of on the one hand seeking to protect its economic and energy interests while on the other not wanting to see an Iranian nuclear bomb potentially destabilise the Middle East. Beijing, along with Moscow, has resisted the use of intense economic coercion or the threat of force to settle this issue and China has traditionally maintained that a diplomatic dialogue is the best way to prevent a potential nuclear crisis.[76]

South Asia

The Chinese government under Xi Jinping has viewed South Asia and the Indian Ocean as a major area of interest in its developing Eurasian trade policies, and there is the question of how this greater interest will affect the political, economic and strategic landscape of the region, especially in terms of Sino-Indian relations which have had a long and sometimes difficult history. The two large states were partners, given their post-colonial status, throughout much of the 1950s, a link which was articulated during the watershed 1955 Bandung Conference which was meant to promote developing country solidarity. Yet despite a 1954 bilateral agreement between Beijing and New Delhi which included Indian acknowledgement of Chinese sovereignty over Tibet, outstanding border issues remained from the previous decade.[77] Bilateral relations deteriorated due to Cold War divisions, reaching a nadir during the 1962 Sino-Indian War, which was fought over their disputed border in the Himalayas as well as Beijing's unhappiness with India granting asylum to the Dalai Lama after a failed uprising in Tibet in 1959. The conflict resulted in the annexation of the Aksai Chin region in the Himalaya Mountains by China, an area which India still claims. As well, the status of the northern part of what was called the North-East Frontier Agency and is now the Indian state of Arunachal Pradesh is also a source of contention between Beijing and New Delhi.[78] China was also highly critical of India's nuclear tests in 1974 and 1998, although Beijing's reaction to Pakistan's nuclear testing in 1998 was more muted.

In 2005, China became an observer within the South Asian Association for Regional Cooperation (SAARC), an organisation heavily dominated by India and including other states on the subcontinent such as Pakistan, Sri Lanka and Bangladesh. India was at first very reluctant to permit Beijing even observer status, but acquiesced as part of a deal proposed by Pakistan to permit Afghanistan to become a full SAARC member. However, in a bid to prevent China from tacitly influencing the organisation, India pushed for and was successful in allowing the United States to also sit as an observer.[79] Other large and medium powers such as Australia, Iran, Japan and the European Union also attained observer status within SAARC. It is likely that as China's diplomacy in South Asia continues to develop, the country's future role with SAARC will continue to be debated among its disparate membership.

Sino-Indian relations have warmed somewhat since the coming to power of Indian Prime Minister Narendra Modi in May 2014,[80] with both states being leading members of the BRICS regime and its New Development Bank, as well as the AIIB for example. The bilateral economic relationship has also strengthened since both countries began further openings to the international economy. However, questions have been raised in India about the country's trade deficit with Beijing, largely due to the nature of the trade itself. Much of India's exports to China tend to be raw materials such as base metals and cotton, while Chinese exports to India have been dominated by high-technology and manufactured goods. Thus, one of the top priorities for the Modi government in further developing trade relations with China is greater access to the Chinese market for Indian goods.

There also remain numerous outstanding security issues between the two states relating to disputed territory. The sensitivity of the border situation was demonstrated in April 2013 when a platoon of approximately 50 People's Liberation Army (PLA) personnel crossed into a disputed area of the Aksai Chin in the frontier region of Daulat Beg Oldi and set up camp before withdrawing. According to Indian officials, the platoon crossed what Delhi perceived to be the Line of Actual Control (LAC) separating Chinese and Indian territory, however the physical border between the two states has yet to be fully demarcated to the satisfaction of both parties. A similar incident took place in September the following year.

There is also the question of India's potential responses to an increased Chinese economic and security presence in the Indian Ocean as a result of the Maritime Silk Road trade routes being considered by the Xi government. Two of India's neighbours, Myanmar and Sri Lanka, were seen by Beijing as potential sites for ports and trading hubs for China, and Delhi has been wary of previous attempts by Beijing to establish port facilities in the Indian Ocean, including an unsuccessful 2012 negotiation with the government of Seychelles to provide facilities for Chinese vessels participating in counter-piracy operations in the Gulf of Aden.[81] In September 2014, Xi had the opportunity to articulate his plans for a Maritime Silk Road in the Indian Ocean during visits to the Maldives and Sri Lanka, two countries which had traditionally been seen by India as part of its sphere of influence,[82] and also considered important components of what was called a "string of pearls" strategy on China's part to increase its presence in the Indian Ocean. However, China has been taking steps not to give the impression that it wishes to cut New Delhi out of the evolution of the New Silk Road process. Beijing's longstanding enthusiasm for a "Bangladesh–China–India–Myanmar" (BCIM) economic corridor was demonstrated with December 2013 talks between officials from all four states in Kunming, which could become a component of larger Eurasian trade corridors planned by China.[83]

Even before the Xi government began to develop its "one belt and one road" strategies, Beijing under the Hu Jintao government had begun to view the Indian Ocean as being of great importance to Chinese strategic interests. As Robert Kaplan argued in his 2010 book on Indian Ocean strategies, China was able to take advantage of a "peace dividend" from having no outstanding border instability issues and place more attention on developing sea power capabilities both in the Pacific and in the Indian Ocean. As well, he noted that much of China's economic security concerns were emanating from the need for ready access to resources, including fossil fuels in the Middle East and Eastern Africa, which required increased Indian Ocean transit. He concluded that while China was satisfied with having the United States take the brunt of providing security in the Ocean for many years, Beijing was now in a position to become more directly involved with Indian Ocean politics and security.[84]

Since Xi Jinping came to power, Indian concerns about Beijing's long-term interests in the Indian Ocean and South Asia have been demonstrated in tacit diplomatic competition in parts of the region, including the Maldives, Mauritius, Myanmar, Seychelles and Sri Lanka. Also, after a massive earthquake struck Nepal in April 2015, both China and India rushed aid to the region. Although the political and economic relationship between the two powers became more businesslike and multifaceted under the Modi and Xi governments, it remained to be seen whether issues including the Indian Ocean, Pakistan and trade will continue to pose obstacles.

China and Pakistan had maintained an exceptionally close relationship ever since Islamabad was one of the first governments to recognise the People's Republic of China in 1950. The depth of China's commitment to supporting Pakistan was demonstrated in April 2015 when Beijing announced an aid package worth US$46 billion for Islamabad, which included a proposed "Pakistan–China Economic Corridor" located between Pakistan's southern Gwadar port on the Arabian Sea and China's Xinjiang region.[85] This aid has been viewed as a reflection of the paramount importance of Pakistan to China's developing "Silk Road" Eurasian trade routes. Pakistan has in turn been increasingly supportive of Beijing attaining full membership within SAARC, a move resisted by India.[86] The Sino-Pakistan relationship has been viewed as the most durable of China's current strategic partnerships

As well, there is the question of whether China and Pakistan may increase their cooperation in Afghanistan in the wake of the pullout of American forces from the country in 2014 and China's growing economic interests in the war-torn nation, including a potentially lucrative copper mine located at Mes Aynak in western Afghanistan.[87] China also views Afghanistan, which still suffers from civil conflict between the government and forces loyal to the extremist Taliban, as essential to maintaining stability in Central Asia. Like the United States under President Obama, the Xi government during its first few years also appeared to be constructing a framework for an "Afghanistan–Pakistan" regional policy, given the intertwining of so many security issues between the two states.

China's emerging polar policies

In recent years, Beijing has been seeking to develop a more comprehensive set of policies in the world's polar regions, especially as both the Arctic and Antarctic have garnered a growing level of international attention as a result of climate change, with the resulting melting of ice at both poles. In the case of the Arctic, Beijing's emerging areas of interest in Arctic affairs have diversified, to include the development of scientific diplomacy through joint cooperation with Arctic states, climate change and the Arctic environment. China completed its first North Pole expedition in 1999, and shortly afterwards began sea-based research expeditions in the region. In 1996, China joined the International Arctic Scientific Committee (IASC), a non-governmental organisation dedicated to coordinating regional scientific research initiatives.[88] Beijing's research interests later culminated in the opening of the Arctic Yellow River Station (*Beiji Huanghe zhan* 北极黄河站) for scientific research at Ny-Ålesund on the Norwegian islands of Svalbard in July 2004.[89] Beijing has stressed that despite concerns raised in North America and Europe, China's Arctic interests are primarily driven by resource diplomacy, and scientific interests will be the main driver of future Chinese Arctic policy.

From an economic viewpoint, China is seeking to develop joint ventures with Arctic states, including Canada, Denmark (Greenland), Iceland and Russia, in regional resource extraction, including fossil fuels, metals and minerals, as these resources become more accessible. For example, in October 2013, the Chinese National Offshore Oil Corporation (CNOOC) and Reykjavík-based energy company Eykon were given official permission to jointly explore for oil and gas in the Dreki region of the North Atlantic between Iceland and Norway, with the Norwegian firm Petoro joining the project shortly afterwards.[90] In February 2013, CNOOC completed its acquisition of the Canadian energy firm Nexen, despite internal debates within the Canadian government. The deal, worth US$15.1 billion, solidified Chinese interests in the potentially lucrative oil sands of northern Alberta.[91] Also, Hu Jintao's visit to Denmark in June 2012 was widely viewed as an expression of China's interest in assisting with the development of Greenland's fossil fuels, precious metals and rare earths as the ice sheet begins to recede in that country, which is part of the Kingdom of Denmark. In January 2015, the Hong Kong firm obtained the rights to a potential iron mine at Isua in Greenland.[92] The region is increasingly being viewed by Beijing as politically and economically valuable, and Beijing's interests in Arctic engagement have become much more visible in recent years.

China also wishes to make use of emerging Arctic sea routes, especially the Northern Sea Route (NSR) via the northern Siberian coast. In keeping with Beijing's interest in expanded land and sea trade routes between Asia and Europe, the NSR is of great interest to China as it seeks to export goods to Europe and beyond, using faster and less expensive routes. In this, China wishes to join other Asian states, including Japan and South Korea, in seeking to take advantage of future trans-Arctic shipping. Beijing is also seeking a voice in the development and legal status of these potential trade routes as well as potential new organisations designed to regulate future Arctic shipping. Beijing demonstrated its commitment to participating in the future economic opening up of the NSR for commercial shipping in August–September 2013, when the Chinese cargo vessel *Yongsheng* (永盛) travelled from the port of Dalian to Rotterdam in 33 days via the Arctic route, saving about two weeks of transit time instead of going the traditional way via the Indian Ocean.[93] In mid-2015, the *Yongsheng* was planning a second test voyage through the NSR. The event marked the first time a container vessel made the journey, and emphasised not only the potential viability of the passage for Chinese and Asian shipping, but also China's growing prowess in maritime trade and strategies. In September 2015, five PLAN vessels transited the waters off the Aleutian Islands of Alaska for the first time.

Finally, Beijing has sought increased participation in Arctic governance and more frequent engagement with regional institutions on the governmental and sub-governmental level. This has especially been the case with the Arctic Council, which is the main decision-

---

Box 8.4 "Luck and misfortune" in the Arctic

"In China, we have a saying, 'Luck and misfortune come in turn'. New opportunities also bring new challenges. Likewise, the habitat of human beings has been significantly influenced by the natural environmental changes in the Arctic. Therefore, it is necessary to further carry out relevant research, so as to deepen our understanding of the process and mechanism of the natural environmental changes in the Arctic in a comprehensive way."

– Chinese Ambassador Zhao Jun, speech at the Arctic Frontiers Conference,
Tromsø, Norway, 21 January 2013.

making body in the region, featuring eight members, Canada, Denmark (Faroe Islands and Greenland), Finland, Iceland, Norway, Sweden, the United States and the Russian Federation as well as observer nations and organisations. Although China could not be a member of the Council, as it does not have an Arctic border, Beijing attempted to gain observer status and ultimately did so in May 2013 along with Italy and other Asian states also interested in the potential for the Arctic as an economic resource and trade corridor, namely India, Japan, South Korea and Singapore.[94] Among the Council members, some states such as Canada and Russia have been more wary of China's Arctic engagement, while the Nordic region has been more open to the idea of developing cooperative projects with Beijing and other Asian actors in Far North affairs.

China has also increased its scientific and diplomatic presence in Antarctica, having signed the Antarctic Treaty in 1983. Since 1985, Beijing has opened four research bases on the continent, with the first being the Great Wall Station (*Changcheng zhan* 长城站) on King George Island and the most recent being Taishan Station (*Taishan zhan* 泰山站) on Queen Elizabeth Land in Eastern Antarctica which opened in February 2014. A fifth base, to be located on Inexpressible Island at Terra Nova Bay, is being prepared for a potential 2017 opening. Unlike Taishan, this station would have the ability to stay operational through the winter months. This would give China an equal number of stations as the United States has on the continent. In November 2014, President Xi and then-Australian Prime Minister Tony Abbott agreed to sign a memorandum of understanding to strengthen ties on joint research work in Antarctica.[95] China also operates an icebreaker, the *Snow Dragon* (*Xuelong* 雪龙), which has conducted survey missions at both poles, and may be joined by a second icebreaking vessel which was being prepared for deployment in 2016.

Conclusions (and what's next?)

While the development of China's cross-regional diplomacy is still very new, the political and economic benefits to Beijing have thus far been considerable. Beijing has been successful in incorporating a level of diplomacy based on shared international interests and the benefits of increased trade to make great progress in expanding its foreign policy beyond the Asia-Pacific region. As well, Beijing under Xi Jinping has demonstrated considerable confidence in engaging many parts of the world outside of the Asia-Pacific region, including in areas as politically complex as Africa, Europe and the Middle East.

China has a number of foreign policy challenges ahead. Relations with the other big powers, including the United States, Russia and European Union, will remain paramount, but other issues closer to home will also require a great deal of attention, such as maritime security issues in the western Pacific, relations with immediate neighbours including Japan and Southeast Asia, and the construction of the "one belt and one road" / OBOR trading routes through Eurasia and the Indian Ocean, which if successful will result in a much deeper relationship between China and the rest of Asia. Beijing is fortunate since unlike during the Cold War it is not facing a direct threat on its borders, but like much of the world China is finding that many security threats are beginning to emanate from non-state actors, ranging from terrorist organisations such as the Islamic State to transnational crime. Without an organisation in Asia similar to the European Union, NATO or the Organisation for Security and Cooperation in Europe (OSCE) to assist the region in settling disputes, regional frictions in Asia will be a constant issue, especially as Beijing's relative power continues to rise. The East and South China Seas have become East Asia's most difficult strategic issues along with North Korea. Also close to home is the Taiwan issue, which has been muted since 2008 but could resurface after the early-2016 elections on the island. Other developing power centres in Asia, including India and Indonesia, may also play a larger role in China's regional policy interests.

On the international level, China is still seeking to expand its international economic interests abroad in a global economy which in some areas is recovering but in others is still facing problems. China's economic expansion since the Dengist era has been rapid, heady, and has challenged and sometimes upended commonly-held views on how states could and should modernise. The core of China's economic successes has been its large market, coupled with a large workforce, both of which were galvanised and internationalised as a result of globalisation and the pro-trade policies of Chinese governments since the 1990s. China's economic power still lies largely in the manufacturing sector, but the country is seeking to move more swiftly into the modern economy dominated by services and high technology.

As a result of the global economic slowdown after 2008, China has also sought to work its economy to place a greater emphasis on domestic growth, but the announcement of the OBOR projects well illustrated that trade will still be the cornerstone of China's economy for the near future. The Xi government continues to fight poverty and underdevelopment, as well as corruption, within China, problems which threaten to dilute its economic successes, and China's economic growth must still be weighed against the fact that the country is in many ways still classified as "developing". At the same time, China is seeking to better "brand" both itself and its international products and services more effectively, taking a page from other economic powers.

China's networking capabilities in the international system also continue to expand. There are now more global and regional organisations, regimes, rules and norms than ever before, which on the one hand serves to constrain state behaviour to varying degrees but on the other offers states goods and power which would otherwise be too difficult or too risky to pursue. China is the first great power to develop within an international system so dominated by institutions, and as it develops it has made masterful use of them in order to improve its power and standing on a global level. Beijing still retains concerns about state sovereignty and remains wary of strategic cooperation, but in some areas those concerns are beginning to subside as China grows more confident of its foreign policy capabilities. China has many more outlets to the international system than during the Maoist era, ranging from government contacts to the opportunities for Chinese to increase international awareness via travel, education and communication. However, in addition to the OBOR trade routes, organisations such as the New Development Bank and the Asia Infrastructure Investment Bank, which have been spearheaded by Beijing, all illustrate that China's confidence in its international capabilities has further placed the country to become more of a norm-maker in the international system in

---

Box 8.5 "Tianxia" ("All under Heaven") and international relations

"Here, *Tianxia* is embedded in an important debate about how China can fit into the world system as a 'responsible great power' that has emerged via a network of liberal IR scholars during the past decade. China is trying to prove to the world (and especially the West) that it is no longer a revolutionary state that challenges international order but is a 'responsible' member of international society."

– William A. Callaghan, "Tianxia 天下, Empire, and the World: China's
Visions of World Order for the Twenty-First Century", *China Orders the World:*
Normative Soft Power and Foreign Policy, ed. William A. Callaghan and Elena
Barabantseva (Washington, DC: Woodrow Wilson Centre Press, 2011), 107.

> *Box 8.6* China's rise: then and now
> "Beijing has done very well inside the global economic and governance system that was largely shaped by America after World War II. But we should have no illusions that China will simply accept this system in its present form forever. Indeed, China has been testing alternatives."
> – Henry M. Paulson, Jr., *Dealing with China: An Insider Unmasks the New Economic Superpower* (New York: Twelve, 2015), 394.

addition to being a norm-taker. As well, China under Xi Jinping is now beginning to view its relations with the United States on more of an even playing field, and economically the two countries will be responsible for guiding the global economy in the years to come.

China's geographic interests expanded considerably over the past decade both in the developed and developing world. Along with the expansion of China's foreign policy in a geographic sense, there has also been a process of deepening. This process can be seen both in the growing numbers of people and groups who are now crafting China's international relations and in the ideas and concepts which they are producing. Since Mao's death, the removal of socialist ideology from China's foreign relations and the subsequent end of the Cold War prompted much new thinking in the country about foreign affairs. It is now impossible for a single Chinese leader to take an overwhelming role in international relations, as with domestic politics, without the assistance of a much larger group of governmental and semi-governmental actors ranging from ministries to think-tanks. This has led to a proliferation of new ideas about China's place in the world and which directions the country should take as it grows in power. Although Xi Jinping, unlike his predecessor, has put a more personal stamp on Chinese foreign policy since his coming to power, it can still be argued that China's international interests have grown to the point where many actors in China are necessary to contribute to foreign policymaking.

The question remains, however, as to the response of the West, especially the US and Europe, as well as other regions to a more activist Chinese foreign policy under the Xi government in many more parts of the world. Will the pattern which emerges as China continues to widen and deepen its foreign interests be that of Western accommodation, competition, or something in between? It can be argued that foreign policy expertise will continue to be crucial to China's government both from a domestic and an international viewpoint. The Xi government came to power along with the so-called "fifth generation" (*diwudai* 第五代) of Chinese leaders, and the president is expected to stay in power until 2022, so there is much more time for Xi Jinping to add more features to China's foreign policy in addition to the considerable number of policies his government has put forward in its first three years. The rise of China continues to be one of the most significant changes to global affairs since the end of the Cold War, and it is for that reason alone that understanding how China interacts with its neighbours in Asia, and the international system, has become so important to the study of modern foreign policy.

Discussion questions

- What were the reasons behind Beijing's decision to expand its foreign policy more deeply into regions beyond Asia?
- How have China's relations with Europe differed from those with the United States in recent years?

- How have Chinese economic policies in developing regions affected their trade and their political development?
- Will a diplomatic competition take place between the United States and China for influence in Africa, Latin America and/or the Middle East?
- To what degree is China's cross-regional diplomacy driven by Beijing's need for commodities and energy?

Recommended reading

Alterman, John B. and John W. Garver. *The Vital Triangle: China, the United States and the Middle East* (Washington DC, Centre for Strategic and International Studies, 2008).

Brautigam, Deborah. *The Dragon's Gift: The Real Story of China in Africa* (Oxford: Oxford University Press, 2011).

Cardenal, Juan Pablo and Heriberto Araujo. *China's Silent Army: The Pioneers, Traders, Fixers and Workers Who Are Remaking the World in China's Image* (London: Allen Lane, 2013).

Dittmer, Lowell and George T. Yu (eds). *China, the Developing World and the New Global Dynamic* (Boulder, CO and London: Lynne Rienner, 2010).

Economy, Elizabeth and Michael Levi. *By All Means Necessary: How China's Resource Quest is Changing the World* (Oxford and New York: Oxford University Press, 2014).

Ellis, R. Evan. *China in Latin America: The Whats and Wherefores* (Boulder, CO: Lynne Rienner, 2009).

French, Howard W. *China's Second Continent: How a Billion Migrants are Building a New Empire in Africa* (New York: Alfred A. Knopf, 2014).

Kerr, David and Liu Fei (eds). *The International Politics of EU–China Relations* (Oxford and New York: Oxford University Press, 2007).

Lai, Hongyi. *The Domestic Sources of China's Foreign Policy: Regimes, Leadership, Priorities and Process* (New York and London: Routledge, 2011).

Lanteigne, Marc. *China's Emerging Arctic Strategies: Economics and Institutions* (Reykjavík: Institute of International Affairs / Centre for Arctic Policy Studies, 2014).

Leiv Lunde, Jian Yang and Iselin Stensdal (eds). *Asian Countries and the Arctic Future* (Singapore: World Scientific Publishing, 2015).

Lo, Bobo. *Axis of Convenience: Moscow, Beijing and the New Geopolitics* (London and Washington DC: Chatham House / Brookings, 2008).

Moyo, Dambisa. *Winner Take All: China's Race for Resources and What It Means for the World* (New York: Basic Books, 2012).

Naidu, G.V.C., Mumin Chen and Raviprasad Narayanan (eds). *India and China in the Emerging Dynamics of East Asia* (New York: Springer, 2014).

Olimat, Muhamad. *China and the Middle East Since World War II: A Bilateral Approach* (Lanham and Boulder: Lexington Books, 2014).

Reilly, James and Jingdong Yuan (eds). *Australia and China at 40* (Sydney: University of New South Wales Press, 2012).

Riordan Roett and Guadalupe Paz (eds). *Latin America and the Asian Giants: Evolving Ties with China and India* (Washington DC: Brookings, 2016).

Ross, Robert S., Øystein Tunsjo and Zhang Tuosheng (eds). *US–China–EU Relations: Managing a New World Order* (New York and London: Routledge, 2010).

Rozman, Gilbert. *The Sino-Russian Challenge to the World Order* (Washington DC: Woodrow Wilson Centre Press, 2014).

Shambaugh, David, Eberhard Sandschneider and Zhou Hong (eds). *China–Europe Relations: Perceptions, Policies and Prospects* (London and New York: Routledge, 2008).

Simpfendorfer, Ben. *The New Silk Road: How a Rising Arab World is Turning Away from the West and Rediscovering China* (Basingstoke, UK and New York: Palgrave, 2009).

Small, Andrew. *The China–Pakistan Axis: Asia's New Geopolitics* (Oxford and New York, Oxford University Press, 2015).

Notes

1 Peter J. Katzenstein, *A World of Regions: Asia and Europe in the American Imperium* (Ithaca and London: Cornell University Press, 2005), 24–30.
2 Joseph Y.S. Cheng and Zhang Wankun, "Patterns and Dynamics of China's International Strategic Behaviour," *Chinese Foreign Policy: Pragmatism and Strategic Behaviour* (Armonk, NY and London: M.E. Sharpe, 2004), 179–206.
3 "We Hope to Increase Economic Ties with Europe (April 18, 2005)," *Selected Works of Deng Xiaoping Volume III (1982–1992)* (Beijing: Foreign Languages Press, 1994), 125.
4 Robert Ash, "Europe's Commercial Relations with China," *China–Europe Relations: Perceptions, Policies and Prospects*, David Shambaugh, Eberhard Sandschneider and Zhou Hong (eds.) (Milton Park, UK and New York: Routledge, 2007), 189–90.
5 "China's EU Policy Paper," Information Office of the State Council of the People's Republic of China, Beijing October 2003, <http://www.china.org.cn/e-white/20050817/index.htm>.
6 "China's Policy Paper on the EU: Deepen the China–EU Comprehensive Strategic Partnership for Mutual Benefit and Win-win Cooperation," Foreign Ministry of the People's Republic of China, 2 April 2014, <http://www.fmprc.gov.cn/mfa_eng/wjdt_665385/wjzcs/t1143406.shtml>.
7 Ali M. El-Agraa, "The EU–China Relationship: Not Seeing Eye-to-Eye?" *Asia–Europe Journal* 5(2007): 198.
8 Carol M. Glen and Richard C. Murgo, "EU–China Relations: Balancing Political Challenges with Economic Opportunities," *Asia–Europe Journal* 5(2007): 332–4.
9 Costas Paris and Alkman Granitsas, "Greece to Proceed with Piraeus Port Privatization," *Wall Street Journal*, 10 February 2015.
10 David Shambaugh, "The New Strategic Triangle: US and European Reactions to China's Rise," *The Washington Quarterly* 28(3) (Summer 2005): 14–15.
11 David Scott, "The EU–China 'Strategic Dialogue': Pathways in the International System," *The International Politics of EU–China Relations*, ed. David Kerr and Liu Fei (Oxford and New York: Oxford University Press, 2007), 13–37.
12 Christopher Bo Bramsen, "ASEM – A New Dimension in Asian–European Relations," *China's Century: The Awakening of the Next Economic Powerhouse* , ed. Laurence J. Brahm (Singapore and New York: John Wiley and Sons (Asia), 2001), 89–97; Marc Lanteigne, "ASEM and the Expanding China–EU Relationship," *Multiregionalism and Multilateralism: Asian–European Relations in a Global Context*, ed. Sebastien Bersick, Wim Stokhof and Paul van der Velde (Amsterdam: Amsterdam University Press, 2006), 83–103.
13 Aiofe White, "Europe's Trade Deficit with China Swells in First Ten Months of 2007," *Associated Press Newswires*, 17 January 2008; "New Statistics Method to Shrink EU–China Trade Gap 36%," *The Wall Street Journal*, 16 April 2012.
14 Mathieu Rémond, "The EU's Refusal to Grant China 'Market Economy Status' (MES)," *Asia–Europe Journal* 5(2007): 345–56.
15 Matthew Dalton, "EU Lawyers Favor Market-Economy Status for China Next Year," *Wall Street Journal*, 9 June 2015.
16 "China, EU Officially Launch Talks on PCA," *Xinhua*, 18 January 2007, <http://www.china-embassy.org/eng/xw/t290010.htm>.
17 Marc Lanteigne, "Northern Exposure: Cross-Regionalism and the China–Iceland Preferential Trade Negotiations," *The China Quarterly* 202(June 2010): 362–80.
18 Bjørnar Sverdrup-Thygeson, "The Flexible Cost of Insulting China: Trade Politics and the 'Dalai Lama Effect'," *Asian Perspective* 39(2015): 101–23.
19 Marc Lanteigne, "The Sino-Swiss Free Trade Agreement," *Centre for Security Studies, ETH Zürich* 147 (February 2014), <http://www.css.ethz.ch/publications/pdfs/CSSAnalyses147-EN.pdf>; Victoria Gomelsky, "Swiss Watchmakers Court China's Young and Trendy Buyers," *The New York Times*, 29 September 2014.
20 Bates Gill and Robin Niblett, "Diverging Paths Hurt China and Europe," *International Herald Tribune*, 6 September 2005, 3; Willy Wo-Lap Lam, *Chinese Politics in the Hu Jintao Era* (Armonk, MY and London: M.E. Sharpe, 2006), 193–5.
21 Nicolas Kulish and C.J. Chivers, "US and Much of Europe Recognise Kosovo, Which Also Draws Expected Rejection," *The New York Times*, 19 February 2008, A10; "China 'Deeply Concerned' Over Kosovo's Declaration of Independence," *Xinhua*, 18 February 2008.

22 Song Xinning, "China's View of European Integration and Enlargement," *China–Europe Relations: Perceptions, Policies and Prospects*, ed. David Shambaugh, Eberhard Sandshneider and Zhou Hong (New York and London: Routledge, 2008), 174–86.

23 Fiona Hill and Bobo Lo, "Putin's Pivot: Why Russia is Looking East," *Foreign Affairs*, 31 July, 2013.

24 "Remarks by the President at the Economic School Graduation, Gostinny Dvor, 7 July 2009," *The White House, Office of the Press Secretary*, <http://www.whitehouse.gov/the_press_office/ Remarks-By-The-President-At-The-New-Economic-School-Graduation/>.

25 John J. Mearsheimer, "Why the Ukraine Crisis Is the West's Fault: The Liberal Delusions That Provoked Putin," *Foreign Affairs* 93(5) (September / October 2014): 77–89; Lawrence Freedman, "Ukraine and the Art of Limited War," *Survival*, 56(6) (December 2014–January 2015): 7–38.

26 "Foreign Ministry Spokesperson Qin Gang's Regular Press Conference on March 4, 2014," *Ministry of Foreign Affairs of the People's Republic of China*, 4 March 2014, <http://www.fmprc. gov.cn/mfa_eng/xwfw_665399/s2510_665401/2535_665405/t1134077.shtml>.

27 Aglaya Snetkov and Marc Lanteigne, "'The Loud Dissenter and its Cautious Partner' – Russia, China, Global Governance and Humanitarian Intervention," *International Relations of the Asia Pacific* 15(1) (January 2015): 113–46.

28 "Foreign Ministry Spokesperson Qin Gang's Regular Press Conference on March 4, 2014," *Ministry of Foreign Affairs of the People's Republic of China*, 4 March 2014, <http://www.fmprc. gov.cn/mfa_eng/xwfw_665399/s2510_665401/2535_665405/t1134077.shtml>.

29 Mu Xuequan, "China Makes Proposals on Political Solution to Ukraine crisis," *Xinhua*, 15 March 2014.

30 "Russian, Chinese Navies Hold Joint Drills in Mediterranean," *Reuters*, 17 May 2015.

31 Rakteem Katakey and Will Kennedy, "Russia Gives China Arctic Access as Energy Giants Embrace," *Bloomberg / National Post* (Canada), 25 March 2013.

32 "Chinese Banks Ready to Invest $10 Billion in Yamal LNG," *Moscow Times*, 7 November 2014.

33 Marat Gurt, "China Asserts Clout in Central Asia with huge Turkmen Gas Project," *Reuters*, 4 September 2013.

34 "On the Question of the Differentiation of the Three Worlds (February 22, 1974)," Mao Zedong, *On Diplomacy* (Beijing: Foreign Languages Press, 1998), 454.

35 "Africa's Task is to Struggle against Imperialism (February 21, 1959)," Mao Zedong, *On Diplomacy* (Beijing: Foreign Languages Press, 1998), 286–7.

36 Xi Chan, "China's Foreign Policy Dynamics and International Order," *International Order in a Globalising World*, ed. Yannis A. Stivachtis (Hampshire, England and Burlington, VT: Ashgate, 2007), 88–9; W.A.C. Adie, "Chou En-lai On Safari," *China Under Mao: Politics Takes Command*, ed. Roderick MacFarquar (Cambridge, MA and London: MIT Press, 1966), 462–82.

37 Pádraig R. Carmody and Francis Y. Owusu, "Competing Hegemons? Chinese versus American Geo-Economic Strategies in Africa," *Political Geography* 26(2007): 508; Ian Taylor, *China and Africa: Engagement and Compromise* (London and New York: Routledge, 2006), 28–31, 38–40; Bates Gill, *Rising Star: China's New Security Diplomacy* (Washington DC: Brookings, 2007), 124–5.

38 Martin Bailey, "Tanzania and China," *African Affairs* 74(294) (January 1975): 39–50.

39 Qian Qichen, *Ten Episodes in China's Diplomacy* (New York: Harper Collins, 2005), 191–229.

40 Jessica Drun, "China–Taiwan Diplomatic Truce Holds Despite Gambia," *The Diplomat*, 29 March 2014, < http://thediplomat.com/2014/03/china-taiwan-diplomatic-truce-holds-despite-gambia/>.

41 Chris Alden, "China in Africa," *Survival* 47(3) (Autumn 2005): 147–8.

42 Sanusha Naidu and Martyn Davies, "China Fuels Its Future with Africa's Riches," *South African Journal of International Affairs* 13(2) (Spring 2006): 69–83; Ian Taylor, "China's Relations with Nigeria," *The Round Table* 96(392) (October 2007): 636.

43 Yun Sun, "China's Aid to Africa: Monster or Messiah?," *Brookings East Asia Commentary*, February 2014, <http://www.brookings.edu/research/opinions/2014/02/07-china-aid-to-africa-sun#_ftnref13>; Liu Yumai, "China's Soft Power and the Development of China–Africa Relations," *China International Studies* 7 (Summer 2007): 84.

44 For example, see Howard W. French, *China's Second Continent: How a Million Migrants are Building a New Empire in Africa* (New York: Alfred A. Knopf, 2014), 5–8.

45 Bates Gill and James Reilly, "The Tenuous Hold of China Inc. in Africa," *The Washington Quarterly* 30(3) (Summer 2007): 37.

46 "China Military Declines to Confirm Djibouti Base Plan," *Reuters*, 25 June 2015.
47 Chris Alden, "China in Africa", 148; Jonathan Holsag, "China's Diplomatic Manoeuvring on the Question of Darfur," *Journal of Contemporary China* 17(54) (February 2008): 71–84.
48 Sudarsan Raghavan and Andrew Higgins, "China in a Tug of War between Two Sudans," *The New York Times*, 24 March, 2012.
49 Ian Taylor, *China and Africa*, 123–6.
50 Harvey Morris and Tom Burgis, "Russia and China Veto Zimbabwe Sanctions," *Financial Times*, 12 July 2008, 5.
51 Joseph J. Schatz, "Zambian Hopeful Takes a Swing at China," *Washington Post*, 25 September 2006, A16; Alden, *China in Africa*, 74–5; Alden, "China in Africa," 156–7; Gill and Reilly, "The Tenuous Hold of China Inc. in Africa," 46–7.
52 "China's African Policy, January 2006," *People's Daily Online,* 12 January 2006, <http://english. peopledaily.com.cn/200601/12/eng20060112_234894.html>.
53 "China–Africa Economic and Trade Cooperation (2013)," *Information Office of the State Council of the People's Republic of China*, 29 August 2013, <http://www.china.org.cn/government/ whitepaper/node_7189938.htm>.
54 Justin Yifu Lin, "Industry Transfer to Africa Good For All," *China Daily*, 20 January 2015.
55 June Trufel Dreyer, "From China with Love: PRC Overtures to Latin America," *Brown Journal of International Affairs* 12(2) (Winter / Spring 2006): 87–8.
56 "BRICS Leaders Hail Outcome of First-day Summit After 4 Major Deals Signed," *Xinhua*, 15 July 2014.
57 Takashi Nishiyama, "The Roles of Asia and Chile in the World's Copper Market," *Resources Policy* 30 (2005): 131–9.
58 Rhys Jenkins, Enrique Dussel Peters and Mauricio Mequita Moreira, "The Impact of China on Latin America and the Caribbean," *World Development* 36(2) (2007): 235–53; June Trufel Dreyer, "From China with Love," 94–5.
59 Brian Ellsworth, "Venezuela and China Boost Ties with Refinery Deal," *Reuters*, 10 May 2008.
60 "China Eyes Brazil's Petrobras to Develop Oil Reserve- Estado," *Dow Jones Energy Service*, 3 July 2008.
61 Peter Hakim, "Is Washington Losing Latin America?" *Foreign Affairs* 85(1) (January / February 2006): 45–7.
62 Marisela Connelly, "China and Latin America: The Economic Dimension," *Multiregionalism and Multilateralism: Asian–European Relations in a Global Context*, ed. Sebastien Bersick, Wim Stokhof and Paul van der Velde (Amsterdam: Amsterdam University Press, 2006), 108–112.
63 Randal C. Archibald, "China Buys Inroads into the Caribbean, Catching US Notice," *The New York Times*, 7 April 2012.
64 "Bodies of Chinese Peacekeeping Police Killed in Haiti Earthquake Arrive Home," *Xinhua*, 19 January 2010.
65 "Chinese President Makes Four-point Proposal for Settlement of Palestinian Question," *Xinhua*, 6 May 2013.
66 Gouda Abdel Khalek, "The Impact of China on the Middle East," *Journal of Developing Societies* 23(4) (2007): 425.
67 Weiming Zhao, "China's Energy Security Moves It Closer to the Middle East," *Daily Star* (Lebanon), 12 May 2008.
68 Peter Cornelius and Jonathan Story, "China and Global Energy Markets," *Orbis* 51(1) (Winter 2007): 18.
69 Zha Daojiong, "China's Energy Security: Domestic and International Issues," *Survival* 48(1) (Spring 2006): 179–90.
70 Flynt Leveritt and Jeffrey Bader, "Managing China–US Energy Competition in the Middle East," *The Washington Quarterly* 29(1) (Winter 2005–6): 195–6.
71 "Sanctions-Hit Iran Turns Increasingly to Asia for Trade," *Al-Arabiya*, 4 February 2012.
72 Sanam Vekil, "Iran: Balancing Against East and West," *The Washington Quarterly* 29(4) (Autumn 2006): 55.
73 Alyssa Rallis, "China–Iran Trade to Hit US$25 Billion," *Global Insight Daily Analysis*, 1 July 2008; Marc Lanteigne, "Energising Links," *The World Today* (July 2007): 7.
74 Manochehr Dorraj and Carrie L. Courier, "Lubricated with Oil: India–China Relations in a Changing World," *Middle East Policy* 15(2) (Summer 2008): 73.

75 "Iran Hopes to Join Shanghai Cooperation Organisation – Envoy to Tajikistan," *Nigoh, Dushanbe / BBC Monitoring* [Factiva], 24 July 2008.
76 "China Urges Flexibility in Iran Nuclear Talks," *Reuters / International Herald Tribune*, 18 July 2008, 3.
77 Michael Yahuda, *The International Politics of the Asia-Pacific* (3rd edn) (New York and London: Routledge, 2013), 44–5.
78 Waheguru Pal Singh Sidhu and Jing-dong Yuan, *China and India: Cooperation or Conflict?* (Boulder, CO and London: Lynne Renner, 2003), 14–15.
79 David Scott, "The Great Power 'Great Game' Between India and China: 'The Logic of Geography'," *Geopolitics* 13(1) (January 2006): 11.
80 Nitin Gokhale, "An Evolution in China–India Relations?" *The Diplomat*, 1 April 2015, <http://thediplomat.com/2015/04/an-evolution-in-china-india-relations/>.
81 Maseeh Rahman, "Chinese Plans in Seychelles Revive Indian Fears of Encirclement," *The Guardian*, 22 March 2012.
82 Dharisha Bastani and Gardinier Harris, "Chinese Leader Visits Sri Lanka, Challenging India's Sway," *The New York Times*, 16 September 2014.
83 Ananth Krishnan, "BCIM Corridor Gets Push After First Official-level Talks in China," *The Hindu*, 21 December 2013.
84 Robert D. Kaplan, *Monsoon: The Indian Ocean and the Future of American Power* (New York: Random House, 2010), 281–4.
85 Katherine Houreld, "Chinese President to Launch Economic Corridor Link in Pakistan," *Reuters*, 19 April 2015.
86 Dipanjan Roy Chaudhury, "SAARC Membership: India Blocks China's Entry for the Time Being," *Economic Times* (India), 2 December 2014.
87 "The Other Power: Security and Diplomacy in Sino-Afghanistan Relations," *The Regional Dimensions to Security: Other Sides of Afghanistan,* ed. Stephen Aris and Aglaya Snetkov (New York: Palgrave Macmillan, 2013), 120–35.
88 "Significance of Arctic Research Expedition," China.org.cn, <http://www.china.org.cn/english/features/40961.htm> (Accessed 1 August 2014).
89 "Yellow River Station Opens in Arctic," *China Daily*, 29 July 2004.
90 Beth Gardiner, "Iceland Aims to Seize Opportunities in Oil Exploration," *The New York Times*, 1 October 2013; "Iceland: China's Arctic Springboard?" *Energy Compass*, 26 July 2013.
91 Euan Rocha, "CNOOC Closes $15.1 Billion Acquisition of Canada's Nexen," *Reuters*, 25 February 2013.
92 Lucy Hornby, Richard Milne and James Watson, "Chinese Group General Nice Takes over Greenland Mine," *Financial Times*, 11 January 2015.
93 Charlotte MacDonald-Gibson, "From China to Rotterdam, and Into the Record Books," *The Independent*, 12 September 2013.
94 "All Eyes on the Arctic Council," *Deutsche Welle*, 17 May 2013.
95 "China Opens 4th Antarctic Research Base," *Xinhua / Global Times*, 8 February 2014; "China Builds 5th Antarctic station," *China Daily*, 16 April 2014; Bree Feng, "China Seeks to Become a 'Polar-Region Power'," *The New York Times*, 19 November 2014.

Index

Bold page numbers indicate figures, *italic* numbers indicate tables.

CPSIA information can be obtained
at www.ICGtesting.com
Printed in the USA
LVHW09s1729050818
586021LV00015B/108/P